Wyrdwalkers:

Techniques of Northern-Tradition Shamanism

Raven Kaldera

Wyrdwalkers: Techniques of Northern-Tradition Shamanism

Northern-Tradition Shamanism Book III

Raven Kaldera

Asphodel Press

Hubbardston, Massachusetts

Asphodel Press
12 Simond Hill Road
Hubbardston, MA 01452

Wyrdwalkers:
Techniques of Northern-Tradition Shamanism
Northern-Tradition Shamanism Book III
© 2006 Raven Kaldera
ISBN 978-0-6151-3944-9

Cover art © 2007 Abby Helasdottir, http://www.gydja.com
Back cover photo © 2006 Sensuous Sadie

Printed in cooperation with
Lulu Enterprises, Inc.
860 Aviation Parkway, Suite 300
Morrisville, NC 27560

DEDICATED TO ALL
MY FELLOW SPIRIT-WORKERS,
WHEREVER THEY MAY BE.

Contents

Part I: Shamanism of the Northlands

Introduction: Northern-Tradition Shamanism 1

Laufey's Lesson 20

Classic Shamanism And Core Shamanism 22

Gods And Wights: Spirit Allies and Spirit Masters 32

Frey's Lesson 73

Part II: Mastering the Elements

Starting With The Roots: Mastering the Elements 79

Mastering Air 82

Kari's Lesson 88

Rind's Lesson 92

Bragi's Lesson 95

Groa's Fourth and Ninth Charms 97

Mastering Fire 99

Surt's Lesson 105

Logi's Lesson 109

Farbauti's Lesson 111

Groa's Seventh Charm 114

Mastering Water 115

Aegir & Ran's Lessons 120

The Nine Undines' Lessons 123

Groa's Third & Sixth Charms 153

Mastering Earth 154

Jord's Lesson 161

Gerda's Lesson 164

Nidhogg's Lesson 168

Groa's Fifth Charm 171

Part III: Mastering the Skills

Divination in the Northern Tradition............................ 175

Groa's Second Charm 183

The Soul Map.. 184

Children Of The Void: Runes As Spirit Allies............. 208

Wyrdworking: Combing The Threads 236

Luckworking: The Dance Of Hamingja 245

The Norns' Lesson 256

Blood and Bloodlines 259

The Red Road: Bloodwalking...................................... 276

Hyndla's Lesson 285

Making Whole: Repair Of The Soul............................ 289

Hamrammr: Strong In Shaping 314

Angrboda's Lesson 331

Part IV: Keeping Whole

Power And Restriction: Spirit-Work Taboos 337

Shaman Health and Shaman Sickness......................... 345

Spouses, Partners, and Other Hapless Bystanders......... 395

Mengloth's Lesson 408

Afterword.. 412

PART I: SHAMANISM OF THE NORTHLANDS

Introduction: Northern-Tradition Shamanism

The man sitting in front of her, cross-legged on the other half of her big embroidered quilt, definitely has a tangled thread of Wyrd. The reading spread out between them strongly suggests this, and she's seen the patterns before. His orlog is weak and his wyrd is blocked, and he is not doing what it is that he's supposed to do. The question is, what is that? She holds her hand over the pattern of runes on the embroidered cloth and decides that it's time to ask a deeper power. Let's see... which of them would know the most about this kind of situation? She reaches out intuitively and the name of one of her secondary patrons comes to her. She begins humming the power song that he taught her to herself, closing her eyes, ignoring the man sitting there nervously. She sings and asks for the aid of that Wight, that deity at whose feet she studied once, at the behest of her patron Goddess. She asks him to take a look at the file of Wyrd open on her metaphorical desk, and see if he can make anything out of it.

The man shifts and clears his throat as she sits there humming to herself. This isn't anything like the last two psychic readers that he went to. They smiled brightly and told him that everything was going to be all right—see, there were three Cups and two Coins in the reading, that meant love and money, right? They whipped through the card meanings, always keeping him entertained. They didn't sit there singing to themselves as if he wasn't there at all.

But then, of course, things weren't all right. They kept getting worse.

That's why he's here.

She's been the last resort more times than she can count. She knows all about it. Just as he starts shifting restlessly and gets ready to say something about leaving, her eyes snap open and hold his, and he can't move. She opens her mouth, and tells him exactly what it is that he needs to do. He doesn't know how she knows, but he flushes red. It's that thing that he'd been trying not to think about, all this time. "I can't do that," he says. "My wife would leave me. I'd lose my job."

"They want you to do it," she says. "It's part of your life path. The longer you wait, the worse things will get. If you use your marriage or your career as an excuse to avoid your path, They'll take it away. If you choose this, it will be easier than if you wait until They come and get you and make it so that you have nothing left to lose." She dislikes having to deliver messages like this, but it's so often true that they come to her already knowing the answer, but hoping that she'll tell them that what they fear so deeply won't really come true. Say it ain't so, shaman, say it ain't so! Except that it usually is.

She watches him struggle with it. Finally the first grudging step comes out: "What would I have to do first?"

The shaman studies his cosmic casefile, laid out on the metaphorical desk that is her rune-embroidered blanket. "Can you get hold of some animal bones and a shovel?" she says. "Because you're going to need to make a mound of dirt and sit on it overnight."

This book is the third in my series dedicated to northern-tradition shamanism. For those who haven't read the first two, this tradition of shamanism is not the religion of the Viking-age Norse or Germanic peoples that is reconstructed from bits of Christianized lore in the modern Nordic reconstructionist religions. This spiritual practice is what spirit-workers of that area did centuries, perhaps millennia, before that. It is written nowhere in the paltry existing scraps of lore, because it was an oral tradition in an age without books, mostly if not entirely lost well before the first chroniclers began to write about the already-fading Pagan beliefs. This tradition is reconstructed entirely from teachings gained directly from the Gods and wights who still speak to us, still connect with us, still teach us things that are found nowhere in books ... until now.

Many northern-tradition spirit-workers and shamans donated their words to this book, and I can only be grateful to them all, because our shared perspective is greater than that of any single one. By pooling our knowledge, we taught each other further, and I am honored to be the one to commit all this to paper and publications. As much of this information is spirit-taught, this is the first time that some of it has ever been committed to paper, or even put into words.

The first book in this series, *The Jotunbok: Working With The Giants In The Northern Tradition*, was written partly because there were so few writings about the Jotunfolk, and their Gods, the Rökkr. However, there was another reason as well: When doing northern-tradition shamanism, all too often you bypass the Aesir and Vanir and run into the Jotnar holding that thread. (Exceptions are Frey, Freya, and of course Odin the shaman-king.) This lends credence to the supposition that the Jotnar are the Gods of the pre-Indo-European people, who most certainly had a shamanic culture. Therefore, it made sense to start with them.

The second book in the series, *Pathwalker's Guide To The Nine Worlds*, was written as a guide for those journeying in the Norse/Germanic cosmology. Its appearance was a little out of order, considering that journeying is a fairly advanced technique, but it grew out of a nine-day pathwalking trip that I did through the Nine Worlds, and of course being a writer I brought a journal with me and recorded my adventures. Then some friends read the journal and begged me to put it up on a website, and of course I then had to write explanatory chapters for the Nine Worlds, and what was journeying and pathwalking anyway, or no one would be able to understand it. Before I knew it, it was the length of a book and strangers were emailing me, asking when it would be available in print. So I did it, but at that point I was aware that there needed to be books describing techniques. Otherwise we were all going to be reinventing the wheel with our own wight-guides, isolated in our bedrooms across the world, and not knowing that someone else struggled with this and managed to find a way.

The third and fourth books in this series, *Wyrdwalkers: Techniques of Northern-Tradition Shamanism* and *Wightridden: Paths of Northern-Tradition Shamanism* are being published simultaneously, because they were meant to be one book but became so huge as to require two. Thus, if you've read this introduction in one of them, don't bother to read it now. Jump ahead to the meat of the information, unless you feel that you need a refresher. This is really just for the folks who are picking this up at a yard sale and saying, "What the heck is this about?"

Actually, the first thing that's likely to confuse them is the issue of northern-tradition shamanism itself. These days, at least in America where I write, shamanism is almost synonymous with Native American spirituality; even the "neo-shamanisms" that can be bought for many hundreds of dollars and that claim to be above any single tradition are basically stolen Native American flavors. The idea that "white people" might actually have their own ancestral shamanism is something that most people don't know about. However, if you go back far enough in any ancestral direction, you will hit pre-agricultural hunter/gatherer/herder tribes for whom shamanism was their daily religion. Most of those religions have been obscured by the smoke of history, but they existed, and the spirits remember. It's time for us to remember, too.

Questions About Northern-Tradition Shamanism

What do you mean by shamanism? Why do you use that word?

I use the word because it is the closest word my birth language has for what I have experienced, what I am expected to do, and what I have become. It is a word that has been borrowed from the Tungus language, but it fills an important hole in our language. For more information on how I feel about the word and its common uses, see the article *Public Horses.* (http://www.cauldronfarm.com/nts.html)

My definition of shamanism is "a spiritual and magical practice that involves working with spirits and is designed to serve a tribe". It's distinct from thaumaturgic magic, which is working magically with directed energy, or theurgic magic, which is working with divinely inspired symbol systems like runes. This is working with Entities, and that's a whole different ball game. Shamanism is also distinct from religion proper, because while it is certainly a spiritual practice, and has always traditionally been embedded in a religious cosmology, it is a practical discipline that serves the people in concrete ways—healing, divining, channeling, and generally enhancing people's lives.

"Shamanism" as a term can be compared to "monasticism"; while it is almost always found embedded in a religious context, it is not a religion per se. It could also be compared to "spiritual scholarship"; which is similar to but distinct from nonreligious scholarship, and also cannot be called "a religion".

In shamanism, it's all about the Entities with whom you have formed relationships. Some of those relationships may be akin to spiritual slavery, in that one deity (it's usually a deity) has grabbed you and made you their tool, while granting you certain powers and protections; as an example, I work for Hela, and she both protects me and forces me to do Her work. Some of these relationships may look like alliances between a superior (deity) and an inferior (mortal), where each agree to provide certain favors in an exchange; as an example, I horse Herne and Frey for the community on one day apiece each year, and in exchange they gift me with certain powers and protections. Some of these relationships may be alliances between equal powers; as an example, I work with many of the Grandparent spirits of herbs and plants for purposes of healing. Some relationships may be the (ideally) consenting use of a smaller spirit in order to borrow some power or trait; as an example, a friend of mine has bad eyesight and "borrows" the vision of her pet rats when she has to go out at night. Regardless of the level of power exchange, it's all about keeping those relationships well-greased and humming along.

Shamanism is also distinct from mysticism in that it is goal-oriented and work-focused. The mystic may share many of the same techniques, especially the altered-state techniques, but his focus is on pure experience. If you ask him, "What good is this? What's it useful for?" he will probably just smile and tell you that it has its own goodness which you have to experience to understand. For the mystic, it's between him and the Universe. For the shaman, the question "What's it useful for?" is all-important. As the servant of a tribe, rather than as a sole quester for oneness with the All, the shaman has to stop short of entirely merging with the Divine Web and instead find ways to make these experiences useful to the betterment of their people. In some ways, it's much more of a bodhisattva than a Buddha path, although the point is not getting everyone off the Wheel of Life and Death. Shamanism is set in a context that values all worlds equally, and sees body and flesh and blood and Earth as sacred; the point is to make things easier for people here and now. Therefore, shamanism is intensely practical, making use of every tool of "ecstasy", as the anthropologists like to call it, in order to make actual change in the world.

(An excellent comparison of the Path of Mystic Quest with the Path of Shamanic Mediation, as the author refers to them, can be found in the book *Six Ways Of Being Religious*, by Dale Cannon. While the book only uses Christian and Buddhist examples, the projected paths can be easily seen in modern Paganism as well.)

What do you mean by Northern-Tradition? Where do these traditions come from?

They come from many sources—Germanic (and Anglo-Saxon, which is part of that); Norse; a little bit of Saami; and a little bit of Siberian. They are from the circumpolar peoples of the western Eurasian continent. Some seem to go back as far as the Mesolithic or Neolithic pre-Indo-European people of northern Europe. Some come from books, lore, research, but most of it comes from the Gods and spirits that are training me and others like me. Occasionally, some will come from that source and then later I discover them in books.

Is this part of the religions referred to as Asatru, Vanatru, Heathenry, etc.?

No, it is not. Those are reconstructionist religions of the beliefs of the Viking-Age Scandinavian people. They are generally based mostly or entirely on the surviving lore about that religion. While this tradition shares many of the same deities and myths, it is different in that it is a spiritual practice, not a religion (as is all shamanism), and it is not based on written records, nor is it technically reconstructionist. If it falls within any religious demographic, one could loosely say that it might be a part of northern-tradition Paganism, which is still a vague term generally referring to reconstructionist-derived northern-European Neo-Paganism, but as those borders are still being defined, we'll just say that northern-tradition shamanism is not part of reconstructionist Heathenry, by their own definition, and leave it at that.

Wait a minute. I'm a scholar, and I was under the impression that the Norse/Germanic peoples of the lore did not have shamans or a shamanic culture.

You are quite correct. The people of the "lore era" didn't even have an entirely pagan culture any more, much less a shamanic one. They had been converted to Christianity. Even if there were still a few heathens tucked away in odd corners, the writers of the books—and the dominant culture—was Christian. To minimize this is to make the mistake of absorbing a lot of Christian values along with your Heathen lore.

There was once a shamanic tribal culture in all of these areas. It was mostly gone well before the Christians converted everyone. Bits and pieces and glimpses of it can be seen and patchworked together, but we don't have a full picture of it from any written lore. That's what I mean when I say that it is lost, and why I have to be spirit-taught it. Of course, the Saami and Siberian peoples have shamans to this day, and there was a good deal of marrying back and forth.

Is this stuff like seidhr?

Seidhr is the term for one of the magical practices that was still in use during the late Iron Age, the time that is used by religious reconstructionists. It is likely that it has strong shamanic roots, and that many of its tools are a holdover from earlier shamanism, and/or learned from the Saami *noaidi*. There has been a lot of argument and debate over that, among academics and practitioners of *seidhr* alike, as well as argument over whether the word *seidhr* should be restricted to the sort of oracular performance that the volva does in *Eiriks saga Raude*, or whether it should extend to other sorts of magic too, and which sorts.

I choose not to enter that debate. Yes, what you'll find here has some things in common with what some *seidhr*-practitioners are doing, and in fact some of them contributed generously to this work. On the other hand, some practices written here are not found anywhere in the lore as being concretely and beyond a shadow of a doubt part of the *seidhr* complex of magic, as they likely died out centuries or millennia previously. So I do not claim the word, any more than I would claim the words *Asatru*, *Heathen*, or *reconstructionist*. This is a form of wight-taught ancient shamanism, and that's all.

Why don't you stick to information that is already written down? What's wrong with sticking to the lore?

Well, the Gods and spirits that I work with don't see it that way. If every time they told me to do something, I objected, "But wait! I can't do that unless you show me where it's written down in a book, preferably with an author who has an entire page of academic credentials," well, let's just say that it would get ugly real fast. So I use the lore as a jumping-off point, and then I keep going. In the meantime, I keep reading, because sometimes I find something that I've already been told to do. It's nice to be validated in that way, but it's not necessary. I'd do it anyway. I can't afford to be lorebound, not with Gods and wights on my tail.

Except for places where certain contributing authors have given me whole essays with references, you won't find footnotes and references throughout this book, either. That's because such things contribute to the idea that this might be an academic research work, if a poor one, and I have no desire to enable that misunderstanding. These books fall into another category entirely, and I am very clear about that. Although I may mention subjects that I ran across in research, this book is primarily material gathered through the experiences of myself and others. We *are* the primary source material.

Aren't you ripping off these ancient peoples and their cultures?

Since these are my ancestors, I would say that I have a fairly solid right to do what I'm doing, if you use the argument that one's ancestral traditions are an inheritance. Frankly, though, I'd do this even if they weren't my ancestors. I do it not because it is any kind of politically correct, but because that's what the Goddess who owns me and the Spirits who work with me say that I have to do. If I had been grabbed up by, say, Native American gods and spirits, I'd be doing that path even though I don't have a drop of that blood, and I'd just have to find a way to deal with the opprobrium that would be heaped upon me.

Besides, the Gods and wights don't give two rat's asses about what I may think that I'm ripping off. However, I can actually imagine "ripping off the past" in a way that would be disrespectful, and it is already practiced by some groups. It consists of doing reconstructionist religion without actually believing wholly in the Gods of our ancestors; one does their practices, but merely pretends to believe in their Gods. It's a twisted, blasphemous kind of ancestor worship. But anyone who wholeheartedly believes in our Gods, and worships them with sincerity, isn't ripping off anyone. They are giving back.

What do you mean, "spirit-taught"?

The Buryat Mongols have a word for shamans who are spirit-taught—it's *bagshagui*. Usually this happens when the shaman's lineage or clan dies out and the spirits who have worked with them all move over to another line or clan, and pick some poor slob that they have decided would make a great shaman. A *bagshagui* doesn't have the benefit of the old guy in the hut to teach them. Everything has to be learned from the spirits themselves, who are wonderfully effective but extremely frustrating teachers.

Since this tradition is largely lost, I as a white American don't have the old-guy-in-the-hut benefit either. I am in the service of the Norse death goddess Hela, and she sends me to various other gods and spirits for training. It's often spotty and confusing, but sometimes it is amazing.

As I learn, I write it down. I am aware that I may have to teach someone else someday.

I've studied a different shamanic tradition from elsewhere in the world, and while there may be some things in common with this tradition, there are a lot of things that you say are true which that tradition doesn't find to be true at all.

That's very much the case, and at no time do I mean to speak for any tradition other than my own. If nothing else, I don't know enough about them. I haven't seen them from the inside, and known them intimately, and lived their patterns. So from here on in, anywhere you see me talk about any sort of shamanism, you may assume that I am referring to *the way it is in this tradition*, regardless of how it is in any other one. There just doesn't seem to be any point in disclaimering every instance of that.

While I like the tales of the Gods and spirits of your tradition, I'm not sure that I believe in them. Can I still practice this tradition if I believe that they are archetypes, or energy forms created by human attention?

No. You cannot. Sorry, I'm going to have to be hardline on this one.

This is a polytheistic spiritual tradition. No way to get around that one. Not only do you have to believe fully and thoroughly in these Gods and wights in order to really practice it, if you come at them with any less than complete faith in their existence, they may be offended and refuse to deal with you ... and for this tradition, it's all about dealing with the spirits. No spirits, no luck. Not only are they all real, they are all distinct from each other as well.

If you are not comfortable with polytheistic belief, perhaps you might prefer working with a more ceremonial-magic system, such as Thelema or the Golden Dawn. If you are drawn to Norse stuff, there is a sect of Norse-style ceremonial magic that combines the two. However, it is not shamanism. I realize that some neo-shamanistic workshops downplay the literal existence of spirits and allow people to reserve their disbelief. That's fine for them, but not for us. If you can't fully embrace the religious and devotional aspects of this tradition of shamanism, don't practice it. Find something that fits better with your world view; there are plenty of them out there.

Why should I believe you about any of this? Isn't it possible that you are delusional?

There's no reason at all for you to believe me. In fact, it would be unreasonable of me to expect it, considering that you haven't experienced what I have experienced. It's as unreasonable as expecting you to believe in any god that hasn't talked to you personally. If you'd like to decide that I am full of it, it's no skin off my nose. The only reason I'm laying it out for total strangers anyway is because Hela wants me to make this information available.

Can I learn this tradition even if these aren't my ancestors?

Sure, knock yourself out. I'm not sensitive about it. If the spirits are calling you, who am I to argue? If it's just that you're drawn to it, it won't hurt anything. After all, the more people who know it, the better. I'm not one of those who believes that the Gods and wights choose people only from these bloodlines—I've seen them pick out too many who weren't even white to believe that one. They take who They take, and who am I to criticize?

What is different about northern-tradition shamanism compared to other cultural forms of shamanism? Or, for that matter, modern northern-tradition religious faiths?

Well, for one thing, we have no rattles. Seriously, the first big difference in the former category is that it deals largely with the Gods and wights of Norse/Germanic pantheons rather than the spirits of various aboriginal religions. Occasionally you might get referred to a deity outside of this tradition, because a few of our Gods are like that, but mostly it's working with the three pantheons of this tradition. There are a myriad of other little cultural differences as well, which are too many to list here.

Where this tradition peels away from modern reconstructionist Norse religion is in the matter of timing. Much of modern Heathenry is reconstructed from a particular era in the early medieval Iron Age. Even before the onslaught of Christianity, it was not a shamanic culture, although a few bits and pieces survived in myth and seidhwork. The shamanic culture and practices had largely died out centuries before, although they were still going strong next door in Finland among the Saami people and further east among the Siberians. Long ago, however, there was once a circumpolar set of shamanic traditions that shared much in common, more even than the shamanic cultures of other parts of the world. If we go back to the Mesolithic or Neolithic era, we find the Indo-Europeans overrunning an indigenous Scandinavian people, and it seems to those of us who are spirit-workers that the original deities of those people were the wights now referred to as Jotun, or Giantkind.

The various waves of Indo-European people brought the agricultural Vanir, and later the warrior sky-god Aesir, and the early gods were relegated to the villainous position, much like the Greek Titans. Yet if you study them, you find that they are extremely Neolithic and shamanic in nature—elemental, shapeshifting, animal-like, multitudinous, partaking of fire and ice and trees and ocean and sacred mountain, wielding stone blades and dark, bloody powers. In the myths, whenever there is an underworld journey, there is a giantess or a Rökkr god involved. When you come to the Northern Tradition and start pulling the string labeled "shamanism", four times out of five you'll get the Jotnar, or the Rökkr Gods (Hela, Loki, Surt, Fenris, Jormundgand, Angrboda, etc.) at the other end. That's why so many of the "deity-lessons" in this book are from the Jotun point of view, rather than mostly the Aesir. These are the Gods and wights that my ancestors worshiped and worked with when they lived in a shamanic culture, and they know more than anyone about this kind of work.

However, they are not the only deities who take an interest in such things. When someone gets pulled into this tradition and their patron is one of the Vanir, it's most likely to be Freya, with Frey as a close second. Freya is the mistress of seidhr, the magical tradition that survived into the Iron Age and which had many shamanic elements, perhaps left over from the early days. She is not only sex goddess and sacred whore, fertility maiden and warrior-woman, she is also the witchy-woman with the magic comb and net who knows how to sing her way into a journeying-trance. Freya and Frey are the repository of that shamanic knowledge which combined with the early sacrificial agricultural religion, creating its own flavor of shamanism which survived piecemeal into the Viking Age. It should be noted that when golden sacrificial-king Frey is the patron of a shaman, the individual is likely to be a gay or bisexual man. There are at least two "cults" of Frey, and one is the faithful husbandman and farmer with a wife and children who has no need of this book. The other path of Frey is that of the (slightly to very) effeminate shaman/priest with his skirt hemmed with tinkling bells, and this is the Freysman who is most likely to go down this road.

When the patron is Aesir, there is only one deity for the shaman to look to: Odin. The All-Father of Asgard is the archetypal shaman-king, warrior and wanderer, magician and ruler, who learned his shamanic magic on a long nine-year ordeal from Freya, Mimir, the Norns, and other older wights. While he comes by it third-generation, so to speak, his talents in this area are nothing to sneeze at. If you're an Asatru and you get dragged down this path, it is Odin who will take you there—ravens, wolves, ordeals, and all.

What sorts of things did northern-tradition spirit-workers do in ancient times? How is it different from what they do now?

In ancient times, spirit-workers—be they shamans, volvas, seidhr-workers, noaidi, etc.—did a variety of things to help their people survive. They called the wild animals for hunting and the reindeer for herding. They called fish into rivers and close to seacoasts. They made sacrifices to make sure the crops grew. They did healing of various sorts—magical and herbal together—for the sick. They did divination for individuals and the tribe, especially when things went wrong, and figured out who had to be propitiated in order to set things right. They named children. They put people through ordeals of passage. They altered the weather. They made women and men fertile. They blessed those who needed blessings. They cleansed evil places. They protected the tribe from destructive spirits and the shamans of other tribes. They talked to the Dead, and to the Gods and spirits, and mediated for the community between these worlds.

They also did a lot of things that were destructive themselves. They fought in battles, charming weapons and calling in spirits to aid their side. They helped warriors to shapeshift into fierce animals. They magically attacked the other side's warriors, and sometimes the members of neighboring tribes who were encroaching on territory. They left their bodies in order to do reconnaissance for their chieftains. They drove people mad. They made vengeance magic and curses for people who paid them, and this, too, was accepted and considered right and loyal. In fact, they probably did as much of the latter as of the former types of magic.

Today, many of these things are no longer useful, which is why I don't have a hunting drum. However, there are still many things that my ancestral spirit-workers did that I also do, including divination of all sorts, untangling people's bad luck and fate, healing, doing ordeals of passage, cleansing spoiled places, and talking to the Dead. I still fare forth on errands to Otherworlds like them, and I still mediate between the inhabitants of those worlds and of this one.

Why did you name this book Wyrdwalkers?

When you are a spirit-worker in this tradition, one of the most important things is to be aware of and skilled in interpreting Wyrd, or the paths of Fate. This is partly for the sake of all the people who will come to you for advice and help with their Wyrd, and partly so that you can properly walk your own. While most folk have a good deal of leeway in their path, being a spirit-worker narrows our Wyrd to a thin line. Because we have more power and the ability to see further, we have more responsibility. We need to pick and choose our actions with care, because they reverberate further. Our Threads have the power to affect more people, and yet be affected by them in time. To be a Wyrdwalker is to understand where we are going, and what we are to be used for, and to see that path clearly.

Can I learn to be a shaman from reading and practicing your stuff?

No. You cannot. Only the Gods and wights can make a shaman. You can, however, learn to be a shamanic practitioner. If you are already being harassed by the Gods and spirits, then you'll be a shaman if and when They say you're one, and you have all my sympathy for what has happened or will probably happen to you.

On the other hand, there's nothing wrong with being a perfectly good shamanic practitioner, and you may well find some useful points in this book.

What about the charms and power songs in this book? Can I use them if I want to?

These charms and power songs were given as gifts to myself and other shamans who spoke to the Gods and wights and then graciously donated their words to this book. You can speak or sing them, but they won't have any effect at all unless you first go to each deity who provided them, make offerings, make alliances, and form a real relationship. This is spirit-magic, not theurgic magic, and it requires the ongoing cooperation of the spirits. Some may speak to you, some may not. This was the deal we made when we asked to be allowed to publish them. In fact, all the "lessons" in this book and the next one were given as gifts by the Gods that we serve and love. A bevy of spirit-workers "interviewed" them, asking them their opinion on the most important things for a spirit-worker to know. Some gave charms, some songs, some important knowledge. All are precious.

Music for the power songs can be found on my homemade CD, "Nine Sea Songs", which is only available for sale on my website (http://www.cauldronfarm.com/music/) for the curious.

What's the difference between a shaman and a shamanic practitioner?

Keeping in mind that the answer *is true only for this tradition* (i.e. other shamanic traditions may draw the line in other places), a shaman is someone who is seized up by the spirits and forced through a long and tortuous phase of illness that brings them close to physical death, or complete insanity, or both. During this time, the Gods and wights modify their astral body in ways that you'd have to be close to death in order to manage. Most tribal cultures acknowledge that there is an attrition rate—i.e. there's a definite risk of death, which is worse the more the beginning shaman fights the process. Once through, they must do their job of public tribal spirit-worker for the rest of their life, or the shaman sickness will occur and cause insanity and/or death. Their lives are bounded by taboos, and they work closely with spirits of many different types, sometimes as a slave, sometimes as a partner.

On the other hand, a shamanic practitioner is someone who learns shamanic techniques, and perhaps has some voluntary dealings with spirits, and does what they do because they want to, not because they have to. It's much easier, and safer, to be a shamanic practitioner, although there are a small number of people who start out in the latter category and end up in the former one. A classic shaman, however, will be able to channel heavier "voltage" and do more intense spirit-work, and have a closer connection with the spirits. They just had to give up their entire life for that ability.

Can I force or coax the Gods and wights into making me a shaman?

Force? Not likely. Coax? That depends. It has been done, in the past; some people have deliberately brought themselves repeatedly very close to death in a ritual context in order to get the attention of the spirits. Some died. Some survived, but insane. Some got the attention that they desired and became shamans, but were so mentally scarred that the ensuing shaman sickness killed them. A few made it. Generally, though, most people wouldn't want to be classic shamans if they really understand what that meant. These books will tell of what it's like in this tradition, this harsh and bloody subarctic tradition that bore so many of my ancestors. They were chosen so that their people might survive. If you are chosen, you will serve some form of a tribe—possibly not of your choosing—for the rest of your life, and that work will come before everything else. Not your parents, your children, your partners, or any other career will take anything but a back seat to this Work. If you slack off, you'll become ill. If you quit, you'll die. We don't joke about this; we've seen too many go down.

If this is you, welcome to the Boot Camp of the Northern Gods. We hope that you survive, but that will depend on your relationship with Them. In the meantime, here's a textbook for you, perhaps the only written one you'll ever get. Don't mistake it for the important information. That, only They will give you. This is only the syllabus, the course outline, the notes scribbled down in the back of the class. But here, take my shaman's notebook. At the end of the day, it might just give you the keys to get through a few thorns.

Shamanism and Service
by Lydia Helasdottir

If you look at the wandering Volva in Erik The Red's Saga, the concept is quite an interesting one—she's welcomed in, but there's all this "When is she leaving?" They go to a lot of trouble for her, ritual trouble, with feeding her the hearts of every animal on the property, in part because they want to propitiate her because she's scary, and in part because they want her to be on her way as quickly as possible. So I think spirit-workers end up feeling used, a lot, but that's part of the deal. We are set apart and used, and it's part of the power. I think that's hard for people to understand; they think that in the perfect tribal world the shaman would be just like the smith or the potmaker, just another job, but they have to be set apart.

There's a story about a young girl in a Native American Plains community who got hit by lightning. People who got hit by lightning were supposed to be blessed and taken by the spirits, but they were also supposed to die, taken by Sky Father or what-have-you. But she didn't die, so the people didn't know quite what to make of her, because here was this being that Sky Father had touched, but she wasn't dead, so was she now bad luck or good luck? So she ended up living in this tent outside the village with her door open away from the village, but they would still bring her food, because they didn't dare not to. She told about how she then began to get bitten by poisonous animals and not die.

It really is part of the deal, though—we are equally respected, and feared, and loathed, and admired ... and admired is the least on the list, occasionally. Some tribes had no compunctions about killing off their shamans if the things they were doing weren't working. So however bad it is now, one is glad to not have to deal with that. There is also the modern issue that people who are outsiders for other reasons decide that they like the shaman job because it's at least about being a powerful outsider, whether or not it's really for them. (I'm quite comfortable with people doing shamanic practices, but this does not make them a shaman.) Most of them don't really understand that you're still tied to the tribe, to the service position, even though they fear you and don't appreciate you. You can't just up and leave, unless the spirits are sending you to another tribe. You have to keep offering your help again and again, even though you will never really be one of them. It's a painful, awful, thankless place to be in, and that's the way of it. Do you really want that job? Most people wouldn't, if they understood that.

But it's absolutely necessary, because the power that you're gaining is so large that if you were not constrained to use it in a service situation, you'd just turn into a power-greedy maniac. There are stories of shamans who go bad, and they tend not to live too long, but they can get up to some bad stuff in the meantime. There are medieval stories about how the shamans and the casters of magic darts were in collusion, because as long as the casters of magic darts were there, the shamans could be called to fix whatever damage the casters had done. This was pretty convoluted, but since the writer was writing in the 1400s it was kind of understandable.

But you can't escape from the service job. No matter how arrogant shaman-people may appear, in the end, you're just humping a sack for a group of people who need the service ... most of whom are ungrateful wankers, who you can't turn down. (Although you can sometimes get some choice as to priority. "OK, I've got fifteen wankers here, which one of them is the least annoying? Maybe the day will be done by the time I have to get to the most annoying and he'll go away, because his problem will be miraculously resolved.") It's similar to the bodhisattva oath, and to the ceremonial magic idea of sacrificing everything into the cup. It's not about you. You look at the shaman role from the outside, and you think "Wow, there's all this power, and this ability to cause awe and do cool shit—heal shit and blow shit up and what-have-you." And the shaman says, "Well, yeah, but…"

I sometimes talk about it like being in the army. Yeah, you get to drive a big tank and carry a gun and look tough, but most of the time it involves eating bad food and not getting enough sleep and crawling through the mud, and you can only blow up what they tell you to blow up, and if you blow up the stuff that you want to blow up, you get court-martialed and shot, and you have to account for every round of ammo, and they might send you into wars you don't agree with, and that's too bad. While it's cool to walk into the bar in your fatigues and camo with your gun over your shoulder, in reality you're just a grunt. And if you walk into the bar with all that stuff, you're a wanker grunt as well! For me, my patron deity just says, "Make sure you carry the ID, but don't be walking around in all that stuff." Of course, it also depends on what the uniform for your job is. Some of us have to wear the crazy uniform and be the community model for what a shaman looks like. Others of us get to be stealth and look normal, except when we need to do our work. It takes both kinds, working from the outside and the inside as well. But we're all outsiders, in the end. It's part of our power. It's lonely, and dark, and absolutely necessary. We are the sacrifice made that humanity might live on.

Laufey's Lesson

Courage Is An Action

as told to Elizabeth Vongvisith

I first encountered Laufey when I went on a journey to Jotunheim. I didn't quite know what to expect. I had not met Loki's mother before, and there is very little information extant in the lore or in modern heathen UPG about her. My nervousness was quickly put to rest, however. She was very kind to me, and I soon felt both more at ease with her and more in awe of her as Laufey's real nature became apparent. It seems strange at first to think that this calm, rather earthy giantess is the mother of the infamous Loki, but once you talk to Laufey for a little while, you will soon see that there is far more to her than meets the eye. This is, after all, the woman who fled Jotunheim while pregnant, alone and without even a weapon to defend herself, and who swallowed her pride and sought sanctuary among total strangers in Muspellheim for the sake of her unborn son.

Laufey has a soft spot in particular for women who are unhappy in love or those in need of protection from their enemies, having once been in both those unenviable positions herself. From her, Loki inherited his tenacious will to survive, his ability to wait patiently to have his revenge, and conversely his extreme protectiveness towards those he truly loves. Her will can be quite as implacable as that of her granddaughter Hela. Her foes are often surprised at her tenacity, but to her friends and those under her protection, Laufey is a bold and reassuring ally. Like Sigyn, Loki's enduring second wife, Laufey reminds us that there are other ways to show strength than on the field of battle.

Laufey's Lesson:

When you think of courage, do you think of brave deeds, daring quests, or battles with overwhelming odds? Do you think of war, danger, adventure? All these things require courage, it is true, but how often do most of you face them, except perhaps in your dreams and daydreams? Much more relevant, and perhaps even more important, is the courage one needs to live day to day, even in times of peace and plenty. Not all tests and trials come from hardship and ordeals. Some of them come in blessings and wishes fulfilled. Some of them come through friends and loved ones, rather than rivals and enemies. Sometimes courage requires patience and endurance instead of bold action.

There is a kind of courage that is much harder to manifest than the kind it takes to run another man through with a sword, or to lead a dangerous expedition into some unknown land. There is the courage one needs to go against the wishes of one's family and friends and to follow the dictates of the heart. That same courage is necessary to stand up alone amidst a hostile crowd and say, This is not right. That is also the kind of courage one needs when one's children grow up and go off into the world, there to live or die as their choices lead them. That is the courage it takes to simply live life.

Classic Shamanism And Core Shamanism: Basic Differences

(Author's note: This article was written for a Pagan publication some years before I started writing this series, so it is not aimed at a specifically northern-tradition audience. I include it here because I believe that it contains useful concepts for anyone working with any kind of shamanism.)

The word "shamanism" has been thrown around a great deal these days, and attached to all manner of things, sometimes with only a vague understanding of its meaning. Most people who go to a class on "shamanic this-or-that" have very little knowledge of what actual tribal shamans practiced in any given cultures, or what sorts of things were and are practiced transculturally among them. A researcher or interested seeker, looking through all the widely varied literature, will notice both similarities and differences between anthropological descriptions of long-ago tribal shamans and modern-day shamanic practitioners. They may also run across specialized terms such as "core shamanism"; "shamanistic practice"; "shamanistic behavior", and so on. It can be rather confusing.

The term "core shamanism" was popularized by Michael Harner in his book "The Way Of The Shaman". It supposedly implies that it contains the "core" shamanic techniques, stripped of their cultural context and teachable to individuals not raised in that culture. On the other hand, the experience of people who work with core shamanism is not identical to that of shamans and their counterparts who come to their work the old-fashioned way, anthropological accounts of which have been gathered for over two hundred years. There are stunning similarities between the experiences of many of these shamans, regardless of their home culture or place in the world. These similarities, and the similarities of the altered-state and magical techniques used by tribal shamans, have popularized the concept of the global "shamanic" spiritual/magical system.

I've chosen to use the term "classic shamanism" to describe the cross-cultural set of experiences described by tribal shamans across the world. It shares with "core shamanism" many of the same tools and techniques of consciousness—journeying, visualization, drumming, ritual, working with animal and plant totems, natural spirits, or ancient gods; natural hallucinogens, cultural symbol systems, and so forth. It isn't the tools that differentiate the two, as core shamanism borrowed those tools from classic shamanism. Instead, it's the central spiritual experience that is strongly different, as can be seen from this chart.

To be clear, however: Not all shamans in traditional tribal societies follow the "classic shaman" pattern. For example, among the Jivaro Indians, as many as a quarter of the men in the tribe may be trained as shamans, and the knowledge can be bought for the fee of a gun and some ammunition. This would make most of them analogous to "core shamans". In other tribal societies, a shaman's son or daughter may be trained in the position; sometimes they are chosen before birth with divination methods (which would suggest spirit-choosing, like the classic experience) and sometimes they are merely selected by their parent when old enough. In some areas of the world, where the tradition has all but died out, a member of the tribe may volunteer to take on the work whether or not they have been contacted by the spirits, in order to keep the tradition alive.

Core Shamanism	Classic Shamanism
Is theoretically open to anyone who is sincere. Some people who are more talented in energy-moving techniques may do better, but no one is technically banned from the practice.	Is open only to those who are clearly chosen by the spirits. Although one can offer one's self to the spirits, they may or may not accept.
Is generally entirely voluntary. The individual chooses the path, rather than being chosen for it by the spirits. Although the seeker may feel "drawn" to shamanic practices, they are not in danger of illness, insanity or death for refusing to follow a particular path. They may choose their own human teachers, and they may stop at any time; although their lives may be poorer for it, they will not usually be penalized by the spirits unless they have made specific bargains.	Is generally entirely involuntary. The individual is chosen by the spirits, often with no warning, and is not allowed to refuse the "gift", or they will suffer illness, and/or insanity, and/or death. They can never stop being a shaman so long as they live, or it will recur.
Is not generally accompanied by severe life-threatening experiences.	Is nearly always accompanied in the early stages by severe life-threatening experiences, including but not limited to chronic serious illness, psychotic break, and/or near-death experience.

Core Shamanism	Classic Shamanism
May engender growth of personality and an empowering change of life path, but is not generally accompanied by a traumatic death-and-rebirth experience. No one specific image, vision, or symbolism predominates across the board in the early stages of shamanic work.	Is nearly always accompanied by a traumatic death-and-rebirth experience, after which the personality is radically changed. A visionary experience of being dismembered and rebuilt differently by the spirits is evident cross-culturally in the accounts of many tribal shamans, and is almost a hallmark of the experience.
Causes slow and gradual change to part of the aura and astral body due to working with the various shamanic techniques. The process is usually largely under the control of the seeker.	Causes radical, unusual, and permanent changes to the aura and astral body. This process is inflicted onto the shaman by the spirits, and is entirely out of their control.
Shamanic practice can occupy however large a space in the individual's life as they wish. It can be a part-time hobby or a full-time occupation, as they decide.	Shamanic practice occupies the main focus, time, and energy of the individual's life for the rest of their existence. All mundane careers, projects, loyalties, and relationships are secondary to the shaman's career of spiritual service.
Primarily taught by human teachers, although in the more advanced stages the seeker may work with divine and/or spirit teachers.	Primarily taught by divine and/or spirit teachers, although in the beginning stages the novice is usually taught the cultural context and symbolism by another shaman.

Core Shamanism	Classic Shamanism
Often taught in groups, or in books.	Never taught in groups; always one-on-one as an oral tradition.
Taboos are rare, and taken on only as a deal with a particular spirit. Violation of those taboos generally only result in loss of power, although bargains with powerful spirits may result in traumatic incidents.	Lives are bounded with dozens of increasing taboos, violation of which generally brings immediate illness, pain, or other physical and spiritual retribution.
Can work shamanic practices alone, or see clients unattached to any demographic group.	Cannot work entirely alone; must be attached to a tribe. If no tribe is in evidence at the time of their shamanic rebirth, one will be provided for them by the spirits. Ability to see clients outside their demographic group varies, usually depending on their tradition and their particular patron spirits.
Can be seen as a path of service, or as a lucrative career.	Is almost always seen primarily as a path of service to a particular tribe.

Core Shamanism	Classic Shamanism
Mental illness is as rare or prevalent as it is in the ordinary population demographic, and unrelated to shamanic practice.	Mental breakdown or temporary psychosis common to the early "death-and-rebirth" stage, after which shamans have been tested and found to be comparatively extremely sane and stable. Mental illness never returns as long as they continue to do their jobs.
Can draw from any cultural contexts, or create their own.	Generally requires one specific central cultural context, although they may borrow from neighboring (and thus not radically different) cultures. The symbolic context seems to be a useful "anchoring-point" for the training of beginning classic shamans, and aids in bonding them with the tribe that they are to serve.
Often seeks to have a relationship with the gods and/or spirits that is "equal", or even "mastery over the spirits" in order to gain access to their powers.	Relationship with gods and/or spirits ranges from propitiating or coaxing to being their outright slave, for which the shaman gains access to their powers.

As can be seen from this comparison, the question of who and what is a shaman is fairly complex these days. One could define "shaman" as a job description only to classic shamans, and call folks in the other category "shamanic practitioners", or something of that nature, or one could expand the term to include full-time workers in both categories. Most Americans would prefer the latter, as there are few classic shamans in the white American demographic.

Of course, then one would get into the equally sticky space of what constitutes a "full-time" shaman. Would those who only teach it for money, essentially as a lucrative financial career rather than a service practice, be counted? On the one hand, they are doing something involving shamanic techniques full-time; on the other hand, being a shaman is traditionally a religious service position. A tribal shaman fills a similar function for his/her people that the local priest or pastor or vicar does here; it has a ministerial as well as a ritual/magical side. One ought to be able to go to your local shaman for aid and be helped at a reasonable price for your wallet, even if that's an empty, broke, unemployed wallet.

This also brings us to the question of why there are so few classic shamans in the white Western demographic. Part of that is need; if a people are getting their spiritual needs adequately met in a non-shamanic context, the Gods and spirits may not feel the need to interfere. A greater reason, however, is sheer risk. Even in shamanic cultures where there is a structure and context to train novice shamans, there is an acceptance of the fact that not all of them make it. The physical and mental stresses of the transformative classic-shamanic experience create a varying death rate even for those who are prepared for it. When refusal of the gift, or inability to get a handle on it, means insanity (often leading to suicide) or death from illness, there is going to be a certain attrition rate.

Additionally, in this culture, we have no tools or context or experienced mentors to lead us through the process. In a traditional shamanic culture—meaning one in which shamanism is an accepted part of the spiritual tradition—the suffering person is identified by and taken on by an already functioning classic shaman. This mentor will teach them the proper techniques, give them a useful cultural context-system to work with (something that is dismissed by most Westerners but seems to be vital to the effectiveness of the classic shaman's work), helps them identify and manage their taboos, introduces them to spirit helpers, and above all provides affirmation that this process is "normal" for what they are becoming. The average American who might get themselves seized as a shaman by the Gods and/or spirits will have none of these things. In fact, they may end up medicated (which will temporarily "abort" the shamanic transformation, only to have it repeatedly recur throughout the person's life until they are insane or dead), or institutionalized, or struggling with life-threatening illnesses that modern medicine is not capable of curing. Often, if an illness contracted as part of a shamanic rebirth is actually cured by medicine, the sufferer will promptly come down with another one.

On top of this, we have little in the way of coherent, easily accessed tradition. The shamanic traditions of our ancestors have been suppressed to the point where they are broken shreds that we are desperately trying to piece back together. The Gods and spirits still remember them, but in order to access that information, we have to have a clear line through to them ... something that may not happen until one has already survived the transformation process. The likelihood is that most Westerners who are struck with the shamanic transformation "illness" simply don't make it. No one shows up to help them, and they are told that everything they are experiencing is not real, and is symptomatic of a curable problem. They try their best to make it all go away, and in the process they make it even worse.

This doesn't mean to imply that everyone who gets cancer or pneumonia or goes mad is a potential shaman. Even in shamanic cultures, there are accounts of people who fell physically or mentally ill in ways that resembled shamanic transformation illnesses, and the local shamans came over to check, and declared it to be an ordinary sort of illness. One such incident was recounted by a Western anthropologist living in a small Taiwanese village. A local woman began to have "fits" and talk to unseen spirits. A group of shamans came from miles away to check her out, and declared that she was merely mentally ill; no actual spirits were in evidence.

However, we also have the accounts of white Americans who are "classic shaman" types; who survived their transformation illness and went on to do their job in a way remarkably similar to that of traditional tribal shamans. In each case, they managed to figure out what was going on and either find mentors somehow or embed themselves into some cultural context that worked for them and for their spirit helpers. Although they may have studied core-shamanism techniques, they often did not find them to be adequate for their needs without some kind of deeply-understood cultural cosmology attached to them. Some threw themselves into the foreign cosmologies (with the permission of the spirits attached to those cosmologies) and some struggled to unearth that of their own ancestors. Either way, many admit that they almost didn't make it.

There's also the ongoing debate over the appropriation of cultural spirituality by people not of that culture, which is a long and tangled skein with good points on both sides. Perhaps it's wrong to steal the cultural context of someone else's culture ... but what if their gods speak to you? Perhaps it's fine to be dissatisfied with a cultural context that doesn't make sense to you ... but what if your own genetic heritage is nearly entirely robbed of its ancient shamanic roots? There doesn't seem to be any one good solution to the problem. Some strides have been made, and are being made, by dogged souls who are piecing together the ragged bits of shamanic lore left to Western culture, and this is a good thing. It likely won't come together fast enough to save all of the next generation of future shamans, but it's a start.

One thing that we all have to do is to think critically, and to be asking ourselves these hard questions. When people say that something is "shamanic", we need to learn to ask them what it is that they mean, and not accept a vague answer. When people call themselves shamans, we need to ask them why they feel that this job title applies to them, and not take pop jargon replies. We need to find out if they understand the difference between core shamanism and its various American and European offsprings, and classic shamanism and its traditional and modern avatars.

I don't intend to get into a debate about whether a classic shaman does a better job than a full-time core shaman when you show up for your reading or your healing or your soul retrieval. Frankly, the jury's still out on that one. I'd like to think that a competent and ethical practitioner of any sort would do their best for you, and tell you honestly when your needs are beyond their ability to fulfill. But we need to educate ourselves about what it is that we actually want from the world of shamanism, and wean ourselves off of the romantic images of inspirational novels. Being a real shaman is work, lots of hard work, often for little immediate reward. It's not a hobby. It's a calling, or it should be, at least to some extent. It's not something that you do in order to find yourself ... or if you go there looking for yourself, it will show you yourself as a tool of the Gods and spirits, not how you'd like to think of yourself in your head.

So... let's talk about this. Let's bring it out into the open and clear away the fog from the terminology. Let's honor both scholarship and personal experience, at the same time, and see if we can make something useful out of all the ragged bits. Because the next generation is waiting.

Gods And Wights:
Spirit Allies and Spirit Masters

All cultural shamanisms are based in a larger religious context, and this is an important point that is missed by many neo-shamanic practitioners. Modern Westerners like to hedge their bets around the existence of the "differentiated Divine", as one friend refers to it, as opposed to the "undifferentiated Divine" which isn't much interested in giving us personal attention, because it's too big. It's especially difficult for the sort of modern Westerner who is on a spiritual quest, because they may have left the religion of their birth with a certain amount of disillusion and trauma, and part of that disillusion may be around Deity and its existence. That means that a lot of modern neo-shamanisms are careful not to use language that alienates too many of their paying students by requiring them to actually believe in the existence of spirits ... which for any tribal shaman would be ludicrous.

Lessons in these modern traditions are phrased in such a way to suggest that "it's all part of alternate realities" or "if it feels real for you, then it's real," with the unspoken "or might as well be," being careful to make no definitive delineation between actual entities and whatever the sock puppets in people's heads come up with during trance. Yet the real spirit-workers that I know are constantly working to improve their signal clarity and figure out what's the clear voice of the wights, what's their voice but garbled by our mortal meat-brains with their loads of issues, and what's the mental puppets putting on God-masks. It's one of our biggest struggles ... because we've heard the voice of the Gods clearly differentiated from our own mental voice.

Perhaps even more importantly, we've seen the results of listening to divine voices as opposed to listening to our own illusions. Certainly for myself, what got me to trust in Hela was seeing the track record. When I was hearing Her clearly and doing what I was supposed to, things got better. When I wasn't, things got worse. Not teaching people to make the distinction—assuming that they even have a line to the spirits, a "throughput" as one spirit-worker calls it—puts them in grave danger of a cosmic smackdown. It's the equivalent of flying without any navigational information or radio contact with the ground. Part of the reason why modern spirit-workers have begun to stress this new title as an umbrella term (besides wanting to avoid the who-is-a-shaman argument) is that working with spirits is by definition what we do. Without these People in our lives, this work can't be done.

Northern-tradition Paganism, the context in which this shamanic tradition is posited, has a polytheistic worldview. This means that each God/spirit is seen as a separate, living, changing entity, not dependent on human attention or worship to survive (although their connection to this particular world of matter may fail without that), and clearly differentiated from other similar Gods/wights. Even if they have the same title, they may not be the same being. The President of the U.S. is not the President of Angola, even if they are addressed similarly.

To be fair, there are a few exceptions where a deity may actually deliberately appear under a different name, and some deities have lists of *heiti*—titles of their different aspects which, when used to call them, will define how they manifest. (That seems to be a Cosmic Law that is bigger than us and Them.) We don't know all the details of these Mysteries, and anyway They don't expect that of us. What we are expected to do is to show respect and honor, and give them our attention and energy, and we will get attention and energy back in return. Treating them like real entities rather than idealized thought-forms or archetypes or even fantasies is part of that respect and honor.

The cultural/religious context in which this shamanic tradition is based is not modern American Heathenry, although it shares many of the same myths and deities. Modern Heathenry, while it is a valid religion on its own (as is any faith which serves its members usefully in a spiritual way), carries some attitudes towards deities that create problems when it comes to spirit-work. Some are modern American prejudices against devotion and supplication, some are modern Western prejudices against apparently non-intellectual mysticism, some are baggage from monotheistic upbringing in a religion largely of converts, and some are early Christian attitudes absorbed from the authors of the surviving texts themselves. Whatever the sources, these make it difficult to form the kind of relationships with the Gods and wights that are absolutely necessary for the spirit-worker to function. A strict reconstructionist religion, while it is itself a form of ancestor worship, has little room for an active and changing relationship with real entities who may refuse to adhere to human writings.

Unfortunately, the northern-tradition Pagan religious context in which this shamanism fits is still quite vague and has not yet found its edges, or even its feet. There is also the fact that if you view the Gods and wights as real individuals, you have to take into account their ability to change and grow. Some of the Gods that I work with seem to be still very much stuck in an ancient era, and unused to modern ways; others are quite comfortable with cars, computers, cheeseburgers, and safe sex. They evolve by experiencing things through us, and to see them as stuck in some idealized eternal video game is to miss the point. Instead, the northern-tradition spirit-worker needs to understand that these Gods are alive and aware and remaking their connection to this world, and coming to understand it anew.

Part of what seems to have happened on a cosmic level during the last millennia was a sort of pulling apart of the worlds. This has been metaphorically acknowledged by many writers, but we don't see it as a metaphor. It doesn't seem to have been due to anything we humans did or didn't do. It seems to have been part of a natural cycle, an orbiting dance, so to speak. During this period, connection with the Gods and wights of the other worlds was not impossible, but was much more difficult, and seemed to require a strong initiating (or even a strong longing) by us mortals; they were mostly unable to come through on their own. Rather than the claim of some writers that Christianity drove off the old Gods, it may be that this pulling away of the worlds left a vacuum that was then filled by Christianity.

As far as we can tell, the Nine Worlds pulled away from our own from the top down—first Asgard, then Alfheim, then Vanaheim, and so on. Legends of the faery folk leaving the world of Men date back to the late medieval period, but the legends of the Duergar packing up and leaving Germany are as recent as the late 1700s, with the rise of the hammer-mills. We have reason to believe that Niflheim and Helheim parted company before the 20th century. We also have reason to believe that they are reversing, again as part of the natural cycle, and coming back into connection again in the opposite order that they pulled away—from the bottom up. Helheim, certainly, is much more active and connected than it ever was before, and we are starting to feel strong echoes from the other worlds. As the lower worlds are mostly Jotun-controlled, it is no wonder that there is a sudden influx of Jotun and Rökkr activity, including increased Jotun bloodlines and the creation of throwbacks.

Then there is the conundrum of Midgard. We refer to this world as Midgard, but more and more people are reporting that they are experiencing Midgard as something else. I can't honestly say that I am a hundred percent sure how this worked, but it seems very much that Midgard is a sort of sister-world to this one, the point at which our world is attached to the Nine, and the one with the most harmony with ours. Certainly it is the world that is most populated with mortal men. There are tantalizing bits of gnosis filtering down that suggest that Midgard and this world were actually the same once but split off, as if the astral body of our world split like an amoeba. Those who have traveled through the Midgard that is the central point of the Nine Worlds, as opposed to simply moving through it in a split second, have reported that the mortal natives live at a much more medieval level of technology than we do, which might allow us to date the split effectively.

At any rate, regardless of the shape of cosmological issues, the Gods and wights of the Nine Worlds are coming through stronger than they have in centuries. They are demanding the respect and honor that they were given long ago, and for some of them, "long ago" may mean very long ago indeed. The Neolithic nature of the wights that I work with clashes strongly with many aspects of the modern world, but some basic primal needs and energies still come through loud and clear. They want to be known, and to communicate, and to be honored and respected by those who are willing and able to make that connection.

About Spirits
by Lydia Helasdottir

Do spirits really exist? Do they have objective reality? I did some good argumentation on that recently, talking about the salvia plant spirit. Somebody had posed the question: Is the salvia entity real? There was a big debate about it, and the way we posited it in the end was this:

Premise number one: The entire manifested universe was, at one time, generated from a single undifferentiated Source.

Premise number two: Manifestation in general is an illusion, in that it is all still really part of the one undifferentiated Source, but in order to have experience, the Source generates the manifestation and the illusion of separation.

As a corollary, we have a catch-phrase that states: Illusion is the coin with which we pay for our experiences, and the ability to have experience at all. So given these premises, then there are things manifest in this universe—like you, me, the fork, the tape machine, the bag over there—that partake of objective reality in our experience. And insofar as those things partake of objective reality to me, Gods, spirits, boggarts, kobolds, and all the rest of the whole coterie have the exact same objective reality, except that they are noncorporeal.

You can add a premise inside of there that says: The apparently objective existence of you, me, and the bag over there is not purely of matter—and this has been proven by physics, there is something energetic going on as well—and then based on all that, you can say that inasmuch as we exist, there is also the existence of manifestation beyond pure matter, which is also a proven thing anyway, so these entities could also exist. And that seemed to catch on pretty well, although it really upset them, because they couldn't argue with it.

But we experience them as absolutely their own people. They get offended when people try to contact them who don't believe in them. Mostly you just get nothing from that, but sometimes they will manifest in an overwhelming way and scare the shit out of the person. "Not real, am I? Oh yeah? Disbelieve the fork that just went flying through the room and stuck in your head." Not only can you piss them off until they won't manifest, there are also things that you can do that make it easier for them to manifest. The particular energetic environment, and your state of mind, makes it easier or harder for you to talk to them. It's just like with people, right? It is not comfortable for a corporate businessman to come to a meeting that takes place in a Hell's Angels bar, where you are distracted by flirting with the girls over there. He will not find it easy to have good communication with you under those circumstances. It's about courtesy and protocol and thoughtfulness.

Yes, there are people who will act as if they believe in the reality of the spirits, while actually doubting that there's anything except this objective reality. And on a purely energetic purview, they're not going to be able to raise much power. It's as if someone phones me up and said, "I'd like to come talk to you and have dinner with you, but actually I'm really not sure that you're the right person to be talking to, and I'm not really sure that you should even have the job that you're actually holding, or even that you are what you say you are, but just in case, I'd like to come interrogate you and have you prove it to me." What I'd say is "Fuck off." If someone came to me and said "I honestly don't quite understand, and I want to learn more, and I'm not sure it has to be the case that something has to exist, and can you help me?" I might still say "Ah, I just don't have the time," but I would tend to be a lot more open to that.

I'm always getting told by magicians that I put too much anthropomorphizing in my dealings with Them. But I choose to interface with the manifest Universe in a way that's easy for me, and if I want to anthropomorphize my Gods, then I'll do that. Please don't believe that I attach any objective reality to the fact that Hela appears to me with a face. I know that me, Her, you, and the fork, are all undifferentiated Source material, really. But it happens to be convenient to me to do it this way. And that just eliminates their whole frigging argument. People will try to convince you that your view of this deity or that deity is incorrect, or that it must not be real because it's so human, that you must be projecting your concerns onto the deity who is actually unknowable. Well, of course there are aspects of any Deity that are unknowable, but She just happens to choose to project a certain manifestation down here because She wants me to do work, and in order to do work, I have to understand what She wants. She happens to find it convenient to take on a human (or humanoid) form, just as I will choose to speak English to someone instead of Swahili or Enochian.

When you're dealing with many different races, it's best to find out beforehand how to behave properly to them. It's just like people. When you go to China, you should find out what's proper customs there. And there's a good policy for the traveler—don't go into places where you can't find out how to behave properly. Until you have a reliable way of finding out—like a guide or a guidebook of some kind—don't go there. If you use divination, be prepared to ask 20 questions. "I'm going to this place; do I need to bring something—yes or no? Does it have to be physical—yes or no? Does it have to be food or jewelry or tobacco?" Go down the list, yes/no, yes/no, yes/no. It could be booze, spices, jewelry, trinkets—but they can be twigs and rocks and sand from other places—small bits of interesting technology like data chips, or willingness to take messages to their family across the pond, etc. Sometimes you end up doing a bit of peace brokerage, which can be surprising, and really make things all worth it.

So what, exactly, should the northern-tradition spirit-worker's relationship be with the Gods and wights? Honestly, the first steps of that are entirely up to Them. The crucial beginning to being a spirit-worker is that entities begin to approach you, and keep approaching—the classic quote by Jenny Blain is "Spirits won't leave you alone, even when you're sleeping." It's up to you to figure out who and what they are—some will let you know immediately, some prefer to be mysterious for a time—and how to treat them. This probably seems unfair, but it's been the way of Gods and spirits since time immemorial. (Just read the ancient or tribal accounts.) Some will be helpful and tell you what it is that they want up front; for some you'll have to guess. Divination helps on all these questions, as does talking to other people who work with the same Gods and wights.

One form of divination that I find excellent for these problems is to do bibliomancy—grabbing a book off the shelf and opening it randomly while blindly putting down a finger on a line—using a shelf full of books on anthropology, history, and religion, or even better, stuff specifically on northern-tradition lore. When it comes to offerings, one tried-and-true method is to go shopping and wander about the stores, and see if you get a sort of mental "poke" saying, "Hey, I want that!" (Of course, this gets us into the corollary of "when the spirits spend all your money", which is a different problem.)

Many (but not all) northern-tradition shamans get grabbed by a specific God or Goddess who claims them. The god-slave (Galina Krasskova uses the term *godatheow*) phenomenon, while not solely found in our tradition, does seem to have a definite trend here. This kind of situation is much more thorough than the usual idea of a "patron deity" who watches over you from afar, is kindly and benevolent and helpful, and may point out your path while not forcing you to tread it. The *godatheow*, in comparison, is very much the slave of their God(s), who may trigger shaman sickness, turn their lives upside down, strip away anything that does not serve the spirit-worker purpose, and herd them by force onto a specific path, not shirking at punishments up to and including death if the *godatheow* rebels.

While Western sensibilities may bridle at that idea, it's not at all unfamiliar to tribal spirit-workers around the world. Many of them will say bluntly that their spirits will make them ill or even kill them if they quit or dishonor their job, or offend the spirits in some way. I read an article recently by Tatyana Bulgakova, *Shaman On The Stage*, translated from Russian and published in a European museum newsletter. It discussed how Siberian shamans had encountered troubles from Russian performance-art agents who were caught up in the revival of traditional folk practices as highly lucrative showmanship, and were asking the shamans to perform their ceremonies on stage as entertainment. Apparently a few of the shamans agreed and were even sent on a whirlwind tour of the west coast of America, where they were thrilled by curiosity-hungry American attention, not to mention the money.

However, they soon became ill and a few even died, punished by the spirits whose rites they had cheapened and wasted. The other shamans began refusing the pleas of the agents to perform on stage, and in response actors were dressed up and paid to wear the costumes, sing the songs, and beat on a drum. Even this had the side effect of making some people in the audience ill. The most sensible response has been from one shaman who had the actors remove certain vital costume elements, and rewrote the sacred songs for performance usage, largely as a prayer and praise of the spirits rather than as a request for aid.

Like any relationship arrangements, there are advantages and drawbacks to being a *godatheow*. The first one is, obviously, is that consent and choices are taken away from you, and They run your life, down to the details. This may include food, sex, clothing, human relationships, career, living location and standard, and anything else. The effect of this on a modern Western individual who is used to independence can well be imagined. The counter to this is that there is a certain amount of comfort in knowing that you are being pushed to be the best that you can be, whether you like it or not, that you are a part of something larger, and that you are burning off karmic debts at a much faster rate than that of most people. You also get a higher "security clearance" when it comes to getting pieces of cosmic information, because your bosses know that They can gag you at any time. If you are a horse, it's very much worth the price, because you as a mere mortal cannot guarantee to protect yourself against random spirits who might want to come in, nor can you guarantee to be able to control their actions once they get inside you. With a patron deity at your back setting rules of use and screening out the unsuitable, you can guarantee that you will not end up in prison, the mental bin, or dead from random spirit-use of your flesh.

The concept of the god-slave is discussed in more depth in the final section of the book *Dark Moon Rising* by Asphodel Press, but here I excerpt one section of my essay on the subject from that book:

> When I fish for the big cosmic reasons—why me, why not someone else?—what comes to me vaguely, over and over, are

the twin concepts of Dire Necessity and Lawful Prey. I know that those labels are confusing, but they are the best that I can do to explain such fuzzy concepts, ideas that seem too big to be contained in my head. I suppose I should first start out by saying that the Gods are not above the laws of the Universe; they are bound by rules just as we are. Consequence happens to them, too. Therefore, the taking of god-slaves cannot be done frivolously or to no purpose. The first principle—that of Dire Necessity—seems to indicate that it can be done only when there is some hole to be filled, some job to be done, that would benefit the greater good in a manner so as to outweigh (at least in a larger cosmic sense) the needs of the individual.

The second concept is even more difficult to explain in words. It just seems that some people are the Lawful Prey of the Gods for some reason, and others are not. Freely offering your oath to a deity, having the deity accept, having them offer at least once to free you, and your subsequent refusal, makes you Lawful Prey and they are allowed to take away your rights and choices. Also, some of us seem to be Lawful Prey without our consent, perhaps due to karmic debts or other reasons, about which I'm not certain. However it goes, I was Hela's Lawful Prey from the moment of my birth, while my sister, for example, was not.

On the other hand, some spirit-workers are not "owned" by any one deity or wight; instead, they have webs of alliance with various smaller wights who aid them in doing their job. These might be animal spirits, plant spirits, Alfar, Duergar, the lesser Jotnar or Vanir or Aesir, land-wights, dead ancestors or other dead souls who have decided to take an interest. Making alliances with many spirits, and keeping those relationships happy, is the major source of a spirit-worker's power, and what differentiates us from magicians, witches, and other assorted magic-workers.

No doubt, as you watch me continually refer to these entities with the phrase "Gods and wights", you will ask what exactly the difference is between a God and a wight. The answer is that I'm not sure where that line ought to be drawn, and anyone who tells you that they are sure is probably asking for trouble. Generally, I use the word "wight" as an umbrella term for any sort of noncorporeal spirit, from a deity on downwards. So what we're really talking about here is what's a God and what's Not.

There are a lot of opinions on this one, and many of them have more to do with personal prejudices than any thoughtful usage. All too often, "Gods" are who the speaker worships, and "Not-Gods" are who they don't work with. I choose not to try to draw that line, because I am aware that there is a huge grey area between those powers that are clearly that big and shiny, and those that are obviously tiny. I generally go with the words of Ari, a spamadhr who corresponded extensively with me for these books: "If it's bigger, older, and wiser than I'll ever be, then I treat it as a god."

Another issue is figuring out what sort of wight you've got when one contacts you. This is a real problem when you're going to a strange place and Something pops up and attempts to communicate with you, and you may or may not even be able to sense it clearly. Throughout the ages human beings have put all sorts of labels on many different creatures, sometimes lumping them all into categories that the creatures themselves might not have agreed with. This is done partly due to ignorance, partly due to lack of appropriate language, and partly due to confusion in figuring out what the buggers are anyway. If you walk onto a mountain and something appears to you as a small bearded male figure with a disgruntled attitude, is it a local elemental gnome or sprite whose territory you've stumbled onto? Is it a manifestation of the land-wight, with a mask that your own meat-brain has shoved onto it? Is it a dwarf from Svartalfheim who has a door to this mountain on our world, and doesn't want it disturbed? Is it one of the lower Fey-creatures—some of them are rather gnomelike—with the same situation? Is it a dead human soul who has been here so long that he's become a sort of guardian to this place? Assuming that it's any one of these could get you in trouble if it's something else, and you try the wrong approach.

The first wrong approach is to say, "What are you?" This is rude— some folk may find it offensive—and counterproductive, as they may not have the language or concepts to explain themselves in terms that you, with your limited knowledge, will understand. It's better to first ask "What do you want?" or "What is it that you would like me to do here?"

and go from there. Sometimes you can get a clear idea of their identity from what wishes they express, sometimes not. Often it isn't really important who or what they are, just finding out what they're aggrieved or worried about, and being able to reassure them that you will not make whatever mess they're anticipating. It's better to have a positive interaction with an entity whose identity you'll never really know than to have a spirit-worker staring at the astral hole in your back months later saying, "Ah, that's elf-shot."

That said, sometimes the only way to find out what a particular wight is may be to observe it over time, and document not its appearance but its behavior, including its alliances and connections. Checking with other spirit-workers can help as well, although the chaotic tumble of words that are our folk names for things may get in the way. Some of these words are currently used to refer to a variety of things, while other things may have several random names. While most entities won't care if you call them by a particular collection of syllables, they may not appreciate being lumped in with creatures that aren't their kind, and if they seem offended by a label, that's the time to politely ask them to explain the nature of their kind of Folk.

Wights can also change categories, in some cases. Little sprites can meld with the larger land-wights and go up the hierarchy. Jotnar and Duergar and Alfar can fuse with the elemental spirits of a place to the point where they become extra-powerful elemental guardians, but lose much of their individual personality and nature. Dead souls can, in some cases, meld with all sorts of things. It seems to me that the (often wrong and sloppy) assumption that these categories all blend together anyhow is due to ignorance not just of the nature of these different wights, but of how they can shift from one category to another.

Below is a quick list of the sort of wights one might work with in the Northern Tradition. This does not constitute all the sorts of wights in the world, or even a large percentage of them, and there may be more NT wights that I'm missing in this list. That said, it's likely that most of your work will be with the wights I describe here, to one extent or another.

Aesir and Vanir

For an excellent baseline description of the Aesir and Vanir gods, including prayers with which to invoke and praise them, I highly recommend *Exploring The Northern Tradition* by Galina Krasskova, one of the major contributors to this book. Until then, suffice it to say that Aesir are the Gods of Asgard and are sky-oriented, and the Vanir are the agriculturally-oriented Gods of Vanaheim. There are greater and lesser beings in each of these pantheons—which are really more like "nations" than the standard idea of "pantheons"; there are the most popular and powerful ones, and then a host of others who we don't know, or barely know, by name. But there's little that I can say about either of these two groups that hasn't been said better in the above book (which lists appropriate prayers and offerings), or in other books about the Norse cosmology.

Rökkr and Jotun

The Jotnar (plural of Jotun, also etin, thurse, etc.) are the Giant-race of the Nine Worlds, and Rökkr is the modern name for their Gods. Like the above nations, and like the Alfar and the Duergar, these are powerful beings with a great deal of wisdom, and it's difficult to make an arbitrary decision about which of them belong in the God-category and which in the merely-a-powerful-spirit category. Some are clearly at one end of that, and some at the other end, and some in the grey area. I treat them all courteously, and leave it at that. For more information on the Jotnar and the Rökkr Gods, please refer to the first book in this series: *The Jotunbok: Dealing With The Giants Of The Northern Tradition*, where you'll find more discussion, prayers, and propitiation than we can put within the scope of this book.

The word *trolldomr*, or the gifts of the Jotnar, became a generic word for magic and witchcraft, and lasted well into the medieval period. There is even a mention of a Norse sorceress calling up a troll in order to gain their aid, and that practice was specifically banned by later Christian law codes. While *trolldomr* is somewhat different from the gifts of the Aesir or Vanir, it has its own useful value.

God-Servants

Many deities or major wights have servants of various kinds who are often wise and useful teachers or helpers in their own right. They may take messages for their divine masters, or handle small issues of counseling, teaching, or general aid for them. Some come in animal form, such as Odin's ravens (Huginn and Muninn, who may well be manifestations of his fylgja), wolves (Geri and Freki), and eight-legged horse Sleipnir, Hela's servant-dog Garm, Thor's goats, the boars of Frey and Freya, etc. Others have humanoid form, such as Frey's elven servants Beyla and Byggvir, or Odin's Valkyries, which may have once been human dead—or, conversely, may sometimes incarnate into human bodies. The most important thing to remember about these wights is that their first loyalty is to their masters, and your words and deeds will be reported. Treat them with the respect that you'd treat the ones who send them. Courtesy counts.

Alfar

A good amount of detail about the Alfar themselves—both Light and Dark—can be found in the second book of this series, *The Pathwalker's Guide To The Nine Worlds*. Like their cousins the Sidhe of Celtic cosmology, they are a highly magical race, wise in many things and strangely ignorant in others, obsessed with aesthetics and better at beauty than anyone else, collectors of lore and magical technology, clannish and private, moving from oddly petty to amazingly generous in a moment. They have many forms, from the gnomelike or pixielike "low fairies" to the tall beautiful courtiers. It's been noted that there is a strange polarity between the Dead and the Fair Folk; those who work with one often don't work often or well with the other, although there are exceptions. It seems to be a matter of affinity.

In ancient times, there were specific nights each year that were dedicated to propitiating the Alfar; one saga tells of a Christian traveler bring turned away from a village because the locals were all engaged in an *Alfarblot,* and didn't want to offend their "guests". In those days, the Elf-folk came over here more often than today, although this too is changing as the worlds pull slowly back together. People who are drawn to the Fey Folk—or, more likely, people whom the Fey Folk are drawn to—will find themselves engaged in a complicated, amazing, and sometimes dangerous relationship. If you're in this category, your best bet is to talk to another spirit-worker who works specifically with the Fey Folk for advice on dealing respectfully with them, because while they can be great teachers of many Mysteries, they are hell on wheels when offended.

I actually get on quite well with the Fey. That's because I offered my hand and my feet to them. I made a big offering to them—and because we have rescued and set free a lot of trapped Fey over the years in the European woods, and they say, "You smell like the fucking Iron Wood!" And I say, "Yeah, but I'm also a human, and somebody has got to do it, so I do it." And they say, "What's the catch? Why is one of Hela's people looking after us!" And I say, "Because we're all on the same side in the end, and I'm a diplomat, so why don't you just chill?" I don't have that much Jotun blood— less than 60 per cent—it's enough, but it's not full on, so they can smell the human on me too. I'm pretty sure that I have Fey blood as well—I'm half German, which is where the Jotun stuff comes from, and half Welsh, which is where the Fey stuff comes from. What a great mix! As capricious as the Fey and as violent as the Jotun.

The Fey can be gracious and lovely and helpful if they want to be. I've also dealt with boggarts, Black Forest tree people, kobolds, gnomes, various giants, both the light and dark Fey—I have a friend who keeps insisting that my Fey blood is dark elf—plus assorted wights from different traditions, because I travel in their lands and they keep showing up. With diplomatic work there is endless cross-pantheon work. I have to keep all those pantheon members in my head, or have little mental flip-cards that you can quickly look through. Boogey recognition cards … what kind of boogey is this? Well, it's not a faery, and it's not from this tradition … what are you? I do have diplomatic access to a wide variety of places, but I can only visit there, so I'll never actually belong there. It's always clear that I'm from the embassy, as it were, and people will adapt their behavior accordingly and not really show me the real stuff, the stuff that goes on behind closed doors.

Sometimes you'll find something that's trapped—in Europe there are a lot of things that are trapped, because in Elizabethan times there were all sorts of sorcerers trying to be Dr. Dee and trapping things and forgetting about them, and the sorcerer never left any notes about it, and he didn't think to put a time-limit on the binding. There are lots of giants and elves and boggarts and gnomes and kobolds stuck and being used as power sources or bait or whatever else in these magical setups. You'll sometimes feel a shudder as you pass by something that's trapped, and you have to stop and ask, "Is this bait to lure in some well-meaning idiot like me so that something big can jump out and get me? Is this something that is even my business?" I don't pick up every stray cat, although I'd much like to, and I can't free everything. It's worth asking your divination method "Do I have to do anything about this?" If the answer's yes, proceed with great caution, and if the answer's no, don't get suckered into something that isn't your fight.

–Lydia Helasdottir

Duergar

Like the Alfar, the Duergar are fairly well covered in *Pathwalker's Guide*. They are the greatest teachers of craft in the Nine Worlds. No matter what it is, they know how to make it more skillfully. They are Makers of the first degree, and Making permeates their culture, their values, and their spirits. That's what people usually go to them for— learning to Make things, especially the more "solid" crafts such as metalworking, stoneworking, jewelry, pottery, and suchlike. There are no better masters for learning how to make enchanted objects where the enchantment is so bound into the procedure of Making that it will never fade out.

The Duergar keep to themselves and rarely approach humans; you'll have to go in search of them, and earn their trust, which is not easily given. Whatever you do, don't go with greed in your eyes. They know all about greed, and they can smell it a mile off. While they may not fault you for it—they understand its draw—they may see no reason to encourage it in you, or invite it into their realm. If you're turned away or ignored, the first thing to do is to check your motivations, and clean them up a bit, and then try again with an apology. As they respect persistence, humility, and hard work, this may win some points with them. However, they take a liking to people by their own obscure standards, and if they just don't want to deal with you, there's no way to make them do so.

An important thing to understand when seeking out or working with the Duergar is this: don't try for a shortcut or a quick fix. Don't think you can do something and skimp on the detail, on the preparation, on the materials, because they will know. Don't try to shortchange your work or the makers thereof or even yourself. Above all, the Duergar mistrust the idea of speed over quality, because it is shallow. You must, if you wish to earn their trust, do things thoroughly and in the appropriate time for that thing. They understand that what is slow is inevitable. Erosion is one of the most powerful forces in the world and it is slow. That's how they function. One must not go to them with human rhythms, wanting everything fast, fast, fast. Duergar don't care if something takes a thousand years to learn. They plod along, and they'll get where they're going.

Also, they despise those people whom Oscar Wilde defined as "knowing the price of everything and the value of nothing." For all I know, they may haggle on price, though I've yet to meet a Duergr that would; but never try haggling on the value of what they do. They may forgive insults—up to a point—but they keep a mental ledger of what you've done for and against them. When one crosses a line with the Duergar, one loses "credit" so to speak by one's poor behavior. There's no way to come back from such bankruptcy. Once the Duergar have reached the point of no forgiveness, there is no rancor; but that person has been crossed off without even the importance of a grudge. When the Duergar close a door, they wall it closed. It takes a lot for a person to get them to that point, but once there, they never, ever go back from that type of exile. They respect somebody with values, even if those values are different from their own, as long as they are not slick and facile but well-thought-through. They come from maggots. High birth, high lineages mean nothing to them because in the end, they always win. In the end, it all comes down to the maggots.

–Fuensanta Plaza

Cosmological Wights

This is the category that covers wights of the Nine Worlds who carry jobs that help that cosmos keep working, but do not themselves obviously belong to any of the above groups. This would include Hraesvelg the eagle at the top of the tree, Ratatosk the squirrel who carries messages back and forth between him, and Nidhogg the dragon at the roots. Nidhogg herself may be a creature of Jotun blood, or like the eagle and the squirrel, something else entirely. This category would also include the Four Deer of the Tree (guardians of the cosmic winds and the very fabric of Ginnungagap), the Dwarf-Gods of the Four Directions, and the large cockerels that act as guardians of the various realms. In general, these beings do not interact with human beings. If they do, it will be because they approached you on their own purposes. If you attempt contact with them, you will likely not get through.

Other examples of cosmological wights might be rune-spirits (see the chapter on Divination) or the *hamingja*, a kind of luck which was sometimes personified. *Hamingjar* could be inherited and passed down family lines, where it was seen as an entity. It could also run away, if misused or struck away by higher powers.

Landvaettir

The Landvaettir or landwights are the spirit of the land itself. Each part of the Earth has an indwelling spirit which wears the soil and bedrock and other matter like a body. The landwight is aware of everything that happens on its piece of earth—or could be, if it cared; some landwights choose to ignore certain things, finding them unimportant, and some are semipermanently hibernating. Some will gladly latch onto humans who make contact with them, and some will ignore humans entirely. As most modern people will not live and die on the same piece of land, our dealings with landwights are often temporary and ephemeral, and this does seem to sadden the ones who like to communicate with humans, as they are much older than we are and take a longer view of things.

If you do own your own land, and intend to stay on it, there is no excuse for you not to make a strong connection with the local wight, assuming it will talk to you. Make it offerings in a hole in the ground—mine likes food, drink, little polished stones, sex, dancing, drumming, and general good energy. In return, it can do things like run your wards for you, give you energy in an emergency, drive off intruders, tell you about what's happening on your land, help the fertility of your crops, keep your livestock from straying too far, and hold your thread when you journey to any place that it can conceive of. (There are some places that land-wights don't understand very well, especially the Void-type areas and very non-material worlds.)

Folktales abound with stories (some of them quite modern) of landwights interfering with the construction of roads and houses. If you have bought a piece of land (or one of your clients has done so), it's best to talk to the wight before doing anything. All forms of Feng Shui and its European equivalents aside, the landwight has a better idea than you as to where a house should go, and which way it should face, and how much the land should be disturbed in order to put it there. Negotiations will need to happen. Large features like boulders may be an energy center for the wight or an indwelling place for the local sprites, and it may be that they can be moved to somewhere equally appropriate with the right propitiation and respect.

On any piece of land, the wight's center isn't that hard to find if you're observant and mindful. Wight-hearts are often the places where things are just a little more naturally beautiful than anywhere else—the trees are greener, the grass lusher, the birds gather there, and it seems peaceful. However, if you haven't found it while wandering around, that may be because it's deliberately hidden. Pick a natural object such as a large stone or tree to concentrate on, and ask to be led there. If the wight wants a better signal from you, it will lead you there. Once you've been admitted to the heart-center of a land-wight's territory, be extra respectful of that space.

There are also larger landwights that look after huge areas of land, but the bigger the wight, the less likely they are to take any notice of you. In some cases powerful spirit-workers have been able to convince large continental-wights to act as protective guardians, but this is rare.

One historical example comes from Iceland, where a seer on an astral scouting mission for a conquering Norwegian king saw the four guardians of that huge island—a snorting bull, a fierce eagle, a dragon, and a mountain-giant with a club—and told the king that he had better back off, as someone there had clearly paid them to ward off any attacks.

In some urban areas, the landwight has died due to poisoning. Generally, their job is taken over to some extent by the city itself, which develops its own spirit. (There has been some conjecture that landwights can morph into city-spirits, and that growing city-spirits can deliberately kill landwights.) City dwellers ought to make nice with the city spirit before, or possibly instead of, dealing with the landwight.

Local Sprites

The "little people", as they are often called, are not the same as the Alfar/Sidhe/what-have-you. They are not "aliens" from another world who visit here; they are actual native inhabitants ... although they are often on good terms with the former group, and are sometimes willing to act as their eyes and ears when they come over here. Some are local to the area and some have migrated—in my area of the U.S., we have both the local Native American sprites and a crowd of Finnish *tonttu* that came over with the significant numbers of Finnish immigrants a century ago. My own farm, being held by Finns since Victorian times, has a bunch of those *tonttu* living in the garden; we've made a small house for them to live in.

Sprites, as I call them sometimes, are part of the astral world of this material plane. They are generally friends with the landwight, or have links to them. They excel in finding things—or, if they have a grudge against you for some reason, losing them. As with landwights, it's good for the spirit-worker to start at home and work with the sprites, perhaps leaving out food and drink for them, being that they can help or hinder any outside workings if they choose to. Their sphere of power is limited to their area, but they can also be your eyes and ears if you are good to them.

Sometimes local sprites take it upon themselves to be the guardians of wild animals in the area, and to a lesser extent plants. As the local ecologists, you may have to negotiate with them in order to hunt or trap, especially if there are species about whose survival is in peril. It's not that the sprites don't understand the food chain, or don't approve of people hunting—they do—it's that they don't like to see things out of balance. Communicate to them that you will only hunt specific creatures, and see if you can get approval for those animals. If you are setting traps, ask that they keep away creatures that are not your intended target.

The local sprites of another place may be more likely to help when called upon than the landwight itself, especially when the landwight has not interacted with humans for a long time and is not attuned to their specific mental wavelength. However, be warned: the legends tell of the Yarthkin, an antagonistic earth-sprite whose job was to drive off the rude and disrespectful. Littering, or pulling up leaves or flowers without asking permission, or otherwise disrespecting a natural site can bring down their wrath upon you. An angered Yarthkin is quite capable of tripping you up and arranging for an injury, or at least making your stay so uncomfortable that you will leave in a hurry.

Housewights

These spirits are of the same family as the above category, except that they choose to dwell in human habitations. The Scottish people called them "brownies" and in Sweden they are called *Nissen*. Some very old houses come with indwelling spirits that have attached themselves to the home in the past, and look after the inhabitants—assuming that the inhabitants are properly propitiating the wights in question. Most new houses don't have housewights, and if you want one, you can call one by stating your intent and putting out food for it on a regular basis.

The question is: do you want the responsibility of a housewight? If you already have one, the point is moot, but once you've brought one in you're stuck with them. They will not only outlive you, they'll expect the same deal (or at least a similar one) of the next inhabitants of the house, so you'll have to plan ahead for what will happen then. If you stop propitiating them, they will start causing mischief, chaos, and disorder— what they can give, they can take away. On the other hand, a housewight is excellent at helping with the domestic arts—keeping food from burning or rotting or going bad, helping butter to come and brew to ferment properly, keeping pets from destroying things, keeping important items from getting lost, protecting the place from fire, and so forth. If you're a particularly domestic person, it might be in your best interest to have the aid of one. Another good situation is having a large household full of people who are all willing to pitch in with remembering to feed the housewight.

Housewights are happiest when you treat them like one of the family. Some older traditions included giving them not only portions of the family dinner, but a bit of the dough when you bake a loaf of bread, a bit of the wort when you brew, and of course setting out porridge and milk. (Housewights really seem to like milk, but not the skim stuff. They prefer it creamy.)

Elementals

These are a similar class of being to landwights, although somewhat smaller and bound up in the expression of one sort of natural essence— fire, water, earth, air, etc. They are not the same as the Jotnar, another sort of elementally-affinitive being, although a Jotun can "backslide" into being little more than an elemental spirit if they burrow too far into their elemental nature and lose the depth of their soul. Elementals have short attention spans and are further removed from humanity than the giants and faeries; their natures are simpler, although they are not stupid. Local sprites are one form of elemental, although they may not be lined up with any of the "classic" four elements.

In the ancient North, many different sorts of elementals were listed in folktales, usually the water-affinitive or earth-affinitive ones, because those tend to attach themselves to specific places—lakes, rivers, trees. The *skogsrar*, or wood-roes, lived in the forest and protected the local ecosystem; they might center their spirit in large "grandfather" trees. The *näckar*, or nixies, were spirits of the fresh-water rivers and streams. There are also versions of these called *Nykur*, linguistically similar, who are actually fey folk rather than elementals; they are water-alfar in the form of horses who like to wander the shores, inducing folk to climb on them, and then rush into the water to drown people. In Celtic mythology they are known as kelpies. It's an example of how difficult it is for the average wanderer to figure out what sort of critter they're dealing with.

Sjörar are the lake-spirits, some of whom have been known to seduce and pull down people into drowning. The *forskarlar* are "falls-men", sprites that guard waterfalls and oversee offerings made there. Mer-people—sort of a smaller elemental version of the sea-etins—populate the oceans, but they are shy and rarely seen. Air-spirits, of course, ride the wind, and fire-spirits inhabit large naturally-started fires, and occasionally large manmade fires. All these elementals can be touched by spending a good deal of time doing utiseta in natural places. As stressed above, they are slippery and have short attention spans, and it is often difficult to get them to understand what it is that you want. Giving you information about what's going on in an area is one of the easier tasks you can ask of them, but even then you'll have to deal with torrents of confusing images. Elementals in general have a very different sort of language than we do, and many don't speak in words per se, although some of the local-sprite type can do that very well, and housewights tend to pick up human forms of communication. They like small shiny things tossed or buried in their element, and of course food and drink.

Among the Saami people, the term for elemental spirits was *saajvh*, and they resided mostly in sacred lakes or mountains. Families would enter into contracts with the *saajvh* where one would swear to serve a particular line in exchange for their attention and energy, thus turning them into a sort of *kinfylgja*, but linked to a particular place. Inheriting such a *saajvh* was considered highly propitious, and especially useful to a *noaide*.

Greenwights

In modern neo-shamanisms, a lot is said about animal spirits (many of it by people who have never actually encountered any of the animals that they desire to work with) but very little about plant spirits. Perhaps they are seen as boring when compared to animal spirits, or perhaps people have less ability to figure out how to communicate with them, or perhaps some people are "animal" folk and some are "plant" folk. Even if this is the case, I would still strongly suggest that those who prefer animals and never intend to use herbs or do healing work ought to make acquaintance with a couple of plant spirits—perhaps trees, if they will be out in the wilds at all—just as I would suggest that those who prefer plants ought to work with at least a couple of animal spirits. It's a matter of breadth of competence and understanding.

When dealing with any given plant, you're actually dealing with two sorts of spirits: the spirit of the plant itself, and the Grandparent Spirit of that plant's species. Plants, like animals, have a hierarchy of intelligence and power; just as a beetle is different from a chicken or a human, a weed is different from a shrub or a tree. Trees are very much like humans in that hierarchy; that's why it's easier to have a useful conversation (allowing for difference in speed of communication) to the indwelling spirit of a tree than to the indwelling spirit of a ragweed plant. That's also why it's easier, in the cases of the small plants, to do negotiations with their overarching Grandparent Spirit—for example, Grandmother Milk Thistle or Grandfather Valerian or Mistress Bramble. If you can form an alliance with them, you pretty much have access to the power of all the little plants they look after.

To start talking to plant spirits, you can either find a wild plant, or (better for beginners) grow one from seed, in a pot or your garden. Tend it and talk to it, and when it is old enough (you'll get a feel for when) ask it to be your introduction to the Grandparent spirit of that plant species—for example, Grandmother Mugwort or Grandfather Lovage. If the spirit agrees, they'll come and talk to you; take a bit of the plant into you and ask them for wisdom about its usage, and aid when you use it on yourself and others. They may give you a rhyme or chant to use (many examples of these will be in *The Northern-Tradition Herbal*) when making herbal remedies or consuming the plant. Once you've gotten to know a few of them this way, many (not all) of the other Grandparent plant spirits will be willing to speak to you through any live child of theirs, even if it's a weed in a field.

Be prepared, though, to have taboos laid on you about ever using that plant unwisely again. For that matter, spirit-workers with lots of plant-helpers generally end up taking on very different attitudes toward plants than most people—for instance, not privileging animals above plants with regard to diet or environmental importance, not cutting trees or picking flowers without purpose, paying attention to not polluting plants in the environment, revering their sacrifice when eating them, and avoiding food-versions of them that are horrendously treated.

Animal Wights

Animal spirits have a much bigger fan club than plant spirits in modern neo-shamanism, with people running around showing off how cool their "spirit animals" are. Oddly enough, they all only seem to get "spirit animals" like Wolf, and Bear, and Cougar, and Eagle, and Hawk. That's not to say that some people are not honestly approached by those animal spirits—certainly I've met a few—but one wonders why there aren't more people working with Rat and Chipmunk and Frog and Cockroach. The big glamorous predatory animals seem to be the ones that all the would-be spirit-workers scramble to obtain ... as if such things could be obtained just by wanting it. No, with animal spirits, it's best to put the call out and see what shows up, and don't be disappointed when it isn't Wolf or Eagle. Every animal spirit has something to teach.

Here we need to differentiate between the term "totem animal" and "spirit animal", the latter of which is heard constantly in every neo-shamanic workshop. Like greenwights, animal spirits also consist of the souls of specific animals (usually dead ones, unless we're talking about the classic witches' "familiar"), or the Grandparent Spirits of the different species. These latter ones are what we're talking about when we say Bear or Crow or Elephant, and some of them are quite powerful indeed. When people refer to "spirit animals", they might mean these overarching wights, or they might mean smaller spirits of that species— perhaps animal ancestors—who have taken an interest in you and bother to show it. (For example, one of mine is Crow, and this manifests as real live crows constantly following me about and shrieking things that I can't always understand, but I know that they were sent by Crow to tell me something, and that Crow is probably doing a favor for a deity in interacting with me this way.) Totem animals are creatures that one admires, emulates, and attempts to make connection with; ancestral totems are animal spirits that were revered (and perhaps worked with) by one's forebears, and could theoretically be called upon for aid in a pinch.

The smaller animal spirits are the most likely to be used for what some spirit-workers have referred to as "reverse-possession"—utilizing their qualities for one's own purposes, while being completely in control of the situation. It's not so much that they possess the spirit-worker as the spirit-worker possesses them. It's been referred to as "wearing them like a hat", as opposed to deity-possession, which would be rather like trying to wear a refrigerator or a truck like a hat. This can be used to augment one's shapeshifting abilities, or temporarily lend some important quality necessary for an act of magic. In order to pull this off, you have to have the consent of the spirit in question, even if it is technically smaller and weaker than you, or you'll anger the Grandparent Spirit.

There are many traditional totem animals, or spirit animals mentioned in lore; obviously these are northern European creatures, although some are found ranging more widely. Some classic ones include Bear, Raven (said to be the two oldest totem animals in the world), Boar, Goat, Reindeer, Elk, Deer, Hound, Sheep, Horse, Hawk, Crow, Eagle, Bull, and Uruz (the extinct European buffalo). Many of these, of course, are the classic "warrior" totem animals beloved by history and by modern would-be warriors. Saami shamans often used the aid of fish or snake spirit totems in order to visit the underworld, and small bird totems such as sparrows to travel to the upper world. Koryak shamans are fond not only of the above animals, but also of the seagull and plover. Wolf-spirits seem to appear again and again in Nordic mythology, to the point where the word *gandir* seems to mean helping spirits in the form of wolves, which one could send out to gain information and do errands. Some of these "wolves", however, seem to be more elemental than animal-spirit per se—thus the words *hallar gandir* (hall wolf) for fire, and *selju gandir* (willow wolf) for wind. So the *gandir* might fall into a different category.

For those of us who live in physical areas that are not the ones our ancestors lived in (like the entire North American continent), there is the issue of working with native animal and plant spirits. While most of the wights that I work with are European-based, when it comes to animal spirits, half of the ones who've approached me are ones who live here. Actually, I was approached very young by Skunk, and who can argue with that? Reindeer walked right out of my European ancestry, but Raven and Crow are everywhere. I've even been approached by at least one animal spirit whose descendants now only live in Africa, which confused me a great deal. We have to balance where we are with where our deities first made connection; little by little, we are reconnecting them to where we are, but this will take time. There's also that animal and plant spirits, while they may work with specific deities in various pantheons (boar with Frey, wolf with Odin and Fenris, goat with Thor, and so on), easily and naturally work across pantheons and without regard to any deity-association whatever. They simply don't care, in the end. They'll come to who they choose, and make that decision according to their own criteria.

Fylgja, or Fetch

The fylgja is neither animal spirit nor animal totem. It is a piece of the human soul that can take the form of an animal, but it is not necessarily linked to the overarching Grandparent spirit of that type of animal. To create a fylgja is a special talent, although it can be learned by anyone who can shapeshift, and many journeyers manifest it spontaneously. The idea is to take a piece of one's soul, shift it out from one's astral body and central consciousness, give it a shape and a perspective of it's own, and send it wandering.

This is a different situation from simply shapeshifting one's entire astral body—"going out in wolf's *hame*"—and journeying in this way. The fylgja is a product of psychic dissociation, perhaps deliberate, perhaps accidental. The piece of soul that is shapeshifted and "hived off" usually (but not always) takes an animal form. It can be sent out to reconnoiter, or journey alongside of someone. Since consciousness-shaping is a large part of shamanic work, one can see how it would be a useful form of altered state to have a small piece of one's consciousness seeing things from an outside perspective, and then able to report back to the main consciousness. However, there is some danger to sending one's fylgja about. It is only a partial soul, and while it may have the attributes of the animal whose form it takes, it does not have the *maegen* of the spirit-worker's main soul, and it can be vulnerable. If it is damaged or killed, the loss of a significant part of the soul can reverberate back to the spirit-worker and permanently weaken them, sometimes to the point of death.

Among the Yakut shamans of Siberia, the word *yekyua* describes an animal-spirit part of the soul that sounds exactly like the fylgja. The *yekyua* (literally "mother-animal") is usually sent out to live in a wild place; the shamans have an understanding that if their *yekyua* is killed (perhaps by a competing shaman) they will die, and therefore it must be protected. One Yakut shaman declared, "My *yekyua* will not be found by anyone; it lies hidden far away, there, in the rocky mountains of Edjigan." They are, however, sent out to fight the *yekyua* of other shamans, assuming that it has the form of a fighting animal.

The other common form of the fylgja is human. Some fylgjar look exactly like the individual—thus the term "fetch", which was something that looked just like you that you saw when your life was in danger. (It may be that for some people, sudden fear would make the fylgja leap out of the body, and in their state of terror they would see it for the first time. Spirit-workers in several other cultures attest to great fear or trauma causing part of the soul to temporarily leave the astral body.) Other fylgjar look like members of the opposite sex (or, one would assume, members of the same sex for nonheterosexual spirit-workers), rather like the Jungian *animus* or *anima*, only actually separated out from the rest of the soul-complex. In these cases the fylgja often serves as a "self-spouse", having an erotic relationship with the main consciousness. This is a different situation from an external "spirit-wife" or "spirit-husband", although inexperienced people have mistaken the former for the latter.

On the other hand, since it is not uncommon for an external spirit to do the same things as a fylgja—right down to being a spirit-spouse or an animal guide—the two were often conflated. And, really, it is not easy to figure out whether the squirrel that shows up in your dreams is your fetch or a squirrel-spirit who has taken an interest in you. I wouldn't say that it doesn't matter which is which—if nothing else, a fylgja is much more difficult to offend, being an externalized part of oneself—but they play similar parts often enough to be terribly confusing. Divination can probably help to figure out which sort of squirrel is perched on your midnight window sill.

A *kinfylgja* is the guardian spirit of a whole family, clan, or human lineage. For more information on dealing with them, see the chapter on Bloodlines. While the kinfylgja is usually seen as a spirit who watches over a particular family, one might also consider the situation among circumpolar shamans, where a piece of "shamanic" soul is passed from one shaman to another, sometimes on the advent of their death, sometimes even whilst still alive.

The Dead

Not all shamanic types work with the Dead, but an awful lot of them do. It has been commented that there is a polarity between the ones who work with the Alfar and those who work with the Dead; perhaps you need to have entirely different sorts of "wiring"—or at least affinities— for those two extremes. In ancient times, the Dead were much more present than they are now, because people made more of an effort to keep them present. Death was seen not so much as something that entirely removed people from existence so much as took them further from it. Some ancestors were still quite approachable, and bothered to take an interest in their descendants, as long as they were remembered. They could be called upon in times of trouble to protect their future kin. It is said that ancestor worship was the very earliest form of religion, and I can believe that.

Spirit-workers might be called upon to deal with the Dead in a number of ways. My earliest dealings with the Dead as a service-provider was dealing with angry, troublesome ghosts. Almost always, in these cases, the Dead soul either doesn't believe that they have passed on, or knows but is still hanging on out of fear or control issues or just sheer habit. After a certain point, their remaining life force begins to fade—there being no body to hold it—and they will lose their grip on this world and pass on to wherever they are supposed to go. In order to keep this from happening, they need to feed off of whatever energy sources come by, which is often the humans who live in their former home. It's often the spirit-worker's job to broker negotiations between the humans and the ghosts, and/or convince the ghosts that they need to move on, and/or forcibly remove them through the door to Helheim if necessary.

The spirit-worker may also be called on to lead lost dead souls to where they need to go when there are no humans involved. This usually comes through as a request from the Gods, usually Death Gods. They may also end up taking messages from Dead loved ones to their descendants, or going in search of information on behalf of clients. For this last duty, it is necessary to have a good relationship with Whomever is in charge of the Dead soul in question, which is going to be Hela ninety-nine times out of a hundred, and She does not like her Dead people bothered, so make sure that you have a good reason and get Her permission, or it won't work. If you've only ever worked with the worlds of the Tree, you can get to other Underworlds via Helheim, but again you need Hela's cooperation. Yes, Hela will help get Christian ghosts to the place that they need to go, which isn't Her realm.

There is a good deal of argument in the modern Pagan and Heathen communities as to where the Dead go after they die. Certainly I've been asked that about a hundred times, and my only answer is still: It depends. Many places. In a northern-tradition context, most who follow the various forms of this religion go to Helheim (which isn't nearly the awful place it's made out to be); a very few go to Valhalla or Sessrumnir or Bilskirnir, and some go to be with their patron deity. (Aegir and Ran get very few these days, as few of our folk are lost at sea any more.) Outside of this tradition, most people go to or through the afterworld that they believe in, if they are religious, and various other places if they are not.

Reincarnation is an even bigger argument, because the lore is unclear on the subject, and there's no definitive proof of it there. However, as a Hel's man who works for the Lady in charge of this sort of thing, I can say that souls who die in this faith can indeed reincarnate ... but that Hela is the only being in the Nine Worlds who has the power to recycle them, and whether the souls in Her charge get recycled, and where they go, is very much up to Her discretion. Well, I'm sure that the Nornir have something to say about it as well, but Hela is usually in accord with their Word.

It's important for a spirit-worker in our tradition to have an ancestor "harrow", or altar. This can have photos of dead relatives, or just their names, or if you're adopted and know nothing about them, just candles or other offerings to honor them. Not everyone can make a connection to their ancestors, however, Some people's ancestors have cut them off, for various reasons. In order to figure out whether this is the case for you (although just not being able to get anything from any of them ought to give you a clue), you can do a Soul Map reading and check the Kinfylgja for a block. If you're in this boat, choose your ancestors. Honor those Dead whose ideas and words have inspired you, and who you feel kinship with. If you have nonhuman blood, make sure that you honor your nonhuman ancestors as well. Calling on them will sometimes give you more information, as some of them may still be alive and interested.

Dead friends count too, perhaps more than family if you don't know who your family was, or if they have rejected you (the Dead ones, that is—if living family has rejected you, wait until they're Dead and check back, as people often change their minds once they've passed beyond petty concerns). The soul of a good friend, or one who was like a relative to you, can be even stronger in some cases than any kind of blood kin. I still call on one beloved Dead father-figure occasionally when I need help facing down an intimidating power tool for a crafting job.

Sometimes you'll find that a Dead soul about whom you know nothing will call to you and end up on your ancestor harrow. For example, along with family and friends, I also honor a woman named Elizabeth Bellingham, who died in the 14th century. I know nothing about her except that she was married, and died young in her twenties, probably in childbirth. She came to be part of my Dead because I went on an outing to a museum exhibit where people were allowed to make rubbings of replica medieval funeral brasses, and I made and framed a rubbing of hers. Apparently my work for Hela means that even bringing in a rubbing of someone's funeral picture means that they are now one of my Dead to honor, something which I didn't expect ... but I added her to the list anyway. But be careful about it. We spirit-workers are held to a higher standard of responsibility than most people when it comes to our Dead. Because we can often see and speak to them, more so than most people, and because some of us can send them on their way, we have the responsibility to treat them with more respect.

Guiding the Dead
by Elizabeth Vongvisith

The most noticeable thing about psychopomps in the Northern Tradition is that really, there aren't that many. True, there are the Valkyries who choose from battlefields which slain warriors will join Odin's Einherjar, but most of us aren't warriors, and most people seem to find their own way to their final destination (Helheim, or perhaps the realm of the deity they were dedicated to) after they die. Some living Odin's-women serve as Valkyries, and I even know of an Odin's-man who has been given this role, but most of us who work with the dead in this way have little material within the extant official lore to compare to our own experiences.

I am most definitely not a Valkyrie, but I am a psychopomp and I serve Hela in that capacity. It seems like a given that if your job ticket includes working with dead folks and you aren't Odin's (or Freyja's, since she chooses half the war-slain) then you're going to be working for Hela. At the very start of my career as a spirit-worker, I was told by Her Ladyship that for the remainder of my life, I will have to make at least one journey to Helheim every year to bring dead people to her realm. I'm not completely certain why some dead merit a guide while others have to make their way there as best they can, but so far, the ones I've taken have fallen into either of two categories.

The first and most numerous group are dead humans who were not necessarily Hela's in life—they may not have been heathens or pagans at all, and perhaps were even been devout adherents of other religions. But if so, their gods have not claimed them after death for whatever reason. Hela seems very interested in collecting these folks, though she will not coerce them if they do not want to come to her. I have picked up a number of them who agreed to leave whatever spot they'd been hanging around in for the last few decades or centuries and place themselves under Hela's dominion and protection instead. I'm pretty sure I'm not the only one who's been faced with that task recently, and it's very likely that as time passes more and more NT spirit-workers who belong to or work for Hela part-time will find ourselves doing this work too.

The other sort of dead has consisted of non-human wights who, for whatever reason, required special treatment—and this type of psychopomp duty usually tends to be more formal, since I have to serve as a sort of honor guard for the important party on their way to Helheim. One of these was a relative of Laufey, Loki's mother. Another time, I was sent to collect a *Teind* of elven souls from both the Ljossalfar and Svartalfar—a duty which I will again be required to perform should the *Teind* come up due again before the end of my lifetime.

The approach I've taken to guiding these types of dead is different in each case. In the case of dead humans whom Hela has convinced to come to her realm, it generally involves a physical trip to collect the dead from the place where they have been told to gather, then the use of a labyrinth through which I can pathwalk to the borders of Helheim, and which will allow the dead folks to follow me there without getting lost. In the case of the non-human wights, I have thus far used *hamfara* (faring forth, or astral journeying) to go to one of the other Nine Worlds and escort the dead from their own realm to Hela, whether in her own realm or at some other meeting place. I really have no idea what future underworld journeys will involve, but it seems likely that serving as a more or less official escort for dead Jotnar or Alfar is going to be a much less frequent task than simply collecting dead mortals who wish to go to Helheim, and making certain they get there safely.

One of the things I do every time I make a journey to Hela's realm is to bring messages for the dead, and to bring back messages for the living who have enquired after them. This is not so complicated as it sounds. Hela seems to have connections with other underworld deities, and whether or not the dead person in question is actually in Helheim or some other afterlife realm seems to make no difference—the right people are always there to receive the messages I bring and to give me their own messages to take back. I would advise anybody who ends up working as a psychopomp to do the same. It pleases Hela and it's a nice service for people who may otherwise never have the chance to speak to those they love who have passed on. Interestingly, there seems to be some kind of prohibition against me seeking my own beloved dead. If I want to send a message to my dead grandmother, for instance, someone else has to take it there for me. I'm not sure if this is a personal issue or if it's universal for all who perform this task, but nevertheless, Hela doesn't allow me to see or speak to my own dead loved ones while I'm there in her land

I have only made four psychopomp trips to Helheim so far, two of which were made for the sake of the "common folk." Though much is made in the Northern Tradition about the great honor given to those who die in battle, it should be noted that the vast majority of heathens (past and present) are not going to be chosen to sit among the Einherjar, but will come under Hela's dominion, unless they are instead sent to reside with the deities they served in life. Hela fiercely defends her dead, and whether they were kings or paupers, great or humble, does not matter one bit to her—all are equally welcome in her realm, and no one is more deserving of her care and protection than another (though admittedly Baldur seems to be under a bit more security than everyone else).

I feel certain that there is another word for this duty within the Northern Tradition, a word which probably predates the "lore era" and which has since been lost, but I haven't managed to recover it, and neither Hela nor Loki will tell me what it is. "Guide" seems to come closest to the spirit of the thing, since I'm not a reaper—I don't separate folks from their bodies, just come pick them up afterwards—and it's not my place to judge them or second-guess why they're going to Helheim instead of somewhere else. But to serve as one who collects the dead for Her Ladyship is a true honor, no less than if one were chosen to bring the war-dead to the halls of Odin and Freyja. Although it's often grueling and even scary, I'm glad to perform this service for Hela, in thanks and recognition for her graciousness in the past.

Disir

For this entry, Galina Krasskova gives us her wisdom on the Disir, who are a form of female ancestor-spirit. The Norse word for the ancient equivalent of *disir* was, at least some of the time as far as we can tell, *alfar* ... which is problematic because it also refers to a nonhuman race of beings living in one or more of the Otherworlds. (Very different from *disir*, which is actually a word for a female deity.) This is likely due to the fact that to an ancient peasant, the various kinds of wight blended together. They were all powerful and mysterious creatures who should be venerated, and it was difficult to tell (and they likely didn't care anyway) which sort of wight was which.

Another theory on the *alfar* issue is that it was started by people who were actually descended from the Alfar, and legitimately calling on them for ancestral purposes. Either way, in our modern era it's confusing and often a problem, especially for spirit-workers who need to make clear identifications between this wight and that wight, if only because they are dealt with and propitiated differently. In my personal practice, I don't use the word *alfar* to refer to ancestors, only to the Fey Folk. I tend to say "...the Disir and their beloved fathers, lovers, and sons." If they want a better term, they can give it to me.

It is common in Heathenry and in many other indigenous religions to maintain ancestral altars and otherwise venerate one's honored dead. Within Heathenry, it is one's female ancestors, otherwise known as Disir, that receive the greatest attention. There's evidence that a special ritual called *Disablot* was performed in Scandinavia in honor of the Disir at the beginning of winter (Yule), and special temples to them were called *Disarsalir*. They are frequently mentioned in the Sagas and in Eddic literature and are often said to come to their descendants in dreams.

Scholar Rudolf Simek, in his 1993 *Dictionary of Northern Mythology*, specifically notes that Disir were dead women or the souls of dead women (Simek, p. 61). Simek goes on to note that the Disir apparently combined the functions of fertility Goddesses, personal guardians and warrior Goddesses and their worship was tied closely into the cult of the Matronae or Mothers. (Simek, p. 62)

It is not uncommon for a specific Dis to attach herself to a family line and serve as guardian of that line. One's female ancestors were traditionally invested with an immense amount of *hamingja* and *maegen*. They habitually maintained a strong interest in the goings-on of their families and watched over successive generations. There are examples of heroes seeking out their guardian Dis for special knowledge or power, such as when Svipdag seeks out his dead mother Groa for advice on how to win the giantess Mengloth. Amongst many modern Heathens and especially amongst spirit-workers, honoring one's Disir has remained an integral part of their ancestral practices.

Maintaining an ancestral altar replete with pictures and possessions once belonging to one's female dead is an excellent way to start incorporating them into one's devotional practices. Setting out food, particularly the appropriate ethnic dishes, drink, incense and flowers, are all appropriate ways of honoring them. Researching one's genealogy and adding that knowledge to one's ancestral practices is a nice way to become more involved with one's dead, one that the Goddess Saga may be willing to assist with. It's important that one's ancestral altar be a living, vital part of one's spiritual life. Talk to the ancestors, tell them about your life, your goals, anything that is important to you. Invite them to become active parts of your family. This has to be an ongoing relationship, not something done once, or once in a blue moon and forgotten about.

Disir are "high" ancestral spirits. They may not even be related to you directly by family. If you are strongly linked into a specific spiritual practice or tradition, you may get adopted by an appropriate Dis. They can be invaluable guides. When you die, one can be a "low" spirit, but can be elevated by the manner in which one's descendants honor you. Most people who try to do Disir work would have to do some kind of elevation of their own spiritual line if they're going to work with their own family line because I don't think that most people in American culture feel that their own family line would be adequate when compared with the qualities of the Disir mentioned in lore. This is a problem with modern Disir worship. Most don't find the rich reservoir of power and experience within their own immediate lines. This actually provides an amazing opportunity to elevate one's line by making appropriate offerings and prayers. It also provides the opportunity to discover powerful women already lurking within the line of one's honored dead.

While one might question the relevance to modern spirit-work of women who died having lived the most mundane of lives, it is the combination of the gifts and struggles and knowledge of all those who preceded us that made it possible for us to be born in the here and now with the skills and gifts we possess. Furthermore, Disir are powerfully protective and can do much to ease the transition between worlds. Spirit-workers with non-human blood should be aware that they not only have human Disir to honor but also those of their non-human bloodline. It's important to remember, however, that there is something to be gained from purely mundane, human Disir. While it may be easier for the spirit-worker to link into the non-human bloodlines, there is worth and value in both. A gifted spirit-worker can strengthen his or her entire lineage, paying homage to those who may not have had the skills or freedom to do the work themselves, but who have been counting on their descendants, three or four generations hence (in other words, us) to do the work to strength the entire line, the work that they themselves laid the foundation for by their struggles and sacrifices.

–Galina Krasskova

Draugar

One subcategory of the Dead are the draugar. In northern lore, draugar are undead creatures who rise like zombies or vampires to feed on the living, still clad in their rotting bodies. Another term for such creatures was *aptrgangr*, which literally meant "after-goer", or the thing that goes after you. There was a lot of fear in the North about unquiet spirits, and no matter how good a person was said to be during life, their unquiet ghost was considered likely to be destructive and murderous. The worst were said to be dead sorcerers, as they would retain many of the powers that they had gained in life, and perhaps gain even more now that they were no longer burdened with a physical body.

Modernly, some spirit-workers have dealt with something that they labeled a "draugr", but there was a good deal of difference in what the term was referring to. The most likely definition seems to be a dead soul which has lost most of its remaining soul-parts until all that is left is a semi-mindless hunger to feed on life-energy. While bodiless, it can temporarily manifest at least partly physically, assuming that it has enough energy, and can drive someone mad or scare them literally to death. (If that last seems unbelievable, imagine a draugr manifesting in a car on a dark, dangerous, icy road, next to a lone driver who freaks out and drives into a tree.)

Draugar can be called down for purposes of vengeance, but usually they are free agents looking for whatever they can get and need to be thoroughly banished. Powerful draugar are tough customers and there's no guarantee that a weak or inexperienced spirit-worker will win against them. In some cases, it might be best to swallow one's pride and get help, both divine aid and that of other spirit-workers.

Guardian Spirits

This is more a job-related category than a specific type of spirit, but the Old Norse word seems to be *verdir*, referring to any and all spirits who are called to guard the perimeter of a working. These can be animal spirits, or any of the above. The first half of the word *varthlokkur*—the song used by volvas to call spirits—contains reference to the *verdir*. The

Saami word for such guardian spirits was *vuojnodime*, "the invisible ones", and supposedly they referred to humans as "the visible ones".

Evil Spirits

All early cultures have the concept of spirits whose purpose is specifically that of destruction, and plaguing hapless humans. (The plague itself was characterized as a pair of twins, one with a rake and one with a broom, cleaning out people's houses.) One of the longest-lived examples of such spirits in the North is the Mara, sometimes said to take the form of a horse, and sometimes the form of a woman. The Mara sends evil dreams to human sleepers, sometimes sitting on their chest and attempting to suffocate them. In some accounts, this creature is a spirit conjured and sent by an evil sorcerer (or even the curse of a non-sorcerer) to deliberately bother someone; in others, it just picks some hapless soul without apparent reason. Like many other creatures who have been foolishly summoned and then get trapped here, the Mara may simply be feeding on whatever it can get in order to survive. A good spirit-worker can open a door to wherever it came from and send it back; if it was summoned without consent, it may well be willing to go.

Disease is a good example of evil spirits as well. While this concept will be further explicated in the forthcoming book on northern-tradition shamanic healing, suffice it to say that while ancient shamans could not literally see invading life forms such as bacteria and viruses (having no microscopes) they might certainly be able to see the life force/souls of those creatures, and label them "evil spirits"—which they are, or at least destructive ones. The fact that they happen to be carting around small bodies as well is irrelevant, both to the ancient shaman and to the modern shamanic healer. It's their life force and souls which we have more direct access to.

Spirits From Other Places

We modern people tend to think of each "pantheon" or "cosmology" as its own safety-sealed little universe, which may leak into this world, but which are all kept entirely separate. Our ancestors, however, didn't see things like this. Instead of the modern reconstructionist trend of cosmological separatism, they freely and willingly invited new gods into pantheons, and integrated the wights of new (possibly conquered) places. An ancient spirit-worker would not have been unaware of the concept of spirits that were not necessarily part of the above list, but might come from an Otherworld hanging on a different Tree, as it were. One might refer to them by the generic word for spirits, *natturar*.

As a modern spirit-worker, I don't have the luxury of spiritual separatism. While the cosmology of Yggdrasil is the one that I generally work in, sometimes clients come to me who live and work in other cosmologies (or whose Gods and spirits live and work in other cosmologies) and I still have to help them, which means broadening myself to be able to do that work. Our world is much smaller than that of our ancestors, who might not ever have traveled beyond the village where they were born, or met more than a few people who had done so. We may speak to people living thousands of miles away by the handful on a daily basis, and few of us live in the town where we were born, or perhaps even in the same country. This means that when someone comes to me with problems around a spirit, the likelihood is that it may not fit into any of the above categories. This means that I have to do some divination to figure out what they are, and how to best deal with them. If you're spirit-worker with a public practice, get used to dealing with Gods and wights from other cosmologies.

The most important thing to remember when dealing with any new spirits is that these are entities with agendas of their own. They may neither understand nor care about your goals and needs, and you have to figure out a way to make it worth their while to work with you. While demanding and forcing smaller spirits to work has been done throughout the ages by magicians (and even some shamans), it's a bad policy. No matter how good you are, there's something out there that can stomp you, and sooner or later you will misjudge them. Besides, even smaller spirits can slip away from you and strike back; it's best to have them as allies, not as angry servants. We are not Gods, and they are not our lawful prey.

All spirits have their own perspectives, their own communities, and their own needs. Those will comes first, and you must never fault them for that. After all, your community—whatever that is—and your needs come first for you. Understanding their values and priorities is important to being able to ally with them. Sometimes those goals and priorities will be in opposition to those of the humans on whose behalf you're working, and that may require some difficult negotiations. Remember that once you have made an alliance with a particular nonhuman community, you owe them some measure of loyalty and service as well. Alliances come with extra responsibilities, so don't sign up for them if you're not willing to do the work (unless you have no choice, that is).

The last thing to remember when working with wights is that the best offering of all is your time and attention. Food, drink, fancy items, great deeds, fine songs, these are all good things, but human time and attention are something that they rarely get. Just listening to them communicate about whatever is important to them, and paying attention, can not only increase your own understanding of the Worlds, it shows them that you give a damn. When I went about to various and sundry Gods and wights to get the lessons in this book, I started with the same question: "What do you think is most important for spirit-workers to know?" I tried to keep an open mind and have no expectations about what they might tell me, and that openness worked best of all. It's a good way to begin.

Frey's Lesson
Sacrifice

Frey is tall and golden and beautiful, and when he smiles it's like the Sun coming out. I met him the first time that I traveled in Vanaheim, and I fell in love. My relationship to him is very different from that of my patron deity. I work for her. I don't work for him, except to horse him once a year, and that's a separate deal that I made for him in return for a favor I asked. I've occasionally wished that I could be a Freysman, but I'm well aware that my nature is too dark and twisted for anyone but Her Ladyship to keep in line. Besides, the fact that I don't work for him means that I am free to just love him, and that's excellent in its own way. I don't think I really experienced the path of pure devotion until I met Frey.

It was a surprise to me when he required me to lend my body for one day a year in return for the favor he did me—not because I didn't think he could ride me, but because I was surprised that he would want to. I'm not tall and young and gorgeous, with the world's most beautiful cock, but that didn't matter to him. Besides love, I asked, where is the affinity? He is a creature of light and fertility, I'm a thing of darkness and sterility, a "black shaman" in Siberian terms (which doesn't mean evil, it just means that you work primarily with underworld deities). He reminded me gently that if he hadn't loved darkness as well, he would never have fallen in love with an etin-woman. "I am the light of Love that descends to the darkness," he said, "as my sister is the light of Love that seeks upward flight."

Affinity? There, too, he had an answer. "You are a sacrifice," he said, "just as I am, although in a different way. All the wight-workers who are chosen and bound, you are all sacrifices. And those who bind you are in haste, and they may not get around to teaching you how to properly be a sacrifice before you are thrown into it, if indeed it occurs to them at all." And it became clear that this was the lesson Frey had for spirit-workers, the thing that he felt they needed to know more than anything else.

Frey's Lesson:

There are three parts to being a proper sacrifice. First, suffering. Second, usefulness. Third, joy.

The first one, suffering, that is the one that catches everyone up. One may sacrifice one's self for a cause, a loved one, for the greater good—but that is different. You are your own to give away, and if you have any sense you do not do that unless the cause is great, and if you waste yourself on a foolish cause you will eat the dust from that and learn better next time. But you do not know what a great and terrible thing it is when the Gods choose someone to sacrifice. We may not do this out of whim—I cannot stress that enough. There must be what your Ladyship calls dire necessity, the knowledge that without aid all will fail. In order to sacrifice the needs of one for the needs of all, there must be a great and terrible reason. The Norns guard those threads fiercely, and any God who would seize someone away from their life path without their leave must justify it to Urd's old, old ears.

The suffering that you go through, the remolding, the changing, the binding, this gives you great *maegen.* You cannot gain that kind of *maegen* on your own; it must be earned through outside circumstance, through some kind of struggle. When the knife comes through me, every year at the harvest, I feel that pain. It is never any easier. Do not think I do not understand your pain, you who have died and returned. Imagine having to do that every year. Imagine seeing the wheat-heads ripening on the stalks and thinking, Soon I will be dead. Over and over. That is the way of things. Something must die that others may live, eh? You know that. You are that. I am that. It is what we have between us, you and I.

Then, after the suffering—the part that you people obsess on so— there is the usefulness. And this is where the *maegen* unfolds. If it was dire necessity that took you, you will gain much power by being useful in the way that alleviates it. For me, the corn must be cut, the grain must come down, the calf must be led to slaughter, or the people will starve. To come back and see them with full bellies, it is enough. It is always enough, and more than enough. Everyone you aid is the reason for your sacrifice. When you ask, "Why?", look at them. It is not enough to suffer. Your thread will not be made clean by mere suffering; that is only the first part. After you have endured suffering, you must alleviate it in others.

Everything you are will be used. You can sing—good. Then you will sing spirit songs. You have rhythm—good. Then you will drum for the spirits. You are quick of finger—good. Then you will spin spells. When you are a sacrifice, you retain nothing of yourself, and in exchange you gain… what? Work. Work so worthy that the Gods obtained leave to sacrifice you for it. Can most people say this of their lives?

Your sexuality too, that will be used as well. Whatever is between your legs will no longer be your own, and that goes for those who do not carry Gods in their bodies as well. It is a tool, a great tool, a magnificent tool … and it must be used that way. The man who places his member in the earth to give her a gift, or in his wife to give her children, that is a sacrifice in its own way. Yet many wight-workers must give up their fertility, aye, and that is why there is a second path in my sight … the *ergi* ones with the bells on their skirts. Do you know how much *maegen* there is in sacrificing part of one's manhood or womanhood, or perhaps all? Of course you do. And this, too, is given up. It is not yours. It belongs to the world now, and to the one who shapes your path.

And then, after the usefulness, the joy. This is the one thing that is not for them, and if you can achieve it you should try. First, because if you cannot learn to take joy in it, the Work will eat you quicker than it would otherwise. The joy is your buffer against the grinding, the honing, the hard use you are put to. It will give you that extra spark when the cycle comes around again and it is the dark time. Second— and this I tell you true, trust me on this—there are laws about what the Gods can and cannot use. Your body, your sex, your mind, your powers, your emotions, your eyes, your mouth, your hands—all these things they can use, if you are a sacrifice. But if you can find joy in it somehow, they cannot use that. It is against the Rules. It works for no one but you. And if you should want to have one thing that is still yours alone, it will be this … if you can find it.

That is the secret… if you can go to the pain and the sacrifice like the bridegroom going to his bridal bed, that can never be taken from you, or used to fuel the ends of others, even if those ends are great and worthy, even if it would save lives. That joy is yours to do with as you will, hoard it or give it, lend it or throw it away, and even the Norns themselves will not begrudge whatever you might choose to do. For this you have earned, by losing the rest of yourself, and by giving that to the world, and then struggling further to find this light. What is thrice-earned in this way is your gold. Follow it. It will be the only thing that you can be sure of holding onto.

PART II: MASTERING THE ELEMENTS

Starting With The Roots:
Mastering the Elements

Shamans and spirit-workers and even witches and magicians the world over, and throughout time, have learned to master the basic four elements in order to get things done. However, mastering them is much more than just doing a few spells, or contemplating the nature of each element, although that's a good way to start. In spirit-work, it's about working with the spirits who deal with that element to find a greater understanding of it.

I should disclaimer, here, that "mastering" the elements is nothing like some Truncheons And Flagons game of creating "fire spells" and "water spells" and so forth. While there are legitimate uses for those, the kind of shamanic work that I was set to do by the spirits around mastering elements is very specific. I don't control them. I work with them, I have established a relationship with them, I call upon them, I continually gain a deeper understanding of them. Like other situations where shamans talk about "mastering" spirits, it's not about waving one's oh-so-wizardly hands and commanding entities to do your laundry. It's more like you'd speak of mastering the violin. You can be lordly at it all day, and nothing is going to happen until you put in sweat and blood and years of effort to come into a satisfactory understanding of and relationship with it. In a very real sense, what you're doing is mastering yourself with regard to the violin, and that is also where we stand with the elements.

My understanding of the elements is likely circumscribed by my northern-tradition background (and foreground), and those of other traditions would likely be asked to do different things. The particular slant that this tradition puts on the elements is forged by the experience of the subarctic and arctic circumpolar environment. Unlike modern Neo-Pagan understanding of them, all the elements—and for that matter all the forces of nature—are understood first and foremost as dangerous. Air is the province of the frost-giants and storm-giants who bring blizzard and snow and lightning, or of Aesir-gods who are about thunder and steel and war, or of the Alfar—the Kingdom of Air—who bewilder and confuse with illusion. Fire is the province of destructive fire-giants, the sort who can reduce a forest to ashes, and fiery gods like Surt and the trickster Loki; fire can cremate you as well as warm you. Water comes to us through the sea-etins of the cold heartless ocean with their teeth and claws and stormy currents, and the spirits of lake and river who are equally fond of drowning people. Earth can be the fertile field of wheat, but as the Vanir will tell you, blood must be spilled for that fertility. It can also come to us in hard, unyielding mountains; giants like Hrungnir whose heart was made of cold stone. Sacred trees became sacred groves in which bodies were hung; plants hold spirits who can heal or kill; animals can come as teachers, allies, or the teeth in the dark that wait to devour you and your family. In the North, there is no such thing as "naturally safe". It's much more the opposite, and it's no wonder that the most popular pantheon was the Aesir, whose nature is that of Civilization and of keeping those "natural" red teeth and claws in check.

Working with the elements from this perspective is, I think, healthier in many ways than much of the prettying-up that modern earth-centered spiritual work leans towards. I don't know how many workshops or classes that I've been to where herbalism was mentioned (not by herbalists, by the way) as some kind of completely safe thing that would never hurt anyone. The doctrine of Nothing Green Can Harm You would have been laughed at by our recent ancestors, who carefully catalogued which plants could heal and which could kill, and at what dosage. To our ancestors further back, it would have been fatal, and such people would have been culled out by natural selection. (Generally the first plant that I bring up to counteract that argument isn't poison hemlock or aconite, or even something like ragweed which can cause allergies, but poison ivy. It's amazing how many of the folks making the claim have already had an unpleasant encounter with that bad-tempered lady wight, but have blocked it from their memory.) This is the kind of mindset that led to the tourist climbing two security fences in the zoo in order to get close-up picture of the cute big fuzzy white polar bear, who promptly grabbed her through the last set of bars and began to gnaw on her leg, or the couple who were mauled by an alligator because they taunted it in order to get a photo with its mouth open. In the end, Nature is still cold and hard and encourages the survival of the fittest.

Looking at the elemental world as something potentially dangerous that requires respect is a good antidote to the anthropomorphizing rife in our society. The shaman's perspective is not to see the wights as humans in suits of fur, chlorophyll, or energy. They may have parts of their natures that are similar to ours, and we do tend to stress that when we write about them, but they are not human and never will be. It may be that we cannot fully grasp their nonhumanness, but that's part of how we master these forces of nature—learning not only to grasp it, but to take it into ourselves, for those parts of their natures can do things beyond humanity.

That said, here is the NT Absolute Minimum Necessary To Master The Elements. The ones that are starred are ones that I am told would be necessary for any shaman; a shamanic practitioner would be wise to work on all of these, and any of the optional ones that they are able to do. I should emphasize that these are months and years of work. It has also been said that once you've mastered them, you simply start all over again learning them in a deeper way. These are what I had to do in order to learn the very first level of each one.

Mastering Air

The element of Air is one of volatility, changeable as the weather. That is its most defining characteristic—it can be anything quickly, but it does not stay that way for a long time. It is the last element to come into your body, and it defines the moment of birth; before that, while you live in a sense, you are not yet your own person. It is Air that cuts you away from the body of your mother, away from being part of another; the first breath and the first blast of cold. Air says, You have your own thoughts now, and no one else will ever be that linked to you again. You are separate ... and this is not such a bad thing.

Air is also the other things that come out of your mouth when you breathe out—words, thoughts, singing, etc. It is those things traded and swapped amongst people—communication—and those things laid down in funny symbols to stay. Yet it all starts from Breath, and Wind. Wind is the medium of the Dead, which they ride; it is the medium of messaging.

Historically, Air was symbolized by the frost giants, born from the slumbering body of Ymir. In the northern tradition, air is not just gentle breezes; it's blizzard, snow, hail, subzero winds, all the harsh and difficult things that come out of the sky. Useful northern-tradition wights to call on for help with things related to Air include Thor, Odin, Frigga, Tyr, Bragi, Gna, storm-thurses such as Kari the North Wind and his various children (and for that matter the other three winds), Skadi, Rind, and many of the Alfar.

The list of Air-element skills below is sorted by what sorts of wights you'll need to call upon to help you with them. Most are required, or you can hardly be said to have mastered anything. A few are optional, and this is noted.

1. Breathwork *

In the northern tradition, breath is *ond*, which has a double meaning both of the air that you pull in and push out of your lungs, and of the energy that flows through your body—chi, ki, mana, prana, whatever you want to call it. There's no coincidence about this; breath is the first way that we learn to manipulate that life force. The first part of mastering Air is mastering your own breath.

While you don't have to learn every obscure yogic breathing technique in existence, you should be able to alter your consciousness by breathing a specific way. You should be able to calm yourself, slow your heartbeat, and get yourself into a space for journeying through breath alone. You should be able to hold your breath for reasonable periods of time, with your body relaxed and your lungs empty. You should be able to breathe out pain. You should be able to use breath to circulate energy around your body, moving it up the front and down the back of your body, and reversing that flow. (One direction is invigorating, the other is calming.) As discussed in *Pathwalker's Guide To The Nine Worlds* and *Wightridden: Paths Of Northern-Tradition Shamanism*, the four-fold breath is a good place to start working.

2. Breath magic *

The next step after using breath and *ond* to shift and enhance the energy in yourself, and your state of mind, is to take it outside of you. Unlike bodily fluids, breath leaves your body all the time. You should be able to imbue your breath with a certain sort of energy, and then blow it out onto something as a spell. This is especially good for purification—blowing something clean. It's also good for quickly charging found items that you've just picked up—a leaf, a twig, a bit of tree bark, a small stone. Similarly, the breath can be charged with negative energy, and then blown out to remove it. This is the step before getting to...

3. Singing—and Spellsinging *

This is a bardic technique whereby you use your voice as a conduit for specific magics. It takes time and practice, and you have to sing a lot. Your ability to sound great as a performer is not in question; I have recordings of many old shamans who are lousy singers (by our modern standards) and yet manage quite well to create power with their voices, and affect anyone who listens. If you're good enough, it can be heard through a recording, though of course it's most powerful in person. You should be able to write a spell in the form of a song, sing it, move power through your voice, and have it work. Listening to a Saami *joik*, if you have the chance, is highly instructive. No shaman should ever be afraid to sing, because it's a basic part of their work. Remember that this isn't a performance of vocal skill, but of *maegen*.

In the northern tradition, this is one of the main forms of *galdr*, or active magic. Rune-*galdr* is the most common form, and can consist of singing the name of the rune over and over, letting the rune itself shape the sound of your voice and influence the energy passing through it. It can also be sung wordlessly, just holding the rune energy in your head. It's easiest to start doing this with runes, because their theurgic magic holds the cosmic "groove" in place while you're doing it, and requires less mindfulness from you, so you can concentrate on feeling the process. Eventually, though, you will graduate to being able to do it with any energy, if you work at it enough.

4. Weather magic *

Although you don't need to have control of the weather (and frankly, you won't), you need to understand it, and have worked with it. You need to be aware of the changing patterns of the weather, and to have affected it in some small way a few times. Smell is important here— predicting the weather by how the air smells. You need to be able to competently read the message on the coming wind with your nose, and your skin. Learn to be aware of what's going on in the atmosphere, even if you live in a city.

5. The Four Winds *

You need to have spoken with them, and with some of the minor winds. As I understand it, nobody ever has a strong relationship with all four winds. That would be too much power, and the winds—who hate the idea of being bound—won't have it. As long as one or more of them cannot be bound by you, they could free the others from whatever spell you were lobbing. So nobody ever gets full patronage of all four of them. That doesn't mean that people don't try; witness the Saami noaide's cap of the four winds. Most spirit-workers only work with one wind, a few with two or three. I've worked with three. The South Wind merely laughs at me and won't work with me. They all have different personalities. By the way, it may be that you have to master spellsinging before you can call the winds, because that's the way you get their attention.

In the northern tradition, lore only gives us the name of one of the four winds—Kari, eldest son of Mistblindi and brother to Aegir and Logi, and one of the great chieftains of Niflheim. While their names are not found in lore, I have experienced the West Wind as a female storm-giantess who travels the islands off the coast of Jotunheim. The East and South Winds are both storm-giants with one fire-giant parent—possibly brother and sister. The South Wind spends a good deal of time in Muspellheim, although she often comes forth bearing its warmth; she is a warrior and is dedicated to her ancestors' task of melting the ice. The East Wind is a skald, eloquent with words and riddles, and friendly with everyone—the Aesir and Vanir like him, and even the Alfar grudgingly allow him in.

Working with the physical winds can, when you are much more experienced, lead to working with the Deer of the Four Winds in the branches of Yggdrasil. Their powers are not, contrary to their name, about the actual breezes that blow. The Deer are the cosmic guardians of the winds of the Tree, of Ginnungagap, of the Void. Those who work with the energy of the Void had best have a good relationship with them, because they monitor who brings in what sort of energy and make sure that doors which should not be opened (at least by anyone less than a

God) remain closed. The Deer are actually four famous runemasters of four different races—Alf, Duerg, Jotun, and human—and while they rarely get involved with people, they may quietly shut down the work of someone who infringes on their territory, without that person knowing. They are there for a reason; if they say that the door you are opening through the Void oughtn't to be opened, they know best.

6. Flight *

Shamans all over the world use bird forms to travel and journey. While some folk prefer to use just wings grown out of their own *hama* for *hamfarir*, others like to take on bird form. Famous bird-shapes include eagles, hawks, ravens, crows, seagulls, and sparrows, but any bird will do. An important part of understanding air is shapeshifting to a bird form at least once, and having the experience of flying, in any world you want. Doing it in a bird's body, with the aid of the bird spirit, will give a more organic experience than artificially growing wings and trying to figure out how to use them; no matter how graceful you think you are, the birds are better at it. It's learning to ride the wind currents, in a way that we can't know with our physical forms. One supposes, of course, that hangliding might be a way to learn it in real-time.

7. Spinning

Learn to spin fiber, at least on a drop spindle. I learned to do this many years ago as a hobby, but he importance of this did not become clear until later. (It was one of the many "hobbies" that I was drawn towards for no particular reason, and would then discover decades later that it was part of my shamanic training, and that I'd been unwittingly "nudged" in that direction.) I discovered that spinning my own thread was useful for about a million small magics. This seemed to be an "air" thing somehow, or part of the training for that element. You should not only be able to spin, but to spin "with intent", putting spellcraft into the string as you create it. (This is an optional one, but extremely useful.) Goddesses in this tradition who aid with such things are Frigga (if you're spinning wool or animal fibers; she spins from the cloud-sheep), or Holda and her handmaiden Harn (if you're spinning flax or hemp).

8. Skaldship

Learn to write articulately and well, and speak in front of an audience in a way that holds their attention and gets through to them. While this is more the part of the bard or skald, it is an important, though optional, part of mastering Air. It is useful for the shamanic practitioner as well, especially if you intend to teach, or do public ceremony for a community. Since we have few spirit-workers, the role of the shaman and the role of the priest are often merged and intertwined in this tradition—as it often was in Paleolithic-through-Neolithic times, before the rise of the priestly class. This role also comes with that of historian—not of ancient lore, but of what is being learned and discovered now, which must not slip through our fingers. The best one to teach these skills is Bragi, the skald of Asgard. As an As who is very close to his Jotun mother, he is willing to work with all sorts of folk. Loki and Odin are also quite talented at this sort of thing, and will work with some folk who call on them in this way.

Kari's Lesson
Wind I

I chose to put Kari's lesson first, because although he was not the first Jotun that I interviewed for this article, his was the first of the elemental lessons that I learned.

Long ago, when I was young—perhaps thirteen, fourteen—the wind was my lover. I didn't know anything more than that about the situation, but when I would go outside the wind would touch me in certain ways. I knew that it wasn't just any wind; it was my wind—or at least that's how I thought about it. All the other winds might blow at me, some of them might even talk to me or sing to me, but only one of them touched me in that way. I was still very much a virgin, and to me the wind's touch was amazingly erotic. I remember that it happened in the spring, and that the wind seemed like a young, androgynous figure. Long, white-pale hair and white skin; cold touch and high, singing voice. I didn't know what to call him, although I tried a few Greek names for the winds, but although they were pretty, they didn't seem right.

The problem was that I was a pretty screwed-up kid at the time, suffering from abuse at home and desperate for energy and attention. I tried to suck energy off of my wind-lover, and he retreated, and finally ceased to visit me. I convinced myself that it had all been something in my desperate teenage imagination ... until one of the Nine Sisters commented to me, "You're going to have to make it up with my uncle eventually, you know."

I choked, and grabbed for my research books. I found out that their father, Aegir, had two brothers ... Logi, a fire-etin, and Kari, a frost-thurse who was the keeper of the North Wind. With a sinking feeling in the pit of my stomach, I knew exactly who I had wronged, and why. It took months for me to get brave enough to deal with it, but finally, as the winter wore on, I went out to talk to him.

I went out with an offering—a serving of our dinner, mutton and vegetable soup with homemade brown bread and a tankard of goat milk. Not fancy, but it was what we were eating. I brought it to the back field and the gate of the winds, and set it down. Then I asked for his blessing, and apologized for what I had done when I was young and foolish.

Absolutely nothing happened. It was as if I was talking to dead air. Finally, I got a bit of a message, though it didn't seem as if it came from anyone so much as just a feeling of what would be right. Leave the dinner and come back again with another one in three days, it said. "Well, I guess I'll go in, then," I said to the empty air, feeling foolish. Just because you're a spirit-worker doesn't mean that you can get everyone on the phone with you.

Three days later, my wife came in while I was still getting out of bed. "The wind is beating against the house," she said, "and I have the strangest feeling that it wants to talk to you." I hadn't told her, or anyone, about my aborted attempt to make amends, so her comment was entirely unexpected. I dressed and heated another bowl of soup, more bread, more milk, and went to take it to the field.

As I walked down the path, it began to snow. Quickly. By the time I reached the back field, I was standing in a whirling cloud of snow. It spun and vortexed and clouded just at the gate of the winds. I put the dinner down, and waited. The wind buffeted me, battered me, blew up the skirts of my coat, and then there he was. Not an androgynous youth, but an old man, white-bearded, white-coated. His coat was startlingly like my own. He grinned at me. "What would you have of me?" he asked, but there was a knowing look in his eyes. The voice was a low grumble.

I swallowed. "Your forgiveness for what I did. Your friendship, and your blessing if possible. And your lesson... I am writing a book..."

"I know about that," he said, and I wondered how much word had gotten around. "You were awfully annoying," he said. "Calling me by all sorts of silly names. But then, you were young. And I was young... "

"Have you aged so much, in only my lifetime?" I asked.

He chuckled. "I am one of those who ages throughout the year, you see me now in winter. But after the equinox I shall become young again, as you saw me when I came to you before. And as for the lesson ... I already gave it to you, back then." He gestured with his hand. "Turn around."

I turned around and the wind got me full in the face. "Breathe," he said, and I breathed in—the wind, the blowing snow, the cold. As I did, I felt him come up behind me and move into my body. The breath left my throat in a long, long sung note ... one that went on and on, vibrating in my head, filling the whole field. I would not have believed that a note could go on so long. Then he moved out of me, and I twitched and shook as I often did after a light possession.

"I am the Breath of Song," he said, and I had a sudden auditory hallucination of the wind shrieking and howling—was that song? "Just as the other three winds are the Breath of Speech, and the Breath of Music, and the Breath of Fire."

"I've always known how to do that," I said, thinking of the ability I've had to push energy out through song, to spin spellsongs, for … how long? I wasn't sure. Certainly since my teen years.

"That's because I breathed it into you," he said, and then he was gone.

Kari's Lesson:

I am the Breath of Song. Breathe in, into your belly. Not just your lungs—fill it all the way down. Release it silently, then breathe it in again. Again. Again. Feel the energy build up in the back of your head. Now open your throat and sing it out, long and clear, pushing that energy forward through the front of your skull, out your mouth. No words; that will come later, in the shaping, with East Wind. First, you sing.

Don't worry about how sweet you sound—sweetness is not necessary. Have you heard the voices of some of the old shamans? Even withered and creaking, they have power. They have learned the way of Song, and once you have learned it, nothing short of muteness shall take it from you. My song is powerful whether I have the sweet voice of springtime, or the rough voice of winter. It is strength and power, not sweetness—that's the West Wind's game.

Sing each note—not in any order, but only to find the feeling of each one. Each note has its own peculiar magic; sing it and find its secrets. You could sing one note a month for the rest of your life, and do nothing but explore each of them, if you chose. But some notes are more powerful than others, due to the quality of their vibration, and that is why more songs are sung on those notes. When you know which note is right for which thing, you will know where to pitch each song. How to find the right note? Run up and down till you find it, of course.

I am the Breath of Cold, and I purify not by burning or raising energy—that's the South Wind's game—but by freezing, cleaning out clear and cold. I am the one who cools the hotter heads, and you can do that, too, with Song. You can slow them down, make them think, make them listen and consider. You can slow down in yourself what needs slowing ... what is being burned up too quick, what needs conserving? I'm the one who can break a fever with breath and singing. I can kill panic in its steps, I can slow anxiety to a trickle. This is the trick, then: Right breathing, right note, right focus of the power in the back of your head. Simple, eh?

Rind's Lesson
Wind II

It was the night of the full moon when I went to the back field to talk to Rind,
and it was bitterly cold and dead silent. The moon cast a silvery sheen on everything,
and the frost glittered everywhere. I brought her a tankard of white goat's milk and
a plateful of sugar-powdered cookies, artfully arranged in the shape of a snowflake.
She came immediately—she had been expecting me—and she was tall, slender,
with long black hair and a flowing blue-white dress that glittered like frost. She
smiled and was friendly, but her presence was like an extra chill in the freezing air.
I was very glad of my warm frost-giant coat, especially when she instructed me to sit
down and meditate on an ice-covered lawn chair in the moonlight.

She stood behind me and instructed me. Her demeanor was friendly, even
cheerful, but at one point I made a small bad joke and she looked at me, and I
immediately apologized. Frost-giantesses are all intimidating, even when they have
decided to like you for the moment. She had me swing a small weight on a string,
like a pendulum, in horizontal circles; this was part of the exercise. I was instructed
to make something special for this purpose, a "stone the color of frost" on a string
that could be swung slower and faster as I breathed. She told me that it could also
be done with a "singing stick", and the image she sent me was of something rather
like a bullroarer, but that was for outside as it took up a lot of space and made a
lot of noise; a small pendulum was better for inside.

Rind's Lesson:

Breathe in. Yes, it's cold. Feel the frost. Feel the tears in your eyes
starting to freeze. That's important, because without freezing,
crystallizing, you cannot stop Time. They say that Time is a river,
always flowing, not a series of crystallized moments like beads on a
string, but really it is both. There is more than one way to move
through Time. There is Unn's way, which is Water, and there is my
way, which is Wind and Frost. Without Wind, you do not move, and
without Frost, you cannot stop.

Why move through time at all? That's something that Unn won't tell you; she is as shifty as the ocean itself. Because sometimes, in order to find the truth of something, you must go back to when it happened. To change things, no, that isn't allowed; the Norns will sabotage your efforts, and it is like nothing for them to do that. Don't waste the energy. And remember that even if you go there and see through your eyes, it is only your eyes, not the eyes of those who told the tale. There are things you might miss or see differently. But this is only something to be done rarely. You do not know how easy it is to get lost in Time.

Breathe out, now. Blow it out. Spin. Don't breathe with the spinning; spin with the breathing. You are gathering the winds of Time, which is different from the winds of space. You are going backwards, so you know which way to spin, yes? Indeed, widdershins, against the turn of the sun. To go forward again—which you must do, the same number of breaths and spins, and you will know how many because you will feel it fall into place—spin sunwise.

To the future? No, I advise against that. There is no one future, there are many, and the one that you visit might not be the one that will come to pass. Besides, you need someone strong to hold your thread and bring you back. It would be a strong mortal indeed who could hold you against the winds of Time. Even a land-wight would get confused; they do not understand the passing of Time well. No, you would have to ask a God for that, and they would have to approve of your reason, yes? Of course, whenever you go backwards, you will always be going a little way further forward when you return, as time will have passed with your body and you must find it in Time. Don't worry, it is much easier to feel this with Time than with Space.

Speed up your breathing, your spinning. This is easier done when there is no wind, strangely enough. That is because when there are winds, you must convince them to aid you, and to spin in the right direction, and if they abandon you once you have gone back, and refuse to return with you again, there can be problems. The winds are more fickle than the waters, but they see more clearly. Each spin is a period of time—how much, how long? It depends. That is something I find difficult to express in your words, your images. But what you are doing now, it is not long. Minutes, perhaps. Hours. There, see, the sky your Eyes see is lightening, not the moonlight seen by your eyes.

Now is your moment. Jerk up on the string and do This to stop. *(At this point in the teaching, she made a flicking, whiplike motion with her hand that was accompanied by some sort of magic. I begged her to show me again, and after watching it a few times, I feared that it was beyond me—not the motion, but the accompanying magic. I couldn't figure out exactly what it was, and it seemed to be so natural for her that she couldn't seem to explain it in terms I could understand. All she would say was:)* This is the moment of frost, of freeze. Freeze! The wind chills the water. Ice. Ice. Not the rune, the moment, that is different. Well, I shall give you a song to sing while you do this, and then you can do it with your voice. Now spin sunwise, start slow, breathe into it, go further and faster. You will know when to stop. It will feel natural to start winding down, until you know you are on the last spin, and then hsst! The frost again.

Do this only to see, and it is best done with another holding your thread, even for the past, unless it is so small a time that you will be able to catch up anyhow. But be warned: this will age you, if you are not careful. Not the going back … the coming forward again. See, you have taken a few hours from your life just doing this tonight. Does that frighten you? Good, it should. If you can save a life, if you can set right a great wrong, if you can find a great thing lost, these are the only reasons. Otherwise, you deserve what you will get.

Rind's Song

The flower opens to the Sun
But Time spins on and soon is lost
The flower falls before the ice
The chill winds bring the killing frost.

Bragi's Lesson

Wind III: Building Bridges With Words
as told to Elizabeth Vongvisith

A year or so ago, Loki sent me to Bragi, who told me that I would become his student and he would be my teacher and patron in the arts of writing, music and poetry. All poets, storytellers and musicians in the Northern Tradition are His people, regardless of their allegiances. He is very unlike his quiet, self-contained mother or his intense, ruthless father. Bragi is good-natured and gregarious, self-assured without being proud or overly conscious of his achievements, ready to laugh and very easy to talk to. His is the most superb singing voice in the Nine Worlds, and he is liked and admired by people of all races—Jotnar, Aesir, Vanir, Alfar, Duergar, the high and the low, the mighty and humble.

Whereas I have been reluctant to share much of my work with others, out of self-consciousness and a fear of not measuring up to my own imaginary standards, Bragi has encouraged me to share my gifts and think of my talent for writing as a tool I can use to make the world a more enjoyable place, rather than something to measure myself by. Because of him, I am starting to understand the true power there is in being a skald.

Bragi's Lesson:

I was born of a mountain-thurse mother and an As father—ancient enemies as far apart in philosophy and temperament as you can get in many ways. Yet my parents' story is an example of how good can come from the willingness to compromise, and how words in particular can inspire friendship and bind hearts where other methods have failed.

When you tell a story to someone, you are forging a tie between yourself and them, and also between the hearer's own experience and the events you're speaking of. Your words become a tangible link to bygone days, different points of view, other people's feelings and concerns, or perhaps all three. You build a bridge with every story told, every song sung and every piece of lore or legend you relate. It doesn't even matter if the story never existed before you spoke it—you are still a bridge-maker, and you are still creating that link for your audience which comes directly through your heart and mind, shaping itself through your words and anchored in the commonality of experience that all of us share—giant and dwarf, mortal man and immortal deity, living and dead

This is why skalds and bards have, throughout the long ages of the Worlds, always been ambassadors of goodwill, welcomed by all and recognized as bringers of frith. Those who tell stories have a unique perspective on the world, for they understand that any story itself is worthless without a speaker and listeners to give it life and make it mean something. And through paying careful attention to the stories he or she tells, a skald understands better than anybody else that all of us are not so different as we would like to believe from our enemies or lovers, or from those who have come before us, or for that matter, from those who will come after. Times may change and worlds may come and go, but the hearts of men and women are the same always. A true storyteller knows this, and uses it to his or her advantage in the crafting of words and the honoring of the art

And so, if you tell stories or sing songs, if you are a world-maker, a hero-chronicler and a tale-weaver, and if you have the wit to pluck from thin air a story recognizable deep in your listeners' hearts of hearts as something that need not have actually happened to be utterly true, then recognize yourself that you are both the carrier of an enormous responsibility and the recipient of a valuable gift. Stories are the glue by which friendships are formed, love is begun, alliances are made, and old enmities put to rest. Stories tell us not only who others are, but who we are as well. Stories serve us best when they show us how alike we are to others, rather than setting us apart from each other. And with each story told, each tale sung, every poem written or every piece of lore you relate, you are building bridges where none may have existed before.

Groa's Fourth and Ninth Charms
Wind IV & V

The first time that I met Groa, I was sent to Helheim for three days of training. I assumed that I would be seeing Hela, but instead an elderly Jotun woman came to me. I knew that she was dead, although her ghost seemed vital and intelligent there in Helheim. She was a sorceress, and it was clear that this was not the first time she had sat with a novice and put them through paces. When I came back and my assistant asked me what I had done, all I could do was shrug and say, "Wax on, wax off!"

Later, when she was certain that I'd mastered a few elemental basics, she started to give me a few song-charms. Further on in that year, I was to stumble across Grougaldr and realize who she was, and recognize the charms as ones that she had given to her son Svipdag—"although," she said irritably, "he is not much for magic." I asked if all nine of them would come to me, and she glared at me and told me to be patient. So the few of her charms that are listed in this book are numbered not in order of their position here, but their position in the lay of Grougaldr, for those who wish to find them. They are all simple, with no explanation needed. If you want to be able to use them, you'll have to get an invitation into Helheim anyway—which means dealing with its forbidding mistress—and Groa will have to agree to teach you, because like all the power songs in this book, it won't work without the will of the wight whose gift it is.

Groa's Fourth Charm: Wind IV
Foes To Friends

When faced with enemies, the greatest conquering is indeed in making them your friends. Never forget this, for the best battle is the one that need not come to pass.

> You see my heart, and I am seen.
> You hear my words, and I am heard.
> You feel my fears, my foes, my flight,
> You fathom deep my path and plight
> And friendship steals across your sight,
> And understanding steals your fight,
> And we will reach across this road
> And hand to hand we bring this right.

Groa's Ninth Charm: Wind V
At Wit's End

For when you must debate with one who may be wiser than you, and you need a head full of quick wits and quick words. This rhyme gives focus and quick thinking, but only temporarily. It will only last for an hour or thereabouts, so you must be expedient about it.

> Riddle and rhyme, I am laid on the line,
> I am sharp as a shaving, I shine like the light
> Of a breath of chill morn, of this moment in time.

Mastering Fire

The element of Fire is different from the other three elements in that it is not a form of matter. While scientists may scorn the classification system of our ancestors, in recognizing four "elements", they were actually recognizing, among other things, four forms that matter can take. It can be solid (earth), liquid (water), gaseous (air), or it can transform itself completely into something that is not matter, but has heat and energy of its own. As such, Fire is the medium of transformation and purification. The three runes of fire are Kaunaz, the fire of the forge whose glyph is a hammer and tongs; Cweorth, the funeral pyre whose glyph is a fire-twirl; and Nauthiz, the rune of Need, whose symbol is a firebow. The first two runes are all about transformation: dross metal into tools, a dead body into ashes and soul. The third rune harks back to when Fire was a necessity, without which we would not be here today.

For a people surrounded by the harsh cold of the North, fire was very literally the only way of survival. We, with our technological plundering of the realms under the Earth for our fuel, have forgotten how each tiny spark was the beginnings of a lifeline for a starving, shivering tribe. From the descriptions of the Northern creation myth, which seems to have been inherited from the indigenous folk that the Indo-Europeans moved in on, researchers feel that this myth means that these folk lived through the receding of the Ice Age, in which heretofore unseasonably warm winds melted the ice and revealed the mountains.

Historically, Fire is symbolized by the fire-etins. Surt the Black, lord of the fire-giants, was the first being to come through Ginnungagap, out of the darkness with his flaming wand Laevateinn, bringing light and creating Muspellheim, the Land of Fire. He is the progenitor of the race of fire-giants, whose blood runs through much of the Nine Worlds. When Muspellheim drew near to the frozen Niflheim, it began to melt the ice and revealed Ymir, thus creating the frost-giants. The collision between the two worlds created the combination of Nature that we know today. In the stories of the Northern Tradition, Fire comes first, for without Fire there is no light, no heat, and no life.

Fire is also rage and wrath, sexual and emotional passion, and the warrior's courage. For the first of these, there is no better ally than Fenris, although his is a difficult trust to gain. For the second (and even the third), one can call upon Freya in her fire-aspect as warrior who rides with the Valkyries, or her love-goddess aspect. For the third, any warrior deity (Tyr, Angrboda, Vidar) who you can work with will do. Fire is also the Sun, and thus Sunna can be called upon.

Fire from the sky—lightning—was likely the first fire, carefully sheltered and carried from campsite to campsite before people mastered the art of making it themselves. The gods of lightning—Thor and Farbauti—can also be called upon to aid with understanding fire, although their lessons tend to be harsher. Loki the Trickster is also a fire-god, and he can aid in may things fire-related (although if you go far enough with this element under his supervision, sooner or later he will refer you to his godfather Surt).

The list of skills below are the most important things in mastering Fire on a basic level.

1. Making Fire *

This is the first part of mastering fire, and although it may raise some eyebrows, it is very important: Learn to make fire with some older method, a method of the ancestors. I chose tinder and flint, because I felt it was the easiest. Firebow or fire-twirl would also be acceptable— heck, they'd be even better. According to Siberian tribal shamanic lore, you are supposed to have special sacred tinder and flint given to you by the shaman who trains you. Ideally, to pass this part, you should be able to make fire with it yourself, and light your own homemade recaning incense with it, with no technological help, at least a few times. All sacred fires should be lit in this way, for personal or group ritual. Just as you can't master water without learning to swim, you can't master fire without creating it with your own hands. That's part of understanding it—praying to the fire-gods or fire-wights as you work, seeing the first sparks, coaxing them to life with your breath, feeding them the right food, getting them to a roaring blaze. I would also strongly suggest that you spend at least a couple of weeks in a (preferably cold) place where your only source of heat and cooking is wood-fire, and doing what is necessary to keep warm and have cooked food with only your own fire.

Here's my chance to tell about my tinder-and-flint experience. I knew a year in advance that I was going to have to learn this, but I kept putting it off. My dear friend Aelfwine, who I considered very much a father figure, promised me that he would teach me the art. I kept waffling, mostly because I had been told that I needed special sacred flint and steel. This was traditionally given to the novice shaman by their teacher, the proverbial old man or woman in the hut. I had none, and it just didn't feel right to go buy some, although I stared at them over the mail-order catalogs occasionally. I rather doubted the spirits' ability to come up with the right stuff, so I waited.

Then Aelfwine came down with leukemia and died. I was so sad about it that I put it off still further, because thinking about it reminded me of the chance that I'd lost. The spirits became impatient with me, it was the only required thing I hadn't done yet for Fire. Then one day I visited Aelfwine's family, whom I considered family as well. I mentioned to Tchipakkan that Aelfwine had promised to teach me firemaking, and she said that as his widow she was honor-bound to keep his promise for him. She got out her firemaking kit and showed me how to do it, warning me that I would end up destroying a lot of flints in the process of practicing it. I didn't manage to make fire that day, as it would take months of practice before I got it right.

Then she brought out the kit that had been Aelfwine's. It was a reproduction of a Dark-Age Saxon and/or Viking kit, with a hand-forged steel and a little toolkit handmade out of twisted copper, a copy of one found in a Viking burial, with tweezers to hold burning material, and an awl, a punch, and an ear-spoon. She held it out to me. "None of our children is interested in this," she said, "and he wouldn't have wanted it to go to waste. You take it and put it to good use." So I went home with my dead father-figure's kit, feeling foolish for having ever doubted. There is no way that the spirits could have come up with anything more sacred to me ... and of course, Hela's way of sending me a special kit would be by way of a dead man. It is things like this that remind me that those I serve do care about me.

Useful Gods/Spirits to call upon for help: For eclectic folks, Brigid, Hephaestus, Shango, Hestia. For northern-tradition-only folks, Loki, Surt, fire-etins.

2. Recaning *

Learn about incense, about doing magic with burning plant matter. The Anglo-Saxon term for it is *recaning*, which is cognate to our work "reek" and is pronounced "reek-en-ing". In doing this, you learn how fire purifies things, how the burning corpse of a plant can become purified and purifying. Make and dry your own incense out of various herbs for different Gods and wights. I started with Mugwort, making my own recaning sticks, as Mugwort is to our tradition as White Sage is to the Native Americans—the first of the Nine Sacred Herbs. Mugwort clears an area of negative energy like nothing else, leaving it clean and ready for creating ritual. It is the traditional burning plant of western Europe. Another traditional recaning herb is Juniper, the traditional burning plant of eastern Europe. Burned together, they pack a wallop.

3. The Inner Sun *

Heatwork, which the Tibetans refer to as *tumo*, is the ability to raise the temperature of your body and make it warm at will. Your body's internal thermostat is in your third chakra, your center of *vili*, and if you can figure out how to tweak it, you can wave heat out from that point. You should be able to keep yourself warm by this means when you aren't actively ill. It's very helpful on long vigils in the cold. It is also good to meditate on the links between *vili* and heat, fire and will.

4. Internal Ley Lines

Get a feel for the energy meridians of the body. While it seems strange to go as far as Chinese medicine for such information, they are the acknowledged experts on the subject. Ever since a five-thousand-year-old body was pulled out of a Swiss glacier and found to have tattooed acupuncture points, many of us have been prodded by the wights of our tradition to rediscover what our Paleolithic ancestors knew, two millennia before the Chinese supposedly "discovered" it. That shouldn't be too surprising—the human body is the human body, and they all have same energy meridians, and the points on those meridians all do the same things, whatever cultural language is used to describe them. While the new generation of northern-tradition spirit-workers is working to "download" the old European names and understandings of them, we will have to work with the Chinese conception, at least for the moment.

You don't need to know the entirety of all 365 points, unless you are called to learn that. Just figure our where your 12 meridians are. Run your fingers along them. Learn a handful of the main points, the ones that are useful for doing things you need done, and learn to call *ond* to those points while pressing on them. This is where you use your inner understanding of Fire to energize those points and lines.

5. External Objects *

One of the powers of Fire is controlling your energy flows, and directing them outwards. There is no stagnant Fire; it moves or it dies. Learn to charge items with particular energies. You should be able to put a certain "flavor" of energy into an object, and thus make the various things that you'll need. A good way to begin is to charge water, or milk, or some other simple drinkable substance. Then you drink it every morning as a kind of spirit-work health tonic, especially if you're feeling logy. Charging small polished (non-poisonous) stones and putting them into the charged water makes it keep longer. (The Siberians use vodka—originally it was distilled fermented mare's milk—but I wouldn't want to drink that every morning upon arising. Still, it's your taste.)

6. Teeth and Claws *

All predators have fire in them, the fire that devours. This is an aspect of fire that it is important to understand, because to downplay the destructiveness of fire in any way is to dangerously miss the point. Demonizing that destructiveness and refusing to see its necessity is to dangerously miss the point in the other direction. Learn to shapeshift to a predator form of some kind, even if it's not your regular animal; hunt in that form and make a kill. If you aren't a skinshifter, work with a predatory animal wight and ask it to teach you about the devouring fire and its necessity to the cycles of Life.

7. Dancing the Fire

This is an optional one, for those who are drawn to it. Learn to use dance as a method of trancework and raising power. Dance starts with fire, harnessing the inner *litr*; some spirit-workers who use dance as a tool have begun to work with fire-dancing as a way to honor the fire spirits. (More on trance-dancing and sacred dance will be covered in the next book, *Wightridden: Paths of Northern-Tradition Shamanism.*)

8. Heat Purification

Learn how to use heat ordeals as purification, such as the sauna or *stofa*, if it's physically possible for you. This is optional, but a good way for people who can do sweats to understand heat—and it's good if you're having trouble with #3 above. The steam spirits can help you to internalize heat and release it when necessary. Learn the full steam rite of this tradition, which is found in the next book in this series, *Wightridden: Paths of Northern-Tradition Shamanism.*

Surt's Lesson

Fire I: Creative Spark And Destructive Flame
from Corbie Petulengro

Surt is immensely old, and quite capricious in his own way. In many other pantheons and cultures, the figure of the Primal Light-Bringer is angelic and entirely beneficent, but in this our Nine Worlds, our Primal Light-Bringer is a grim and cantankerous fire-giant. There's a side of him that is almost stereotypically fire-giant—well, after all, they are all descended from him, so he isn't so much stereotypical as prototypical—that chuckles gruesomely and blasts things with fire, that seems gleefully bent on destruction. There's also a side of him that swaggers up arrogantly and with sudden blazing generosity, pitches you a wad of creative energy—zing!—as a freebie, and you're left standing there are juggling this red-hot thing that you'd better use for some high purpose before it burns out or burns you. He is straightforward, his language plain and almost coarse, and I almost underestimate the grim depths of his mind. Almost.

Then there's the other, older, side of him. I see that part when suddenly he pauses and darkens, becomes smoke-blackened rather than flaming, and his old, old eyes slide sideways and look at me, and through me. That's when he says something that reminds me that these other, more surface, sides of him are just camouflage, just a mask over the being that was born from the darkness and rent the first hole through Ginnungagap, and begat the world of Muspellheim that warmed and began all other life in the Nine Worlds. That's when I remember, again, that he is older than Urd, the oldest surviving frost-thurse, that he saw her born from a great distance in his own world. He told me once that after she had mated with two brothers and brought forth two daughters, he sent her one of his sons to be the father of her first-born son, to eventually lead the frost-thurses into new worlds. I remember also that he was born not only to begin life in the Nine Worlds, but to end it as well. In the end, it will be Surt who decides when Ragnarok goes down, and no other. To him is given the dread task of endings.

Surt sometimes comes to aid me when I am stuck on my creative work, blocked in, unable to get any further and cursing myself for it. He tosses me the tiniest spark of that primal creative fire, the stuff that lit Ginnungagap. When it leaves his fingers, it is just the faintest spark, but by the time it crosses the space between us, it is a raging fireball that I must open myself to take, desperately jamming open my chakras in that split second and praying that I don't become consumed. Surt doesn't have time to wait around for me; either I am ready for those blockages to be blasted away, or I can sit in my ice and suffer. The size difference isn't really a size difference, either. That spark hasn't grown any between his hands and my belly. It's just that he's that much bigger, and I am only a mere mortal.

You may think it cruel of him, that he'll toss someone a spark and not really care all that much if it burns them up or not. And yes, I am aware that he doesn't care. It's all fine to him. I've seen people consumed by such sparks—eaten by their creativity until the manifestation of the project was all that mattered, and such things as body, health, and lovers were forgotten in the bright blaze. Yet those that survived long enough, he shrugs, they left such a fine mark on the Universe! There is no compassion in Surt. That's not his job.

Yet if I can open myself to it, for that moment I am a daughter of Sinmora, burning with the urge to make manifest. Fire roars out my fingertips into music, into art, into words that burn on the page. I used to like to think of the sons of Surt as the destructive sides of Fire, and the daughters of Sinmora as the creative sides. Then Surt decided that I had held onto that illusion for quite long enough, and thoroughly burned it down to ashes. Idiot, he said to me, and he gave me a lesson that left me humbled. I thought that I understood creation and creativity, but now I realize that I knew nothing. The fire of Muspellheim that I had used would not be so divided. And this—according to Surt—is the first Mystery of Fire, the one that seems the simplest but is so hard for everyone to truly grasp.

(One note about Surt's galdr-song: The version I enclose here consists of the beginning line, the first verse, the runing, and the ending line which is the same as the beginning. Assuming that you work with him and get his permission, you can sing this song, and this is the minimum that you will need to sing it ... but if you're doing it right, there will be another whole section between the verse and the runes. It will leap out your mouth, it will be different every time you sing it, it will be from his Fire. Oh, and you'll need to have some kind of fire—even a candle—to look at while you sing, duh.)

Surt's Lesson:

You want the secret of Fire? I ought to tell you to stick your hand in a flame. Still, I can't guarantee that you'd learn anything from that, could I? If observing the nature of Fire—and that includes Sun and light and all things that give vision, it includes the warmth in your body from the chemical fires, the sunlight that the leaves devour to grow, the magma under the earth, all of that—won't tell you the secret, then I'll have to set it out plainly. Fire doesn't keep deep secrets, not like Water or Earth, or even changeable Air. Fire doesn't care who sees, who knows. Fire writes it plainly in huge letters, all over Creation, all over Destruction. *I was here. I did this.* You only miss it because you're not looking.

This is the secret. You mortals, you always want to separate creation and destruction. They are two different forces, you say; they are opposing, they cannot be in the same space at once. This is because you would really like to have the one without the other, or so you say. You think you would, but if you could, it would be disastrous, of course. The truth is that they are not opposites. They are not even different sides of the same coin. *They are the same thing.*

This is what fire teaches. If it can create, it can—and will—destroy, in the same breath. Every choice that begins also ruins the choices that might have been. That which brings forth light and heat must devour something else to do so. The life that is you might have been someone else, someone that may never be given birth because you exist. At the very least, it will lead inevitably to a death—yours. There is no having one without the other, because they are the same stuff. You don't really understand this with all your being; you think that things are linear. I can forgive that; your lives are short, and broken up by forgetting deaths. I argued with Urd about that, but she seemed to think that it was important, the continual forgetting and starting over, so here I am teaching you about it again, and again. Let this be the last time for you, eh?

So when you sing this song I've put through you, remember that every act of creation you put that spark to will also be an act of destruction, and you'll have that on your hands. That's no excuse not to use it! After all, I started these worlds, and you know what my job will be, if things get old and tired and too far out of balance. Does that mean that they were better off never happening? Bah. No regrets. The burning will have been worth it, every moment.

Surt's Galdr-Song

And the worlds were born in fire and in ice.
Tear open the darkness
Rent with the light
Force the warmth and the flame
Upon unwilling ice.
The first spark
The first fire
The first ashes of desire
The first hope
The first turn
The first tree black and burned.

Kano Kano Kano
Kaunaz Kaunaz
Ken Ken Ken Ken Ken
Cweorth Nyth
Nyth Cweorth
Isa Isa Isa Isa Isa
And the worlds were born in fire and in ice...

Logi's Lesson
Fire II

This was a very short lesson. We had lit a fire on the winter solstice, and after other folk left the field, I was set to watch it. The moment I was alone, he was there, sitting in the fire. Skinny, bony joints, bony pointed face, long gnarly fingers that flicked out at me. His hair was a snapping, sparking halo about his narrow shoulders. "Get your drum," he ordered. When I played, he told me "Faster," and then "Faster!" again. When I was drumming at the absolute limit of my concentration, he laughed, tapping his fingers in time on the fire-logs, and spoke to me. After he was done, he vanished, and he took the fire with him entirely. I have never seen a bonfire shrink to dead smoking coals in less than three minutes before this.

Logi's Lesson:

Fire eats things. Of course you know that, but when people talk about inner fire, what do they really mean? Or—to put it differently— what *ought* they to mean? I'll bet you're thinking about anger, or pride, or any of those things. Sorry, all wrong. Your inner fire is your metabolism. It's what burns your fuel. And what I'm going to do is to give you two rhythms, and two songs, to work with that. One will speed metabolism up, if repeated over a long period of time; one will slow it down. Why bother with this? Because you might need it. You might need to get something bad out of your system, or put on more muscle; you might want to conserve food during a stint in the cold. You have no idea what kind of things will be asked of you, what kind of circumstances and how long they might go on! Some things are good to be able to tweak. Mind you, this won't change anything strongly; only subtly. It won't give someone a hummingbird metabolism if they're a complete slug, or vice versa—but it will help, a little, over a period of time. Even once will help a bit. All right, I'm done; it's too cold here for me. Hah!

Logi's Songs

Haste now to the fireside,
Haste now to burn bright,
Come now devouring,
Each grain a-scouring,
Bowl and spoon and all.

Bank all the coals yet,
Orange as sunset,
For winter we keep you,
With ashes we sleep you,
Hoarded like dragon's gold.

Farbauti's Lesson
Fire III

I'd wanted to talk to Farbauti for some time. I'd gone to see his old enemy, Angrboda, the night before my doctor's appointment to complain about how often ill I was. She told me that I was strong and that I could bear it, and then brought up the totems of the Nine Clans of the Iron Wood. She had allowed me to see and draw them already, on the condition that I have them tattooed on my body. Each would be a protective power. Now she said that the first one would be Farbauti's, the Lightning Clan sigil. "Not yours?" I asked.

"Mine will be last," she said. "You need Farbauti's now."

The next day I went to the doctor and got my diagnosis. I have lupus, the chronic and fatal disease named for the Wolf. I thought of Angrboda, my maternal grandmother, of the Wolf tribe, and my Iron Wood blood, and wondered. When the names of one's medical diagnoses match with one's spiritual path, it gives one a strong wish to beat one's head against the wall. The lupus had ramped up in the past year, and I was already allergic to most of the medications used to treat it.

That meant that I had to create a relationship with Farbauti, and soon. I tried to contact him mentally, but the connection was fuzzy. I heard his presence faintly telling me that the time for contact would be soon, in a few days. I wondered, ironically, if it required a thunderstorm in order to bring his presence to me. Unfortunately, it wasn't the season for thunderstorms, I thought to myself.

A few days later, I woke from an afternoon nap in the middle of a thunderstorm.

I immediately sought for Farbauti, without even getting out of bed. He was there sending his presence into my mind, loud and clear. Unlike many Gods and wights, he came to me; he did not demand that I go to him, but then he is always a wanderer, like his son. I saw his face—red-haired, red-bearded, broad and huge, but there his similarity to that other thunder-and-lightning god, Thor, ended. He was much more the classic giant, older and craggier, with a mouthful of none-too-straight and quite pointed teeth, including the classic ogreish lower-jaw canines. His smile was delighted, and terrifying. He wore traditional Iron Wood fashion— rough-cut skins laced into clothing, with dangling, swinging, rattling strings of beads and bones, and on Farbauti, clanking pieces of iron. His massive arms were exposed, with leather bracers banded with iron; they looked strong enough to rip down a tree without breaking a sweat. His eyes were brown, almost black, and glittered. I could smell an iron scent about him; whether blood or weapons I couldn't tell.

The thunder cracked outside, and I could see the dark-grey sky lighting up. Every rumble was his voice, speaking to me, telling me what he wished me to know. He came right to the point; there were no exchanged pleasantries beyond "Listen to me!" I listened. Even as he was speaking of these harsh things, he was smiling, and chuckled often. I wanted to ask if he delighted in smiting, but figured that was a very stupid question. Strangely enough, his enthusiasm was infectious enough that it pulled me away from the tension in my belly that was the knowledge of my illness.

Farbauti's Lesson:

You are my lawful prey. Everyone is my lawful prey, you see, because everyone ages, and everyone develops diseases that are wrongness in the body. No matter how hale you are, sooner or later you will get old and things will begin to go wrong—unless, of course, you are cut short by my granddaughter Hela or one of the other Deaths. The afflictions that come from the evil spirits that invade, through the nose and mouth and parting of the skin, the attor and the onflying, the poison and the tiny creatures, these are not mine. For them, you speak to my granddaughter. My part is the power of degrading, of the disorders that strike later in life yet were built inevitably into your bloodline, of strokes and heart attacks, of the eyes and ears slowly going, of the organs slowly failing, and hardest of all for you mortals, the breaking of the mind into senility.

It is the most terrible weapon of all. Others may break the body with strikes, perhaps even damage the mind by beating at the head, but no one but I give the terrible gift of slowly sinking into forgetfulness, until one is as helpless as a babe. It is not the same as sinking into insanity, is it? It is much, much worse. Anger me and you will be my lawful prey.

What angers me? Believing that you will be spared my attacks because you are better or more worthy than others. Believing that those whom I strike as my lawful prey are less worthy than you. I do not play judging games with lives, pah! Believing that if you do well in life, or even if you take care of your body, you will escape me. I am a part of life; few escape my attacks, and if they do, it is more out of luck than out of anything that they did or did not do.

Yet I give solace and protection from these things as well. How to gain my protection? Ask for it, make sacrifices for it. Yes, I know, most people do not know Me, but ignorance is no excuse, not for me. There is a certain capriciousness to my nature; that is because I am close to Nature, like all my kind. We are relentless, we are restless, you cannot be expected to understand everything of why we do what we do. Also, you must bear your burdens well and gracefully, without letting them ever stop you completely, until they finally do so anyway. Then you can call upon my granddaughter, eh? Or have the courage to go to Her arms of your own accord. I respect those who step out of life into Her arms. It is not a cheat for me, it is a victory for them.

So… your foes. Yes, my gifts are about more than your own weakness, your own pain. I am a foe of some worth because I can see weaknesses where others cannot, and exploit them. That is where my wisdom can help you. I can see the tiny cracks in the wall, too small for the defenders to notice, but you can use those. What one single thing would cause a chain reaction that would bring them down? Can you see it? I can. Start with that—strike hard, strike fast, before they can see you and protect themselves. Then you stand back and let the chain reaction happen. The runes to use for this are Stan and Haegl—you find the keystone, then you strike it out of the arch. Invoke me when you do this, and I'll guide your hand.

Oh, and those stone arrowheads … yes, the elves use them to strike disease and wounds, and so do I, so do many different kinds of folk. There are more who know how to curse with a stone arrowhead than you'd imagine. Why that? Because it is attuned to the ancestors— no matter who you are, your ancestors started out with stone tools— and thus it strikes to your bloodline, to the things in your blood that make you weak. Those arrowheads can also be used as protection, to ask my favor, to strike those who would strike you. If you are under my hand, you are my prey and mine alone for such things, and no other will dare to shoot you, and only I will decide when the blows will fall. And fall they will, for all mortals grow old, but I have the power to keep them at bay for a while, if you honor me. So wear the stone arrowhead, or the stone knife, on yourself or marked into your skin. It will protect you from the blows of your foes. Pour to me in the thunderstorm; Odin's son is not the only weather god in the sky— remember this. Before he came to the North, I was there. I was there first. I am the Cruel-Striker, and I will teach you what is your lawful prey.

Farbauti's Song
(for protection from his strikes)

Hail the tree so high
The torch against the haze
Burn and be consumed
Fill Farbauti's gaze
Let me be low today
Let me be low today
Let the lightning pass me over once again.

Groa's Seventh Charm
Fire IV: Against Freezing

For creating heat within, when all energy-moving efforts to that end are expended.

Sun within, well of the warming,
Sun out of storm and the fire begins.
Sun within, flame of the heavens,
Fly through my halls and burn hale in my skin.

Mastering Water

Water is a tripartite element, in that it has three different forms. In its liquid form, it sustains life, be it the ocean from whence we came (and which gave our ancestors a great deal of their food supply), or rivers and lakes, or underground streams, wells, or springs that provide so much of our drinking water. While all things may spring from the Earth, they are nourished with Water. It is also the most distorting of elements—things seen through water are rarely clear, and when you strike water, it just gets out of the way of your strike and closes around your hand. Squeeze Water and it flows through your fingers. It is the essence of all the things that we need to live and survive that are difficult to pin down, a mystery, as opposed to the concrete life-sustaining things that are Earth.

In its second form, steam or mist, Water cloaks, distorts, hides, and creates danger. To look at the ancient northern attitude towards mist, one should look at Niflheim, the world of Water. Parts of it are lakes filled with islands (and treacherous icebergs), part of it is frozen ice and snow, and much of it is blanketed with rolling mists. It is barren and frigid, populated by frost-giants and a huge dragon that eats rotting bodies. Its well—Hvergelmir the Boiling Cauldron—is the source for all the rivers of the Nine Worlds. (The Indo-Europeans considered water that came up from the ground—springs and wells—to be sacred, just as was fire that fell from the sky.) Yet it was from this barrenness that everything sentient in the Nine Worlds that was not descended from Surt once grew, out of the melting ice. Water is at the base, at the root, one level above the Dead.

Ice, the solid form of water, seems to have sometimes been

considered a separate element to the people of the North. Certainly they had just as much experience with water in its form as snow and ice as liquid, and they were certainly not unaware that it was simply water that had hardened due to cold, but to them it seems that it had processed through a great alchemy and was now another element entirely.

Unlike modern Pagan thought which seems to stereotype the Powers of Water as all-nurturing and all-kind, the people of the North were clearly aware of Water as deadly. Many of them were sailors in cold northern seas, and knew the fury of the tossing waves that could drown a boatload of men with seeming effortlessness. The Gods of the Ocean—Aegir, Ran, and their daughters the Nine Undines—were shown with claws and sharp teeth, and their bloodthirstiness was legendary, even as they were propitiated desperately. Smaller water-spirits of lakes and rivers also did their share of pulling people down and were to be feared and avoided. Every lake, river, well, and spring had its own spirit, and if you gave it gifts, all would be fine. If not, small children or drunken adults might disappear into its depths.

Other water-gods include Mimir, whose severed oracular head lives in his Jotunheim well, and the mysterious Jormundgand, and Njord the sailor god. Njord is far less elemental a deity than the water-giants; he guards man's relation with the sea, and is mostly benign ... but his power only extends to the surface. The deeper one goes—and this is true for internal as well as external water—the more dangerous things get.

Water is also known as an element of healing, in spite of all this ... and yes, it does have a nurturing side, because water is linked to emotion and that's one of them. Still, we should take counsel from the old ways, and never forget that there are positive and negative aspects to all elements, and that one cannot simply deal with the former and ignore the latter. Water is as much whirlpool as wellspring, and one cannot master this elusive element without understanding both. As with all the elements, I follow them with lessons given by Gods and wights. However, Water was particularly difficult for me to master, and there are a lot of extra lessons in it, largely from the Nine Sisters who helped me out. While I list some basics below here, the rest of the basics are found in their wisdom.

1. Learn to Swim *

This sounds obvious, and perhaps seems not even necessary, but if you can't survive in water on water's terms, it will refuse to teach you. Really. Learn at least to dog-paddle. If you're actually going to be working with water-spirits, you will not be doing it in your bathtub.

2. Observe Water *

Go to a river where the water flows over lots of rocks. Watch it, for hours. Watch how it moves, how it flows, how it tumbles. Watch how it shifts, for no apparent reason, then close your eyes and listen to it. Listen to its heartbeat and its rhythm. Listen to how it plays over the rocks. Lay down on the rocks and let your hand fall into the water, let your hand rest on top of it, barely breaking the surface. Feel how it moves around your hand—how it flows, how it beats it and slides around it. Smell it in different moods and seasons; after a rain or sun. Then do this in various types of waters—lakes, rivers, streams, oceans, rain. Meet each one and feel its differences.

Then go to the Museum of Art and look at how artists have portrayed water—Edward Hopper, Monet, Turner, for example. How do they describe and depict the water? How is it different or the same as you felt it? What did they do right or wrong?

Do not attempt to grasp or hold water. Allow it to slide over you, to feel you and meet you. Yes, it sounds strange but, like meeting a dog, stand up to it and let it sniff you. Show no fear. The fact that it feels like it's slipping away from you is important— follow it. It's meant to slip away. I remember spending hours on end floating in water. Just... floating. Listening to sounds filtered through it, feeling the sensation of being held by it, losing the sense of time and place, transcending. That's all part of water.

–Aleksa, spirit-worker

3. Many Waters *

Collect water from as many places as possible: From the ocean. From a lake. From a large, fast-moving river. From a lazy stream. From a well dug deep into the earth. From a swamp. From rainwater. From melted snow. From a sacred spring. From the place that you were born. From many springs all over the world. (If you can't go to all these places, have friends bring or send you the water. I asked Aleksa, who lives within miles of the town where I was born, to bring me up a bottle from the water fountain in the hospital.) Put the waters together in bottles and keep them for sacred work. You will be told how to use them.

4. Into the Cold *

Just as part of mastering fire is learning to heat yourself, part of water is learning to cool yourself. Cold is one of the Powers of Water, as my lesson with Kolga the Ice Mermaid taught me. Cooling oneself isn't done from a specific chakra; it's more about slowing down all the chakras. If you use any particular point, it's the one on the top of your head, feeling cold slowly work its way down your body. Some people have luck using their fingers, and letting it creep up their arms to the rest of their form. This is a way of calling on your inner water, and it is good for surviving great heat. Sometimes you may have to do utiseta in a hot area and season.

5. Internal Flow *

While Fire can help you to understand where your energy meridians are, and to direct that energy outwards, it is Water that will help you to control the flow of chi along them. This is a Laguz trick—learning to keep things moving smoothly, and doing something about when they are blocked. Learn to move the chi around in yourself, perhaps through yoga or tai chi or some other practice. Learn to follow and recognize the flow of chi in others, and when it is blocked; learn to gently push through that if you can. This will require looking at a lot of people's energies, and having them allow you to work with it. Be very careful before you make any strong move, and perhaps check with some form of divination.

6. Fish In The Ocean *

One of the best ways to learn water is to shapeshift into something aquatic. Many Saami shamans had a fish as one of their necessary astral forms (and so did Loki, and the famous Duergr Andvari), and some ancient seidhworkers had whale forms. For a people who lived next to the ocean, in places where the earth was permanently frozen in places, the sea was a good way to get to the underworld. (Likewise, the Inuit of circumpolar North America also see the ocean as afterworld.) Whether it's whale, dolphin, seal, or any sort of fish, work with an aquatic astral form—ideally with the help of an aquatic spirit guide—and learn about water from underneath. It's the only vantage point that really describes it.

Aegir & Ran's Lessons
Water I: Giving And Receiving
from Ari

Aegir and Ran rarely appear together, even though they are a couple; usually the come to me separately. They are busy wights, and their tasks take them in different directions. Aegir is a homebody, keeping his castle, feeding those who gather there. He provides the atmosphere, they fill it with stories and joy. His hall is a place of good fellowship and imagination. On the other hand, it is Ran who goes out on the daily patrol of the seas. Her hair lies all through the weed in every ocean, and she can go anywhere just by pulling on a strand of her hair. She travels through space, as long as it is through water. Go to any ocean and call her, and she will come, instantly—if she feels like it. Don't do it without good reason, though, and expect her to take something from you if you have nothing to give her. Because that is what she does: take. Or, rather, receive. As Aegir is the giving aspect of Water, Ran is the receptive one. Or is it taking? After all, her name means Robber.

We like to make a distinction between taking and receiving. Society tells us that the first one is "bad" and the second one "good", because although we should all be passively open to whatever is gifted to us, we mustn't "take" because that would be selfish. To a certain extent, that's true—we shouldn't take what is not ours by right. On the other hand, some of what is ours by right is never going to get shoved into our hands; we must reach out and take it, or we'll never get it at all.

The key, of course, is to know what is ours by right and what is not. And that's what their lesson is all about.

Aegir's Lesson:

Without Water, there would be no life. All human life once came from the sea, as driftwood washed up to be discovered by Odin and his brothers, as figures drawn forth by giants from the waters and saved by Bergelmir by placing them in a tree, as four-legged fish and later small apes who came dripping out of the ocean. All the creation stories of the North have humans washed up and out of the sea, because the sea gives forth more life than any other place, even including Earth itself. The places on the Earth with the most varied life are built around waterways, such as the teeming wetlands. Water gives forth without request, because that is Water's nature. You may think that it is Earth's nature as well, but remember that Earth does not give forth anything unless it is watered. It is Water that stimulates Earth's giving.

Every time you stand under a stream of water, say: "There will always be enough. Blessings flow over me without end." Remember that I do not have to feed and water the hungry Aesir, and all the other souls who come to my hall. I do it because I can. In order to get that from the Universe, you must give because you can, regardless of who may or may not be worthy.

Ran's Lesson:

So, you ask, what has all this about giving and taking to do with the powers of Water? Why, that is simple, and you can prove it to yourself. Go into the water, open your hand, and then close it about the water. When you do that—when you take something but only hold it, you keep it at a distance and make it safe. It cannot get into you, unless it breaks your skin. But when you do this with Water—see there—it flows away from you. There is no way to grasp it in your fist. You can hold it cupped in your hand, but not for long. Eventually it will run out. If you truly want to hold it, you must drink it. Take it into yourself. What you receive passively does not touch you, and you cannot hold it. What you take, becomes part of you.

This is part of the lesson of Water. As it gives, so it takes. As Water passes through you, it takes some things away. These are mostly things that you no longer need, but not always. And, as my husband says, the oceans are always giving. That is why they are allowed to take. You are allowed to take exactly to the amount that you are always giving. As Water is all-giving, it is also all-taking. When you give that much, you are allowed to take that much. Water takes the very substance of the Earth, bit by bit, and carries it away.

So how do you know if something is yours to take? Simple. Put a spoonful of sea salt in your mouth and say, "From now on this is a cave of the sea, and it will ebb and flow with the tide of giving and taking." Then, whenever you are not sure whether something is yours to take, ask your mouth. If it is not yours, the spit will dry up in your mouth. If the tide flows forth, take and be glad of it. Ask whether you should give something, if you are not sure if it should leave your hands; if the spit dries up, keep it to yourself. If it flows forth, open your hands. You see? Just as simple as that. Only it will happen whether you are asking or not, you know. Someone will offer you a gift with the wrong strings attached, something you desperately want, and you will suddenly stand dry-mouthed and dumb. There will be no way to deny it. So be careful what truths you ask to know.

The Nine Undines' Lessons
Water II–X

In the past several years before this journey was written, I had managed to do Air (pretty well) and Fire (barely), and I was making long slow progress with Earth. It actually seems appropriate that it is long and slow. However, I hadn't even begun to touch Water. It was my weakest point. I had no idea where even to begin. I got the feeling that there was some cosmic glaring going on in my direction at my procrastination, and so I asked for help. Help, please. Someone, anyone, show me where to go with this.

I realize that Water takes many forms, and that for some people, such asking might be answered by the spirits of lakes and rivers and streams, of fresh water. Perhaps their lessons might even be different. (I would also strongly point out that this is just as valid and useful a way of learning about Water.) However, for me it apparently had to be the sea. I have always been drawn to the ocean, and I am incapable of living more than two hours from the coast. When the call was answered, it was the Nine Waves, the nine daughters of the sea god and goddess Aegir and Ran, who answered.

I was told that they would not come to me; that I would have to come to them. I was told that I would have to make nine separate appointments at nine separate beaches, and that they would not wait very long, so it had better be scheduled soon. I printed out a map of the New England coastline and pendulum-dowsed over it, marking out the places where the pendulum went crazy. Then I enlarged the map—thank goodness for online map programs!—and discovered that they were in fact beach points, many of which I'd never heard of.

I went to the first beach with my wife Bella—she'd heard that it was Monomoy Island and wanted to come with me and fish—and then did the other eight a month later, in one long six-day marathon that nearly blew my head apart with the intensity of one lesson after another, one spirit after another singing at my brain and body ... and I ended up with nine important pieces of understanding about the nature of Water, and nine power songs that I have chronicled here.

The thing that stands out to me, in the after-period when I try to put words to what I've learned, is that so many modern elemental-magic systems emphasize water as the kindest, most loving, and even most passive element. Water is healing and flowing and yielding and all that, right? The lessons that the Nine Ladies taught me were quite the opposite. They were the embodiment of the Great Water, not the small water that we separate out for our own uses, that we make safe. They were the sea that eats people, the water that drowns you, dashes you against the rocks, takes you down. They were Water with Attitude. We tell each other our pretty little fantasy stories about how lovely Water is, but the deep truth is that when there is enough of it in one place, it is every bit as dangerous as fire, and perhaps more so. Each of the Nine Ladies had that quality of danger about her, whether up-front and obvious or more subtle. They all had teeth and claws. Behind the lesson of what they were trying to teach me was another, more pervasive message. *I could eat you. If I wanted to, I could drag you down and take your life, not out of malice, but because it is in my nature to do that.* Ocean's embrace of us always intends to be fatal, whether we slip through her fingers or not.

This was underlined by my problems with finding the proper offerings. I tried to give them home-brewed beer or mead, in little bread bowls that I'd handcrafted myself, but they didn't want that. What they wanted was blood. I discovered this accidentally with the first visitation, and afterwards I went to the ocean with a bag of diabetic stickers and gave each of them (except Hevring) a few drops of blood. I don't know whether it was the salt water or their good wishes, but the pricks on my fingers were fully healed and invisible in a matter of hours after I shed each offering.

Water II: Blood
May 30, 2005, Monomoy Island
Blodughadda's Lesson

So today I went to the first beach. The pendulum had indicated a point on Cape Cod, right at the "elbow". I blew the map up and dowsed again, and it pointed out an island, which turned out to be—wonder of wonders—an actual well-known wildlife sanctuary. Ferries run out to Monomoy Island on a daily basis. There are miles of bird sanctuaries, and a seal sanctuary (which humans aren't allowed near, although we did see a dead seal on the beach where we parked). I hadn't heard of Monomoy, but Bella had, and she asked to come with me and offered to drive me out. So we started out this morning at 6 a.m.—it's a 4-hour drive—in order to catch the ferry over.

We were the only people going out besides the serious hip-wader-clad fishermen, and they all wanted to go to the mud flats where the fishing was better. We told the ferryman that we just wanted to be dropped off on a private stretch of beach, and picked up 4 hours later. He cooperatively marooned us on a lovely shore flanked by flocks of nesting birds, me with my crane bag and large wicker trash can with straps in which I carry my water drum, and Bella with painting equipment. She did watercolors and fished while I did what I had to do.

I had made an offering bowl out of rye bread dough the night before, and I filled it with local-brew ale and placed it on the beach, right where the tide was coming in. I got the idea that this wasn't enough of an offering, but I wasn't sure what to do. Whoever she was, she was holding back. Messing further with the bottle cap from the ale, I accidentally gashed my knuckles and bloodied the bowl of beer, and bam! She was there. Crawling up from the surf, the ugliest mermaid I'd ever seen. Not that I'd actually seen any real ones before, of course.

She looked nothing like any mermaid pictured in fairytale books. It brought home to me that Aegir and his clan were sea-etins, not some sort of faery or elf. She would have been tall if she had been standing upright instead of wriggling up in the surf, and was powerfully built in the shoulders, less like a slender girl and more like an Olympic swimmer. Her breasts were long, hanging dugs, under necklaces of teeth and fishbone. She had a fishtail, but it looked like that of a shark, with a fin protruding between her shoulder blades. She had very long hair, the dark rusty red of dried blood, that swirled around her in the water like seaweed. Her face was broad and rather flat, with a very wide mouth that was full of rows of sharp pointed teeth, and it gave her a grin like a manticore. Her eyes were the steel-grey of the foggy sea behind us, and shifted exactly with its coloration the entire time that she was there. The pupils were slitted. "Come here," she purred, "and let me clean the blood off your fingers for you."

I wasn't quite that brave, but I held my hand in the seawater and let the red stain float over to where she lowered her face and lapped at it. Her tongue was bluish-purple in the grey surf. She moved from the blood to the ale, drank it, and ate the bowl in three bites. Her fingers were clawed. Her hips wriggled as she moved in the shallow water, and I could only stare stupidly. I swallowed and retreated back to where my drum stood in the sand, and asked politely what she would deign to teach me.

She laughed at me, and told me to find my pulse with my fingers, and then follow it with the drumbeat. The rest of the interaction was not as interesting from a personal standpoint; I spent the whole time trying to concentrate on what she was telling me to do. She gave me a power song, or rather she put something in my head and the drumbeat that allowed a power song to come to me. She told me that there would be a very important thing just around the curve of the shore that I must take home, something that would be incorporated into a fetish for me, that I would know it when I saw it. I was thinking it would be a seashell, but when I rounded the curve there were a gazillion horseshoe crabs mating in the surf. One of them had been eaten by seagulls and the cleaned-out shell was laying on the sand; I knew immediately that I should take it home.

For all that she was clearly a salt-water creature, I gathered from what she told me that she was about the sea's relationship to the rivers that emptied into it. As such, she was also about blood, which are the rivers of your body, and empty into the heart which is its ocean. Each of the other Nine Ladies would also be about the sea's relationship to something, although sometimes that was vague and subtle.

Blodughadda's Lesson:

The rivers talk to the sea, you know. They trickle on down, or they come crashing back like a lover coming home, and they tell us tales ... about the overhanging trees, the rounded stones, the dappled sunlight, the deep roots under mountains, the pale spear-lined caves. We know all about the world wherever water goes, because it eventually all comes back to us. No matter how far away it flows, we get it back in the end. All the rivers are our errant lovers.

Listen to the blood in your veins. It is your inner ocean. Your blood is very like seawater in its consistency, its salts, its proteins. Yes, yes, you say you know this, but it is much, much more than symbolism. It means that you have the power of the ocean within you, all the time, and you can call upon its power at need with the taste of your blood. You want to learn to use the power of Ocean? First you learn to control the ocean inside.

Find your pulse. Listen to it, get its rhythm. Make the drum match it. A water drum must always first be aligned with the rhythm of your pulse before you do anything else with it. Eventually, you will be able to align it with the pulse of others, when a healing is to be done, but right now you focus on your own. Follow it with the drumbeat, and then see if you can change the drumbeat slightly and drag your pulse along with it. No, don't try to alter your breathing. This is not about air and breath. This is about changing the flow itself, changing the pulse of the riverbanks within you as they flow to and from the ocean of your heart.

You can't get that right, you can't control your blood flow that easily? Of course you can't. Did you think that you would get it right, the first time out? You need to practice this, day after day. Find the rhythm and change the flow. Use the power song that is coming to you. Unlock its clues, use it in all the ways you will figure out. The ocean is enormous. With your eyes closed, and an awareness of your body, of all the rivers of seawater inside you, you realize how huge they are as well. When you can chase down your pulse and lock it to the drumbeat, and then take the throb of your inner tides with you, then you can start to think about the water outside your veins.

Blodughadda's Song

Root of the willow, drink from the riverside lee,
Root of the willow, drink from the riverside lee,
The river runs on till it opens into the sea.

Fruit of the hawthorn, curb the scarlet flow,
Fruit of the hawthorn, curb the scarlet flow,
The tide rushes in and the tide goes out so slow.

Red stain spreads as the ocean's song I sing,
Red stain spreads as the ocean's song I sing,
Blood in the water make my offering.

Silt from the riverbank, wash to the sea and then
Silt from the riverbank, wash to the sea and then
Feed the blood-haired maiden once again.

I am the river and I am the endless sea,
I am the river and I am the endless sea,
The rivers flow out and then return to me.

Water III: Fair Weather
Herring Cove Beach, Cape Cod, June 2005
Himinglava's Lesson

We left home with the weather warning throbbing in our ears: an entire solid week of rain. I wondered if I ought to cancel and postpone, but it was the only week that my boyfriend and assistant Joshua was able to get off from work, so I forged ahead anyway. Yet when we got to Herring Cove Beach, the very tip of Cape Cod and the furthest east one could get in this state, it was beautiful. The sun had been hot throughout the entire drive, and by evening when we arrived it was cooler, but still gorgeous. The sea was as warm as it ever got, and the glasslike waves sparkled in the sun.

This time, I knew better about what gift to give. I sat on the sand and drummed and sang to call her—I sang Rudyard Kipling's "Harp Song of the Dane Women", which made reference to her mother, in the hopes that she would like it. When I felt her presence, I had Josh prick my finger, and I walked into the waves with my offering.

Himinglava is the youngest and prettiest of the sisters. I knew it was her as soon as I saw her, as would be the case with each of them, even though I would have no idea which sister I would be facing until she arrived. She was long and slender and graceful with long curly hair of a chestnut-orange that glowed coppery under the perfect green-glass waves. Her eyes were just like Blodughadda's, the same color of the sea behind them and changing with that water as she moved. She had teeth, though, and claws, and those strangely inhuman features—the wide face and mouth, the wide-set eyes. She giggled, but I had no delusions that she was harmless. She flipped out of the water and turned back in, and I saw that her lower half was a dolphin's tail.

She is the fair-weather goddess, which means exactly what it says. She is fickle, and the worst wound that she can give some poor seafarer is to desert him completely just when he thought that everything was clear sailing ... and leave him to the tender mercies of her sisters. She can arrive just as suddenly, in the wake of a storm, bringing a calm sea and an ironically bright sun to gleam on the wreckage. She is about the sea's relationship to the sun, and although she is the youngest sister, her eyes see back to the very beginning, when the sun's rays reached down through the water and stimulated life.

Himinglava's Lesson:

Under the water, the sun is not like it is in the air. It is a faint light, fainter the deeper you go, that gives life yet may come or go without warning. If you chase it to the surface, suddenly you're in the air … and most of what lives down here cannot live up there. So if you break through to bask in the sun, it can kill you. Even if you're of the kind who can breathe beyond the barrier, you can't jump high enough to get to it, and it will always be beyond your reach. Not to mention that too much exposure can burn you.

That's what joy is about. There are places where it's dark, and there is no joy, and life grows up there anyway without light … because they make their own light. Where there is no sun, you have to make it yourself. The sun comes and goes overhead, and you can only see it from afar, and that's a good thing because to get to that much joy would destroy you. The waters of your being protect you from that ecstasy, because there's a part of you that would risk self-immolation for it, and something has to hold it back.

Joy is a gift, and so it is never deserved or undeserved. It comes because the Universe feels generous. To go on about whether or not you deserve joy … that's foolish. It will come and it will go, and it is not controlled by your merits or follies. Be glad when it comes, and when it goes you know it'll be back eventually, and that's all. And if you find yourself in the dark place where it never shines … make your own light. See those sparkles on the water? Cup your hands and hold them, What, you think they're just tricks of the light, you can't hold them? Of course you can. Now bring them into yourself, up your fingers and into your arms. When you sing this song I'm giving you, release some of them into the air, or better yet, onto salt water.

This song will bring fair weather and disperse darkness, whether it's the sky or your head, but it won't last, because it never does. Don't curse it when it goes away. Let it fly, so that it will want to come back to you. Release the sun to the western horizon, and it will reappear the next morning. But if you're watching where it went, with nostalgia and regret, you'll have your back to where it comes up, and you'll miss it.

So always be watching for it in someplace opposite to where you saw it last. Remember that.

Himinglava's Song

Green as glass and green as glass, the sun shines through the wave,
A window on the sea to see the light in the deepest cave.
The weed leaps wanton 'neath the wave
    like the maiden's chestnut mane,
For sun and sea and song the spell from which all life once came,
And I bid this darkness to depart in Himinglava's name.

Blue as glass and blue as glass, the shining waters flow.
I catch the silver sparks that glint on endless indigo.
Fair weather maiden's touch a feather's softly falling flight,
The clouds disperse and fly before the sun's eternal might,
And I bid this darkness to depart in Himinglava's sight.

Water IV: Fear
Sandy Neck Beach, Cape Cod, June 2005
Hronn's Lesson

The good weather didn't hold, as was expected. The next morning it was raining and cold—Himinglava was clearly nowhere to be found today—and we trucked down to Sandy Neck ... named, I expect, for the narrow strip of sand at the top of the beach. The rest of the beach was composed entirely of pebbles, down into the water. The place was completely deserted, and I had to wonder if the rain was engineered for the privacy of the mermaids. Joshua set up the fly with poles in the front, weighted by rocks in the back, a fabric lean-to with a floor-tarp and blanket underneath. I drummed and sang, figuring that it was too cold for swimming and I would just get my lesson up here in shelter ... but it was clear, after a while, that I was going to have to go in. I had Josh prick my finger and I stripped and walked in naked.

She was there, coming toward me in the water with a strange wriggling motion, and there was fear in the pit of my belly. I was more scared of this one than even of bloodthirsty Blodughadda. She swam in a circle around me—I was chest-deep by then—and surfaced, and I stared into a round mouth full of bared teeth. Her face was more pinched and her eyes more bulging than that of her sisters, and her fair hair was cut short and flapping about her inhuman face. The eyes, they were the same. I was getting used to the eyes.

Her touch was slimy as she slapped lightly at me with her clawed hands, and her tail whipped back and forth in the water beneath her, a tapering dark line. If Blodughadda had been shark and Himinglava dolphin, Hronn was eel. "Are you frightened of me?" she asked. "Good. You should be. I'm the whirlpool, I could suck you right down to the bottom of the ocean." I felt the waves around me take on a rougher rhythm, grabbing me around the waist and pushing me about. "You think you know all about fear just because you've died once? Don't be a fool. You're not done with it yet."

Hronn is Lady of the Whirlpool. Like her twin sister Hevring, she is a mistress of currents, but Hronn is mistress of the currents that suck you down into the water, rather than those that carry you horizontally across it. She seems to be connected also to the life of the deep sea bottom, especially the black waters where we cannot go and still live except with technological equipment.

Hronn's Lesson:

All those warriors, they talk about fighting fear, as if it was some opponent that could be slaughtered. When you fight fear and win—or when you think that you've won, anyway—all it means is that you fought your way clear of the whirlpool … this time. The whirlpool is still there, waiting for you. That's escaping, not winning. To win, you have to go all the way down, all the way in. You have to go down to the center of it, to face the worst of it. The situation is terrifying? What's the worst that could happen? Can you imagine it? Now go there. Go there in a way that you can't just walk out of when the game gets too scary.

That means that just imagining it isn't enough, although it's a puny start. You need to do it, or do something like it. You need to feel it in your body, to force yourself to take those steps forward, to touch something. You need to walk into that fear with your flesh, making a mark on that flesh that you will always recall, with heart-wrenching physicality, every time you think about it. You remember, don't you? You remember how you lost the fears that you lost, how you came that close to Death? You remember Her Ladyship's bony knuckles clicking on your ribcage as She tore out your heart. You can recall that sensation, sharp as a convulsion, every time you think of it. That recall is a scar, a mark, a brand laid on you as a passport through that fear. Every deep fear requires such a mark, but it must be one that drives you on when you touch it, not one that paralyzes you. If it paralyzes you, you did it wrong, and you must rip it open and go into the maelstrom again, all the way to the bottom of the whirlpool.

That's the secret. You walk and keep walking, you keep going all the way to the bottom, and then you come out the other side. It really is that simple. It really is that difficult. And nothing else will ever do. If you sing this song, and sing it and sing it, while you're going there, it will carry you. It won't give you courage—you have to do that yourself—but it will create the current that pulls you through even without courage.

Hronn's Song

By the cold grey waters
    I draw you in.
By the pulse of your blood
    I draw you in.
To the eye of the storm,
    I draw you in.
To the fathomless deeps
    I draw you in.
Sharp the wet stones,
    I draw you in.
Chill my grey mantle,
    I draw you in.
Sea takes your breath,
    I draw you in.
Sea chokes your words,
    I draw you in.
Sea kills your song,
    I draw you in.
Silence your doom,
    I draw you in.
Find you again,
    I draw you in.
Find you again,
    I draw you in.
Find me here
    I let you go.

Water V: Sorrow
York Beach, Maine, June 2005
Hevring's Lesson

We arrived in York in the evening and checked into the campground, and then ate dinner. I knew that I was supposed to be on the beach after dark, not during daylight hours. York is a well-touristed public beach, so I figured it was just as well. As it was, there were a few packs of children playing with a dog in the moonlit surf. The dog ran up to me while I was doing my introductory drumming and sniffed me. I turned my head and told him quietly that I was calling a dangerous mermaid, and that if he didn't stay away, she might eat him. He took off immediately, and didn't bother me again.

When I was done calling, I sensed Hevring in the surf. Far, far out in the surf. I walked out up to my chest, and was still several yards away, but I got the feeling that she didn't want me any nearer, so I stayed where I was. Her voice, her lesson, carried to me over the wind.

She never actually came close to me, and I never saw more than her head and shoulders and upper torso. Her hair was long and jet-black, and cast forward over her face so that I couldn't really make out her features. The darkness added to that; she was just a shape poised there in the water. I felt that if I cast out further, she would retreat. Her skin was pale, and she seemed to be wearing some garment made of white strands that flowed out in all directions from her shoulders like a cape of string. It took me a while to realize that she was actually wearing a giant jellyfish as a garment, and its tentacles extended in all directions. About that time, I realized also that she was sobbing.

Hevring is sorrow, but she is not pretty sorrow—the pale trembling lip, the trickling tear, the bravely-borne look of sadness. She is weeping, screaming, ranting sorrow. She is wailing, undignified, consuming despair. These days we don't like to overplay our sorrow for the public, because we feel vaguely guilty about shoving it in the faces of people who have no reason to care. We forget that once people screamed and wept and rent their clothes at funerals, that they even hired mourners to play that part of fully-loosed grieving. Hevring was the only one of the sisters who didn't want my blood. She wanted my tears, freely given to the ocean.

In spite of this, Hevring is important to sailors, because she is the mistress of the wave-current, the up-and-down of the surface of the ocean. If you can placate

Hevring, she will turn the surface currents and take you where you want to go. Placating her involves shedding your tears into seawater, and not fake tears either. You must weep for a real grief. If you have no grief in your life worth weeping over, she considers you shallow and not worth her attention.

Hevring's Lesson

How dare you be ashamed of grief? Grief is one of the currents of life. Without grieving, there is no depth. We forget things and they go away as if they never were. We cannot truly remember our losses with love and respect until we have mourned them properly and completely. Mourning is not something that you rush through, hoping that it will soon be over. If you do not go through it completely, immersively, it will be unfinished and it will linger in you, making poison. You will not be able to remember your loss cleanly, you will turn your mind away from it, and it will be yet another blind spot in your vision.

You must abandon yourself to grieving, wholly and completely, and trust that there will come a time when it is entirely done. Remember that while grieving, you are strong. You are less likely to be swept away by the needs of others. You can get close to your own center, your own needs, when you are grieving. This song will walk you through that time, though it will not take you any faster than it ought to be done.

Hevring's Song

Heartbeat, feel my heartbeat, like the turning of the tide;
Pulsebeat, feel my pulsebeat, like the salt wind in my eyes.
Heartstrung, I am weeping, I am tatters, rent and torn;
Soul-pierced, I am dying, but somehow I still live on.

Ai, in our grieving, in our sorrow,
We are stronger than we've ever been and
Ai, as the storms rise, there is no compromise
Any longer nor ever again.

Flying, I am floating, I am ashes on the wave;
Crying, I am wildness, like the wind I rail and rave.
Poised here in the moment, there is nothing left to choose;
Bleeding, I see clearly, I have nothing left to lose.

Ai, in our grieving, in our sorrow,
We are stronger than we've ever been and
Ai, as the storms rise, there is no compromise
Any longer nor ever again.

Water VI: Obsession
Fortune's Rocks Beach, Maine, July 2005
Bylgja's Lesson

Fortune's Rocks Beach was lined with rugosa roses and elderflowers, and the sea was inviting in spite of the grey weather. The few folk taking walks on the shore quickly left, leaving it empty, and I sang my calling song and went straight into the water. I sensed that this sister was of a different temperament from vicious Hronn and anguished Hevring, and I was grateful.

The first thing that I noticed as I went into the sea-green white-foam-lace waves was their height—it was a rough, wild day for the sea. The second thing was that there were faces of white horses in the waves, and then their forelegs as they reared up. They pounded toward the shore, and then I was surrounded by thundering wave-horses. Among them, with a shriek of gaiety, was a mermaid diving through the water, coming past me. She spun somehow in the surf and then was off again, swimming with the tide. The water blurred her form and I couldn't tell if she was riding one of the wave-horses, playing with it, or shifting her shape back and forth to become one. I did, however, get the strong feeling that they were an illusion that she had created herself out of sheer fun.

She paused long enough to acknowledge me, and then insisted that I play with her in the water, jumping the waves. I've done this game before. It requires that you let the wave come at you, and then you jump just before it crests and let its peak pass you and break behind you. If you misjudge the time to jump, the breaking wave catches you and dashes you to the shore, grinding your face into the sand. I managed to get it right about two times out of three.

Bylgja is plump and round, like a seal, and indeed the seal is one of her animals, as are sea otters and the mythical wave-horse. Her hair is seal-brown and velvety-looking, and her round breasts are good-sized as well, contrasting with flap-breasted Hronn and skinny Hevring. Coral bits hung around her neck, from her ears, and were wound through her hair. Her eyes were currently as sea-green as the glassy waves behind her, but they were the same eyes as her sisters.

She is the Lady of the Breaker, and while she was in a good mood when I saw her, she is the one who decides when and where a tidal wave may strike. A tidal wave is, according to her, the doing of all nine of the sisters working together, but it is Bylgja who is in charge of such a thing, just as Ran her mother is in charge of storms at sea. Bylgja is also about the life of the tidepools and the coral reefs, the sea life that lives on the ocean's edge. While her sister Unn is the keeper of the tide's rhythm, Bylgja is the thundering passion of the tides themselves.

If there is one word that could describe her, it would be obsessive. She is passionate, and her passions can become larger and larger until they destroy things. "I am like my mother in that," she said. She is all about obsession, in fact, and spoke to me about its sacred nature. Everything she does, she does totally, without reservation. All Jotunkind are to one extent or another, but Bylgja is especially good at it. Her lesson is about tapping into that obsessive focus so intense that you practically become what it is that you're focusing on. In terms of the natural world, Bylgja seems to be about the wave-form of the ocean's surface, the up and down of its throbbing rhythm.

Bylgja's Lesson:

What you call obsession, that's part of the way of water. Water starts small, just a trickle, and then it gets bigger and bigger until it washes away everything in its path. That's what all water wants to do; that's the ambition of the tiniest drop. It doesn't ever just want to run happily in the beds that it has already carved. When it overflows its borders and sweeps everything away, that's the expression of Water's greatest joy. It may be hard on you, but it's Water rejoicing. You think that the Water is being angry at that time, but that's only because you think that Water is only passive.

But obsession, like anything, can be a tool. It's a knife with two edges, and you can cut both ways. You can use it to do something you don't want to do, but ought to. It won't make you want to do it, but it will make you do it, and in a pinch that can be enough. First you drum it—it's a rhythm that starts slow and gets faster, bigger, louder. Feel it like a tidal wave within yourself. Let it rise and peak. Feel it like joy, like nothing else in the whole world is more important than this thing, this moment, this ride. It's total focus, with your heart as well as your mind.

Use it while you can, because like all things Water, it will pass and change. Water is never static unless it is ice—and that's my sister's lesson, you'll get to that. But the wave rises and breaks, and that's the way it is.

Bylgja's Song

Ride, ride, ride, ride, shore in my sight,
Ride, ride, ride, ride, with all my might,
Ride, ride, ride, ride, through to the end,
Ride, ride, ride, ride, breaker will bend.
Ride, ride, ride, ride, arrow in flight,
Ride, ride, ride, ride, lifting the light,
Ride, ride, ride, ride, crash on the shore,
Ride, ride, ride, ride, dive through the door,
Ride, ride, ride, ride, ride!

Water VII: Time
Pemaquid Point Beach, Maine, July 2005
Unn's Lesson

The sun was actually out for a change when we arrived at Pemaquid, although it played hide-and-seek with the clouds. As soon as I arrived and set up my drum on the sand, whole clouds of seabirds descended on the place. There had been only a couple when we arrived, and I was surprised ... but later I was to discover that the seabirds are Unn's special creatures.

Unn is a slender, delicate mermaid, like Himinglava. Her mouth was smaller and more bowlike, but I had no doubt that it was filled with razor-sharp teeth. Her face was more heart-shaped, but still with those inhuman eyes and flat features, and her hair was like a cloud of light brown curls that dried and fluffed out the moment she raised her head above water and shook it. Her fingers were long and tapered, like her delicate fishtail, and she was wreathed, neck and waist and arms, in strands of tiny shells that clinked and clicked. "They are for counting on," she said mysteriously when I commented on their beauty.

She rotated slowly in the water in a strange dance, letting me walk in and out of the rising and falling water. Of all the sisters, Unn's lesson was the hardest to understand, because it seemed the most esoteric. Parts of it were sung and other parts spoken, and I am sure that I did not understand much of it. It was odd to go from the blunt, striking lessons of Hronn and Hevring and the others to Unn's vague concepts of time and dimension. She is about the relationship of the sea to the sky, and the rhythm of the tides (although not the force of the tidal waves themselves, that's Bylgja), and to time. She spoke of using the tidal energy as a way to travel through time, which was utterly unexpected by me.

Unn seems to have a close, friendly relationship with Mani, the Moon-etin. She mentioned it briefly, speaking of their mutual love of calendars and counting the passing of days and the cycles of time. Her friendship with him seems to connect to the Moon's control of the tides, and also a love of song and travel. "I sing numbers to him, and he sings them back," she said, and I smiled at the idea that this delicate little mermaid might be a math nerd.

Unn's Lesson

The sea is the keeper of all memory. You'll sing that, but do you understand it? No, of course not. How could you, unless you've experienced it? Oh, that's a nice idea, you'll say, that's a romantic thought, but you don't quite see. So I'll show you, as much as you can see with your human eyes. Here, we are in the daylight, the sky is blue. The moon is three days short of full, even though you can't see it. The tide is going out, it is half gone. So we will look backwards to a time when the moon was the same, and the sky was the same, and the tide was the same, and the place was here. That's how you lock onto it. If you want to see a particular time, you have to find when all those things were the same. That's too difficult, too many details? Well, did you expect this to be easy?

Here, I'll shift to a time two months ago. The season matters, but not so much as you think, surprisingly enough. Now I've drawn the veil in—can you feel it clinging to you, like a web over your shoulders and your sight? Now we are partly in another time, that day two turns of the moon ago. One turn ago, the sky was dark and raining. Why that matters more than the season, that would take too long to explain to you. But you can feel the double layer of time. Be careful—it's fragile. It will break if you don't move carefully, and then it will vanish.

Can you change time if you go back? Of course you can. If I gave you the song to be able to do that, which I won't. This is just for seeing, not for doing. That means you can't get stuck there. That's more important than your being able to mess with time, isn't it? Can you look ahead? Yes, you can, but then you have to deal with the Norns. They might smack you, they might not. You take your chances. There are other ways to look ahead that are safer anyway.

My seabirds all understand this, although they are too silly to do anything about it. They can't keep enough of a focus to do it, but they will notice when you do, and maybe try to follow you. Don't worry about them. They can take care of themselves. They can't count, but they have the counting in them, if you know what I mean. They just know about days and numbers. Crows do too, although they use it for

different things. This song will show you where you can go, what days
and moments you can reach from each shore, each place. It will help
you pull the veil in, pull in the other time. But don't be silly about it.
This is not for everyday. It can put feathers in your brain if you do it
too much.

Unn's Song

> Hey-ho, heave and blow, wind to the westward side,
> Gull wing go to the ebb and the flow,
> > and the tern return with the tide.
> Kestrel and kite keep the counting road
> In the breeze with each beat of their wings,
> We swim through the centuries like they were days
> And the gift of the gulls is the song that we sing.
> Hey-ho, turn back the veil,
> And backward we sail, back we go.

> Hey-ho, heave and blow, wind to the westward side,
> We leap from the land over sea below,
> > and into the salt wind we ride.
> Mark the moon his meandering road
> Many moons in the making of mine,
> The sea is the keeper of memory
> And the tides are the rhythm of time.
> Hey-ho, turn back the veil,
> And backward we sail, back we go.
> Hey-ho, heave and blow, wind to the westward side,
> Gull wing go to the ebb and the flow,
> > and the tern return with the tide.

Water VIII: Revealing the Hidden
Owls' Head Beach, Maine, July 2005
Duva's Lesson

Owls' Head Beach turned out to be a rocky area next to the lighthouse at Owls' Head. As usual, it was cold and misty and the one family at the beach suddenly decided to pick up and leave as we arrived. This seemed to be the way of things during this beach trip; the weather kept all but a few away, and those few somehow suddenly decided to leave as soon as we arrived. At one beach, there was only a single swimmer in a wetsuit, and he too suddenly about-faced and walked out of the water and toward the parking lot as soon as we showed up. I suppose that the Undines can make the water quite unwelcoming if they want some privacy.

A morning fog covered the water, as it had when I met Hronn. Large, rounded, seaweed-covered rocks lined the water's edge and extended far out into the water; it was treacherous to climb over them and I slipped several times. Perched precariously with my toes digging into the rocks, I waited for Duva the Hidden One to appear.

Like Hevring, she did not come close to me. Some of the Undines are more sociable than others, and Duva, Kolga, and Hevring tend to keep their distance. Duva was a pale figure wreathed in mists, speaking to me from the fog that slowly blew away as I listened and sang. Her long fair hair seemed to wrap her entirely around like a garment. What I could see of her appeared to be slightly scaled and bluish, and her hands bore webbed fingers. She was the most fishlike of the sisters, and although I am not sure what her specific pet creature is, I assume that it must be some kind of fish. Perhaps all fishes are dear to her, for all I know.

Duva is the Lady of Islands, and she shows sailors the way to safe havens on those points of land. She may not, however, be so kind as to abandon someone on an island that they could actually survive on, or one that is close to their home. She is both the keeper of all that is hidden and the revealer of hidden things, and this is her magical specialty. One thing that did strike me was how much she loved pearls. One thinks of mermaids as dripping with pearls, but her sisters all tended to wear more primitive shell and stone jewelry. Duva wore strand after strand of pearls wound about her slender torso and through her long hair. She toyed with them as she spoke.

Duva's Lesson:

I know what it is that you want from me, and although I am loath to yield up my treasures, you have come all this way and my sisters have agreed to give you gifts. So I must do so as well, for what eight agree to, nine must agree as well; it is the way we have always been. There, I have already revealed more than I wished. I know what it is that you want from me: to know how to reveal what is hidden.

I will give you the song you wish, but you must understand that there is a price for each time you use it. The price will not be told to you until after you have found your way through. I give that much to you. The rest you will have to discover on your own.

This is not for revealing every thing that anyone thinks, or knows. It is for when you are lost at sea, when you have no idea where to go or what to do, when you are desperate enough for any haven. It will not take you home. It will take you to safety, wherever that is; the closest safety. It will reveal the way that has been hidden from you, but it is up to you to take it. This song will show you the way out of the fog and the storm, but the knowledge must be used wisely. What it will not do is show you where the hidden treasures are kept, the secrets of Wyrd and the Cosmos. Those are mine to know and to hold onto; I will not share them. You will have to get them from others, more loose-handed and loose-lipped than me.

I have already told you too much. I will say no more.

Duva's Song

Duva, Duva...
Lead the way to the hurricane's lee,
I am lost at sea, I will pay your fee.
Show me the way to the hidden sands,
Follow to your hand, though strange be the land.

Duva, Duva...
Lead the way to the shrouded cove,
Take my sight in tow, through the fog I rove,
Open the curtain and show me the way
To the sacred land, and the price I'll pay.

Duva, Duva...
Mists that cover the island fair,
Like your pale mist-hair, you will find me there,
I fear not the mist and dew,
May your way be true, I will trust in you,
Duva, Duva...

Water IX: Cold
Lucia Beach, Maine, July 2005
Kolga's Lesson

As I approached Lucia Beach, the rain started up again and the temperature dropped. For all that it was the beginning of July, it was cold enough to be March or October. My fingers were stiff as I drummed and sang the calling song, and when I made my way into the water, it was bone-breakingly cold. The clouds deepened as I slowly dragged myself in, lowering the temperature still further. By the time I was in up to my thighs, I couldn't feel my feet any longer and the skin on my legs was burning. I knew without being told that the sister I was visiting at this moment was the Cold One, the Lady of Ice Water.

Kolga, Duva's twin and her elder sister by a few minutes, indeed the eldest of Ran's daughters, appeared without fanfare a little ways away from me. She was neither as distant as Duva or Hevring nor as close and personal as Blodughadda or Hronn. She was bony and angular, her skin a pale grey-blue and her hair silvery-grey, with the look of frost on both of them. Her face was gaunt, the skin stretched over her bony features, and her eyes were narrowed in speculation. When she spoke, her voice was harsh as a crow's, unlike the others who all seemed to have mellifluous voices. I could see the frost-thurse in her background; those bloodlines had come through the strongest in Kolga.

"You can't come in any further than that?" she asked scornfully. "I thought you had mastered Fire."

I was actually running my body-heating abilities on high just to be able to stand there in the frigid water with her, and I told her so. She snorted, unimpressed. "You know what you're here to learn," she stated. It was not a question.

"To cool myself," I said. "To be able to use cold." Heating myself had been a fairly easy trick for me, as I run hot anyway. The opposite, however, eluded me. I was often overheated in the summer, dependent on air conditioning to function. This was a problem.

Kolga looked at me severely, like a student that she could tell immediately was going to be a problem. Her mouth pinched like that of a schoolmarm. She seemed to be utterly motionless up to her hips in the frigid water. "This won't come easy for you," she said.

"All the more reason that I should learn it," I said, my teeth chattering. Her eyes traveled up and down my body, the only thing about her that was moving. Even her mouth hardly moved when she spoke. Kolga is about the sea's relationship to ice, the frozen northern parts, and to its temperature in general. She was silent for a long while as I struggled in the water, and then finally she turned in one graceful movement and I saw the flip of a fishtail for a moment. Then she settled back to her motionless floating position, this time only her head and shoulders showing, and began to speak to me in a cold, deadpan voice.

Kolga's Lesson:

First, cold is about slowness. Don't expect to this to work while you're running around. Stop. Be still. Empty your lungs, all the way down. Push all the warmth out of you. Water can be warm, yes, but it would rather be cold than warm. In fact, most of the water in the Universe is in the form of ice; you know that.

As you sing the chant, focus on your solar plexus. That's your internal thermostat. Find the right note to start on; it will be the note that sends a chill to that point of your body. Sing that note for a while, then start the song on it. You may have to sing it a few times, if it's a really hot day. Feel your solar plexus slowing, feel ice start to form around it. Breathe that cold out to your toes and fingers, but especially your neck and head. Run it up and down your spine, and don't let yourself shiver. Shivering is your body's attempt to warm itself. Make yourself stay still, the stiller the better, until you're cool enough that you can move and not undo it all.

Kolga's Song

Oooooooh…
As the ice-bulls ride on the cold grey meadow,
As the ice-hills glide on the cold grey plain,
Let the ice-grey maiden wrap me in her mantle
Let her rime-cold fingers stroke my spine.
Oooooh…

Oooooh…
As the ice-winds whip all the clouds to tatters,
Let her strip the heat from my suffering bones,
Cold as ice yet always moving,
Let the ice-grey maiden turn water to stone.
Ooooooh…

Water X: Erosion
Reid State Park Beach, Maine: July 2005
Bara's Lesson

Reid State Park Beach was another rocky one, with lots of sheer cliffs and stones underfoot, and piles of driftwood on the upper sands. The sea was pretty violent after days of rain and storm, and was smashing itself hard into the cliffs. I had barely finished my drumming call when Bara came sauntering up to through the surf, if indeed one could name a sort of bouncing swim as sauntering.

She was an enormous mermaid—not just tall (or long, I suppose one could say), which she was, but wide around as well. Hugely fat, billowing rolls of flesh, great breasts bouncing in the water, long dark brown hair draped over her broad, muscular shoulders, which were also draped with hundreds of strings of beads. Her face was round and fleshy, with at least two chins, and a big crooked-toothy grin. Wide sea-dollar earrings dangled from beneath her draggled locks. Her tail was that of a whale's, and she carried a big club that looked like the toothed jawbone of some enormous animal.

She hailed me merrily, and slammed her club onto the rocks, and the waves leaped up and hurled themselves at the cliff with a roar. In spite of myself, I laughed. She looked very much as if she was enjoying herself thoroughly. "Come dance with me!" she cried, and although the water was bitterly cold, I tried my best to come in and swim a little. She rolled over and over in the water, great flukes splashing, rolls of pale mer-flesh billowing, and then she rushed at the land again in a great wave and slammed her club against the cliffs once more.

Bara is all about the sea's relationship to the dry land, which she explained to me saucily in no uncertain terms. We tend to talk about the sea as nourishing the land, but the land directly by the ocean is not terribly good for growing cultivated human food, although in a balanced ecosystem there is plenty of wild food at the seaside. But Bara's feelings were something else entirely, and reminded me yet again that the ocean does not exist for our benefit.

Bara's Lesson:

The sea's relationship to the land is always one of antagonism. Yes, I know, that makes you shake your head, you think that all things in Nature work in harmony with each other. Well, they do. Harmony does not always mean kindness. The wolf is in harmony with the rabbit when she catches and eats him, yes? At least, they are in harmony with Nature's plan for them. And what the sea wants to do, what all water wants to do if it admits it, is to take the land apart.

So it tries, bit by bit, piece by piece. If the sea has its way, the land would all be floating in tiny bits within its waves, or at its bottom, the way it used to be before the land became arrogant and heaved itself up. In the end, the sea remembers the time long ago when all the earth was ocean, before the land was forced up high. The sea wants to go back to that time, and because part of water's nature is endless patience, it will keep trying until it succeeds.

But patience doesn't have to mean peacefulness! My pets, the whales—they once came out of the sea and grew into predators on the land. Then they came back to the sea and became predators there! That's a story I like. What you need to know from me is that patience takes muscle, it takes strength. What kind of surety does it take to know that you are the oldest element, and that you are intent on destroying the whole world? This song is about wearing down the endurance of obstacles, not like a mouse who gnaws a tiny hole, but like the ocean waves who get out there and bang away, day after day. This is a song for your own endurance as well, and the ability to wear down the task, bit by bit, when you are feeling weak and tired. This antagonism is good, it is good for the world. It is joyful antagonism. Those who say that all things must be accomplished only with serenity, who do not understand the sacredness of joyful antagonism, they are not looking at the real world, the natural world. We Jotnar understand this. So should you. So slam away at it!

Bara's Song

Carry you out to the white-capped waters,
Wash you away to the wild wet womb,
Batter you, bash you, beat you down,
To be worn by the waves is the way of your doom.

Chorus:
For I am the strength of the mighty ocean,
The patience of ten centuries,
Though once it birthed you, spat you, flung you,
Return you now to the endless seas.

Stone, you are lucky to be backed by cliff and
Cliff, you are lucky to be backed by land,
But I will grind you grain by grain,
From cliff to stone, from stone to sand.

For I am the strength of the mighty ocean,
The patience of ten centuries,
Though once it birthed you, spat you, flung you,
Return you now to the endless seas.

(Author's Note: I put the lessons of the Undines up on my website two years ago. In that time a surprising number of people who live on the coasts have told me that they read my accounts and have begun to honor them. I have built a floating altar to them – a huge mobile made of driftwood hung with shells, figures, tiny bottles of seawater, shark's jaws, and many glass sea floats. When people come into that room, they are often transfixed by it, and then start bringing me more things to hang on it. We are now joking about me having started the Cult of the Nine Sisters, which seems to be spreading. So this is my gift to them. Hail to the Nine!)

Groa's Third & Sixth Charms

Water XI: Whitewater

To calm wild rivers and streams long enough to gain safe passage.

River flood the plain and hill,
Well I ween thy wrath and rage,
River run around me still,
Let me ford the singing flood
And pass with peace thy silver rill.

Water XII: Safe Sailing

For safety when passing over any sea.
Best done with an offering to the sea-wights.

Salt water seek me not,
Save for a sweet caress to say
Safely sail thee where thou wilt,
For thou seekest the white wave's way.

Mastering Earth

The element of Earth is one of solidity, precision, and the slow deep cycle of nature. All parts of that cycle are useful and important—not to mention sacred and magical—and there are wights that specialize in every part of that cycle. There is no way to master this element by avoiding the less attractive (to us) parts of the Earth cycle, from green growth to flowering to fruiting to withering to rotting down to dust and worms, and over again. Useful northern-tradition deities to call on include Jord, Gerda, Aurboda (or any mountain-giant or earth-giant, for that matter), Nidhogg, Iduna, Nerthus, Frey, Freya, and some of the Duergar.

The "curriculum" for mastering Earth is, as one might expect, extremely practical. It deals with how the spirit-worker manages to bridge the gap between the Otherworlds and the physical world of their body, the bodies of others, and the physical Earth. While any of the elements can be useful for healing, it is Earth that really pulls the weight in this area, at least with the healing of the physical body. On a smaller scale, it is the element to work with for all magics involving money, emotional stability, commitment, permanent growth, and gradual removal (when ripping or burning something away would cause too much instability). In this tradition, Earth can be both fertile soil and hard stone, the field of grain and the mountain that looms above it, hulking and foreboding, the home of mountain-giants and trolls who blend into the rock when you're not looking for them.

In the list of Earth-element skills below, I have filed the various things to learn under the sort of spirits that can help you to learn them. Some can be learned on their own, but most will require some help from spirits, and some cannot be done without a spirit-alliance of some sort.

1. Landvaettir and Land-knowing *

Develop a relationship with the land-wight on a particular piece of land. If you don't have land of your own, learn to develop casual and propitiatory friendships with local land-wights in preserved nature areas. Feed them, give them drink, give them whatever energy you can. Do utiseta and talk to them about what's going on in their neighborhood. Remember that not all land-wights will talk to you: some may be hibernating, some may not want to speak to humans, some have not been communicated with for so long that they may dismiss you like the buzzing of a fly, especially if you're only there temporarily.

Others may have relationships with their own human beings, and may react territorially. Be assured that they will tell "their" humans that you are there, and what you are doing. Land-wights can be protective, and sabotage the magical workings of people who are doing things on your land that you'd rather they weren't. They can also strike out physically against those who attempt to harm, or even look as if they might be attempting to harm, "their" people. One visitor to our land playfully threatened my wife with one of her spears—he thought that it was a prop, not the sharpened implement that it is—and she was not amused, and on his way back across the field the land rose up and tripped him, causing him to tear all the tendons in his knee.

Smaller land-wights can adjust to human speed of thinking, for a time anyway, but larger ones may live so much slower than us that they may have trouble communicating. The solution to this is for us to slow down, meditate, and let the images come as they will, not trying to rush the situation. A land-wight who is your ally can ground you when you can't ground, give you energy in emergencies, and hold the end of your thread when you go to any place that it can comprehend (which isn't all of them) and pull you back if necessary.

Land-wights are also useful for teaching the skill we refer to as "land-knowing", which is a way to tap into a section of the Earth and sense what's going on there with the ecosystem, both physical and spiritual, for one affects the other in turn. Learning land-knowing can tell you where glitches are in the system, including magical accidents that are creating problems, or doors to other places that need to be closed or guarded, or pollutants that are causing mass death in a particular area, for example.

2. Plant Spirits and Herbalism *

For a spirit-worker, the biggest reason to work with plant spirits is to use herbs for healing, usually medicinally. Some spirit-workers also work with plants and plant-spirits as entheogens for altered-state work, but that aspect of plant-working will be covered in the next book, *Wightridden: Paths of Northern-Tradition Shamanism.* A deeper delving into medicinal herbalism, including information on the plant-spirits of many traditional northern European herbs, will come after that in *The Northern-Tradition Herbal.* However, in the meantime, the spirit-worker who has any affinity at all with plants—or who wants to work with herbalism, which is a mainstay of shamanic work all over the world— would do well to make the acquaintance of some plant spirits.

As mentioned in the chapter on Gods and wights, there are two different sorts of spirits that we are talking about here—the plant itself, and the plant's Grandparent Spirit. The plant itself will give its life for you, while the Grandparent Spirit of the plant will actually aid you in directing the energy and chemicals of the plant. Any shamanic practitioner who works with herbalism—and two out of three "classic" northern-tradition shamans will be herbalists as well—needs to have a relationship with the plants that they use and prescribe. This means learning them carefully, personally, one by one, and can take years. But you need to be able to prescribe not just from the proven medical usage of a plant, but from its spirit-usage as well. Learning the plant kingdom is part of successfully mastering the first level of Earth.

3. Animal Spirits and Shapeshifting *

As discussed in the chapter on Gods and wights, animal spirits are good allies to have, and they are another important key to gaining a deep understanding of the powers of Earth. They can tell you things about

Earth that you never knew, with senses that are keener than ours. As part of mastering Earth, the spirit-worker should cultivate a relationship with at least two animal spirits, if it's at all possible, considering that they choose you rather than you choosing them. Tribal and ancient spirit-workers often had a good handful of animal spirits to work with, often from widely varying species. One example of this was the Saami female noaide Rijkuo-Maja, whose animal helpers were supposedly the crow, the eagle, and the woodpecker. Another classic combination of the noaide was a bird of some sort to help them fly to the upper world, a fish to help them swim to the lower world, and a reindeer to carry them in this world.

Shapeshifting can be learned without the aid of spirits, but it's easiest and goes fastest if they can teach you. However, if you want to learn yourself, instructions can be found on the chapter on that subject. While it's not a part of mastering Earth per se, it's a skill that generally goes along with dealings with animal spirits.

4. Rocks *

Not fancy crystals. Rocks. Start out by talking to them, especially large boulder-type ones which have enough mass and chi to possibly be able to hear and answer you. Then learn the properties of stones, starting with ordinary ones you pick up around your area. Actually read about the geological properties; that information's useful too. What sort of stones are found in great numbers in your area? What are their properties? What does that mean for the bedrock of your area?

Actually, you can learn about fancy crystals too, but that comes later. Start with ordinary stones and learn to sense their spirits and their vibrations—that's such a New Age word, but it makes sense. Different stones have different properties that do feel sort of like they vibrate at different speeds. You'll be using them later, for other purposes—charging them with intent, for example, or divination—so learn about the nature of all sorts of rocks first.

The very first rock divination that I did started when I was a kid at school, and had long lonely hours on the playground to kill while being ignored by most kids and avoiding the bullies. There were plenty of weeds and rocks in the field where we played, so I hung out with the weeds and rocks, them being less dangerous than the crowds of poorly supervised feral children. I would pick up three rocks of about the same size at random—or perhaps it was more "intuitively" than "random"—and compare how they felt. I called them "light", "medium", and "heavy", although that had little to do with their weight and everything to do with what I felt when I gripped them in my fist. I decided that the lightest was a "yes", the heaviest was a "no", and the middle one would indicate the yes or no depending on which of the other two it landed closest to when I tossed them onto the dirt.

Many years later I ran across this method in a book, named "lithomancy" or divination with stones, and laughed my ass off. It still works, though, and it's not only the world's simplest divinatory method, it's also excellent training in feeling the vibrational level of rocks. It's even better if you can identify their mineral content and keep a journal of what sort of minerals seem to be "lighter" or "heavier", even in small chips, and which can be either. However, if you use this as a divination method, part of the "luck" of it seems to be throwing the stones back to the ground where they came from, and choosing another three every time you use it, rather than keeping a set of three to work with. There are other shamanic techniques that use sets of special stones, including some of the healing techniques (to be discussed in *Mapping the Hollow World: Northern-Tradition Shamanic Healing*), but this one seems to thrive on randomness.

5. Food and the Body *

Food is sacred. Part of understanding Earth is understanding the flesh that we live in, and that starts with food. A spirit-worker should develop a relationship with food that is different from the unhealthy attitudes of most modern people. This may involve learning to tell, nonjudgmentally, what sort of food your body wants and needs, and which it will merely process, and which it dislikes. Try not to let your ideas about what food "ought to be" good for your body get in the way. It's also important to learn to feel the energies in food, and feel the difference between food that is "live" and food that has all the life processed out of it. There are energies in food beyond the simple nutrients, and you can learn to use those. The Vanir gods are particularly good to talk to about this sort of thing.

6. Sex and the Body Again *

After food, water and sleep, sex is the next part of understanding how the body works and using its energies. While sex magic will be covered more fully in the next book in this series, it's very much an Earth path. There are three sorts of sex magic in this tradition, corresponding to the three major pantheons in our cosmology, and what sort of sex magic you get will depend on who you learn it from.

Even if the idea of using sexuality magically or spiritually is intimidating to you, start with this: Every time you have an orgasm, dedicate it to a particular deity. That includes the ones that you give yourself. If it takes too much concentration to dedicate it just before it happens, dedicate it before the sex starts. (If it doesn't come off for some reason—our bodies are not machines, and they have their ebbs and flows—then just dedicate the next one. They aren't going to blame you for sexual difficulties.) Then the next step is to thoroughly learn your body's sexual responses, and that alone can take some time. Mastering Earth, for the first round, does not need to mean becoming experienced at sex magic. It simply requires being able to go deeply into the primal needs of your body, experience them as sacred, and learn its sexual energy flows.

7. Fertility Magic *

Without fertility, nothing grows, including all the food that you eat that is worth eating. Something had to nourish the soil, and that something is rot and death. Understanding fertility magic is to learn the song of the cycle, in your bones, starting with the seed planted in the earth and ending with the rotting down. A spirit-worker can only learn this cycle hands-on. Start by planting a seed, if only a pot by your bed, and feeling its growth energy. Learn to sense what it needs—water, sunlight, nutrients. Follow its energy all the way through the cycle—

planting an annual is good for that. You'll want to recreate that energy for creativity, healing, and growth in other areas.

For the last part of the cycle—the rotting down—I find that keeping a compost bucket is the best thing. Sit with the compost heap and feel its energy. You'll want to use that, too, someday when something is taking too long to go away, but is too unstable to burn down and needs to rot faster. Rot energy is important to a shaman; we have to learn how to deal with it when we deal with illness. When your compost bucket has become black earth, turn it out and plant a seed in it to start the cycle again.

Jord's Lesson

Earth I

from Ari

Jord, the Jotun Earth Mother, came to me not in some wild place as I'd expected, but in a public park. Granted, this might be because she had to catch me where she could, and I'd been city-bound for a while. I was sitting in the park in mid-autumn, looking up at that perfect blue sky with the orange-yellow leaves against it, my back against a maple tree. I'd wanted to sit against the enormous oak a few feet away, but there was trash scattered around its base. So I stared at it instead, and then suddenly, sitting against its rough bark, Jord appeared.

Jord is immense—billowing flesh, great wide hips, breasts that could feed a million children, eyes and hair the color of dark chocolate, reaching to her feet and vanishing into the roots of the oak tree. Voluptuous doesn't begin to cover it, yet she was beautiful and very sensual. One could feel the urge to sink into her lap, into her body, and she would let you. It wouldn't be a violation no matter who it was, because she could envelop you. The hard part would be not getting lost in her. She wore a green garment that looked like a piece of turf that had somehow been ripped up wholly, flowers and weeds still intact, and draped about her. Of all the giant-gods—heck, of all the Norse gods period—she is the one who is closest to Gaea, to being the embodiment of the Earth Mother.

Was there a bit of Thor in her face, in her eyes? I couldn't tell.

The lesson that she taught me was about grounding. I was surprised, because that's a fairly elementary technique and I was hoping for something a little more advanced. I'd learned to ground years ago, when I'd started out in a Wiccan coven. Yet when I objected that I already knew this, she laughed at me and said...

Jord's Lesson:

Ah, little man, you think that you know everything about becoming one with the Earth? Because you can sit down on a fine day with the Sun shining and nothing wrong in your life and do it? Because when everything is peaceful you can quiet yourself and reach down? That's the easy part of it, little man. That's the child's part. But I am a

Giantess, even if I am tree and soil and all beneath it. I am of Earth, but I know that Earth quakes and one must hold on.

You want to know about Odin, then? And me? Ah, he was not One-Eye yet, he was young, so young. Nearly a virgin. He thought that he was not a virgin, but then he had never been with me, had he? No, it was I who made him a man, that youthful murderer with the winter sky in his eyes. His uncle, his father's brother, brought him to me all callow and nervous. I had just borne a child from that one, I was still feeding her at my breast, but my womb was empty and that makes me restless. I took the boy into my arms, I cleansed him of some of his blood-guilt—not all, even I cannot take away all the stains on a Thread, Urda must have her say—and I changed the winter sky to summer. I admit, he was more of a son to me, but then most of you boys are. You have no idea how old I am. I am Nott's first child, born just after she rose to the sky.

And then I sent him forth again, cleansed and taught how it is to love a woman. Those who came to his bed afterwards should thank me, for it was my hands who guided him in that. We arranged his wedding, Bestla and I, married him to that babe who lay sleeping peacefully in her cradle while I made merry with her future husband not a few feet away, and I bore him a son, and sent that son to Bestla to raise, for I saw that Odin would have great need of him, and he was too young and quick, then, to care for a child.

But I bore him Thunderer, yes, he is one of mine. And there is part of the lesson: I came from the sky, yet I am Earth, yet I bore again Sky. I am the pole between them, the one who can reach up and down, take what is Up and bring it Down, anchor it, secure it, return it again. There is no land-wight who will not speak to me, if there is a single blade of green anywhere on its face.

You passed by this grass a month ago, yes? Why did you not sit and link yourself to the earth then? Of course, you were weeping. Your heart had been torn in two, and it was all you could think of. You could not focus enough to ground then, only when it is easy—and that is the problem. Sit there and I will link you hard to the Earth, and I will give you a song to put you back there when you need it most, when there is no peace, when you think that it is impossible. It will tie you to the pole from sky to earth and back again, which is Me.

Jord's Song

I am the daughter of Night and Water
And all the storm taught her of legend and lore.
I was born of the stars in the lake reflected,
They never expected I would root by the shore.

Like the tree reaches arms to the sky in yearning
The rain returning caresses of doom
Green I awoke and so greenly opened
To the wings and the sky born again from my womb.

From the sky to the leaves and the tree is a river,
A giver of rain to the roots that curl,
And the roots are a tree that is warmed by the fire
That is sired by Void at the birth of the world.

Lock you and link you to the stars reflected,
Lock you and link you to the earth below,
Laid to the ley lines your spine and your spirit,
Lock you and link you to the downward flow.

Gerda's Lesson
Earth II

Gerda always comes to me when I'm working in the herb garden. As the Lady of the Walled Garden, the peace of that space appeals to her. I was in the process of creating a shrine to her in my herb garden, including a new variety of elderberry shrub with black leaves and purple flowers—how's that for an etin-woman!— whose botanical name is Sambucus nigra var. "Gerda".

One thing that I do know about Gerda is that she plants herb gardens wherever she lives. Her favorite is the extensive one at her father's hall in Jotunheim, but she also has one in Vanaheim at Frey's house there, and one in Alfheim at his residence. Although she no longer goes to Asgard, there is a small walled herb garden at Sessrumnir that was given to her by Freya during her stay, and it is still lovingly tended in her honor. She always tends to speak to me either from one of her gardens, or from the woods near them, where she may be collecting wild-grown forest plants.

I see her sitting on a bench near me, as our two gardens coalesce in time and space. She is a tall solid-bodied woman with a round pale face, always clothed modestly in long gowns from neck to ankles. Her eyes are dark, and penetrating, with thick dark brows; her nearly-black hair hangs past her knees in a thick braid, or more than one. Only Frey ever sees it hanging loose, ever sees the mysteries of her body, for Gerda is a very private person. With him, she is a passionate lover; with others, she is almost nunlike in her distance. She speaks quietly, but there is force and sharpness behind it; it would be a foolish man who thought her submissive. She is not shy, just serenely guarded, self-enclosed. Her body is often still, except for her hands which are now stripping the leaves off of some herbs with graceful, deliberate motions.

Three black cats prowl around her ankles. "They are from Sessrumnir," she says. "My wedding gift from my sister-in-law, to keep me company. They have not adapted well to Jotunheim, poor things, and stay in the hall or my garden. There are too many dangers in the woods for me to let them out." I am reminded of her other form, that of the black leopard, and I realize that Freya saw her sister-in-law quite well.

Gerda's Lesson:

Mine is the middle way, between tame and wild, and I will teach you about the place between those two.

Men see one good in something, and they want to make it even better, perhaps at the expense of other goodlinesses. They see that something is lovely and useful, and they make it lovelier until it is no longer useful, or more useful until it is no longer lovely, or more of both until it is too fragile to live. This I will not have. This tree you are planting, which bears my name: its colors may be altered, but its virtues are still good. If they had been one whit less fine than the wild elders over there, I would never have allowed you to dedicate it to me.

Understand this: there is no more perfect form than what Nature has created. It has been subject to tests the length and severity of which you Man could never hope to duplicate. That wild thyme there, it may not be to your liking, but it will survive the winter and laugh. That is what Nature breeds for, above all else—survival. Wild is always more perfect. Never forget that.

Yet it is within our rights as folk with hands and eyes and minds to take what Nature gives and change it. I will not say improve upon it; no, that is a hubris of Man. We Jotunfolk, we know that when we change a wild thing, we are creating weaknesses in it that we can exploit. This garden thyme, here, it makes more perfume than the wild thyme … and more of its energy goes into making it, so that less is available for it to survive the winter, do you understand? You have made it weaker, less perfect, so that you can exploit it. That is what the walled garden is for. When you weaken something, you must care for it. It is the same as if you wounded and weakened a man, and must now pay his weregild. The weregild you pay for these plants is the wall that protects them from wind and cold and the mouths of animals, and the careful tending you must now give them.

You must control the space, in order to raise the fragile creatures Man loves. Yet you have come to the point, now, where it has gone too far. You have made so much that is against Nature's wishes that you must now extend your protective walls over the whole Earth, and this cannot be achieved. The further you reach, the more you will fail. You have overbalanced in the direction of husbandry, and you must take some steps back before it all collapses.

You no longer eat any food that Nature grows without your aid. Perhaps this is not such a bad thing, for there are too many of you anyhow. But you no longer eat any wild food that can be cultivated, that could be made between you and the spirit of the woods and fields. All of your food is now from agriculture, and most of it cannot be grown without artificial additives. You are too dependent on them, and when they vanish, you will starve. Could you live if you ate nothing that could not be grown in your own dung? Some could, perhaps, but there is not enough of that to go around. You have seen to that. Back off. Back up, or you will starve your children.

I am not saying that Man must return to the wild. There is not enough wild left in your world for all the Men. You have seen to that. Besides, you have made yourselves too weak. In your mercy, women breed with narrow hips who would have died otherwise, and make daughters whose childbearing will always be dependent on a knife. Children are raised too carefully, so that they do not know how to survive. I am not like my cousin Skadi in this—there is a place in my heart for the walled garden, the delicate seedlings, the special ones that are worth protecting—but there must be a balance. You think to remove yourself from evolution, and this only means that you will be weaker when evolution finally catches you.

If you would raise your children in the walled garden, rather than letting them run in the dangerous forest, then you must have fewer of them. I cannot say this enough. If you would not take life, you must prevent it. There is no room in the walled garden for everyone's child. That is why we pull the weeds. And if you exile some children to the woods and fields, those that survive will grow stronger and wilder than your delicate seedlings. Think, before you bring life into the world. How will the life you bring forth compete with the life that others are bringing forth? On the day when it is your child against their children, you will not be there to protect them. The forces of Nature will see to that.

Mine is the middle way, and that is the way of pruning, of weeding, of winnowing. If you would change things, if you would take on the role of Nature, you must not be too fearful or too lazy to do what Nature does, which is to cull that which is not perfect enough. Too often you let things grow and breed that are far too imperfect. Better to kill off three-quarters of your crop, and eat something else this year, and have a finer crop next year. Better this than to let it come forth too weakly. Better still not to change it so far that it cannot compete with anything of the wild.

Nidhogg's Lesson

In the back field of the farm where I live, there is an altar to the powers of Rot, in many pantheons. It doesn't look like an altar. It is a small group of chicken-wire cages, weighted down with stones. In the cages are the severed heads of all the animals that we slaughter on our farm—sheep, goats, chickens, ducks, geese, rabbits. The cages are there to deter predators; the real power lies under those cages, in a whole city of busy ant mounds which spend their time carefully stripping the flesh off of those heads. When they are clean and white, we remove them and hang them on the trees. This little unobtrusive pile of natural recycling has horrified a few people who have stumbled across it, but it is part of our way of life. Waste nothing.

I was making my way across the field when the pile of cages caught my eye, and I was drawn towards it. Kneeling, I watched the flies buzzing about it, watched the ants crawling on the latest pile of half-eaten heads. It was summer, and the mosquitoes were fierce. My body, uncomfortable in the cloud of bugs, warred with the part of me that wanted to stay and do some kind of obeisance. Suddenly, a shining movement caught my eye, and I turned my head. A shimmery silvery-blue dragonfly was hovering about me, lazily sucking in mosquitoes. It dropped briefly onto my shoulder—I didn't dare move at that point—and then lifted, going back to its work. As it silently moved around me, devouring the little vectors of disease, suddenly Nidhogg was there, silvery-blue as the dragonfly, sniffing at the severed heads. The long coil of its tail slid past me, roughly, sensually, like a snake uncoiling, huge enough to knock me off my feet. I had the strong feeling that I shouldn't speak, even to greet it, and I was right. In time, it spoke to me, golden reptilian eyes glinting. Like its mistress, Nidhogg smells of rot, of the piled corpses on Dead Man's Shore.

The words came as poetry, as images. Nidhogg can speak, in hissing serpentine whispers, but it does not speak like a human. Unlike Jormundgand, it has language, but the translation crackled and strobed in my head, breaking up the meaning. This I wrote afterwards, as much as I could remember:

Nidhogg's Lesson:

There is no such place as Away.
All you throw, all you cast off,
They will come back to haunt you,
For they fall no further than your feet,
No matter how hard you run.

You are a plague upon the land. You foul
Clean water with your waste, wasting
Its purity; you do not return it
To the Earth who will gladly consume it.
You take no responsibility for it,
Your shit, your vomit, your mucus,
All the detritus you scatter like ugly
Autumn leaves from an evil tree
That does not properly rot. The Earth
Is pitted from your disease, cities like scabs
Barren patches that once waved with green hair,
Open wounds of bleeding strip-mines, poisoned veins
That once flowed clean. Land-wights sleeping,
Or dead, emptying the land of its soul.
Your are a mange upon the land's pelt,
A skin cancer that devours, and yet you think me ugly?

This is the truth about rot, children.
It all comes down to roots. I am the Gnawer
At The Root. Where are your roots?
Where is the soil in which you sprouted?
Even if they are sound and perfect—and how many
Can make that claim, in truth?—you cannot use them
As a garbage heap for all you would not see,
While you reach blissfully towards the sky.
Your roots are poisoned with the denial that you drop,
And I promise you that it will one day choke you.

If you try to settle into your roots, you feel it,
The gnawing feeling that all is not right in your sunlit world.
That is the kiss of my jaws, little fool. You may try
To run from it, run from those roots, but see,
There is no such place as Away.
Only when you go down, down to the bottom,
Wading knee-deep through the corpses of your waste,
Your greed, your convenience, your blindness.
You must choke them down, eat them all,
And only then shall you be clean.

Would you give me tribute, would you ask
For aid, that I might take from you that rot?
This is the only tribute that I care for.
For one day, you waste nothing.
Can you do that? Nothing that leaves your body
Shall be wasted—bury or burn it all—and nothing
Shall fall unwanted from your hand
Without being reduced to ash or given to rot
In a place where it shall best be used. No clean water
Shall be fouled by you, unless it goes into the ground
To be cleansed by the Earth. One day,
Sunup to sunup. Can you do that, plague children?
I will take as much from you as you give me,
Which is to say, one day's worth. Not enough
To stop your choking, but my bargain stands
To be kept as many times as you would have it.
No matter how high you climb, no matter
How much you revile me, here I am,
Coiled about your roots, dragging you down
When you would rather forget your own wastes.
Run, little locust-children, run in fear from my truth,
The truth that stinks, but you will always find
There is no such place as Away.

Groa's Fifth Charm
Earth IV: Breaking Chains

This charm works as well on magical bonds as it does on physical ones—that is to say, it takes its time and works through them slowly, depending on their strength and the strength of those who bound you. But be warned ... if you have cast magical bindings on yourself, those might be accidentally undone by this as well. No, it will not undo the geas of a God; don't even try that.

Bonds that bind shall fall away,
Chains that choke must rust release,
No lock holds my limbs,
No fetters find my feet,
Free I am to fly and find
Some safety in the fading day.

PART III: MASTERING THE SKILLS

Divination in the Northern Tradition

As a "professional" spirit-worker—meaning someone who actually sees clients who come to my door—the single most frequent things that I am asked to do is divination. People want to know why things aren't going well, or what could be done to make them go better, or what should they be doing anyway? They need answers, and you have the phone. Sometimes you can get through and sometimes you can't.

As a diviner, it's best to get used to giving people bad news. They don't show up on your doorstep because everything's great in their lives. (That's the difference between the spirit-worker and the psychic who does parties.) In fact, I am repeatedly faced with people who actually have a good idea about what's wrong, but are hoping that I will tell them that what they fear isn't really the case.

The first thing that I've found to be useful is to have several different kinds of divination that you're skilled at. When I first started out, I didn't know what I was to become; I only got strong proddings to "learn this" or "study that". One of those things was divination, every possible form that I could find and master (although some of them, to be fair, I'm only mediocre at.) Eventually, when I got clear on what I was supposed to be doing, Hela told me that I was to master 27 different oracles. While the average spirit-worker probably won't be asked to go that far, it's useful to know as many as you can stuff into your head. Sometimes, in periods of signal fog when no other spirit-workers are around to ask for divining, switching methods can help. Some methods are more useful than others for specific types of questions or information—you get a lot more out of a large sortilege method like

Tarot than a one-shot yes-or-no method like tossing a rock into water and counting rings. Some clients will respond well to one method and not to another, and some clients' "astral files" may respond better to some method for whatever unknown reason.

For the record, I do use divination methods that are not specifically northern-tradition, and that's because most of my clients aren't from that demographic. Because there are not that many of us, spirit-workers in general (and professional ones in particular) do not have the luxury of serving only one small homogenous group, especially if we are god-servants whose patrons want us to be a public utility. It behooves the diviner who is not privileged to stick 100% with a northern-tradition clientele to utilize a variety of divining methods in order to work with a variety of people and their internal imagery. To that end, I'm not going to recommend any particular method over any other. Try them all, and see what sticks.

Even if you only do runes, bother to learn both the runestone method and the runestaves method. They are useful for different sorts of questions, and are both appropriate. Also appropriate are many of the little folk-omen divinatory methods that have bounced around in books of folk magic for some time. While they may seem ridiculously simple (and perhaps embarrassing due to their common home in baby-step magic books) they can be just the thing when you get up from your utiseta with a question in the middle of the forest and you didn't bring the rocks along. They are elemental, and many such elemental spirits approve of them and will facilitate messages in this way. They include:

- Divination with wind, including writing possibilities on leaves slips of paper and letting them blow away; the last one remaining is the answer.

- Divination with fire, including scrying in candles or bonfire, throwing herbs into a fire and watching the smoke for images, holding a candle over a bowl of water and seeing what forms the drops take, or scrying in the ashes of a fire. Fire itself is a good trance-maker, especially if you work with fire-gods.

- Divination by water, including tossing rocks into a pond and counting the rings, or just staring into water and scrying, especially if you work with lake-spirits or the local land-wight. If you use the ocean, you can make marks or place small objects in the sand and see which one is still there after the tide washes over them.

- Divination in the leaves of trees. Lie under the tree and look up (during a time of year when there are leaves) and watch the leaves move in the wind until you go into trance and see something.

- Divination with stones. Not runes or anything fancy, just rocks. This involves picking up rocks and saying, "What does this rock say to me?" or something equally ridiculously simplistic. Then when you have a handful, you can do divination. Some Siberian tribal spirit-workers work with the technique of tossing a few dozen small stones down and scrying what the pattern looks like as an omen.

It comes down to where your affinities lie. When you start working with elements, you will notice immediately that there are some you take to quickly like a duck to water, and some that repel or confuse you. (That's no excuse for not getting to know them just as well, however.) Using divination with your primary element(s) will be your old standby, but you'd best learn others as well so as to be able to do readings for people with other affinities, or get messages from spirits with elemental leanings other than your favorites.

Of course, the above methods, while they may be quite useful for solitary divining or dramatic as group ceremony, are not terribly practical for the average client reading, especially as that may require more details than such simple omens can give. I find that sortilege-method divinations (meaning those with a number of differing possibilities that are picked randomly in a pattern) such as runes, Tarot, etc. are the best for that sort of thing, and if you know several, all the better.

Some spirit-workers are allowed to get paid for their shamanic work, especially divinatory work, and some aren't. Some choose only to barter. The question of whether or not to charge is a tricky one. In societies where shamans and spirit-workers are part of the landscape, there is a social assumption that yes, of course, you are going to pay them something. Considering the nature of most of those societies, the payment is as likely to be barter as cash, perhaps even more likely. However, in Western society, the closest role that people have to us is the professional psychic, who is likely living on what they can get from clients, and is often willing to soften the message in order to get paid better, or have a repeat client. Spirit-workers, on the other hand, will often be pressed into saying things that the client didn't want to hear by the hovering Powers That Be, and may be punished if we don't say them. That puts us into a different category from most ordinary diviners.

One of the biggest issues when people come to you is finding out what they really need to know. Often they've got a small problem that they're asking you about, and a big one that they're too sensitive about to even mention ... but when you do their reading, it's: "Well, there's nothing about job possibilities at all, but looky here, this says that somebody is cheating on their lover!" While there are many ways of handling this, some more thoughtful and diplomatic than others, I think it's important for the professional shaman to keep in mind that you are not a professional psychic. In other words, if any part of your mind is worried about keeping clientele, or monetary concerns, you may compromise your job. The Gods and wights did not give you these gifts so that you could impress or coddle people and make a few extra bucks, and they may well be most unthrilled if you turn it into a money-making situation. That doesn't mean that you can't be paid for it—assuming that your particular patrons are all right with that—but that you need to put the cleanliness of the message first, and the patron's baggage second, and worries about money way down the list.

You need to be able to say, "I'm sorry, I'm not getting any messages today; it's not a good day for me. Are you willing to reschedule?" or "No, I can't answer that question," or "You don't seem to be taking this seriously. I am not doing this for recreational purposes, I'm doing it for religious purposes. Perhaps your issues would better be addressed with a different reader?" or even "All right, that's enough. Get out!" and not worry about the consequences. There should be no client that you need to coddle so much that you are willing to turn aside a message for them, or tell them merely what they want to hear. Remember who you're really working for, in the end.

The top issues that people bring to me are:

1) *I don't know what I'm supposed to be doing with my life.* This is the one that they're most likely to come to you, rather than to a random psychic, about. It's a request to look at the threads of their Wyrd, and tell them about their *orlog.* My usual procedure is, first, to ask if it's even allowed for me to tell them. For some people, figuring the path out themselves is the important thing, and being told would ruin it for their particular road. This means that either you'll tell them and they'll get that glazed look that says, "I'm not listening," or you'll open your mouth to speak and get the cosmic gag order, or the reading will clearly say "Classified!" In that case, try to explain to the disappointed person in front of you about some people needing to find their own way as part of their lesson. It may be that you can do more specific readings about what they're doing now, or are drawn to, and if those things are moving in the right direction or not. However, I've had completely opaque readings for extremely directionless people, which rather makes sense in a sideways fashion, if the Gods are saying, "Make up your mind and choose something already!"

Then I use one of several methods to get into what I jokingly call the Akashic Library in order to look at what I jokingly refer to as their File. Being a modern human being, sometimes I visualize it like that, because it helps me to facilitate what I jokingly refer to as "the download" if I can imagine a file laid out, with certain marks on the cover and colored pages inside. The information may not be quite that clear, of course; sometimes it's like reading a file where half the papers are in another language—and which half they are keeps shifting as you look. A more traditional visualization can be found in the chapter on Wyrdworking, as can more detailed examples of what to do in case of this sort of reading.

The Soul Map, which can be found in this section of the book, is a technique that Hela gave me for doing readings. It works well for basic-level Wyrdworking and for readings that start out, "I don't have a real question—I just want to know where things are going with me," or something equally vague. If done in the two-round system, it will give plenty of information and many jumping-off points from there, which the client may not have thought of.

2) *How do I fix my health?* Maybe it's just me, but decades ago when I was just reading Tarot for a few bucks a pop, everyone wanted to know about their love lives, jobs, and health, in that order. Now that my shingle says "shaman", if only through word of mouth, health has popped to the top. There are many ways to do a health diagnosis without actually touching the person, many of which will be covered in the sixth book in this series, which is on healing. One is utilizing runes or other divination methods to tell about what's wrong with them, and what can be done about it. (The runic correspondences to parts of the body will also be out in the sixth book; for those who can't wait, they're on my website.)

Another method is to have the client lie down and run your hands over them, a few inches above their body, and interpret through your own Sight and/or whatever any allied wights can tell you. Ask what parts need the most immediate attention, and don't be surprised if it's not the parts that they're complaining about the most. Health problems can be caused by something else entirely from what's actually hurting. I'll sometimes do a row of runes, one at a time, starting with one for the area that is having problems, and asking, "Where does this problem stem from? Where does *that* problem stem from?" and so on.

Then it's a matter of figuring out what to do with it. If you decide that you want to dispense herbal advice, make sure that you know what you're doing by studying a whole lot of herbalism first. (The fifth book in this series will give some aid with that.) Being as these are litigious times, I might suggest that spirit-workers not charge money for anything that might be construed as giving medical advice. This means disclaimering any health readings from the beginning, and working out how you and the client wish to handle it.

3) *I want to know who my patron deity is* or *I want to know the name of this God who's bothering me.* Not everyone has a patron deity, and this is the bald truth that needs to be said up front, perhaps before you cast the reading. Some Gods will take almost anyone who asks, although They may not give them all that much personal attention. Some Gods are extremely picky and will ignore anyone whom They didn't choose themselves. Some Gods will humor you fondly, but not do much more than that. If they have a patron deity just trying to get through, then while you might want to do an initial reading to confirm this, what they really need of you is trancework. Some spirit-workers can do this with the client right there, and actually find it easier due to the "anchor" of their presence. Some prefer to do it quietly later, without distractions, and report back to the client with their findings. Clients tend to prefer the former, but sometimes they will just have to make do with the latter.

If there's no patron deity in the offing, and they really want one (and you've questioned them to make sure that their reasons for wanting one aren't about peer pressure, impulse, parent issues, or other bad scenarios), then you can read to ask who might be willing to take them if they proved themselves worthy, and what that would entail. This is a controversial issue; most modern Neo-Pagans would rather believe in the ideal of the all-loving God(s) that take you the way you are, and never ask you to change yourself or do anything inconvenient. We spirit-workers, however, know better. While a reading may not change anyone's religious worldview—and if they resist on those grounds, let it drop—the information is there for them to think about, should they want to try it. Yes, the Gods have the right to ask us to prove ourselves worthy, and especially in this tradition, they often demand such things. I've found that all too often, the items that come up in the "proving" category are things that aren't world-shaking, just very difficult for that particular person. You can almost tell from the way they draw back when you say it. All too often, the Gods don't want us to battle hordes of external demons, just the internal ones, in order to prove that we are worth bothering with.

You might also want to explain what may happen if they get a patron deity who decides that they are more than just a fan, and wants them as a tool. That's something else that people often don't believe, and those who do believe it romanticize it, and then are shocked at the reality. Give them fair warning, even if they don't take it.

Similarly, the person who's being bothered by a God and doesn't know who it is may not be ready to know. The deity may be concealing their identity deliberately, possibly so that the individual in question does not make assumptions from the words of others. I've seen this happen more than once; it happened to me. Hela did not show me her face or let me know her name for the first 28 years of my life, because she wanted me to get to know her intuitively first, before I read ugly Christian-based writings about her. I know a few Pagans with very real patron deities whose masters still will not tell them who They are. It happens sometimes. Commiserate, and remind them that they don't need a name to give them service and devotion. Many Gods have names that are simply titles, like Frigga and Freya (Lady), Frey (Lord), etc.

4) *Love life, career, and legal cases.* Here we get into the sort of things that most ordinary readers get as well. As every diviner finds, questions of love are often the most frustrating of all to read on, because they're the most likely to be asked with a hoped-for answer already hovering in the room, and the most likely for clients to react with hostility when that answer is not forthcoming. One friend of mine who reads for a living joked that, "When I hear 'But I love him!' that's it. They get nothing more." Here, as with all things, be as helpful as you can be without diluting the message. Integrity is more important than coddling people's feelings, and those who know better will value your honesty.

Remember that you serve both the community of human beings and the community of spirits, and somehow it's up to you to make them work together. There will be times when that's difficult, and some of those times will crop up in the middle of a reading when a wight says,

"Tell them this!" and you have to figure out how to honestly tell them that without breaking them, or with the least possible amount of breakage. It's a balance between being effective at getting through to them, keeping every ounce of your own baggage about the situation out of the way, and remembering that your job is not a popularity contest. You are the living phone line, and it is your goal to continue to strive to be as clear as possible in that capacity.

Groa's Second Charm
Road and Thread

This is a charm for when one is wandering, and has no idea where to go save that there is somewhere, someplace that calls to you ... but you cannot find the road. While this will not consciously show you that road—be it physical or otherwise—it will guard and protect you while you seek, and if it is meant to be, it will slowly guide your footsteps all unknowing to the right path.

As my Thread runs through my fingers
Day by day, year by year,
So the Road runs right beneath me
Dream to dream, come ye near,
Fate and fortune guard and guide me,
Nor lost become beneath my load,
Urda's hand from hanging hide me
I am already on the Road,
I am already on the Road,
I am already on the Road.

The Soul Map

A Northern-Tradition Shamanic Divination
Method

The outline for this divinatory chart was downloaded into my head while I was in Helheim. I asked my patron deity for a useful diagnostic method for clients, and She gave me this. I have no clue to its antiquity, and I suspect that it may have been created for me personally. Deities can do that. While some people have commented that the circles and lines vaguely resemble the Kabbalic Tree of Life, there is nothing kabalistic about it. I do not see it as synchronous with the spiritual maps of other cultures. The center row does tend to line up with the chakras, but the folks in India did not invent the major energy centers of the body; they are present in all of us... and it is interesting to note that there are two, not one, for the sixth row.

The terms used are partly Norse and partly Anglo-Saxon. I go back and forth between them in my daily practice. I include the alternate terms where I have them available. Some are only found in one language or the other. Choose which rolls better off your tongue.

This is a map of the human soul, and all its accessories, which includes the body. I'm not interested in debating how authentic it is, because the sucker works, and it works really well. I've found it to be a crucial first tool in figuring out what's going on with someone, especially when their problem seems to be spiritual rather than simply psychological in nature.

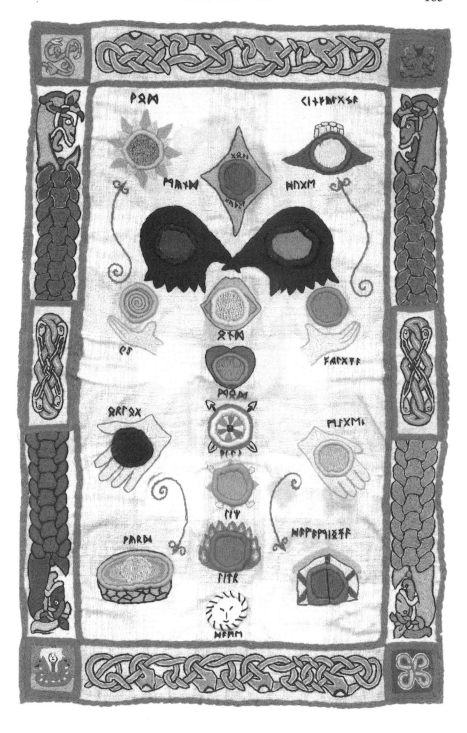

Raven's Embroidered Soul Map

How To Use The Soul Map

For a full-out reading, I do two rounds of divination for the client using this map. The first round is done with a set of indicator stones, which will give a general overview of the client's condition. The second round is done with runes, which give more specific information about what can be done to improve things. If the client comes back to me repeatedly, I generally only do the second round for them on future dates. The first round is usually only repeated if there is serious spiritual upheaval in the person's life.

The Soul Map should be a good jumping-off point for a variety of questions, which can be asked with the runes, or any other divination method that works for you and the client. For instance, one might find a blockage in the physical area, and do separate divination for a potential solution; or one might ask about a Wyrd stone, in order to find out who to talk to.

I made my soul map out of linen, hand-embroidered with the spaces. It took months, and before anyone asks me to make one for them, they had better realize that it would cost a good deal. Ideally, the practitioner ought to make their own, and one can start with any piece of cloth or paper, with the circles marked out in magic marker.

Stones For The First Round

There are 41 stones used for this round. I started out using small blobs of colored glass, of the sort that one finds in the cheap gift and craft store, because they were inexpensive and I needed a number of identical items in different colors. I've now graduated to using stones for this round, too. The colors (or types of stone) were chosen out of what I had around; other practitioners can choose what speaks to them. The number of each type, on the other hand, was chosen by dowsing, and you might want to stick with those.

1. Normal (18). Functioning within normal limits. Not exceptional, but not unhealthy either. Could possibly be made better with work, but no cause for alarm. If this falls on a space referring to non-physical abilities, it might mean possible talent but lack of training and practice;

in "normal" people those abilities are generally latent.

2. Weak (5). Functioning below normal levels. One would hope that with work one could improve in any way. However, after a year of working with this system, I've discovered that the weak stone tends to come up referring to something that is an unfortunate but inherent and permanent problem—a genetic illness, a hardwired learning disability, brain damage, irreversible physical disability, etc. These are the weaknesses that we come with, and that teach us about the nature of limits. The issue here seems to be not so much about trying to improve the problem as accepting it as a limit and learning ways to compensate and still do what needs to be done. Ingenuity, not denial, is the key here.

3. Exceptional (6). Functioning at better than normal levels. This can indicate natural talent or learned ability; either way, the individual shines here.

4. Blocked (6). There is a physical, mental, or emotional block in the way. Unlike weak stones, I've found that blocked stones indicate something which could be moved by the individual if they had motivation to do so, and were willing to put in a great deal of uncomfortable work. While the problem might look insurmountable, it isn't; it's just difficult. Whether the individual is ready to deal with the problem right now is a different issue; perhaps it is urgent, and perhaps it can wait until they are more prepared. This should be checked with runes in the second round.

5. Wyrd (5). This is the signal for divine intervention, the interference of the Gods and spirits, and/or some sort of serious karmic debt. Basically, if a Wyrd stone turns up in an area, it means that circumstances there are out of your control. There are plans for you, and they are going ahead whether you consent or not. The best thing to do under these circumstances is to do separate divination on Who wants you to do What, and how to go about that.

6. Missing (1, smaller than the rest). This is fairly serious, and indicates that the client has lost a part of themselves. More information—probably a separate reading with runes or other methods—should be done on the issue to decide whether retrieval is necessary or possible. This is covered at length in a later chapter, "Making Whole".

Stones For The Second Round

Here I generally use my runes, because I'm used to them and they work well with this system. I am rather clear from what Hela has told me that this system was not designed for runes per se, and that any divination system with simple symbols will work for it. Names aside—and I got the idea that these names were much younger than the actual map—this seems to be a technique that is older than the runes and their introduction by Odin. However, I use them because they do work nicely here.

Generally, the indicator stones tell you where a problem is, and perhaps what sort, and the second round tells you the source of the problem, or more details on its nature, or a possible solution. For example, assume that your client gets a Blocked stone on the Litr space in the first round. In the second round, they get Berkana, the rune of growth and nurturing. This would suggest that the problem is not physical, but one of lack of growth; their life (and probably their sex life) has been stuffed into a little box, and they need to grow past their current idea of themselves in order to regain that vitality.

For another example, assume that your client gets a Wyrd stone on their Fylgja space. This would indicate that Something is looking at them, and wants their attention for an important task or lesson. The second round could help determine who it is. If they were northern-tradition folk and drew Ansuz, that would be a clear indicator of Odin to me, as that's his rune. If they weren't, further divination might have to be done to get an idea of who was tapping them on the shoulder.

Although I generally start out with only one rune per space, it's not uncommon for me to pull more than one if the first one needs clarification. Sometimes the meaning is obvious, and sometimes it cries out for more information.

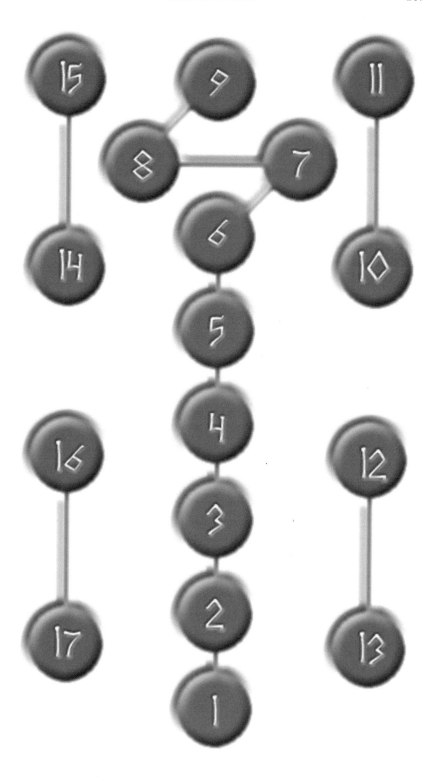

Chart Positions

1. Hame (Old Norse *ham*, pronounced *hahm*; Old English *hame* or *hama*, pronounced originally *hah-meh* or *hah-mah*, and in modern English pronounced *haim*)

Your astral body. Not your aura; the part of you that lies within your physical body and is (sometimes) twin to it. Some people's *hames* are less like their physical bodies than you might think, and this can create discomfort. This position on the soul map shows, first, how harmoniously your *hame* works with your physical body, and second, how much control you have over it. If you are reading for someone who is not a practitioner of energy work or magic, default to the first definition. If they are someone who works with energy or magic, the second definition is very important, as blind and careless energy work can alter your *hame* in ways that can affect your physical health.

The *hame* is the part of your soul that can be shapeshifted into another form, with work and training. Shapeshifting your *hame* will not change your flesh into that shape—obviously, the flesh is a lot more solid—but over time, if you spend a lot of time in another shape, it will attempt to make slow changes. If the shapeshifting is actually something that it is possible for your body to change into, it will gradually start to work over time in small and subtle ways. On the other hand, if it's not something that the human body—or even your personal body—was built to become, then it can create problems and dysfunctions. For example, constantly becoming a hoofed being and then forgetting to (or being unable to) properly correct the bone structure afterwards can cause slow damage to the physical knee and ankle joints. Attempting to make a solid adult body taller or shorter can cause problems with the spine, and so forth. Shapeshifting isn't something to play with regularly unless you know what you're doing.

For the first round: Most people will get Normal here, which means that the *hame* is in reasonable harmony with the body, but there isn't any great ability to work with it. An Exceptional stone denotes ability to move it around and adjust it, either naturally and unconsciously, or consciously after training. (Many athletes and martial artists fall into this category.) Weak suggests a difficulty with controlling the *hame*, and suggests that it is far more affected by the *lich* than the other way around. Blocked means a problem with the *hame*; perhaps it is too different from the *lich*, which can cause dissociation. Working on issues of the body and of body hatred in general can help, as can doing energy work, but be prepared to uncover some unpleasant emotions. Wyrd on this area denotes that the Gods and spirits have plans for this person's *hame* which may or may not be under their control. Natural shapeshifters, those with a predisposition to become god-possessed, and those locked into their bodies for cosmic purposes may turn up with a Wyrd stone here.

For the second round: The runes should describe in greater detail the individual's issues with their astral body. They may describe the way in which it tends to act, or the way in which the individual handles it. For example, Eihwaz or Algiz here might suggest that the *hame* is mostly used to created heavy shields for defensive purposes, while Peorth might suggest random tiny changes, and Ansuz might mean the ability to travel astrally on errands.

2. Litr (Old Norse *litr*, pronounced *leet-r*)

Litr means literally "health" or "blooming hue". From what I have learned from delving into people's *hames* with both hands, as it were, *litr* is more than just good health. It is a particular kind of energy which gives vivacity and "color"; it seems to come from the lower pelvic area, and as such can be seen as that which Ayurvedic practice terms "kundalini". It is sexual energy, as this is its most natural channel, but it can also be channeled in other ways. It encompasses such concepts as "virility" (but is not limited to men; women need *litr* just as much), "lustiness" (not just for sex, but for all things physically and emotionally pleasurable), and general enthusiasm for life.

Without *litr*, the person's experience of life is dull and wearying. Their sex drive may be low, or blocked, either by emotional issues or by hormonal problems. Often a general problem with the *litr* shows up first as sluggish sexual energy. They may be generally fatigued and unenthusiastic about everything; this is not so much an issue of all-out severe depression as a mildly pessimistic grey pall thrown over their life.

For the first round: A Normal stone is obviously average sex drive and vitality, and an Exceptional one might be lean in either a sexually intense or a particularly vivacious direction, or both. This placement could also suggest an innate talent for sex magic. A Blocked stone is the client who is lacking in *litr*, as described above, due to either emotional problems, or hormonal or neurochemical issues. A Weak stone indicates someone who has always been chronically lacking in *litr*, perhaps prone to fatalism and pessimism. Wyrd on this stone might indicate that these energies are directed in their expression, or dependent for their existence, on the Gods and spirits. I have often seen this for people who are god-spouses, or sacred prostitutes, or who use sexual energy as part of their spiritual vocation.

For the second round: The rune should describe the nature of the client's *litr* – if it has trouble, the reasons why, and if anything can be done.

3. Lich (Old Norse *lyke* pronounced *lee-keh*; Old English *lich* pronounced *leekh*, with guttural *ch* like the German *ach*)

The actual physical body. Stones that show up on this space are generally medical issues, as this is the place of the purely physical container for your soul.

For the first round: A Normal stone simply means average health. An Exceptional stone is the athlete, or the person in glowing health, or the one with more stamina than anyone else. A Weak stone might be a chronic health problem, perhaps something the client was born with, which must be compensated for. A Blocked stone is ill health due to long-term habits, and the health can be improved with time and effort and discipline. A Wyrd stone suggests that the current health issues are a lesson imposed from the outside, and dealing with them will require figuring out and learning that lesson, and changing the appropriate behaviors.

For the second round: The rune pulled by the client may show the area of health most in need of improvement, or the one that will be most relied on to support the stress level in the near future. Separate readings can be done for health purposes; this will be covered in the sixth book in this series, *Mapping the Hollow World: Northern-Tradition Shamanic Healing.*

4. Vili (Old Norse *vili*, pronounced *vee-lee*; Old English *willa* pronounced *wee-lah*)

Vili is the will, the inner force that motivates you, pushes you through hard times, and allows decisiveness. One of Odin's brothers is named for this quality.

For the first round: A Normal stone is average willpower and decisiveness. An Exceptional stone suggests that this is one of this person's strengths, and might also suggest that any laziness or slacking on their part is consciously or subconsciously motivated by other things that they are getting out of delaying. On the other hand, a Weak stone on Vili suggests the opposite; this is the person who is continually pushed back and forth by the currents of life, and needs outside help and support to stay on track. A Blocked stone indicates that the individual has deliberately given over their will to someone else for some reason; this can be found in victims of trauma and abusive relationships, but it can also be found in those who thoughtfully choose to live under some kind of strict discipline for spiritual or emotional reasons, such as monastics, devoutly religious folk, career military people, or consensual submission. (Be careful not to jump to assumptions on this placement until you have questioned the situation; admonitions to "take back your will" might be useful for a battered wife, but not a Buddhist nun. The difference lies in whether or not the will has been given over unconsciously due to damage, or consciously due to a strong inner understanding of one's need for discipline and structure.) A Wyrd stone here suggests that the Will has (or needs to be) given over to a Higher or Deeper Power for some reason, for an unspecified period of time, in order to accomplish what needs to be done.

For the second round: The rune that comes up will show the way in which the client's will acts, and the way in which they make decisions. Haegl, for instance, might indicate a strong will but chaotic judgment and random, knee-jerk opinions. Tyr suggests the warrior-type who will fight to get their way every time. Laguz is the one who goes with the flow, but it might suggest passive-aggressive behavior. Beorc might show the client whose will is strongest when channeled through nurturing activities; alternately, it might signal someone whose will is growing stronger with time and attention.

5. Mod (Old English *mod*, pronounced *moad* like road)

This word is cognate with our modern word "mood", and it does refer to the emotions, although with less of the connotation of "lack of control" that we hold today. This point shows whether one is in touch with one's feelings, and how one sees them. It is also a good indicator of how well one interprets and handles the emotions of others.

For the first round: A Normal stone shows a fairly healthy, if not terribly introspective, relationship with the emotions. The client is neither uncomfortable with socially and situationally-appropriate emotional displays nor particularly repressed in showing their own, although they may not be interested in having more than a semi-conscious idea of why they or others are feeling any particular way. An Exceptional stone does not necessarily indicate that the person is overemotional; rather, it is an indication of someone who has a deep knowledge of their own emotional nature, and also has the ability to understand that feelings of others, even when they come from alien motivations. The client with the Weak stone on this point may vary from the overemotional individual who simply reacts without understanding their emotions (or, often, being able to control their emotional outbursts), to the emotionally repressed individual whose repression is based (perhaps justifiably) on a fear of becoming the first type should they relax their guard. I've also observed Weak stones here on people with mild autistic-spectrum disorders, which come with an inability to interpret the emotions and social cues of others.

A Blocked stone here doesn't necessarily indicate that the person is entirely blocked emotionally, but there will be one large area that is behind bars, generally because they fear it, or wish it didn't exist, and have refused to deal with it. Ironically, I've found this placement frequently in people who come across as open, caring, and empathic, and who may follow spiritual paths that encourage this attitude. Usually they've dealt with the selfish negative parts of themselves by locking them in the mental basement rather than consciously working on them. A Wyrd stone here can sometimes be the mark of the healer, the person whose emotional nature is "used" by the Gods and spirits for the good of the community, often without their understanding of what is going on. It can also indicate someone whose current emotional troubles are due to spiritual interference.

For the second round: This rune can further interpret the individual's emotional issues, possibly pointing to a problem area, or suggesting the direction in which the client needs to go in order to be emotionally whole.

6. Ond (Old Norse *ond*, pronounced *ohnd*; Old English *aethem*, pronounced *aah-them*, with *ae* like the *a* in *pack*)

The word "ond" means literally "breath", and it is mythically what was breathed into the lifeless human body in order to make it live. The idea of the Gods breathing the soul into the body is found in mythic traditions all over the world, and it is clear that what is breathed in is not air, but life force. Whether it is called prana, mana, chi, qi, ki, huna, orgone, life force, or anything else, those who work with it know what it is. It has as many flavors as there are beings in the Universe, and it runs through all things to one extent or another.

Any energy worker (such as a Reiki or Ch'i-Gong practitioner) will tell you that the various flows of *ond* through the body and soul affect and are affected by their health. This placement speaks of the flow of *ond* throughout the client's *hame*; is it sluggish, or vibrant? What does it need to do better? If the reading is centering on the client's health issues, the Ond placement is as important as the Litr and Lich placements for informative purposes.

For the first round: A Normal stone means that the client's energy flow is functioning within normal, healthy limits. Any problems are minor, and likely only physical in nature. An Exceptional stone indicates the person who has a natural talent for energy work, and who consciously or unconsciously works with their own flow of *ond* in some way. A Weak stone is the client whose *ond* moves slowly or sluggishly, and who may need regular aid in keeping it moving, be that energy work done by others or some form of physical exercise that speeds up the flow. A Blocked stone indicates one or more blockages of energy, which may need to be worked on by a professional, as they can contribute to physical and mental problems. A Wyrd stone indicates someone who has the potential to be (or already is) a conduit for divine energy; this placement is sometimes found in those rare people who "horse" deities and spirits for purposes of spirit-possession or god-possession.

For the second round: The rune drawn can help determine the nature of a blockage, or the nature of the individual's energy flow.

7. Hyge (Old Norse *huge*, pronounced *hoo-geh*; or Old English *hyge*, pronounced *hee-geh*)

The two ravens that sit on Odin's shoulders and spy for him are named Huginn and Muninn, or Thought and Memory. They represent the two parts of the cognitive process, Huge and Munr, or Hyge and Mynd; we get the word "mind" from the latter word. They also work very well with modern conceptions about the right and left sides of the brain. The Germanic peoples were well aware that the cognitive process is twofold: one must be able to reason, and one must be able to retain. The Hyge and Mynd must both be in order, and to work together. Of course, people being the imperfect creatures that we are, generally one is stronger than the other and pulls most of the workload. Hyge is the rational part of the cognitive process; it is the thinking, reasoning left-brain part that can examine input and draw conclusions.

For the first round: A Normal stone here indicates intelligence and reasoning ability that is well within normally functioning limits; not exactly genius, but no problems. An Exceptional stone indicates the individual with the sharp, and possibly even brilliant, mind. A Weak stone indicates difficulty with the rational thinking process; there may be learning disorders that affect reasoning and the ability to conjecture consequences, or the emotions may hijack things too often. A Blocked stone is a mental obstacle, usually around mental discipline and education; the client may have had a bad experience with the learning process in general in their youth, and may have given up on stretching their mind and learning anything new. A Wyrd stone in this placement suggests the potential to think clearly about spiritual matters that might overwhelm less intellectual minds, and translate them in understandable words while not losing the spiritual experience to skepticism.

For the second round: The rune drawn here gives more information on the nature of the client's thinking process. The result should be compared to the rune on the Mynd placement, as the two should work together as one entity.

8. Mynd (Old Norse *munr*, pronounced *moon-r*, or Old English *mynd*, pronounced *meend*)

Mynd is the memory, which includes the daily short-term memory and the overall long-term memory of past events. While we tend to think of the thought process as being the most important part of the mind, anyone who has had a stroke and impaired their ability to retain information, or who was born with difficulties in the area, will tell you that thinking is as much about your mental filing system as it is about your thought process. Not being able to find the right thing in your memory banks can stop the creative process cold.

For the first round: A Normal stone indicates that the memory is functioning healthily and well. An Exceptional stone indicates the person whose memories often come in better-than-average clarity and detail, with almost hallucinatory envelopment. In rare cases, they might have an eidetic or photographic memory. A Weak stone here indicates a neurological difficulty with memory—perhaps the memory failures attached to attention deficit disorders, or other learning problems. A

Blocked stone indicates a repressed memory, usually one that is pushing at its prison and needs to come out. A Wyrd stone may indicate the ability to remember past lives, or perhaps to tap into ancestral memories in one's bloodline.

For the second round: The rune(s) drawn will tend to describe the nature of the individual's memory, unless there was a Blocked stone; in that case, the rune will tend to describe the nature of the blockage.

9. Godhi/Gythja (Old Norse *godhi*, pronounced *go-thee*; Old Norse *gythja* pronounced *geeth-yah*)

These old words for some form of spiritual practitioner (often used today basically as synonyms for "priest" and "priestess") have an alternate meaning; they have also been used to refer to the higher self. What that means, in simple non-Newage terms, is this: If you are being the best you can be, and fulfilling your entire spiritual potential, what would that look like? Your higher self is the part of you that knows, or at least senses, what that would resemble, and is strongly drawn toward paths that would get you there. For some people, this part is quiescent or suppressed; for others, it is awake and seeking but still fairly vague in its yearnings and direction. This placement on the soul map gives information on that part of you.

For the first round: A Normal stone indicates that the higher self is whispering, but not speaking loudly enough to interfere with the ordinary journey of life. (The "ordinary" condition of humanity is to be going about their daily business, with awareness of the sacred, but not swallowed by it. Mystics and gythjas and spirit-workers and such are not living ordinary lives.) If they have come to a point where they want more guidance, they will have to search hard for it. An Exceptional stone indicates the individual who already senses keenly where they need to be going, and perhaps is already on the path. A Weak stone indicates that the higher self's voice is being overridden by other mental voices, such as the demands of ordinary life or the internal fears and desires. A Blocked stone indicates that it has been entirely shoved into a closet, usually because the individual in question fears where that path may lead and refuses to go towards it. A Wyrd stone is the indicator of someone whose higher self is being called by the Gods and spirits in some way, and achieving their full spiritual potential is entirely in the hands of the Otherworldly beings.

For the second round: The runes drawn generally refer to the path that the higher self is drawn toward, unless the previous round had a Blocked stone; in this case the rune will generally be relevant to the blockage in question.

10. Fylgja (Old Norse *fylgja*, pronounced *feel-gyah*)

Spirit guides. These are the forces that work with us in this lifetime. The placement can indicate deities, including one's patron deity, or spirits, or ancestors.

For the first round: Unless you see an Exceptional or Wyrd stone here, you can assume that spirit guides are not playing an important role in the client's life, and perhaps are not likely to. If the stone is Blocked, the client is not ready to hear or deal with spirit guides, and s/he needs to do internal work in order to figure out what is blocking that channel. An Exceptional stone suggests someone who finds it natural and easy to talk to noncorporeal beings, and a Wyrd stone tells of being chosen by particular Gods and/or spirits, perhaps for teaching, perhaps to do a job.

For the second round: The rune ought to tell more about what sort of spirit guides are involved, or why there aren't any, and/or if anything can or ought to be done about that. If a separate reading is done and a lot of negative runes come up, it may be that the client is not meant to follow that path at this time.

11. Kinfylgja (Old Norse *kinfylgja*, pronounced *kin-feel-gyah*)

This is the point of ancestry, the collected wisdom of your genetic forebears, and your spiritual relationship with them. Some people are called by the spirits of their ancestors, and feel strongly drawn to the spiritual wisdom passed down in the memory of their bloodline, whether they recognize it as such or not. Others may not be tapped by their ancestors nearly as strongly, and some may be destined to walk away from their cultural bloodline entirely and do something else not found in their ancestry. These differing relationships can be read in this space.

For the first round: A Normal stone tells of an ordinary relationship with one's ancestors; there are no geases passed down, and no particular need to serve the family bloodline in any way. The ancestors can be called upon, but they have little obligation to the client beyond that of a general interest in the continuance of the bloodline, and they may or may not answer. An Exceptional stone is someone with special gifts passed down genetically through the family line, perhaps psychic gifts, or perhaps gifts in more mundane areas. They may have skipped generations, but usually they can be remembered in recent family members. These gifts come with a responsibility to the family line of those who passed them on; they must be used in particular ways in order to do right by the ancestors who passed them on, and not misused. Sometimes the gift can be honorably refused; sometimes this is an offense. On the bright side, the ancestors have a vested interest in this client, and are more likely to be of use.

A Weak stone is an indication not only of few ancestral gifts of worthy use, but that one's ancestors are really not worth calling upon, and the client should look elsewhere for aid. This is sometimes seen in adoptive children, and can be a signal not to bother to pursue that path. A Blocked stone indicates that the client is taking a path entirely different from—and perhaps antithetical to—that of their ancestors, and will find no help or aid at all in that direction. This is often the placement of the rebel who breaks away from all family traditions, faiths, and even relationships, in order to fulfill a destiny that involves starting their own. Both Weak and Blocked Kinfylgja folk, at best, have the potential to shed old spiritual and genetic patterns and start a fresh dynasty or clan that is not tied to the past.

A Wyrd stone on this point suggests that it is not just the ancestors, but the Gods and spirits of the ancestors, that have the vested interest in this person. There may be genetic gifts, such as someone with an Exceptional stone, but it is the ancestral Gods and wights that will have the final say in whether and how they are to be used.

For the second round: The rune(s) drawn will tell how the ancestors and their Gods may be of service to the client, or alternately why they will not be, and where they should turn instead.

12. Maegen (Old English *maegen*, pronounced *maah-gen*, with *a* as in *pack*)

Maegen is a concept that most modern people have lost, although the idea of "honor" seems to be a remnant of this idea. The concept of *maegen* rests on the idea that there is tangible personal power that is earned by deeds of honor: walking one's talk, giving one's word and keeping it. Every time you break your word, you lose *maegen*. If you continually shy away from commitments, never actually putting yourself in a position where you need to be held to your word, you fail to build up a supply of *maegen* and thus are not in a much better position than the individual who breaks their promises. You can also lose *maegen* by committing unethical and harmful acts against others, and gain it by refusing the temptation to do those things when the chance is given to you.

Maegen is more than just mere social capital. While showing oneself to be a keeper of one's word is good for building public trust, the concept of *maegen* stresses that this is a power to be built even in isolation, and that it is not dependent on the opinions of others. The idea is that every time you give your word and keep it, you build up a fund of power behind your word that gives it more cosmic impact. In this way, the *maegen* supports the *vili*. One's *maegen* can often be sensed by others, and those with strong *maegen* will be instinctively trusted more by those who sense it. It's more than just reputation, it's an actual force attached to the soul that can be felt and used.

For the first round: A Normal stone indicates an ordinary amount of *maegen*; the client is average when it comes to giving and keeping their word. Nothing awesome, but nothing terrible. An Exceptional stone here is someone with a very strong adherence to their code of honor; their word is their bond, and they can be trusted to walk their talk. A Weak stone in this placement suggests the commitment-phobe, or the one

with lazy ethics who likes to squeeze out of promises, who lives their life
avoiding being pinned down or having their feet held to the fire. They
may place feelings as having more value than commitments, with the
idea that if it no longer feels good to do, one ought not to have to do it
any longer, regardless of how that impacts other people. A Blocked stone
in this area indicates a long history of oathbreaking, even if only in small
ways, that has built up to such an extent that the individual will have a
hard time overcoming it, but it is still possible with diligent work and
painfully correct ethics. A Wyrd stone in this area suggests that the
client's relationship with the Gods and spirits is such that broaches of
maegen will be directly followed by divine consequence and retribution.

For the second round: The rune(s) drawn for this placement generally
show where the client needs to look for ways to build up a greater fund
of *maegen*.

13. Hamingja (Old Norse *hamingja*, pronounced *ha-ming-ya*)

The word *hamingja* has many meanings, but all seem to center
around the concept of some kind of luck—not the sort of luck that
comes out of nowhere, and you either have it or your don't, but the sort
that can be created or earned. Another way to describe it might be good
fortune, and another might be "mojo", in the modern sense of
something laden with fortunate power. *Hamingja* can imbue an object, or
a person. For example, a gift has more *hamingja* than something that you
bought, because it has the energy of the giver's intention and good
wishes behind it. A gift that was used frequently by someone or worn on
their body has even more. An heirloom passed down over time has yet
more *hamingja*, for the same reasons. Gifts given by children out of real
feeling for the recipient seem to have an inordinate amount of *hamingja*.
A bride was considered to have a great deal of *hamingja*, and the wife was
the keeper of the household's *hamingja*, because she was closest to the
hearth, the center of the home.

Maegen may be built in isolation (although it is best done with other
people), but *hamingja* is something that must be granted through one's
links to community. For a person to build up a fund of this quality, they

must be seen as valuable and worthy by others. Sometimes it is built up by the exchange of gifts or favors (done with a whole heart and not grudgingly, or there will be no *hamingja* in it), but more often it is done by one's work for the community as a whole. Your luck grows as people count you among their assets.

For the first round: A Normal stone indicates an ordinary level of *hamingja*; the client has some community ties, but is not in any important positions of trust. If questions show that they are actually in an important position of trust, a Normal stone may not be good enough; they may need to work on building up their public value. An Exceptional stone means that the client has a great deal of "communal luck", and is considered of great value to the people around them. A Weak stone often indicates the loner, or the person with few community ties, or the outcast. This can be due to low social skills, mental problems, personality issues, childhood damage, or simply a life path that is more concerned with personal development than with communal belonging. A Blocked stone indicates that the client has done some great public error in some community that has damaged their *hamingja*, but not beyond repair; they can choose to make it up to people, or to start over in a new community and try to build a new fund of *hamingja* there. A Wyrd stone in this placement indicates that any hamingja the individual will get from their community will be entirely dependent on their relationship to the Gods and spirits. (For example, it is said in many places that shamans lose their luck when they die and are reborn, and they get all future luck from the spirits that they work with.)

For the second round: The rune(s) drawn generally show the source and nature of the individual's *hamingja*, and can also show whether it needs to be built up or not. Having a great deal of *hamingja*, while a good thing, is not everyone's *wyrd*. One notable rune to have in this section is Othila – that refers specifically to a line-*hamingja*, a luck-spirit attached to one's bloodline.

14. Ve (Old Norse *ve*, pronounced *vay*; Old English *wih*, pronounced *weeh*)

The word *ve*, or *wih* in Old English, denoted something that was otherworldly, mystical, and possibly dangerous. It is also the name of another of Odin's brothers. In terms of the soul map, the *ve* is what my assistant refers to as "your Spooky". In other words, it's your innate psychic ability, which seems to be genetically inherited and is different for each person.

For the first round: A Normal stone seems to indicate that the client is normal for the vast majority of the population ... in other words, pretty much entirely psychically repressed. Normal psychic function for modern Western humans is very little; they may get the occasional hunch, or message, or once in a while a word or two from a god or spirit, but for the most part it does not play a part in their daily lives. An Exceptional stone is the individual with real psychic potential, which they may or may not be using. Sometimes great potential manifests as pressing talents that cannot be ignored, and may even cause instability.

A Weak stone means that the individual was not born with a great deal of innate potential, and anything that they do in this vein will require hard work. A Blocked stone suggests that there is talent, but it is consciously or unconsciously blocked, often by fears or distaste. Sometimes it is completely repressed; some people have even made use of their own talent to repress itself, which sounds odd but is very possible, depending on the talents in question. A Wyrd stone on this placement indicates that the individual's *ve* is entirely given to them, and controlled by, the Gods and spirits; these are often folks who become chosen to be spirit-workers of some sort.

For the second round: The rune(s) drawn will further describe the talents in question, and possibly their best usage. If the first round had a Blocked stone, the rune may describe the nature of the blockage.

15. Wod (Old Norse *odhr*, pronounced *oh-ther*; Old English *wod* pronounced *woad* to rhyme with road)

The first syllable of Woden/Odin's name, the *wod* is the ability to merge with Divine Consciousness in some form. This can take the form of spirit-possession, god-possession, or simply mystical union with the Universe. While this sort of thing is pursued by mystics throughout the ages, they have all learned one thing about it: if you achieve it at all, it will be by the will of the Powers That Be, and it's not possible to live constantly in that kind of state. Indeed, it's something that can only safely be experienced for short periods of time, as long-term exposure tends to slowly loosen your soul from your *lich* ... and that does become permanent after a while, a condition that is called Death.

Wod can be more loosely defined, if you blur the edges a bit, as the ability to easily achieve altered states in a spiritual context. Those last few words are important; anyone can get drunk or down a tab of acid, but that's no guarantee of touching the Divine Spirit. Consciously controlled altered states, which are the shamanic worker's stock in trade, are very different.

For the first round: A Normal stone indicates that the client has an average ability to move into altered states, which generally means not very easily or with any control. An Exceptional stone is the individual with the talent in this area, even if they are not using it for spiritual purposes per se. They may have been constant vivid daydreamers as children, or have a knack for trancing out while dancing, drumming, or staring at patterns. This can be cultivated into a knack for other kinds of controlled trancework. A Weak stone indicates that the individual is not the sort for whom altered states come easily; it may be that during this lifetime they need to be well grounded in their body and learn about the limits of the physical. A Blocked stone suggests that there is talent present, but it is being repressed due to fear. This is not always a bad thing—altered states can be dangerous—unless it is becoming an issue in their spiritual lives. A Wyrd stone indicates that the client has the potential for—or is already engaged in—some form of spirit-possession, god-possession, channeling, or being used as a conduit.

For the second round: The rune(s) drawn will usually describe the client's relationship with altered states, and perhaps their relationship with their deities, if they have any.

16. Orlog (Old English *orlaeg*, pronounced *or-lahg*, or *orlog*, pronounced like it looks)

The concept of *orlog* is sometimes confused with the *wyrd*; they are related but subtlely different things. One could say that the *orlog* is the path to *wyrd*. In Eastern terms, your *orlog* is your personal karmic record to date. It is the dance that you do with Karma, the law of cause and effect, and it contains everything that your have gained and lost towards achieving your ultimate goal, whatever that might be.

For the first round: A Normal stone indicates that one's *orlog* is proceeding at an ordinary, functioning pace. The client is learning the lessons that are needful, and moving in the right direction—not spectacularly, but not avoiding or backsliding either. An Exceptional stone indicates the individual who has jumped onto the wild horse of their destiny and is thundering down the track at a fast pace. It is important to remind them that although they are moving in the right direction, they can still be knocked off by poor attitudes or bad judgment. A Weak stone indicates someone who has not yet grasped the concept of cause and effect, and that everything you do comes back to you in one form or another. They may be making bad errors, and need to think deeply about where their lives are going. A Blocked stone here indicates a great fund of bad mistakes, unlearned lessons, and general damage that needs to be worked through before progress can be made. A Wyrd stone in this position suggests that the Gods and spirits are speaking to the client and attempting to give aid, but they need to listen and accept what is said.

For the second round: The rune(s) drawn can indicate the current lessons on the path, or suggestions for direction, or one's general behavior towards the laws of the Universe.

17. Wyrd (Old English *wyrd*, pronounced just like the word *weird*, from the Old Norse Urd, the first of the three Norns)

Your *wyrd* is your final destiny. Embracing the idea of *wyrd* does not require you to believe in an already-written, unchanging destiny. Everyone's *wyrd* is different; some are "destined", if you will, to be allowed to choose their own path with no outside interference at all. Indeed, it sometimes seems as if the world is made up of those who have a set destiny, with the script in the can ready to act out and penalties if you stray from the path, and those who are entirely free to wander with no guidance at all. Generally the first group spends a lot of time moaning about their lack of free will, and the second (larger) group spends their time moaning about how they have no idea what they're supposed to do with their lives.

Your *wyrd* is the thing that your higher self knows about, and attempts, when you let it, to pursue that path. It may not be the thing that you were raised to think that you ought to do. It may not be any one thing; the majority of people have flexible destinies. They may need to learn certain specific lessons, but the learning can be done in many different ways and contexts. For some people, the only *wyrd* is to learn about choice and to have experiences, as many as possible.

For the first round: A Normal stone on this placement indicates that the client, like most people, has a flexible *wyrd*. They are not destined to do any one particular thing with their entire lives; whether they achieve fame or fortune or even karmic understanding will be largely dependent on their own choices. An Exceptional stone on this position is the individual who is meant to do something special with their life, although they may still have the choice to refuse it. Success is not absolutely guaranteed; even the blessed can screw up badly. A Weak stone in this position indicates the wanderer, the one who has all the choices and none of the guidance, the clean slate whose mistakes will be paid for the next time around. A Blocked stone suggests that the individual has deliberately walled off the path to their *wyrd*, usually out of fear of what it might be. A Wyrd stone on the Wyrd position is the fated life: the Gods and spirits have a use for you, and you are going to be their tool whether you like it or not.

For the second round: Ask a question about your destiny, and the runes will answer! Unless, of course, you draw Gar, in which case be prepared to hear someone laughing just out of hearing range...

Children Of The Void:
Runes As Spirit Allies

When Odin hung suffering on the Tree, coming as close to death as he could without passing over, and in that liminal state managed to rip open a hole in Ginnungagap for the Runes to come through... what were they, really? The answers tend to fall into the categories either of "divinatory symbols" or "magical talismans". It seems that no one ever thinks to see them as spirits in and of themselves, which perhaps is the hubris of the magician ... or perhaps a sort of camouflage that the Runes themselves have erected. It seems that no matter how long one works with them, unless it occurs to one to see them as spirits rather than mere symbols, one never does. As soon as it occurs to you, however, sometimes there they are, as if to say, "We wondered when you'd figure it out." (Or sometimes it doesn't work, and usually you find it quickly slipping out of your mind, as misdirection and forgetfulness seem to be the Rune-Spirits' first and foremost mode of dealing with someone who is not ready to meet with them.)

Yet the Runes are the spirit-allies most called on by those who work with the northern tradition, no matter that they have no idea that the Rune-Spirits exist as such. Have you ever stared at a rune-reading and had no idea what it said? That's the moment to call on the spirits of the Runes themselves and ask them what it means. I'm sure that you can see, now, how this would be useful when it comes to galdr-magic as well. This chapter is my experiences with these spirits, and how they came to me, and how I work with them.

Rune-spirits are a good example of a partnership relationship with spirits; they are very powerful, but not enough to command, compel, or own a human being, nor can they be commanded or compelled. They are generally quite willing to do what it is in their nature to do, and so long as you keep that in mind, you can work with them. If they choose to work with you, great; if not, you can't make them. Once you start working with them as spirits rather than merely constructs, they will expect more of you in your rune-workings. They will have something to say about the enchantments that you use them in, and they will go on strike if they feel that you've done something wrong. On the other hand, they can be invaluable for advice on creating magic or doing divination; nobody understands the Runes better than the Runes themselves. Working directly with them gives your magic a kick that merely playing with sacred sigils doesn't, but you will need to use them more carefully.

For those who have never dealt with the Runes as divination and magic, this chapter will not help you with that. There are plenty and enough books on the subject, as well as people willing to teach, and there isn't room for that here. And, frankly, if you are trying to be a northern-tradition spirit-worker of any kind, you should already be familiar with the Runes, or be studying them and using them now. This is advanced rune-working for those who already know, and no apologies about it. As with all things, since I work with the Futhorc runes, I will go back and forth between the Norse and Saxon names, and people will just have to follow along and deal with that.

Beyond Aettir: Rune Categories

In looking through runish lore, many old Norse terms come up, many of which are fuzzy in their meanings. If unsure, the best thing is to ask the Runes themselves, and let them give the definitions. Some of these troublesome words include *audhstafr, flærdgstafr, gamanrunar, hugrunar, malrunar, limrunar, svartrunar, trollrunar, leodrunar, heidhrun* and *myrkstafr,* and *galdrastafr.* As far as I can figure out, from my own working with Runes in both symbol and spirit, these are categories both of the Runes themselves for their properties, and of how they can be combined. For example, Fehu and Gyfu are both used for wealth, but a bind rune of the two would be even more powerful, and would also be referred to in the same category. Obviously, some categories have been lost, so all we can do is to define the ones that remain, and look for what else we can figure out.

Audhstafr means "stave of riches"; the *audhstafr* runes are Fehu, Gyfu, and Jera. Use them in combination in order to bring wealth and abundance.

Flærdgstafr means "stave of deception", and the *flærdgstafr* runes are Hagalaz, Nyth, and Thorn. Thorn is also the Troll-rune, the rune of the Thurses (Thurisaz), and writing it thrice before any other rune will invert that rune's power, recalling the power of the bottom of the Tree to turn things around, no matter what they are—death is change, and all change is death to something.

Gamanrunar means "joy-runes"; the *gamanrunar* are Wunjo, Sigil, and Chalc. These are antidepressant runes, and in combination they can have a "lightening" effect on nearly anyone.

Hugrunar means "mind-runes", and are used for mental excellence. *Malrunar* refers to runes that are used for persuasive speech. These seem to be the same set of runes in different combinations. They are Ansuz, Os, Yr, Ken, Dagaz, and Stan. Combine them into bind runes for improving the mind, speech, communications, etc.

Limrunar means "healing runes", and the limrunar are Uruz, Berkana, Laguz, and Ac. They are also called *Liknstafr*, or "health stave". Combine them into bind runes for healing work.

The *Svartrunar* are the "dark runes", meaning runes that are used for shadow work, heavy magics that make use of the darkness, and also negative magic. The *Svartrunar* are Peorth, Ear, Ior, and Cweorth; you will notice that both death-runes are here, the rotting grave and the funeral pyre—slow decay and quick burning, as well as the binding Serpent and the Rune of Fate. These can be used in combination to do serious shadow work—binding or revealing or destroying when necessary.

From here, one could look at the remaining runes and conjecture other groupings; for instance, Mannaz, Othila and Ing combine into a grouping that speaks of the People and the Flesh—bloodlines, sacrifice, and reincarnation. Tyr, Algiz, and Eihwaz are protective/defensive. Raido, Ehwaz, and Isa are movement-runes—stop and go.

The term *galdrastafr* means a stave of magic, a bind rune stave. Some of the *galdrastafar* in *The Galdrabok*, the old Icelandic grimoire, seem to have no resemblance to the Runes per se, being vertical lines off of which various signs and symbols hang. The vertical line is what creates the "stave" in all of these terms, as well as the assumption that these were once carved on sticks for magical purposes.

Two terms that seem to go together, at least in my practice, are *heidhrun* (or *heidhstafr*) and *myrkstafr*. Rather than simply going with their literal meanings—"bright-stave" and "murky-stave", they seem to be referring to the positive and negative aspects of any given rune. Therefore, Heidhstafr Fehu might mean riches or solid values while Myrkstafr Fehu might mean materialism and greed. Myrkstafr Thorn is obvious, but a Heidhstafr Thorn might be that which pricks the lazy into action.

Other terms that bear looking at include *leodruna*, which means "song-rune" and may refer to a sung galdr using rune names; *hlautar* meaning "lots", which is a random term for runes and refers to the sortilege "luck" nature of using them as divination (and makes one wonder if runes were used for sacred lots to choose sacrifices); and *teinar* meaning "twigs", which seems to be an ancient slang term for magical staves. There is also the mysterious word *Jotna-villur*, which literally means the shadowy enchantments of the Jotnar, and some people's UPG suggests that this may refer to some or all of Hel's Aett.

Runes As Spirit-Allies

by Galina Krasskova

Working with runes takes immeasurable skill and endurance. Odin, after all, had to die for them, hanging as He did on the World Tree for nine nights of agony. They are neither easily won nor easily wielded. They can be ruthless and brutal teachers, and for all those who decry naive folks dabbling in runic mysteries, the runes themselves are quite capable of keeping the unworthy and untested from gaining any useful headway. Working with them is almost like engaging in a cosmic tug of war of the will and the power it wields, or sometimes it can be like playing with razor blades. They do tend to be rather pitiless, or at least the majority of them do until one has been tested, and often even then. Although their spirits may wear human faces, there is nothing human about the runes and that is important to remember. The only humanity they hold is the blood that has been given them by countless *vitkir*.

Needless to say, runes are far more than a simple method of divination or even a system of magic. They are keys to accessing and working the Wyrd web, but even this function only barely touches on their true nature. The runes are alive. It's not enough to simply cast them. At the higher levels of runeworking, one must realize that they have an instinct, an intellect, and a will all their own. They can be powerful allies or adamantly vicious enemies; but suffice it to say they are anything but static and inert sigils. This is something that most people who work with runes don't get to the point of realizing. They're sentient. They are allies, in the traditional spirit sense.

There are many levels of skill in working with them, as they will open so much and no further to the novice. One must keep coming back again and again to explore them, and only when that relationship is solid and well-developed will the individual runes begin to allow the *vitki* a little more access. This is obviously a lifelong endeavor. Runes are most popular today as a divination tool, and they are amazingly effective at that. However, the same caveat applies: they won't allow one to read them until they've in some way begun testing the erstwhile reader. I've heard experienced Tarot readers complain about how difficult it is to read with the runes; they are unable to figure out why they could read so well with Tarot and other methods, but hardly at all with the runes, even after much study. This is the reason.

Furthermore, the runes are entirely uninterested in seeking out humanity. They are quite unique in their nature, and when they unite with the *vitki* in whatever way they are being called – be it for magic, *galdr*, and divination – that rune-worker is touching, however briefly, a world that existed before the coming of the Gods. They are touching spirits that thrived in that which existed when the worlds collided at the beginning of time. There is something primordial and ancient yet at the same time forever youthful about certain of the runes. It is as if all time and all experience is bound up in them. As little as they may consciously seek out humanity, part of their being is still bound up in the flow and fabric of time, and human experience is part of that.

The very nature of the runes is organic. There is a reason Odin was on the Tree when He snatched them up. There's a reason they are fed blood. All of that is organic, so the language of the runes is also organic. In allowing runemals to access their power, it isn't a question of the runes coldly shutting someone out for lack of skill. Rather, it is them allowing the runemal to slowly grow into the meaning of runic interpretation and nature. The runemal must learn their language. Consider, for example, the rune Teiwaz—courage, honor and justice. That rune does not conform to whatever the runemal's idea of justice is; the rune itself is fed with its own conception of justice. The rune will most probably not work for a *vitki* until they understand what that means. This is, in a way, a fail-safe mechanism to prevent the novice from treading in waters he or she may not be ready for. Runes, when they contact or are contacted by human beings, try to make sure that human beings understand their nature and how far they can manipulate that nature while still being true to the rune itself.

So early on, a rune-master must learn not to either ignore what the rune is saying (i.e. the language of the rune) or to become overly manipulated by it. When you're chanting the rune, even if you are aiming for a specific goal, you cannot ignore where the rune is trying to take you. They work within their own natures. At the same time, you can to an extent get the rune to understand what you're trying to accomplish and point them in the right direction. Runes work by understanding, not by domination. A rune like Thurisaz will more likely work for you if you're going to it fully understanding and accepting all the capacities of that rune and what that means. If you yourself do not feel you can harness or even put out destructive energy, and thus feel that Thurisaz won't do it because you don't want it done, then you may encounter serious problems. The rules of good conversation with another human being are very helpful when working with the runes. You neither cut off the other person too soon nor allow them to talk on endlessly. The give and take of good conversational dynamics is exactly the relationship that the *vitki* has with any given rune at the moment of perfect working. The runes cooperate more when you understand and accept the full potential of what they are, rather than trying to ignore certain aspects because you yourself may not find those things in your own nature.

For this reason, rune-workers may find it easier to work with certain runes rather than others. Commonality of nature and personality may lead to certain relationships becoming stronger than others at an earlier stage. For instance, I work quite comfortably and well with Ansuz, but I find Mannaz to be extremely difficult to access. Both myself and the rune are willing but we haven't yet found a point of commonality upon which to build the relationship. I don't yet speak its language fluently. Sometimes, these things take time. And sometimes, though the runes will come when you call them, they may not open their energies to you for a very long time. Often, when I was first learning how to work with the runes, my initial *galdr* sessions would involve no magic at all, but rather simple exploration of the rune itself.

The fluidity of *galdr* prepares one exceptionally well for rune work. The voice becomes the perfect conduit for their power, even if all one is doing is tasting their essence and nature. Through *galdr*, which need not be particularly euphonic, the rune worker may access points on the web that would otherwise be far out of reach. One excellent exercise is to spend several days with each rune. *Galdr* entails singing not only the rune name, but mentally filing any images, sounds, smells, or feelings that may come to mind while concentrating on and reaching out for the individual rune. Eventually, words will fall by the way side and the voice will convey pure, raw power without the limitation of human words to intervene. Runes have rhythm and vibration and movement, and this too is extremely important when one is getting to know them. They are extremely kinetic, and while they do not possess a body as other spirits might, their energies can flow through the body. It can be helpful, and can even augment certain magics, to know how to give that energy the outlet of chanting, singing, dancing, movement etc. Their language is not restricted to the verbal. In listening to *galdr*, you're listening to the sound and vibrations of the threads of the runes, not the vibrations of your own vocal chords. This is why it can sound incredibly dissonant. It's not important how it sounds to human ears, but how it reverberates on the Wyrd web, and it takes time to develop the ability to hear that.

Anyone seeking to access the runes should have at least a basic understanding of Wyrd before delving deeply into the runes. Runes can follow the rune-master almost anywhere (and they do, because they assume the rune-master understands about Wyrd). It's different from being amoral; rather it's more that they trust the rune master to understand the consequences of putting whatever it is he or she is casting into the web. They won't necessarily stop you once you've gained their trust. Some people, when they work magic, have the attitude that "well, if the universe is allowing me to do this, I must have some sort of cosmic permission." Runes are not like this. Their attitude is more along the lines of "if you're foolish enough, or bold enough, to cast this, then you can reap what you sow." The runes will do their job, as it is in their natures to do, and sit back and watch the proverbial fireworks. Learn how to balance Wyrd and move within its strands and eddies before seeking out the runes. The initial stages of developing a working relationship with the runes can actually teach this to a great degree.

There's an advantage to the fact that runes are sentient. When you're doing magic with them, the rune-master and the rune itself both absorb part of the responsibility. By that same token, however, when casting one must be very sure to take the responsibility that is yours to take—but, equally as important, to give what isn't yours to the rune. The rune can hold more of that—a lot more—than you can. This is important when it comes to magical backlash. You may be able to take the backlash for a botched casting in the amount that is rightfully yours to endure, but if you inadvertently shoulder what belongs to the rune itself, you may well be crushed beneath that weight.

It's necessary here to insert a caveat: At some point or another, they all like to be fed, usually blood. Certain ones demand it before lending their energies to tasks, so be prepared for this. If you want to work with them well, it's your blood they'll be wanting to feed on.

Runes find the language of our modern society very, very alien. This is important because when you start working with them, they will often give you very specific images and few of them are connected to 20th century America. They also assign very different values to things like money, death and sex. They more readily communicate those ideas within the concepts of ancient Norse cosmology. They cannot be forced to adhere to the value system of 20th century America. They will utilize the cultural construct for our species that is the closest to the language they speak.

Pain is also a tool that certain runes will utilize, for it opens the consciousness of the rune-worker in ways that friendlier tools do not; likewise with ecstasy and sexual pleasure. Understand that human morality is not part and parcel of a rune's conceptual makeup. All one has to do is to look at what Odin had to go through to initially access them to understand the perils and challenges of this work. They do not open readily to a person overly concerned with maintaining safe appearances or a comfortable status quo. There is something about that place in which they dwell that favors those who tend to extremes, and most of all, favors the shift in consciousness when one fully commits to the work at hand.

The runes influence one another, and ultimately one must understand their interrelationships with every other rune, and also with the Gods that tend to favor certain runes. Ansuz, for instance, is generally considered Odin's rune. Understanding why on a viscerally organic level can do much for increasing one's understanding of the rune itself. Just as the Web is constructed of interlocking and layered threads, so the runes exist in a dynamic interwoven, interrelated, shifting paradigm of energies. In this respect, they reflect the complexity of the Web itself. It is impossible to separate runes from Wyrd. They are living extensions and reflections of it.

Finally, when one seeks to understand and work with the runes, it's important to realize that sooner or later, one will encounter Odin. That has the potential to take one's rune work to an entirely new level of experience and intensity. Certainly, Odin can provide, even in the early stages (should He be so motivated to do so) advice on the best way to approach the runes themselves. This of course, may attract His attention in ways the rune-worker might not be prepared for. It's best to understand that He is the ultimate Rune Master, and sooner or later the road to every rune of the Futhark ends with Him.

The Rune Spirits

Fehu/Feoh: The Herder or Whore

The Rune-Spirit Fehu is feminine in nature, somewhat materialistic, and quite domestic and home-loving. Fehu keeps and sells herd animals, and that simple fact is a defining quality of her nature. She is more than a simple shepherdess; she owns ample flocks and herds, and thus is wealthy and has power in the tribe. She may appear with cows, or goats, or sheep, or reindeer; what matters is that she knows their worth, and does not settle for anything less than the best. A mature woman of ample proportions, usually clad in green, she likes comfort and even luxury. She loves physical sensuality and her bed is open to many, but like the Sacred Whore there is a price to pay, although it is probably worth paying. Fehu gives abundance, but it is less the abundance of sudden windfalls than of fair trade in an atmosphere of bounty, one's honest efforts paying off better than one expected.

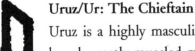

Uruz/Ur: The Chieftain

Uruz is a highly masculine warrior-spirit, manifesting as a tall, broad, greatly muscled man who stands a good head taller than all the others. Brown and bearded, he wears the skins of animals like a barbarian king, and there is a bull-like quality to his face and nature. His totem is the great aurochs, the now-extinct European buffalo, and like the aurochs he will bellow and trample anything between himself and his goals. He is the irresistible force which sweeps all before it like leaves, the strong back that never bows in weakness. However, unlike a berserker, he has the strength of self-control as well, keeping himself in check. Uruz knows that to be out of control is in itself a weakness, as is too much unharnessed rage. His forcefulness can be disconcerting to those of weaker will who summon him; they often expect a brute and instead get a stern, forbidding mountain of a man who can push his case and sometimes bully them, if they prove weak in his eyes. His leadership charisma is intense, and inspires loyalty. Uruz loves the mountains of Jotunheim of all the places in the Nine Worlds.

Thurisaz/Thorn: The Berserker

Thorn is an unpleasant customer. When he laughs, it is probably because someone has suffered some humiliating turn that has brought low their pride. When he is frowning, you can expect that there will be smiting, a bevy of small nasty pricks to drive someone insane. When he has worked himself into a rage by dint of that same method—contemplating and obsessing on all the horrid things in the world—he goes on a bloody rampage unrivaled by any Rune-Spirit save Hagalaz. Thorn lives to bring down the prideful, the hypocritical, the rigid, the cruel, the lazy—and, yes, the naive. Tall, muscled, bearded, his eyes glint red and his fingers drip with blood. If you can bear it, though, no one is better at getting you motivated to do something that you hate. If you ask him to, he will keep at you until you do it; no fog of procrastination can stop his onslaught. He is also something of a reverser, with a gift of turning things around. This means that he can turn around a bad situation as well, if he cares to—but only if the suffering is levered onto someone else. He is married to Nyth, and one way to control him is to invoke her as well. Thorn loves the wastes of Niflheim, where he can be alone with his rage and bitterness.

Ansuz/Aesc: The Winged One

Ansuz is fond of appearing as a bird of various sorts. When this rune has taken a human face to speak to me, it has been an androgynous winged being, not so much a shining angel-type as a half-bird shapeshifter with nervous energy, fluttering or rushing from one perch to the next. Ansuz carries all the power of the bird in flight, and sings a great deal; practically everything Ansuz says comes out in the form of a galdr-song. Ansuz is the Spirit of Freedom, wings outstretched and flying upwards; even the glyph suggests a bird ascending. When not looking at you or some other specific object, Ansuz always looks upwards. As the Messenger Rune, Ansuz has been known to carry messages to and from different parties, or at the least can be asked to guide a spell to the right place, but Ansuz won't tap someone on the shoulder unless they have made some sort of connection with this volatile spirit, so the delivery is more like dropping something in someone's lap and rushing off; they may notice it, or they may not. As the world at the height of the Tree, Ansuz is most fond of Asgard, and the eagle Hraesvelg that lives in the branches above.

Raido/Rade: The Wanderer

Raido is a cheerful dark young male figure, eyes on the horizon and heart always on the next adventure. He appears dressed in warm clothing and worn shoes, perhaps with a stick in his hand, perhaps with a bag over his shoulder, always on the move. Unlike the Horseman who has a specific place in mind and a set time to get there, Raido is happy to wander about as his feet take him. He fully intends to get someplace important, and usually he does, but in the meantime the journey is the important part. To him, it's all about collecting experience, and to do that he has to make no assumptions as to where he might end up. He is a wonderful traveling companion, but not so good for the long haul of a boring life, as his attention span is fairly short. While he loves every world on the Tree—they all have their joys and wonders—his favorite is, strangely enough, Helheim at the bottom of the Hel Road. To most people, this would be where all roads end; Raido calls it his beginning road, where he starts out, and being there means that all roads are ahead of him.

Kaunaz/Ken: The Smith

Ken appeared to me as a blacksmith working at his forge. He is tall, strong, and well-muscled, with a piercing, straightforward gaze, and long hair drawn back out of his smudged face. I got the impression that he might sometimes appear in a somewhat Duergar form, and indeed his favorite place is in Nidavellir in their caves and forges, but for me he appeared as fairly human. He slammed his hammer down on the anvil and spoke of how truth is the fire that forges, that burns and melts away the dross, and the hammer blows of Life are what make us stronger. His manner is very direct, with no frills; he speaks things exactly as he sees and is somewhat scornful of the need for fancy verbal footwork. His words can be painful, scorching like flames or falling like hammer blows, and he spares no one. Ken comes in with noise and ringing and after he is gone, the air at least is clear, if some of the more sensitive souls are fallen in a faint. There is often the smell of smoke and iron when communicating with him.

Gebo/Gyfu: The Giver

Gyfu appears to me as a northern housewife, plump and smiling amidst piles of blond curls, usually bringing some fine dish or fancy trinket, or working on a homemade gift for someone. She loves to give gifts, but they must be properly appreciated or there will be no more forthcoming. She is not interested in the bargaining of fair trade; although they are both spirits of abundance, Fehu's mercenary side makes her shake her head. In Gyfu's world, people give each other things because they care and because it makes one feel good to give. One gift leads to another, and everyone gets everything they want eventually. If she is offered something out of duty or obligation, it is not as good to her; she is subjective and emotional and demands equal emotion for her generosity. Even a delighted thanks and a sincere compliment is return enough. She is a good spirit to call upon for ways to increase hamingja, and frith in the community, but she can be confusing for less emotional people to deal with. She loves the craft-halls of Svartalfheim and the fields of Vanaheim, and divides her time between those.

Wunjo/Wyn: The Lightbringer

Wyn came to me in an aura of radiant golden light, a slender figure with long pale hair. She was female, but androgynous, and I got the impression that she could just as easily appear as an androgynous male figure as well, a slender brother to the sister presented. There was something vaguely elflike in her large eyes and graceful movements, and certainly the world that she loves most is Ljossalfheim, and that is where she can generally be found. She is a dancer, sometimes carrying a torch that sheds light everywhere, and sometimes she herself is the torch, wreathed in light like a figure of St. Lucia. When she moves, her figure leaves a track of light on the inner eye that takes a while to fade. Wyn is always smiling—at worse times her smile might be slightly sad, at better ones it is positively beaming—and she is the bringer of light into dark places, and joy into sadness. She is the one who lifts depression, casts away dark clouds, and shines clarity into shadows, bringing forth creativity and laughter. If there is nothing but sorrow about when you call her, and she cannot bring any light, she will merely vanish; her attention span is not a long one.

Hagalaz/Haegl: The Stormbringer

Hagalaz is generally considered to be the harshest of the Runes, and she is not one to be trifled with. She appears as a pale-skinned woman—almost corpse-pale—with long black hair that is either whipping in high winds or plastered to her head with rain; the only time that I saw it floating gently was when she appeared in the middle of a blizzard. Hagalaz brings down storms on people—sometimes chaos, sometimes radical change, sometimes just misfortune. She is a creature of strong passions—she weeps, screams, rages, laughs hysterically—but the thing to remember is that her smiting of people is never random. She always feels that there is a good reason that this person should suffer this trial, although you may not understand or agree with her purposes. To her, either the storm makes you stronger, sweeps away the unnecessary, and clears the air for new growth ... or it destroys you, in which case you were weak anyway, and part of the flotsam to be cleaned out. The most dangerous of the *svartrunar*, she has a strong affinity with the worlds of Helheim (which she finds peaceful) and Niflheim (which she finds invigorating), and occasionally with lightning-struck Jotunheim as well.

Nauthiz/Nyth: The Crone

Nyth is an old woman, stern and upright and glaring, a teacher but not an easy one. She teaches survival skills in a school of hard knocks—when you learn something from her, you will definitely know it well, but it may not be a pleasant experience. She is a tribal judge of the power-behind-the-throne sort, one of the old women that the chief dared not mistreat for their sharp tongues. Her narrowed eyes will look you up and down and judge you quickly and harshly, and then tell you exactly what it is that you need to learn in order to improve your sorry condition. It may be something that seems humiliatingly foolish and basic; it may be something that you despair of ever reaching. She will not, however, offer to teach you; that is something that you must ask for yourself, and then submit to whatever lesson she inflicts. Nyth is the power of the needfire, the warmth without which our ancestors would not have survived, and the skill it took to make it. I am under the impression that she is the wife of Thorn, and the only one who can keep him in check. Her favorite world is Muspellheim, which warms her chilly old bones.

Isa/Is: The Ice Queen

Mistress Isa is, like her name suggests, very much the Ice Queen. Tall, pale, eyes blue as shadows on snow, hair black as the water under the ice, she is robed in white and silver. Her demeanor is stiff and haughty; she dislikes most people and shows it. However, she is not petty and will either help or leave, perhaps with an excoriating remark in the process. Like Nyth, she is a No-sayer, setting limits when they need to be set. "Everything needs to stop sometimes," she says. "Unbridled growth leads to imbalance. Some things must remain still that others can move about them." Appealing to her vanity may make her more likely to help you, as she does actually enjoy using her powers to stop things in their tracks. Never insult her dignity or imply that she ought to loosen up, or that freezing glance will alight on you, and shrivel you. Mistress Isa prefers the snowy parts of frozen Niflheim for her perfect vacation getaway.

Jera/Jer: The Farmer

Whenever Jera appears, she always has some kind of farm implement in her hand—a digging stick, a hoe, a shovel, a threshing flail, a winnowing basket, a bag of seeds to put lovingly into the earth. Although farmers can be any gender, Jera appears as female; a mature woman with calloused hands, sun-browned face, sturdy work clothes, hair braided back so as not to interfere with the Work. And Work it is; she is the Laborer, the hardest-working of them all. To Jera, nothing is left to luck. All worth must be earned, and there is nothing sweeter than the harvest when you have put in your time and the reward can be gathered in. That is the true measure of worth, she tells us. Yet she does not toil merely out of duty. Jera honestly loves the earth that she tends, and she lives day to day in the cycle of weather and time, and shows us how labor can also be sacred. She is most fond of the world of Vanaheim, where the soil is the most fertile and the Wheel of the Year the most keenly felt, and all the farming energy patterns the land like a patchwork quilt of good intention.

Eihwaz/Eoh: The Protector, or Bridegroom

Eihwaz is the husband of Mannaz the pregnant bride, and the protector of their future children. Tall, sturdy, and honest-faced, he bears only his staff of yew as weapon and as proof of his virility. Unlike Tyr who fights out of honor and service to the tribe, or Algiz who guards out of territoriality, or Thorn who battles out of rage, Eihwaz lifts his staff only out of love for those he cares for. He puts his body between his family and the enemy because his love for them is so great that he would die to protect them, yet mostly he wishes for a happy and content home. That is foremost in his thoughts; he does not see battle as glorious but as a temporary obstacle between one content home-bound day and another. He is unsophisticated but loyal, as much or more a lover than a fighter. Though he is poised on the threshold of leaving youth altogether, there is still an innocence about him. Like his wife, he loves Midgard more than any other world, for it is there that the folk most need protecting.

Perth/Peorth: The Weaver, or Priestess

Perth appears as a woman robed in black, silver of hair and of middle years. Sometimes she is spinning or weaving at a loom, although she will not tell you what it is that she is making, or for what purpose. It is likely that her work is linked in somehow to that of the Nornir, perhaps a pale reflection thereof. She will also sometimes appear with a handful of lots made from the pastern bones of sheep, which were used to choose sacrificial victims. If you want her to aid you, she may request that you take your chances with the lots, and see what comes up. While such a request should be pondered for a good long time, life is nothing without risk. Perth is a priestess, and is wise in the ways of Wyrd and hamingja; she is also a good aid for any diviner to have, especially when they must translate inscrutable messages. As one might expect, Perth likes to be near the Well of Wyrd in Asgard, although she will also travel to Mimir's Well and other places of wisdom.

Algiz/Eolhx: The Guardian

Algiz is a warrior, but unlike Tyr, who is quite willing to go on aggressive maneuvers so long as the cause is honorable, Algiz keeps solely to the defensive warding of set boundaries. He is the border guard, the marker of territory, and as such has a strong affinity with all animals who mark territory, especially predators. He is tall, dark, wild, and reclusive, sometimes showing himself in wolf's *hame* and sometimes antlered, staring through pine boughs from where he watches and guards. He speaks little and does much, and is excellent to be set to watch one's back. There is often a strong animal smell, or sometimes an evergreen-forest scent, when he appears. Generally there will be a few moments of lag-time between calling him and noticing that he has appeared, and you missed it. When aroused to battle, he is a fierce challenger, standing his ground and barring the path, and none shall pass without getting past him. He has a strong affinity for the wilds of Jotunheim, and all deep forests.

Sowelu/Sigil: The Valkyrie

Sigil appears as a Valkyrie, all white and gold with a sword in her hand, and great swan-maiden's wings. Unlike Wyn or Dagaz, the other "bright" Rune-Spirits, she is fairly stern and sometimes even grim, even as she glows mightily. She is known for only appearing briefly; she stays rarely more than a minute when summoned by human beings. She has little use for weaklings and whiners, and will only come to the brave of heart. "Victory is what you make of it," she says cryptically, and then she is gone. If you are lucky, she has pointed out the one thing you need to do in order to be victorious, often she comes and leaves without saying a word. As one might expect, Sigil prefers Asgard to all the other worlds, and she is revered there by all Odin's Valkyries.

Teiwaz/Tyr: The Warrior

It's not surprising that this rune was named for the great god Tyr, Lord of Swords, for Tyr-the-rune is very much like Tyr-the-God. He is quite male, blunt, grim, courageous, valiant, and honorable to the last drop of his blood. He does not like to lend his magic to any aggressive purpose that could be deemed dishonorable, and will silently, stubbornly refuse it; if you incorporate this rune into a bindrune for a stave and he does not approve of it, it simply won't work. He is energetic but not merry; he laughs little but cares greatly. Tyr is a good teacher of the martial arts, especially the psychological side of it: the giving of courage tempered with reason and honor. He has great patience with those who are giving a fight their best shot and losing; he has none at all for those who waste his time. Tyr is fond of both Asgard and Jotunheim, as that is where the greatest warriors lie, and he refuses to choose between them.

Berkana/ Beorc: The Mother

Berkana is the most feminine of all the runes; her very glyph is a pair of breasts, and she overflows with nurturing. She is especially linked with the magic of trees (especially birches, of course) and contains the energy of the tree reaching yearningly toward the sky. She is growth with no limits and no boundaries, and as such she will give until she has no more, and then quietly fade away for a time, and nothing will bring her back until she has recuperated. She is especially fond of mothers, children, and the needy; she hangs in a sort of aura of pearlescent light and pours out love to those who ask for it. Berkana is the greatest of the *limrunar*, the healing runes, but she can only heal in accord with Wyrd, so if she cannot help, look to the threads for information. If she does not like the purpose of the magic she is being tied into, she will weep, but not strike back. However, some of the other more aggressive runes may strike back on her behalf, so be warned. Berkana is most fond of the realm of Vanaheim, although she has an odd fondness for the tall trees of the Jotunheim forests.

Ehwaz/Eh: The Horseman

Despite all fiction to the contrary, the Horseman Rune-Spirit is no romantic highwayman. He comes across as a cheerful, plain workingman whose job is traveling from one specific place to another, usually on horseback. Sometimes he is a carter bringing a cargo of goods from one place to the next, urging on his plodding carthorse—the original teamster/trucker, bringing Progress one mile at a time. Sometimes he is a courier, galloping on his swift-footed steed, delivering his message and tearing off with the reply without even getting out of the saddle. Unlike Raido, who takes long journeys for the experience of it, perhaps without even being sure where the journey will end, Ehwaz prefers to know where he is going, have a decent map, and get there and back with the mission safely accomplished. The goal is the point, not the trip; he is supremely goal-oriented and stays focused on that. He has a good deal of patience, though—sometimes the horse is just a plodding plowhorse and that's that—as long as he knows that it's all towards the greater goal. Ehwaz is most at home in the world of Midgard, as that is the world from which no other world is too far away, the centerpoint of connections.

Mannaz/Mann: The Bride

I expected Mannaz to be male when I called that Rune-Spirit forth, and I was taken aback to find a young female presence, garlanded with flowers, and very pregnant. "I am the Hope of the People," she said simply. It took me a moment to get over my surprise, and then I remembered that the word *Mann* has only meant "male human" for a millennium; before that it was *wer* and *wif* for man and woman, and *Mann* was a neutral word for person; pluralized it was The People, as in the word for the Germanic tribe *Alemanni*—All-The-People. (The story of how "person" came to mean "male person" and "female person" came to mean "married female person" is one not even worth going into for the pain of it.) I remembered, also, that the glyph for Mannaz is the man and woman being handfasted.

So here she was, the pregnant bride. Much younger than Berkana, ripe with her first babe but not yet a mother, just a maiden blossoming to the far edge of maidenhood. Mannaz is the one who carries the future of the People, the one whom they would protect, the one who holds out her hands in frith to bring tribes together on her wedding day. She is the one with constant hope, the mediator who resolves confrontations, the one who is ready to give of herself for the sake of her people, and all people beyond that. Of all the places in the Nine Worlds, it is Midgard that she loves, for her heart is given to those most beleaguered and in need—not out of pity or mercy, but out of the urge to bring peacemaking and justice, and set things right.

Laguz/Lac: The River-Daughter

The Rune-Spirit of Water appears like a river-spirit or lake-spirit, blue-garbed and glistening wet knee-deep in the river, or long hair swirling as she arises naked and sparkling from the lake. Her laugh is the rush of whitewater and her touch is cool and soothing, but there is a coldness to her that reminds us that she is not Berkana or Gyfu. She may laugh or weep in front of you, but it is for her own reasons and nothing to do with you; to grasp her is to see her slip through your fingers like water. She is a healer, but not from compassion so much as casual generosity; if her healing waters fall on you and work; wonderful. If not, she cares little. Her song is hypnotizing; she is solitary but seductive, drowning you in caresses, perhaps actually drowning you in some way if you are not careful. Laguz's ambivalent nature is shown by her favorite lurking places: she greatly enjoys Ljossalfheim's enchanted rivers and streams and springs, but her secret place is the cold waters of Niflheim, around the frozen waters. It is rumored that she is the daughter of Mistress Isa, and just as cold in her own way.

Inguz/Ing: The Corn King

Ing is one of the Rune-Spirits who carries a very clear archetype: that of the Corn King who is cut down that others may live. Like the God Ingvi/Frey whose name he carries, Ing-the-Rune plays the same part, that of sacrificing himself that others may live. Golden and beautiful with haunting eyes, he is perhaps a bit more wistful than the God with whom he shares this title. He rarely comes to people unsummoned, and rarely when actually summoned. His job is to aid with sacrifice when it is necessary, and walk the individual through the often painful process. Ing is a romantic, an idealist, one who is willing to give everything that someone else be saved. He often appears wreathed in grain or even bound into a corn-sheaf; he may also appear as a golden lover on the night of his sacrifice. He has a strange and erotic relationship with Perth, whose hand wields the sickle that lays him low. Ing is very much a creature of Vanaheim, where he is honored as First of the Runes.

Dagaz/Daeg: The Awakener

Dagaz is an androgynous Rune-Spirit who comes in a flash of light. Unlike Wyn, who is always surrounded by a glowing nimbus, Dagaz flashes onto the scene in a blaze that startles, then quickly dies down to a humming glow. Indeed, Dagaz practically hums with restrained energy in between dashes, as if being confined to one place for too long would build up so much energy that there would be an explosion. Bright-haired and bright-eyed, quick-fingered and intense, there is an almost hyperactive feel to this spirit. The presence of Dagaz brings an immediate heightening of energy and awakeness; it is impossible to be sleepy with that humming force right next to you. Dagaz prefers the world of Asgard to all others, largely because of its presence near the top of the Tree where morning comes first and longest.

Othila/Oethel: The Grandmother or Grandfather

Othila is another one of the spirits who can appear as either male or female depending on circumstance, but unlike the elf-maiden/elf-youth Wyn, Othila always appears as an aged elder of the community. Sometimes she is the Grandmother, keeping her memories at the heart of the home, guarding the hearthfire and the grandchildren. Sometimes he is the Grandfather, passing on the tales of wisdom, adjudicating inheritance, dividing up land for homes for the next generation. Othila is a quiet, introverted spirit who knows much about bloodlines and ancestry, and has the longest memory of any of the Rune-Spirits. Othila is strongly tied to the past, and does not like to work with modern things or concepts, although that can be negotiated with difficulty. Othila is also very home-bound, and prefers to work with a family on a piece of land that they own, rather than with someone transient. Othila prefers the world of Midgard to any other, especially the oldest places there.

Ear: The Reaper

Ear sometimes appears as male, sometimes as female, sometimes as a figure of indecipherable gender. Either way, Ear is clothed in black, bearing a blade, with eyes that chill to the bone. When male, the blade is a sword, when female, a sickle, when androgynous, a curved knife. Ear is the one to call when something needs to go and you do not have the heart to do the dirty deed yourself. Ear is patient, and strangely compassionate, but it is unwise to summon this spirit unless you have something for Ear to take away, or the Reaper will take something anyway. Ear will, however, listen patiently while you mourn, be a witness to your pain, and never tell you that you should be getting over this now. Ear also does the work of burying the Dead and returning them to the Earth, and is good to call on for a link to the Ancestors. As one might expect, Ear is most often found in Helheim, the Land of the Dead.

Ac: The Chieftess

Ac is similar to Tyr in that she is a warrior, but rather than being the warrior in service, she has progressed to being the leader of warriors, and then of the whole tribe. Her energy is also similar to that of Uruz in that strength fairly reverberates from her, but rather than aggressive strength it is more that of endurance, of the oak tree that bears the storm and does not fall. She is a mature female, appearing to me dressed still in her warrior's leathers and cloaked in brown, with a great oaken staff on which she leans, both weapon and mark of office. Sometimes it seems to be the pole that holds up the whole sky, and around which the stars wheel; either way, one gets the sense from her of utter reliability. When all is chaos, she can be depended on to take charge calmly and sensibly, and brooking no argument. She is the power of stable leadership, secure in itself and its confidence, as immovable as a mountain and as decisive as the sweeping staff. She is most at home in Jotunheim, and of course has an affinity for all oak trees.

Ior: The Shapeshifter

Ior is the guardian of all liminal states—that which is neither this nor that, and the passage between—so when Ior comes, Ior is always somewhere in between male and female, or human and animal, or solid and ethereal. Ior's shape changes constantly, and it is impossible to follow the shifts; you will become mesmerized, and then dizzy, if you try. Sometimes conversations with Ior are best done looking away for periods of time. Ior is excellent for helping you shape your *hame*, and is often summoned for this. On the other hand, another of Ior's gifts is binding, so Ior is capable of binding someone into one shape or another; Ior simply chooses not to do this to Ior-self. When Ior does bindings, there is a definite "twining" or "clinging" feel, like ivy, and then you are solid in the way that you want, until you undo the binding and let it drift away into nothingness, and begin to shift again. In spite of Ior's shifting nature, Ior likes being around Midgard, especially around the Serpent.

Os: The Skald

Os appeared to me as a middle-aged man, proud of bearing and keen of eye, hair touched with grey and long moustaches, and with a mellifluous voice that could put you into a trance if you listened to it too closely. He is the one who teaches about public speaking, making people hear you and making your words penetrate past their boundaries. "It does not matter how they remember that the idea came to them," he says, "only that it gets in. In fact, if they remember themselves as coming up with it, rather than you telling them, all the better, for then they will defend it all the more fiercely!" To this end, he can assume many faces: fatherly, authoritarian, humble, impassioned, mystical, direct, sober or cheerful, and all are tools for him to reach his audience. Os is musician, singer, speaker, writer, anything to do with words and sound, internal and external. As the greatest of the *malrunar*, he bestows the gift of great speech, but only for a short period of time when the need arises.

Yr: The Archer or Craftsman

Yr always appears to me as a very Duergar-like man, small and wiry and craggy and silent. He bears a bow and arrows, and his hands look as if they could bring forth all sorts of wonderful things—potter's hands, carver's hands, sculptor's hands. He is capable of sitting and staring at something for an unbelievably long time, with a gaze that could drill holes through walls, and then with a grunt he reaches out and Makes something of it. The long stare was his way of learning all there was to know about it, so that it is as nothing to tweak some small thing and change it. His patience is immense, and his aim is keenly accurate. He speaks little, but when he speaks it will cut to the quick with a single phrase. As one of the *hugrunar,* his powers lend focus and aim when bound with other skill-oriented runes. Yr is most fond of the world of Svartalfheim, both the above-ground forests (where he can hunt with his arrows) and the below-ground havens of craft.

Cweorth: The Fire-Keeper

Cweorth always comes with fire. Making fire is what he loves best. That may be carefully tending the communal flame that warms the tribe, cooks their food, keeps predators away, and is crucial to their survival. It may be lighting the funeral pyre for the beloved dead, and marking his face with their ashes in mourning. It may also be burning someone's house down, or even the entire forest, in vengeance for a slight. Fire and its passion is central to Cweorth's nature, as is smoke and ash. He is summoned when something needs to go away fast, now, never mind the pain, just rip it out and burn it down, and he is usually glad to help, although he may not seem so. Cweorth is reserved and guarded, laconic of speech, a thin dark wiry man who crouches by the fire, feeding it wood as if it was his child. He is close with his feelings and does not speak often, although he will sing loudly when the pyre rages and leaps high. His home is, of course, Muspellheim, where he is greatly loved by Surt.

Chalc: The Dreamer

Chalc is another of the Rune-Spirits who can show themselves as male or female depending on the circumstance and the summoner. Chalc is a dreamy adolescent with a high-flown imagination who speaks in poetry and vivid images. Sometimes Chalc is a young girl with faeries in her eyes, sometimes a young boy set on future adventure. Beauty and glory are very important to Chalc, as is the idea of love, but it is not wise to depend on Chalc to carry things through difficult and grubby times. However, Chalc's greatest gift is a deep well of faith in the future, and in one's ability to pursue joy, that many folks would do well to learn to tap into. Chalc's greatest love is the world of Ljossalfheim, for that world contains thousands of dreams and images, and is the most beautiful of all the worlds.

Stan: The Gatekeeper

Stan is one of the androgynous Rune-Spirits whose gender is not apparent. Stan often appears as a grinning, hunched, gnomelike figure wearing a cloak which sprouts moss and weeds, with a face that looks indeed like it was carved out of stone ... but that lumpish figure is not to be underestimated. Stan is wisewoman, cunning-man, hedge-witch, the one who knows many old secrets and keeps them close. Stan is the Gatekeeper to the Mysteries, and knows much but teaches little; you will mostly get riddles and conundrums and metaphors out of that chuckling mouth. Stan loves any arched gate, any door in an outside wall, any circle of standing stones, and will sing unintelligible songs in a high, shrill voice. If Stan shows up without being invited, it means that what is going on now is crucial, reverberating out beyond one person's inner world, and Stan wants to be there to see it happen. Stan prefers to be in Ljossalfheim, and has a great love of the common Alfar and faeries.

Gar: The Door

Gar never shows itself with a human face; it is purely a spirit-presence, sometimes a pillar of light shading to dark at the bottom. Gar is a living spirit-doorway, a connection to the Gods and the Cosmos, the entrypoint of *wod*. Gar is rarely called on, and when called, rarely comes; it is not possible to command the gateway to the Gods to open. One must summon, pray, and hope. If Gar does come, Gar is the best spirit possible for signal clarity in receiving messages. Gar belongs to no grouping—no aett, no stafr-group. It is simply itself, apart, "all alone and ever more shall be so," as one spirit-worker referred to it, quoting the old song. No world holds any more interest for Gar than any other; its affinity is with the World-Tree itself.

Wyrdworking:
Combing The Threads

This is the way that we see it: Start with the three women who stand alone, beyond all the other Gods. Even Odin does not dare defy Them. Even Hela must bend to Their will. They do not generally meddle in the affairs of men—it is not Their job to intervene, to change things. They know what was, what is, and what must be, and also what is not yet set—where the choices are, where things can be made different, although They will not tell you about it. Urd, Verdandi, Skuld—They demand no worship, They show themselves to few eyes, but They are of immense importance in the end.

See yourself, a thread wound through Their tapestry, which is so huge that you cannot take more than a tiny part of it in, so colorful that it hurts your astral eyes to gaze upon it. Where you surface above it, that is your birth, wound with that of the parents who bore you, the people who raised you. Perhaps it is still twined with theirs; perhaps it has moved on. Perhaps it twines with other threads—your lovers, your friends, your children. Perhaps it gradually shifts color as it goes on. Perhaps the place where it dips again below the surface is already set; perhaps the end is still loose, waiting for the right moment to bow out of the upper world.

Is Fate set, you ask? Are things preordained, or am I the captain of my ship? That depends, say the three women. They are frustrating that way, speaking only in conundrums, but perhaps you will get a better line from Them if you are lucky. No, put that thought aside, luck means nothing when you are facing their implacable gazes. Depends on what? you ask plaintively.

On many things, They say. Who you are. Who you are meant to be. What you carry with you from lives before. What your blood gives you. When and where you live.

What you need most to learn.

It's not so simple as preordained or free, you realize. Some people's Wyrd is to live the life that is put before them, reading the script that they are given and deviating as little as possible, herded along the road by the Gods who bound them. Some people are given all the freedom in the world to make all the mistakes that they will—and pay for them later, perhaps in another lifetime—but they get no help, no guidance. Most are in between.

If you are a spirit-worker, you have already moved to the fated side of that path. Perhaps not completely—there is a continuum between part-timers who can negotiate some of their terms and the walking Dead who must do what they do or die entirely—but to engage with the Gods and wights, to get their attention and their direct handling, to work with them as closely as it is possible for one made of flesh, this ties your Thread down. Their Threads are larger, longer, heavier than yours; your tiny mortal strand is borne down beneath the weight of twisting with theirs. Already, you have fewer choices. If they bring you all the way to Death and then ransom you back from its edge, you will have almost none left. The walking Dead live on a narrow path, a knife's edge.

But people will come to you, and ask questions about their lives, and in order to answer them, you must see their Thread. And this is not as easy as it seems.

Wyrdworking, or reading (and affecting) people's Wyrds or destinies, has been a mainstay of northern-tradition shamanism from the beginning. When the volvas were called forth to read people's fates while in trance, they were the last in a long line of spirit-workers who looked at a member of their tribe and saw not just a person, but an entire lifetime, with all its possibilities and restrictions. To see someone's Wyrd is to do far more than just give them a mundane reading about whether they will get this job, or what they should do about their love life. At worst, it is to see in vivid color what obstacles lie on their path to their destiny. At best it is to see that goal in its entirety and describe its path to them.

There is no doing any kind of Wyrdworking unless you have a reasonable relationship with the Nornir. They are the ones in charge of all Threads, and They rule that tapestry with an iron hand. If you have ever received any information about anyone's Thread—and I'm talking about large-scale things, not small divinations—you got it by Their leave, because They chose to give it to you. Nor do They want you to go messing with people's Threads without Their permission. Being a Wyrdworker does not give you leave to arrange things as you choose.

There are certainly all sorts of terrible stories about northern-tradition spirit-workers who could work all sorts of curses on people by messing with their Threads and thus destroying their luck (or any number of other things), but what isn't discussed in these rather self-important tales is that this sort of thing always has consequences. Sometimes the Nornir will step in and put a stop to such interference, and nothing will come of it at all. That's the better of the two outcomes. The other one is worse: the Thread of the afflicted person is simply tied to the Thread of the curse-wielder, and the rot slowly spreads over time from one Thread to the other. The curse-wielder will find it impossible to get rid of the other person, whether from their life or just from their thoughts, and things will eventually go just as bad for them as they intended for the other.

The only way that this doesn't happen is if a deity is involved, and they have bargained some part of their *maegen* for this curse. However, that's not something to bet the rest of your life on, unless you are very, very sure it's what that deity wants you to do. (Ask for confirmation, lots of confirmation.) If you must curse someone yourself—and while I do not recommend this, on the whole, I realize that some people will want to do it—the safest curse is to make it so that all their past debts catch up with them quickly. This means that they will be put in a position where they have to deal with all their baggage, and the fallout from every injustice they have enacted. Any lesson that has been repressed or put off will suddenly be right in their face, perhaps all of them at once, and they will be unable to escape from it. If they have truly wronged you, that will be working itself out as well.

Of course, that also means that this will also happen to you, but we spirit-workers live by different rules. As a rule, our Wyrd is faster than that of other people; the consequences of our actions come quicker, and we are less able to live in comfortable denial. Therefore, we should be used to being forced to deal with things coming back around quickly, and really it's good for us spiritually. We require a good deal more "cleanliness" in that regard than other people, considering the energies that we work with and the responsibility that we take on. Therefore, the best way to work such a curse is to deliberately (and hopefully temporarily) tie one's own Thread to the intended recipient's Thread and speed up Wyrd for both of you. The Nornir have never been known to interfere with that, as long as I have worked with Them.

There might be other reasons to speed up Wyrd, and not just as some sort of punishment. (Indeed, even if you mean it as a punishment, usually the Nornir work in some other lesson as well, often one that shows you your motives much more clearly.) It may be that the person who has come to you is wandering about lost, unable to find their path, and divination shows that they are in actuality ready to walk it, just lost. (Most who come with this question are, unfortunately, not ready to act on the answer, but you'll find a few who just need serious direction.) It may be that some other things are interfering with their path, things that will take longer to be overcome than they have time for. This must be done only with their informed consent, and the results must be explained to them first—that all their debts will come due in rapid order, and there will be a time of clearing-out, after which clarity may be achieved. If they consent—perhaps out of desperation; this sort of thing is really only a last resort—ask the permission of the Nornir and see if They will allow it.

If it is to be allowed, go into trance and find their Thread. Hook it to your own, and begin to twist your own Thread tighter and tighter. (This is one reason I recommend learning to spin—it give you a good physical metaphor for the Work, one that you can recall during trance.)

The twist will travel from your Thread to theirs. Then, well before you reach a breaking point, let it untwist. As it reaches the moment of straightness, before it begins to twist the other way, break their Thread off of yours and let both of them spin in isolation. You will have achieved a speeding up of Wyrd for them—and for yourself as well. If you have been doing your job properly, it shouldn't be a life-threatening difference for you.

If you are at all good with crafts, learning some sort of fiber arts is the best possible tool for accessing Wyrd. The best of all are handspinning and weaving, but even embroidery or quilting are good for working with the Nornir. First, you do them as a service to the Nornir, because that's the way that you pay them for this privilege, and you need to start with a sizeable payment up front. (Housecleaning is also a good payment, or for that matter any kind of serious cleaning; more suggestions can be found in the chapter on the Nornir in *The Jotunbok*.) As you work, you dedicate the energy of each stitch or spin or casting of the shuttle to their Work. That doesn't mean that you are going to be privy to their Work as you do it, but you may feel like you're somehow also blindly working on Something Else at the same time as you are doing your own fiber arts. Don't think that you are influencing the flow of Wyrd by doing this, however; you're just the battery. They do the Work.

Then the next step is to do some divination to see if your gift is even accepted. Look particularly for the Peorth rune, or the Wheel of Fortune Tarot card, or some such thing. If you get a positive reading, go do some utiseta and see if anything happens. I usually hold some handspun yarn while doing this, and try to visualize seeing a piece of Their tapestry. Not the entirety of it, because the entirety is so huge that it would blast a human mind to see it. I concentrate on the Thread of someone that I know. Some people start with their own Threads; others aren't allowed to see or work with their own. Still, a Thread that is well wrapped with yours—lover, child, parent, close friend—is a good place to start. It may appear to you as an actual thread in an actual tapestry, or something completely different. Some modern computer-literate folk visualize it as clicking on a file with someone's name on it, and it comes up on a mental screen.

If you start with a loved one, it's best to let them know that you use them this way, because you're going to get glimpses of their Thread in the process. Then, when you can see better, you switch to finding the Thread of your client, calling it by name. Even if it's not their "usual" name, it's attached to their Thread. If you can't find it, call on the Nornir and ask for their help in sorting through. Sometimes I'll almost feel a hand shoving the end of that Thread into mine when I do this.

Then I run the hand of my *hame* along their Thread—sometimes I also run my physical fingers along the handspun yarn at the same time— and look for tangles, knots, or other problems. There will be intertwinings of their Thread with that of others; ignore that. Look for places that look tangled and painful. Touch the tangle or knot, and you should get some kind of information coming to you about what caused it. If you're lucky, you can get an idea of what can be done about it, but generally that information can only be achieved by coming back and doing a divination.

Don't get any ideas about going ahead and unknotting their Thread. First of all, you cannot see everything that it's hooked to, or what that knot might release that shouldn't be released. You can see a lot about a Thread, but it's hubris to think that you can understand everything. Second, the Nornir don't like it when you mess with other people's Threads. They're the only ones who are allowed to do that by right, and they may stop you—or, as pointed out earlier, they may *not* stop you, in which case there's a good chance that they will just do something to your own Thread in a balance of justice.

But thirdly and most important, it is not your *orlog* to fix the Threads of other people, any more than it is your *orlog* to pay all their other debts. Even if you were able to untangle their knots, there is no *maegen* in that for them. By interfering, you rob them of the chance to earn *maegen* of their own by solving their own problems. Your job is to find out what is wrong, and to give them the best possible information on how they can set things right, and do what it takes to support them in that goal. If you want to untangle a Thread, work on your own.

Some people come into the world with knots and tangles already in their Threads, either from the deeds of their ancestors that have been passed down, or their own deeds from past existences. Other knots and tangles are created by their own actions and decisions. There is nothing that cannot be put right; it just depends on how much effort is needed to go into it, how much they are willing to sacrifice. For some with very bad tangles, the price may be too much. Usually, though, you'll find smaller knots that can be taken care of with some simple attention and propitiation.

One example was a man who came to me feeling like he had done something in a past life that was haunting him. I went into trance and checked, and as soon as I lay a hand on that tangle, I saw him leading a bunch of soldiers into a gas cloud, killing most of them. There were Dead who were angry with him, Dead that he had reincarnated quickly in order to avoid. We lit a bonfire in the back yard and I opened the gate for the Dead who wished to speak to him, and he apologized to them and poured whisky and cigarettes into the fire as an offering. The fire began to stink strangely—we found out that the last people to use the firepit had unknowingly put acrylic batting into it—and we found ourselves enveloped, for a moment, in a caustic burning cloud. Then it passed on, and we felt peace. It was a small thing, but an important one.

Another woman came to me in her forties, worried about the fact that all the women in her family went inexplicably mad at around her age. Her younger sister was already showing signs; she felt that the fact she was the only childless woman in the family for generations had something to do with the fact that it hadn't hit her. Since she was skilled in trance, I drummed her there herself to find things out. It turned out that an ancestor on a small island off the coast of the British Isles had bargained with the local faeries to get her children and herself safely to America when the land was confiscated, and then never paid the debt. It was turned over to her unwitting daughters, and granddaughters, and great-granddaughters, who had no knowledge of it, but who still bore the brunt of not paying it. Standing by a bonfire while I drummed, she asked them how to pay the debt, and got her answer, which was complex but still within her power to perform.

On the more difficult side, another who came to me with a debt and a terminal illness was told that he would have to suffer for that debt, and offer his suffering up as a sacrifice, and not know until the end whether he would be spared or die. It was a matter of faith. Last I saw him, he is still alive, and still making the offering. Yet another very difficult call was an elderly man from India who had broken a bargain with Shiva, and he wanted to know if he would be spared dealing with it again in his next life. Shiva appeared behind my shoulder shouting "You tell him no!" and then said in a lower voice, "And you tell him that his life is not yet over, and there is still time." I tried to relate the message as gently and positively as I could, but he merely wept and said that there was no hope, that keeping his bargain would bring great grief to his frail, elderly wife. I tried to tell him that he would bring greater grief to her by using her as an excuse not to act, as the Gods sometimes remove these excuses when they become impatient with you, but I do not know how that ended.

For most or all of these remedies, while the action is important, the attitude with which it is done is far more so. If you are told to apologize to someone that you hate, you cannot do it with an attitude of "I'm sorry that you're such a twit." A sacrifice offered with the wrong attitude does not count, and may have to be done over again in worse circumstances. A sacrifice done in self-pity—"Oh, isn't it terrible for me that I have to do this awful thing!" may be the most insulting and unacceptable of all. It is your job to get this across to people, as well as you can.

Wyrdworking is part of the art of Sacred Mending, in that it can be used to mend old hurts and set things right. It can help people to burn off debts, increase their *maegen*, gain *hamingja*, and find the path of their Wyrd. What it requires more than anything on the part of the spirit-worker is patience. Be prepared to deal with the difficult reactions of those who are told things that they don't wish to hear. It's not your job to force them to do the right thing; it's only your job to hold up the lamp and point out the path, and then only offer further assistance if they ask for it. In the end, it has to be their task. Still, by aiding people in untangling themselves, you aid the world in becoming less snarled. Remember that fixing the Threads is not best done by yanking on them, but by taking action in the world that reverberates across them. It is the flesh hands, not the ones of the *hame*, that do the work of Mending in the end.

Luckworking:
The Dance Of Hamingja

Some cultures put a lot of emphasis on luck, and some don't. The Northern Tradition's attitude is another place where we share things in common with Chinese and other Asian cultures, in that luck is very important to us. It is a way of getting an edge on misfortune, of convincing the Universe that you ought to have a little less justice and a little more mercy, that things ought to swing just a little more in your own favor whether you deserve it or not. But Fortune, as any religion that deals with her/it will tell you, is a fickle wench. Clients will often show up on your doorstep and say, "My luck seems to have run out." Then it's a matter of figuring out what sort of luck they had, and what happened to it.

Sometimes the problem isn't a lack of luck per se, it's just a period of bad things happening, and the "normal" amount of luck isn't enough to let the person skate by. Many people attribute to bad luck what ought to be laid at the feet of poor judgment and decisions. If scrutiny with divinatory methods does not turn up a problem with luck, it may be time to find out whether inevitable consequence is taking its turn and some things are coming due. This is a hard concept to get across to people, especially when they're hoping that it's just luck and not their fault.

There are many different kinds of luck, and all of them can swing to the good or bad side of the spectrum. First, there's karmic luck—in this tradition, one could call it Wyrding luck—something done in this lifetime or a past one that gave you gifts or obstacles, usually set in such a way to aid you in doing something that you ought to do, or conversely prevent you from doing something that you shouldn't. Wyrding luck is the hardest of all to work with, since it isn't just about making a propitiation but actually understanding a lesson and making an atonement. If the person isn't in a place where they're ready to work seriously on that lesson, then all the magic and propitiation in the world isn't going to help. If they are ready to work on it, their luck may change.

This may be as simple as the lack of luck being what happens to people when they aren't doing what they're supposed to be doing. Lydia Helasdottir comments: "If you are moving along in the way that you are meant to move, and there is nothing in your family background actively preventing you from having luck, then you should be OK. But that's a lot of ands and ifs. So we sometimes have people come to us and say, 'Look, I just haven't got any luck and I don't know what's going on.' We ask them 'What are you actually doing with your life? Is it making you happy? Are you fulfilled?' If the answer to that is No, that's the first thing to get straightened out. Do you like the people that you're living with, or the job that you're doing? Is there at least a hobby that you like? If it's not that, then we go look to see if there's any particular wight or person or entity actively harassing this person. It might be something like a family feud with the local boggarts that his great-granddad had started by cutting down the boggarts' favorite tree without asking. Then you can make a diplomatic mission about remedying that insult. Sometimes just acknowledgment is enough."

The second sort of luck is astrological luck. While the northern tradition doesn't have a surviving astrological system in lore (although there are spirit-taught systems that we are slowly filling in), astrology still works and I strongly recommend it to any spirit-worker as a way to get good information about any client. Jupiter is the planet of luck, and if it is currently being badly aspected by another planet, or if there is another long-term bad aspect going on that brings down difficult times onto someone's head, then it's just a matter of surviving a time of trials. There are propitiations and remedies that can be done in these cases (although this book is not the place for so huge and not particularly NT a field), and at the very least, you can give them an idea of when it will end, and what lessons need to be learned in order to make it go smoother. Some people have difficult aspects with regard to luck built into their natal charts. Be honest with them about it, and stress that while they may have to work for everything they get, they will know firmly that they've earned every bit of it. Such a client needs to concentrate on their *maegen*, on building will and personal power through commitment, rather than depending on luck. Stress also that while it's not comfortable, *maegen* is more reliable to depend on than luck in the long run.

A third kind of luck might be locational bad luck. This is somewhat difficult to diagnose, but very easy to remedy. Some places are just bad juju for some people, while another person might live there just fine. This is a concept echoed in such esoteric arts as Feng Shui and astrocartography. Ari, a northern-tradition seidhmadhr, has dealt with locational bad luck, saying: "It's as if your energy clashes with the land-wight's energy. It's not something that you can fix just by giving it a lot of propitiation, because it's not actively angry at you. It's just that you are not its kind of people, and you never will be. Moving is simpler than living that way, because it can slowly drain you of all luck. If you're living on ancestral land—and most of us aren't—you may be able to get your ancestors to interfere and protect you. But if it's just a house lot that you bought, sell it and buy a different one. If you're renting, get the heck out. You'll save money in medical bills and accidental expenses."

Some people, on the other hand, are born with lots of natural luck, usually inherited through their lineage in some way. This is the fourth kind of luck—inherited luck, or blood-luck. It's as if the Gods look out for them throughout their early lives, giving them a beginning with lots of padding. This may look like a wonderful thing from the outside—especially if you're the person with less luck, watching them skim happily through life—but like all gifts, it's a two-edge sword and there's always a Dark Alfar at the baby's naming, hiding behind the cradle. Inherited luck can run out, especially if it's abused or overused, or if the person goes through a period of bad luck for an external reason that more than counteracts the innate luck. Then you've got someone who has no idea how to live without the periodic rescue in the nick of time, and they can crash pretty hard. It's instructive to see how quickly their cheery optimistic temperaments devolve into whiny, depressed helplessness in short order. It's not easy to go from a lifetime of lucky to a period of unlucky, and even worse, sometimes that unlucky period can be permanent. One of the most difficult things that I've had to tell the occasional client was that their luck was gone. Used up. No more for you. From now on you toil with the rest of us and live off your own harvest. Become an Ant, Grasshopper, or freeze to death. A few folk in that situation actually considered suicide rather than learn to adapt, and almost all continued to mourn their lost luck for a long time. In many ways it's as much a curse as a blessing.

Blood-luck can also be bad. We all know families with terribly bad luck. I was born into one, so I know it well myself. For some reason, people with inherited good luck rarely end up marrying people with inherited bad luck; in fact, it's usually the opposite, a sort of like-draws-like situation. It's not uncommon for two people with bad blood-luck to meet and breed, which means extra problems for the kids. Bad blood-luck is often the result of a blood-curse carried through the line, and this falls into Wyrdworking and combing the Threads for information.

A period of luck in someone's life can end suddenly if that luck is abused. I've had friends refer to this as "shitting on your luck". Abusing luck isn't about relying on it too much—while that has its own danger of becoming too used to it, as explicated above, it doesn't count as abuse per se—it's about not sharing it. Luck is fed by generosity, which comes to us through the virtue of hospitality. If good things come to you, you extend that good fortune by sharing with others. One example of "shitting on your luck" came from a young couple who moved to a new city with a few dollars in their pocket and an old car full of books. Within the first week they found friends who let them crash on their couch, and found jobs through amazing serendipity. An apartment unexpectedly opened up down the street when a student dropped out and went home, and a death in another house resulted in all the furniture being put out on the street for them to take.

Once they were settled into their new furnished apartment, however, the test began to come around. Other friends or acquaintances of theirs showed up homeless and needing a place to crash, just as they themselves had been taken in... but they turned them away. Their apartment was too small; it would be a bother; it would strain their budget to feed people. There were a hundred excuses, and they failed each test of their generosity. After that, a period of insane bad luck followed, and of course they were taken by surprise and had no idea what had gone wrong.

This brings us to the northern-tradition concept of *hamingja*, which is also described in the chapter on the Soul Map. *Hamingja* can be considered a fifth kind of luck, and it is both earned and given. I've often pointed out that one could earn *maegen* alone on a deserted island, but to gain *hamingja*, you need the good will of other people. The simplest way to start earning *hamingja* is to offer yourself to a community of people, even if that's only a few friends, and give them the best that you have. This is where one has to differentiate between the people who see you from a distance and may say nasty things about you, and the people who know you. Look at those folk, the ones who see you regularly, who you care about, who care about you. What do they say of you? Would they say that you can be depended upon, that you keep your word, that you are a trustworthy person? Would they go to the wall for you? That gives you *hamingja*, and you need to earn it. While it's not easy to come by, *hamingja* is a fairly stable kind of luck. You could lose it by alienating most or all of the people who gave it to you in the first place, but it won't up and leave on its own.

Hamingja also comes through gifts. When someone gives you a gift with real goodwill, it has *hamingja* in it. Heirlooms had extra *hamingja*, because they had been given as death-gifts again and again, passing through the hands of the ancestors. Brides would bring to their new homes a wealth of heirlooms, to be passed on to their children. The wife herself was the repository of all *hamingja* in the house, as she kept the hearth, which was where the *hamingja* of a family resided. If she left her husband, she could legally take back everything she brought, and as such would rob his family of all her *hamingja*. Bridegrooms paid a bride-price for their brides not because they were "buying the woman", but because they were reimbursing the bride's family for their *hamingja*-loss. Often, the bride-price would be expected to be paid not just in gold or cattle, but in *hamingja*-laden heirlooms from the bridegroom's family, and this exchange of ancestral wealth would create bonds between two bloodlines, just as much as having children would do.

This is bound up with the power of the Gyfu rune, which is really the rune of *hamingja*. We may think of a gift as an obligation that we need to pay back immediately, so as to be "free" of all obligations. To our ancestors, this was a crazy idea. The web of obligations was what kept people alive. This is Gyfu's message: being constantly in debt to others is fine, so long as others are constantly in debt to you. The sincere exchange of gifts creates this ongoing web, which hold us up and sustains us, and binds us into a community. Therefore, if someone lacks *hamingja*, or their *hamingja* has been damaged—perhaps through bad behavior in front of their community—they need to be advised as to how to best build it up again. This will take work, and the propitiation not of Gods but of people. Even if someone will never be your friend, and thinks that you are an irredeemable person (and even if you think the same), a *hamingja*-gift, honestly given, will help your own luck to come back. It doesn't have to be a big public gifting, and indeed perhaps it's better not to do that. There is no *hamingja* in embarrassing someone, or wanting a public eye in order to impress people with your generosity. (One good way to do a quiet *hamingja*-gift to someone is to send a check to a utility company for their account, or a rent check to their landlord, or a mortgage payment to their bank.) If you think that they will not accept any gift that comes from you, gift their spouse, or adult children, or good friends, and say, "This gift is for you because you are lucky enough to have X as your friend, and I give it in their name."

A sixth kind of good luck comes as a divine gift, and the bad luck that's the flip side is the wrath of the deity in question, or another one whom you've angered. This is somewhat more serious than the situation Lydia describes above wherein a boggart has been angered by your great-grandfather. Deities don't just go off on people for no reason. Either you've broken an agreement with them, or you've defiled one of their sacred spaces or rites. As the latter is fairly rare, it's usually the former. You can often see the handprint of divine wrath in the area of life that is most affected; it's usually one in which they specialize. (The love lives of those who piss off love goddesses are truly an exercise in wretchedness. Seriously.) If it's a matter of atoning for messing up a site or rite, that's much more doable than the former problem, which can really only be solved by you living up to your end of the agreement. In rare cases something else can be negotiated that is equally satisfactory to them, but mostly they just want what they've been promised, and once you've entered into that agreement, it is a Solemn Oath, and you are their Lawful Prey to torment until they get what they want.

A seventh form of luck is Trickster luck. Here in America, most Pagans refer to it as heyoka luck, using a southwest Native American term. This is a particular kind of luck bestowed by people who work closely with Trickster deities, and/or who can call down the Trickster archetypal hat onto their heads temporarily. Trickster luck is probably the strongest temporary form of luck in existence; it's like an incredibly powerful probability-warping field around the individual who is so blessed. If you can call it blessed, that is. Those who work with Trickster deities—Loki is the ultimate master of this in our tradition, of course—will tell you just how many ways they pay for that luck. Being beloved of a Trickster can bring you amazing luck, but it's also rather like being on an exhilarating roller coaster ride... all the time, and you can never get off. Well, perhaps you could try to jump, but it's not recommended.

Trickster luck works best through the unconscious. People with trickster luck instinctively learn not to question it, scrutinize it too closely, or perhaps even think about it at all. The (often bizarre) actions that feed Trickster luck are done impulsively, completely off the cuff, and then the person spins away to the next thing without looking back, or explaining themselves to the bewildered onlookers. Like faery glamour, looking too closely at the process ruins the luck. Of course, they have to be very tapped into that energy (which usually means a link with a deity) so that they will just automatically "know" which bizarre action to take, without considering it. If they aren't properly tapped in, and they get it wrong, it can have the opposite effect. Most certainly it will not come with the circle of protection that is part of that probability-warping field, and it might get them into deep trouble. At the very least, it will be humiliating. That's how someone with Trickster luck knows that they got it wrong—it crashes, burns, and makes them look like an idiot.

Like the Trickster himself, Trickster luck comes and goes without warning, and cannot be summoned or invoked. Even belonging to Loki won't guarantee that it will always be there, as the Loki-folk will wryly tell you. The best attitude to feed it, however, is explained by Loki himself in his lesson in the next book, *Wightridden*. Being keenly true to yourself and your eccentricities is the best way to keep it with you, although nothing to do with Trickster luck is ever guaranteed.

Andvari Luck
by Galina Krasskova and Fuensanta Plaza

A rarer and far less flamboyant type of luck is one that we name after Andvari the Duergr. It is based on knowing what is belongs to you by right and what belongs to you by accident. Those with Andvari luck develop a very special relationship to money, responsibility and resources. Luck in the northern tradition is based on causality and consequence, responsibility and balanced give and take. It flows directly from the state of one's Wyrd, the actions of one's ancestors, and one's own character. This is all the more true with Andvari luck. With this type of luck, one cannot take actions designed solely to increase one's luck. The actions must be done because they are the right actions to take, because the contrary is a screaming injustice or wrong. It is also the knowledge that money and resources, like luck, are in constant flow.

We think of money as finite: you have $10 and that's it. But that $10 can become a gift for someone, a meal for someone else. It can grow and change and evolve. If it doesn't grow and flow, the flip side of this type of luck is that of Fafnir: grasping, greedy, obsessive stagnation. Fafnir's treasure does not evolve into anything, and therefore it rots. Andvari luck is based on loving money and resources, but not in coveting or wanting to have more to keep up with your neighbor. It's loving money as you love a friend and giving it the freedom to grow and evolve.

This type of luck acknowledges that you don't have control over wealth, any more than you have over a friend. It involves acknowledgment that part of this money is yours and part you are only holding for others, and you must facilitate it going where it needs to be. Whether you have a little or a lot, part of it is not yours to keep, even if you have so little you can barely exist. The smile of courteousness you give to someone may be that which you owe out of your limited resources to someone else. This is part and parcel of the flow. This is knowing what is yours by accident and what is yours by right. It involves appropriate utilization of resources: putting spare pennies in a jar rather than leaving them strewn about (out of respect for the pennies, not to hoard them); it means turning off the lights when you leave a room, out of respect both for the electrical bill and also for the limited resources of nature that are not yours to waste. It involves a degree of mindfulness with every action, every day.

One gains this type of luck either by ancestry, or by approaching Andvari with an honest plea for learning and assistance. This will come with a geas. As mentioned above, it will forever entail mindful responsibility of every single resource and its utilization. In the *Jotunbok*, there is a story about Loki going to visit Andvari with money stolen from the Aesir to commission a pretty bracelet for his wedding to Sigyn. Andvari wouldn't take that money, because that was not Loki's to give by right. It had no value to Andvari. What he demanded (and got) was Loki's service for the time it took to craft the bracelet. This was Loki's to give by right and it was far more valuable to both Andvari and Loki than stolen coins.

One cannot court both the easy and fickle Gods of luck, like Fortuna, and Andvari both. Ever. You may lose one and not gain the other. The two may respect each other, but they do not mix. It's like oil and water.

Luckworking, in general, needs to come with a program to help the person change their life. As one spirit-worker puts it, "What I don't like about the luck readings is that it's getting awfully close to 'hey mister shaman, make me lots of money'. You can give them a program—and it usually starts with energy work and breathwork and purification, so that you have a chance of figuring out what you're supposed to be doing and gaining some clarity on it, then some simple mindfulness exercises and meditations so when they ask questions of themselves, they've got some chance of hearing the answer—but they rarely do it. Most of the people who come in for luck problems just want a quick fix, and that's part of why they fell into this pit in the first place."

This is where the spirit-worker needs to have a different slant than the average "psychic". If someone really wants to change their luck, every part of their life and their values needs to be scrutinized. How careful are they about their behavior, about taking responsibility for their actions and keeping their word? Do they share their wealth, or hoard it? How generous are they, not just with material goods and resources but with general aid and attention? Can they be relied on to help out when called upon? What values did they grow up with, and if they were bad ones, have they entirely discarded them? What lessons of life do they need to learn that they are avoiding? Who loves them? Who values them? Who would fight on their behalf?

It's difficult to change people's luck, because it's difficult to get people to change their lives. Sometimes it's just a simple thing that is easily remedied—move somewhere more propitious, wait out this astrological transit, make nice with this wight. Sometimes it's far harder, and sometimes you run across someone whose Wyrd is such that there is no making them any luckier. For example, it's not unusual for many "walking-dead-man"-type shamans to have no luck except what they can earn; that's because dead people have no luck of their own, something that I learned to my dismay. For some people, it is not their *orlog* to get rescued; they must make it to their goal under their own power, step by step, perhaps with the aid of others whom they must humbly ask and then pay well. And, really, in the great scheme of things, one could say that there is more honor in that road than the one cushioned by unearned gifts which are taken for granted, and eventually withdrawn.

The Norns' Lesson
Wyrdwalking

The Norns are choosy about who They work with. It's almost impossible to coax them into taking you on as a student. Generally, the teaching has to be brokered by your patron deity. It's important to remember that the Norns do not owe anything to anyone else, God, wight, or human, and no one can tell Them what to do. In many ways They are the most powerful beings in the Nine Worlds, because They are the agents of cosmic laws that even the Gods must abide by. Wyrd trumps everyone and everything, every time. Therefore, the Norns can afford to be choosy. Therefore also, it is understandable why They are so, given the importance of their Work.

This lesson is not written in the format of all the other ones, because no matter how hard I tried, I couldn't get Their words to come out in a dictated lesson. I expect that is because They don't want it that way, for whatever reason. There's also that the Norns don't exactly communicate in straight sentences. This is something that others have noted. It's unclear why. I'm sure that They are quite capable of it, but They prefer to communicate in images and cryptic words. It's highly annoying, and very difficult to transcribe to any useful purpose. Therefore, what I write here can only give you the flavor of what it is to work with the Norns. Truthfully, since They take on very few people—and that includes spirit-workers—it is unlikely that you'll get lessons from them, but if you do, make sure that you never abuse the privilege. Remember that these are beings that no one else in the Nine Worlds—not Odin, not Hela, not anyone—can tell what to do. Even the Gods are subject to them and their weaving.

I worked for the Norns twice, each time for about a month. I paid for those lessons with my own labor, in handwork and in cleaning. That seemed to be what They wanted most: fiber arts handwork such as spinning and embroidery, and cleaning of anything that needed it. I would dedicate the energy of my working to Them, and while I was working—doing dishes, scrubbing, stitching—I would get the strange feeling that I was also cleaning or sewing something else as well, something that I was not allowed to see. The first time I spun and stitched; the second time I set up a loom and wove. Both times were heavy on the cleaning.

Several hours of scrubbing and stitching earned me a few scant minutes of lessoning. I would lay down and go into trance, and almost immediately I would have the sensation of falling from a great height toward the huge tapestry that is Their Work. It was so immense that I could only focus on a tiny piece of it at a time; its multicolored expanse stretched away in a curve like the rim of a planet that I was diving at. Each time, I landed on my own Thread, because They wanted me to start there. I was told to look for Threads that were attached to mine, or wound around it—my partners, my child—and study them, since I knew them fairly well. I was warned not to look forward to their deaths, or mine, as we were not to have that information yet and anyway, the future was not entirely set and to look at it might change things for the worse. There was a cold tone to that order that kept me from looking that far along the Threads, no matter how great the curiosity.

Then I was told to look at Threads that merely crossed mine, even if only for the moment. Some barely touched—acquaintances, people who had recently crossed my path, or were going to do so soon. This is what I would be looking for in a client, and if they were sitting in front of me I could use my own Thread as a reference point, since we would be crossing each others' paths at that moment. I was told to follow it as it wove along the surface, crossing other Threads—to this day I cannot describe the more-than-three-dimensional appearance of the Weaving, but somehow the Threads managed to cross each other in my sight without going beneath the surface of the fabric, which would mean births or deaths—and look for tangles and knots. Then I could "land" on that Thread and touch that knot or tangle, and "see" the problem.

Then came the next part—how to solve it. My first thought was to yank on the Thread and try to pull it out, but I was sternly discouraged from doing this by the Norn-voice. There was a vague and tumultuous vision (most of Their instructions, if you could call them that, came in the form of being hit over the head with brief and intense flashes of vision) of blindly pulling on something which pulled on something else which pulled on something below the Weaving and threw a whole bunch of other things out of whack, and me realizing that something was going wrong, letting go, and having part of that Thread recoil and wind around mine, sticking me to the problem. Right. None of that. So what to do?

A hand around mine—Urd's? Verdandi's? Skuld's?—and my hand was wrapped around the knot and thrust beneath the surface. It was like sticking my hand into icy water, and it hurt. Wait. Wait. (What am I waiting for?) Then, slowly—agonizingly slow, considering that my astral hands felt like they were freezing—a vision came of the individual doing some action, or series of actions... what they should do to unwind that knot. Them, not me.

The second lesson of the Norns, I cannot write about. They won't let me, and what They want, They get. But this one should give the beginning spirit-worker a good idea of what to expect from them, unless They do something entirely different with you... and why wouldn't They? No man can predict Them, even in their inevitability... which tells us something about true inevitability, doesn't it?

Blood and Bloodlines

Every culture's magical tradition is different. Not only do they differ in their signs and symbols, their Gods and wights, but there are always some mysteries that are deemed brutally important by one magical culture and dismissed by another. This means that each one has their own "specialties", which not all the others may share.

One of the most ambivalent "specialties" of northern-tradition shamanism is the magic of blood and bloodlines. Our Gods beget children on us as part of long-term breeding experiments; our divine pantheons argue about whose bloodlines are the best; we even have a patron goddess of genealogy. Some other cultures share these traits to a lesser extent—the Chinese, for example, have the Taoist immortals who sometimes mess with human bloodlines and create hybrids. In contrast, Kemetic (ancient Egyptian) magical tradition is entirely lacking in bloodline work; their Gods consider the entire field unimportant and prefer to concentrate on other specialties.

It is one of the things that most unnerved me when I started in training with the Northern deities. Bloodlines matter to them in ways that feel difficult for me, a modern American who was raised to be as anti-racist as it is possible to be while being Caucasian. To modern American sensibilities, one ought to be able to do anything regardless of what's in your genes. Even when we are chided for stealing the traditions of aboriginal peoples, it's stressed that what gives them the exclusive right to those traditions is their upbringing, their enculturation in an environment and a society where those traditions are pervasive, not their DNA. The issue of non-genetic people "adopted" into aboriginal cultures, and aboriginally-descended people who have not grown up in that culture but "rediscover" it later is a matter of confusion and argument.

When I learned the name—and saw the face—of the Goddess who had claimed me, I was rather chagrined that She was, indeed, one of the Gods of my Germanic ancestors. It made me vaguely worried, and I consoled myself with the fact that I had also had dealings with deities whose original batch of people never (as far as I knew) slid a single chromosome into my background. It is also true that this trend has continued, in that Hela does occasionally send me to work with deities outside of Her own pantheon, but that seems to be a Rökkr-god trait in general. In the meantime, I was slowly drawn further and further into the cosmology of those ancestors, almost against my will. I found that it was as complex and far-reaching as the multitudinous Greek and Egyptian pantheons that I'd studied in school. All too often mythology classes, books, and readings will stress the classical pantheons and ignore the Norse or Celtic ones save for a handful of stories and deities, usually treated more as children's folktales than as complex, adult myth cycles. The more I looked, the more I found otherwise.

Any cosmology with layers of deities and myth cycles that span long periods of time, especially when there are issues of conquered/conquerors and indigenous/outsiders, will reflect the problem of cultural—and sometimes even racial—tension. Sometimes it does more than that. Sometimes it lays it outright on the table, and that's uncomfortable for all of us. The usual response is to cling to the most favorably presented (which is usually the most recent conquerors), and demonize the oldest ones. Thus Zeus defeats the Titans, and Brahma and Vishnu take precedence over the older Shiva. In the Norse pantheons, the fact that the Vanir fight the Aesir to a standstill and require a truce is unusual, and one can only wonder about the history that was synchronous with that twist of the cycle. However, the Vanir seem to be presented as a similar sort of people to the Aesir, if culturally different, whereas the Jotnar are entirely different racially ... and when a god of the Aesir spawns with a giant/ess, the child is always a god of the Aesir, not a giant.

In *The Jotunbok*, I explored the UPG of those who work with the northern-tradition gods and the way that they do things, and the subtly racist attitude that some spirit-workers have noticed in the Aesir. Although some would consider it rude to say out loud, there is a common understanding among those gods that Aesir blood is stronger (or at least less malleable) than Jotun blood when it comes to breeding, and thus the children are always more sky-god than giant-god, and accepted as such. This strength of the Aesir (and Vanir, whose blood is equal to theirs in lack of malleability) bloodlines is used to explain why they and not the far more numerous Jotnar, and the equally powerful Rökkr, rule the top of Yggdrasil and are worshiped more strongly by the puny mortals of Midgard. (Although in terms of actual influence over every world in Yggdrasil, the Aesir cannot be said to "rule" the majority of individuals.) In other words, the very core of the northern-tradition myth cycles turns on a racial conflict and an assumption of superiority by the conquering caste.

This has been very, very hard for me to deal with personally ... especially as someone who is owned by the main deity of the despised "lower" race, and who carries their blood within me. I look at the fringe elements of the Heathen demographic—the racist neo-nazis—and although they are few and far between, and most of the northern-tradition folk try strenuously to dissociate themselves from this "fringe", the fact that they are there at all seems to reverberate back to the echoes of this ancient racial conflict that still burns today in the Nine Worlds. Of course, if you scratch any religion deep enough, you get to something unpleasant that you'd rather wasn't there, whether it's the Hindu caste system or the rapes of Zeus or Orthodox Jewish men thanking Jehovah that they were not born women, or Luke 14:26. No faith is immune to the bits that make you cringe ... but as spirit-workers, we need to at least be aware of the popularity of genealogy issues in our cosmology, if only because our Gods play with breeding experiments.

Part of that breeding is to get better qualities into the human species, including (but not limited to) magical powers. There is some evidence that the Gods keep up with our bloodlines, and where such powers came from. In *Hyndlujoth*, the tale of Hyndla, the goddess of genealogy, she recounts that: "All of the volvas are descended from Vidolf, and all of the vitkis come from Vilmeith, and all the seid-carriers (a term we will explore further in the chapter on *ergi*) come from Svarthofdi." Of the three, the first one is actually mentioned in Saxo's writing. He was an ex-soldier who managed to teach himself magic powers. The other two are lost in the mists of time, but it's likely that they had nonhuman bloodlines.

Another more clear example in myth is the god Rig/Heimdall, who is made mortal and sent to be raised in Midgard, where he sires children in every (carefully justified) class, thus getting more of Odin's blood into the population. There are numerous examples in historical lore of rulers whose claim to thrones was the blood of Gods in their veins, such as the Ynglings who gave England its name, descended from Ingvi/Frey during his sacrificial ceremony. As the worlds come slowly back together, Jotun blood and Rökkr blood is showing up more readily in the populace as well, and one can only assume that as other worlds pull into line, we will see more Vanir, Alfar, Aesir, and perhaps Duergar blood in the new generations. Ancestors matter to our Gods, all of them, whether we like it or not.

However, when I say that the "bloodlines matter", that doesn't mean that they are only interested in people with specific northern European bloodlines. Certainly, those do interest them, but sometimes they will also grab someone who has none of those bloodlines and work with them, especially when one is talking about the Rökkr Gods and Jotun wights. Remember that they are very close to Nature, with all its inherent chaos and randomness, and Nature sees diversity as wealth. To them, grabbing a worthy person of foreign blood is a good way to integrate them and their gifts into the Northern lines. Separatism is in opposition to the natural cycles of both this world and of the Otherworlds. Even among the Aesir, the children of their etin-brides are accepted as heirs to Asgard, and allies who prove their loyalty are valued.

Besides, I believe that this is one of the ways in which we have the chance to actually teach our Gods something new. I've mentioned this before and gotten rounds of incredulity from those who see the Gods as unchanging and unchangeable archetypes, but to those of us for whom they are real People who can learn new skills and ideas, influencing them through our thoughts and deeds is not unthinkable ... not because we are "changing the thoughtform", but because if enough of us who work with them do it, they will notice. If enough of us say that it is wrong and dishonorable to consider another race inferior just because they are very different, then maybe the message can get through. The Gods are capable of learning too. The *lwa* and *orisha* of the Afro-Caribbean religions have adapted to their Catholic overlay, because that was the only way for them to be able to come down. Our Gods, too, can see us refuse to carry on old hatreds, and they will notice.

When it comes to spirit-work, you will probably run into people who have need of wisdom about bloodlines, whether you like it or not. Some folk have old blood-curses running down their genetic histories, for example. This isn't as punitive as the Old Testament idea of "the sins of the father being visited onto the sons", it's just that sometimes people do things that get tangles stuck in their Wyrd that are passed down through generations, messing with people's luck over and over again. The most prevalent reason for this is a deal with a deity or wight that was forgotten, ignored, or deliberately broken, and the mess was passed on to the individual's children. This may seem unfair, but it's just natural law. It's not fair when a pregnant mother takes a medication or a man is poisoned with Agent Orange while in a war, and their children are born with deformities, but it happens. The best thing to do is not to frame it in terms of blame, but in terms of fixing problems.

While much of this is covered in the chapters on luckworking and wyrdworking, suffice it to say that if you think that a "curse" is stuck to the bloodline, then you need to follow that line back through history in order to find the source. It's not unusual for bloodline "curses" to manifest over time as a gradual increase in genetic health disorders, some of which are strangely resistant to any form of treatment whether it be magical, natural, or technological. It's also not unusual for people with these curses to become attracted to each other and spawn children—a fact which I cannot explain except perhaps in terms of "like attracts like" on some cosmic level—therefore multiplying the levels of blood-curses. Biology being what it is, just untangling the threads will not make genetic diseases go away, although it may make them less resistant to magical healing and perhaps prevent them from being passed on.

It's your job as the spirit-worker to explain things to clients with these problems as honestly as possible. If there is anger towards the past, stress that forgiveness is part of working this through, if only because it's unhealthy to go around carrying that kind of anger towards people who are long dead. People do things for reasons that seem right to them at the time. They may have been in desperate circumstances, with many lives depending upon them, and barely understood the deal that they were offered, or even the nature of the dealers, but only knew that this was their only chance at survival. And really, survival was the baseline of what our ancestors had to give us. If they didn't survive, we wouldn't be here, or at least not as we are now.

It's important to keep those things in perspective. There are choices that you make every day—in the food you eat, the place you live, the activities that you take part in—that will help decide the future for your own children, and everyone else's. We can't fairly berate our ancestors for being short-sighted until every one of us is walking far more lightly on this Earth—and who knows what devil's bargains we will need to make in order to keep our world going for our descendants? This is a point than can be stressed when dealing with ancestor anger: the best possible way for you to channel that anger is to be more mindful of your own choices, so as not to make mistakes as destructive as theirs.

On the positive side, once in a while you will find that a genetic line has a *kinfylgja*, or guardian spirit who watches over the line. Sometimes this is a dead ancestor; sometimes it's a nonhuman spirit who has formed a relationship with a dead ancestor and looks after their descendants out of fondness; occasionally it may even be a deity or major wight (or family of deities/wights) who has attached Themselves to that lineage. In the latter case, you can bet that it's because that human lineage bears Their blood in it somewhere back along the line, due to ancestors who coupled and conceived while being possessed by Them. A *kinfylgja* will often intercede when blood-curses or other problems become life-threatening enough to interfere with the survival of "their" people; they have also been known (especially in the case of deities) to matchmake for purposes of breeding qualities into "their" line. (My own family seems to have Hela and her entire family as *kinfylgjar*, as we are thick with Iron Wood blood in both lines.) A family may have no idea that a *kinfylgja* exists, much less that they are being aided by one, so it's up to the spirit-worker to check on that. If there is one, help can often be negotiated, or at least clear insight as to what needs to be done in order to clean up a mess.

The Power Of Bloodlines
by Lydia Helasdottir

There's a strong emphasis on ancestors needing to be, if not propitiated, at least acknowledged in this tradition. While it is uncomfortable and politically incorrect, it would be foolhardy to deny that there is power in the bloodline. In our work, we have this whole concept of the Lines, and the Lines are basically genetic, and they are what control and have guardianship over the heavy power in the land. There are some lines that are very strong over here in Europe. They just periodically incarnate again and again into the same family; there's always one of them back. And the families know that; these are the great matriarchs. Number One matriarch will bear Number Two matriarch, who will bear Number Three matriarch, and by that time Number One is ready to get born again, so they really dictate and tyrannize, to a certain extent, these entire line structures.

This is why you tend to get these creepy, slightly inbred guys in some places in Europe. You'll be traveling along and you'll get to some village, and you'll notice these slightly inbred-looking, not terribly gifted person, but the stink of power on them is huge, and what those are is the servants of those lines. They are the reservoirs of power in those lines, the sleepers, whose job it is to pass the power and the bloodlines on to the reincarnating ones, and a well that the linefolk can draw from. They're the peasant of that bloodline rather than the aristocrat. And that's a pretty corrupt setup; it wasn't always corrupt, but it's very corrupt now.

There's a school of thought in combat magic that says that lineage stuff is basically impossible to defend against, because it's inside you. Unfortunately, as I mentioned, most of the lines are corrupt. Like it or not, I think that the strictures of those high-class lines were based upon a king tied to the land, and were kept in order by that, and since we don't have that any more, anywhere, they became corrupt. The power of the lines, which was originally there in order to serve the land, is no longer constrained to do that. It's like aristocracy that's gone decadent because the King isn't doing his job. It's the corrupt aristocracy of subtle energy mechanics. It shows itself in the increasing distance from the richest to the poorest, the amount of wealth and the societal power that is held by a very small number of people. You can see it in all these "narrowings" at the top.

What can be done about it? Competent magicians with awareness of their backgrounds and line affiliations need to work together to assist the deities to chastise those lines to behave. Many bloodlines have subtle gifts, but these lines have, as part of their gifts, temporal power. They had received power in order to do the work of keeping the crops growing and the cycle going, and when the Kings were no more, they just used that power of wealth and fertility to suit themselves, because the power itself didn't get taken away, just the requirement to use it for the greater good.

And there's no actual reason for them to stop, by the way, either. It's very hard to motivate them to not do it. The money keeps pouring in, they have good succession, they have done a breeding program so that they generate powerful babies, the houses are there, the lands are there. Why should they do anything else? It's very sad, because those were originally the families who had sworn fealty to the kings and the queens, as representatives of the land as a holy thing. They are often at war with each other, though, which is fun, because territory is never enough. The Balkans is a land war, always will be. That won't stop, because it's the same people incarnating over and over, and the hate just gets bigger and bigger … or the greed does. And it tends to happen, since their magical power comes from their line and not from their attainment, that they tend not to pay that much attention to Deity because they can get power without having the collusion of any deity. It comes with the office, with the hat, with the old structure. Bloodline power is such that it can't even be switched off all that easily.

How do I feel about bloodlines in our faith? It is what it is. It's in the Germanic traditions, it's in the Celtic traditions, it's in all the northern stuff I've ever seen. I don't believe that it precludes people who are not from that bloodline from accessing the technique. I think the deities are quite capable of choosing who they work with and altering them properly, if they want them to access that stuff in a way that someone with the bloodlines could. It's much harder to work with a particular system if you don't either have the "code" for it, or have a deity connection to create that. It's sort of like being pre-hardwired to interface with those deities if you're from there. If you're not, you have to build an interface, or the Gods have to install one, which they are perfectly capable of doing. You don't have to have that "code" to work with any given deity who wants to work with you, but the "code" helps people work more powerfully with the system.

If nothing else, purely from a psychological point of view, the Monkey Mind getting in the way is one of the most common reasons for loss of magic, and if Monkey Mind says, "But I'm not of this culture!" you can say goodbye to 70% of your throughput, before you even start talking about DNA. Just thinking "This is my bloodline, this is my right, I can get power from this!"—well, applied emotion is power. The deeds of my ancestors, the things I have to live up to—or fix, or atone for; these are all very great stores of work to be done and power to tap into.

There's also the power of tapping into the land when several generations have lived there, but I don't think that's a racial thing, I think that's a familial thing. The distinction is subtle, but significant. There is the problem of most Americans being on land that is foreign to their ancestors. Some of the bogeys came over with the people, but they're not the land. Now, the land does reach out to people. It's more interested in how "juicy" you are than who your ancestors are. Still, if the land has a choice between a whole lot of people who are "juicy", then it may well prefer someone who is "juicy" in the same flavor that it's used to. I have noticed that when going to the places where my ancestors come from, there's a huge ramp-up of my power. Now it may be just because those are powerful spots in general, but I feel it internally. Some pressure from power comes in from the outside and you can ward it off; but this comes from the inside and there's no warding it, because it's in the blood.

Blood is controversial for other reasons. Norse/Germanic religion in general has been said to be bloodier than other ancient faiths, and more preoccupied with death and violence. I'm not sure that I agree with that, as many ancient religions have been revived in a very euphemized way with all their modernly-unacceptable practices carefully covered up and denied. It may just be that fewer of the individuals who have revived Norse/Germanic religion are heavily invested in making it seem unbloody or nonviolent. However that may be, there is no question that the shamanic side of northern religion is probably fairly violent and bloody. When most people cut their own runes, they traditionally smear blood into the carving in order to charge it, and that's only one of the many ways that a spirit-worker will use it.

As a shaman, I've learned that my blood is one of the best sacrifices to a God, although I wouldn't necessarily hand it over to any spirit. While many Gods are fine with food or alcohol or the promise of some deed in their name, some of them want your blood, period. There is no way to get through spirit-work without learning to regularly shed a bit of blood for sacrifice, especially when working with darker deities—and you can include Odin in that category when it comes to blood-offerings, along with a few of the Vanir if you're one of the spirit-workers who interfaces with their sacrificial sides. And, in general, I've never seen any deity of this tradition turn down a sacrificial blooding of a sacred object, altar, place, etc. Your blood is your life force, and a bit of the code that built you. It's the most personal thing you have to offer. They like that.

However, there's no reason to open your veins every time you want to show appreciation. A little of the powerful red stuff goes a long way. I use a diabetic sticker for blood magic; a drop or two is enough. I've also found that when you start propitiating in this way, you may be in the middle of doing some ritual or magical working (or perhaps just handling a natural object that *could* be made sacred, like a tree branch) and suddenly "accidentally" cut yourself. I take that as a sign that Someone wants an offering, now, and don't get angry or upset over it.

Actually, these days, I tend to see any accidental shedding of blood as a sign that Someone wants Something done. Even if it's just a hangnail or a cheese grater scraping my knuckles, I'll ask if there's something that I should do with this blood. If nothing comes up immediately, I'll save it—perhaps on a bit of cloth, which is allowed to dry in a safe place—because more often than not something will happen later that week which requires a bit of dried blood. I encourage spirit-workers to do this as well, especially those of us who are classic shamans who have died and come back. The blood of a walking dead man is very powerful magically (as is all our bodily fluids, enough so that there are reasons far beyond physical disease to keep them off of other people), and it shouldn't be wasted.

This may seem harsh of me, but I do believe that there is no place for squeamishness in a spirit-worker, especially when it comes to blood. This is a sacred and powerful substance, and we should never have an attitude of revulsion towards it. Yes, one could speculate that the fainting or fleeing reaction of some ordinary folk to blood might be considered a spiritual remnant of avoiding that which is taboo, *wih* or *ve*, too sacred for ordinary people to touch ... but we aren't ordinary. The proper attitude of a spirit-worker toward blood should at the very least be the attitude you'd take toward a horn of consecrated mead, especially if that blood is spilled in sacrifice. It is powerful, it is beautiful, it is the source of Life. To let disgust color your interactions with it is blasphemous, and you should work on purging that attitude at once.

To bring up blood and sacrifice will, of course, bring us to the question of sacrificing life itself, rather than just a small amount. (Here's the point in this book where some people are going to put it down and run away, or perhaps skip ahead, and that's all right: take what you will, I didn't write it for you.) The first difficult category is animal sacrifice. In the modern Neo-Pagan community, the practice of animal sacrifice is such a pariah that it is often used as an example of "what we don't do", a delineation between us and any "bad" spiritual groups. This has led to some hostility in both directions between the Neo-Pagan demographic and most Afro-Caribbean groups. It is also beginning to create rifts in and around some reconstructionist groups who are rediscovering this practice. Some do it because "that's the way that it was done back then", and they're going for authenticity, which I suppose is an odd form of ancestor worship. On the other hand, some of us do it because we've discovered that our Gods want it.

In general, a deity will not ask something of you that you cannot give them. If you live in a tiny apartment in the middle of a huge downtown metropolis, and the only meat you ever see is plastic-wrapped at the supermarket, they aren't going to demand that you slaughter a sheep in your back yard, three days from now. Also, not all Gods want such things; some would rather have worthy deeds done in their name, or maybe just a cup of good wine. On the other hand, if you live on a farm and butcher your own livestock next to Pagan holy ground—or you have friends who do it—some Gods may well ask for such things, especially if they were routinely offered them in the past. They are not going to accept any reasons for refusal that revolve around your comfort, either. This is, after all, a sacrifice.

I am not even going to address the issue of whether or not animals should be killed for food, as that would take up far more room than I have here, and is not germane to the span of this book. Suffice it to say that I am a farmer and homesteader, and I raise and butcher my own organic meat, and make sure that all my animals live well and die cleanly, and that will give you the main part of my stance on the subject. I don't live this way because my ancestors lived this way. I do it because I like to eat meat, my body responds well to it, I have a taboo about eating it (an agreement with the Hunter), and I don't trust meat from the meat-packing industry to be as clean as my own. However, this does mean that since we kill our own animals, we have no excuse when our Gods say that they want something sacrificed to them.

Some Pagans have pointed out that while our ancestors lived hand-to-mouth and even one livestock animal was a huge part of their wealth, that's not true for us today, and so animal sacrifice has no place in our lives. While the first part of that is true, I disagree with the second part. Our modern attitude towards death and the food chain is abominable. We have no contact with how our food is produced, and with how many things die so that we may eat—and that includes plants, many of which

I've found to be more intelligent than many small animals, just before I devoured them. Harvesting animals and plants without religion is considered to be fine, even if their bodies are processed horribly into corporate McBurgers and plasticized hydrogenated soybean oil, so long as it makes enough money. Our wrongheaded, disconnected, overidealized, undersanctified attitudes are offensive to the Gods of agriculture, the Gods of death, the Gods of hunting and herding, and many others as well. When we do this thing that is so hard for us, this thing that society says is wrong, when we force ourselves to witness and pray and see holiness and learn to have a respectful attitude towards it, we make a great sacrifice—and one that we need to keep making, again and again, until things in this world have changed.

The first time that I performed an animal sacrifice was in desperation. A very dear member of my chosen kin was in the hospital with leukemia, and he had taken a turn for the worse. In the morning, we received word that he was failing, and that we ought to come up and say goodbye. We got ready to go, and then discovered that our buck goat had come down terribly ill in the night. We were torn—was saying goodbye to him worth letting this animal suffer?—but as he'd been one of the people who'd taught me about farming, and how to care for animals ethically, we knew that he'd want us to stay and wait for the vet. She came, pronounced the goat terminal, and suggested that we put him out of his misery with a quick bullet. (It wasn't the first or the last time we'd had to shoot a livestock animal that was ill and couldn't be fixed, not just because we wanted meat.) As we got the gun and led him to the butchering place, I did a quick rite to Hela, asking her to take this sacrifice—not just of the goat's life, but of our tears and sorrow in having to do this—and give a worthy man one more year of life.

It worked. The next morning, we got a call that he had miraculously rallied and had come back from the edge of death. While his acute leukemia was not cured, he got one more year of life, and died at home in his wife's arms. After that, I never spoke ill of the practice of blood sacrifice again.

In answering questions about animal sacrifice, I've had to clear up a number of misconceptions. Here I have to disclaimer that I can only speak about what I have learned through experience with regard to animal sacrifice in my own tradition. I can't fairly cover that of any other religion; their attitudes and practices may be different. But first, the animal must die quickly and cleanly, with no pain, treated with respect up until the final moment when we put a bullet through their head—not period, but the most painless way. The meat is not wasted. It is shared among the people, as a sacred feast. The offal is not wasted; it is taken into the forest to propitiate the forest spirits, who never fail to send an embodied representative in the night to take care of it. The bones are not wasted; they are given back to the Earth or burned in the sacred bonefire or used to make sacred objects. The blood is not wasted; it is used to sprinkle the people with blessings, and to fertilize the Earth. The hide is not wasted; it is scraped and dried to be made into a votive object or drumhead. The energy is not wasted; it goes to be with the Deity in whose name we have made this sacrifice. The soul is not wasted; it goes on its way, with our blessing. To do otherwise would be offensive to the Deity we are honoring.

The most important thing, however, is the attitude of the people present. If you are going to do a blot with real blood as part of a group ritual—and all too often these days it falls to the spirit-worker rather than the godhi or gythia to do the difficult things, and this too is part of our job—screen the participants closely. Talk to them about how they feel about this, and what they are going to do if they are overcome with inappropriate feelings. Having a backup plan for them—such as just falling to their knees on the ground, eyes down, and reciting a prayer or singing a song to the deity over and over—is a useful thing. Far better that over half the folk kneel and pray or sing and concentrate on their words rather than their feelings than to have people start screeching or talking loudly about how they're going to throw up. Giving an honorable and comforting alternative to participants who turn out to be less sure of themselves than they thought is a good thing for all concerned.

If you, the spirit-worker, is told that you must sacrifice an animal to a Deity—and I can't promise you that this won't happen, because it's happened to a few that I know, especially when they were working with deities of Death who felt that their attitude toward same was lousy—

then it's going to be all about your attitude. Do whatever you have to in order to be able to do it reverently. It's even all right to weep, as long as it isn't crying over "Oh, the poor cute little bunny!" or even worse, "Oh, poor me that I have to do such a terrible thing!" Self-pity during this rite is blasphemous and will make it unacceptable. You will have to do a lot of difficult and painful things as a spirit-worker, and that's part of the deal. We are judged by how we get through them, so scrutinize your issues and tackle them.

When I finished writing the above piece on animal sacrifice, I figured that I was done, because of course we don't sacrifice human beings any more, right? In fact, giving up the (highly effective) magical act of human sacrifice is in itself a great sacrifice, one that we've made for social peace. My Boss, however, had different ideas on the subject, and told me that I had to write about it. I objected—surely you can't mean that, Lady!—and she replied that we sacrifice people all the time. Everyone who risks their life in the service of others' lives is a sacrifice. Soldiers, firefighters, police—anyone who knows that at the end of the day they could be dead, and that it is their job to put their bodies in harm's way, is a sacrifice.

Of course all those people want to live long lives, but the hard truth is that many of them don't. Part of taking on their jobs is the knowledge that they may be killed any day, and that can be seen as a sacred act. It can be a holy thing for them to be sanctified to the Gods when they take on these tasks, so if it happens their deaths are doubly useful. It's something to keep in mind when folk in those jobs show up as clients, and have various sorts of emotional malaise from the strain. There can be peace in understanding the nature of sacrifice, especially when it's your job this time around anyway.

Bloody Ritual
by Lydia Helasdottir

In the Pagan community, they say that the northern traditions are bloodier than the other ancient traditions. Whether that's true or not, they did come to use blood a lot for ritual purposes. I think that sacrifice is only worth anything if it's something that's dear to you. When you're living in a place as harsh as, say, the tundra, you don't really have very much that's dear to you that you can drop without starving or dying. Blood, you can live without some of your blood, so our tradition does have a fair bit of bloodiness about it. If you include in the northern tradition the island with all the Saxon stuff and their sacrifices, it does tend to go that way. We do use blood; we use blood for offerings to some of the more bloodthirsty deities, and as a transfer medium for energy, because it holds prana, it holds energy for a while after it leaves the body. So for us to transfer life-energy from us to an object, it's pretty handy. It's like radioactive paint.

There's also the fact that blood has a DNA component in it, so you are offering also the line of your ancestors; it's not just you asking for whatever it is, it's everything that has come to bring you to be. And when it comes down to it, it's the only thing that it really yours to give. Hacking actual body parts off makes you less useful to the Gods, as you need to heal those wounds, and then you can't use things, so it's the closest you can come to offering your own life. Bloodletting itself is a very potent conscious-altering mechanism. If you give a pint of blood, you'll know about it. It makes it a meaningful sacrifice, and it has a vast amount of power. The Aztecs used to use blood and cacao mixed together, and that's still a pretty potent mixture.

There's a difference between blood drawn from the vein and moon blood—a big difference, in terms of magic. Moon blood has a lot less prana. It has already been prepared to leave the body; in a sense it's already rejected out of the circulatory system, and it is already dying on its way out. Plus, that's going to happen anyway. It's like finding a Twinkie on the road and offering that. But then again, some deities prefer that, because they don't want you to be wounded.

There are issues in working with blood, though. First, anything you do with blood can be traced back to you, which is not always advantageous. Second, it does seem to make a pretty permanent link to whatever you've done. This can be handy because you can keep tabs on it from a distance, but on the other hand, if you're doing something like warding your rooms with your blood, then if the wards get broken it has a direct path into your veins. So in that sense it can be disadvantageous.

The Red Road:
Bloodwalking

by Raven Kaldera and Elizabeth Vongvisith

The more scientists study our DNA and our genetic code, the more qualities we find that are inherited, passed down to us through our bloodlines. These qualities can include psychic gifts, "ordinary" knacks and talents, personality quirks, diseases, and dysfunctions. Untangling a client's wyrd may have a lot to do with figuring out their genetic karma, and certainly it's useful for a healer to be able to trace physical disorders and see if they are genetic, teratogenic, or environmental in nature.

Bloodwalking is a form of trance-journeying that takes you down the bloodlines of your own or someone else's ancestral chain. During this procedure, you follow the strands of your bloodline back through your ancestors, seeing pieces of their lives and souls and essence which have been passed on to you. This can be used to look for diseases, or for karmic debts, or general confusion of *orlog* or *wyrd*. Bloodwalking works even if the individual in question is adopted and has no idea what their genetic bloodline is like at all. It can't necessarily tell them much about that—the information gained through bloodwalking is often more intuitive and subjective than the average names-and-dates genealogy— but it can perhaps tell them something.

Positive genetic qualities sometimes come with a price tag attached; the ancestors who bequeathed them to us may want us to carry on some kind of work or take on some kind of taboo in exchange for use of the gift. (Some people, on the other hand, are entirely free of karmic debts to their ancestors, and it may even be part of their *wyrd* to break off entirely with the *orlog* of their genetic line.) They may also come with vague ancestral memories, especially with bloodlines where people incarnate down the family line.

As far as I can tell, there's no rule dictating why some families have reincarnations that closely hug their family line and some incarnate all over the world, seemingly at random. Then again, the mechanics of reincarnation don't necessarily follow our meat-brain ideas of linear time. One individual that I knew, with a genetic background that was completely Scottish-Irish, had many incarnation memories of being in medieval Ireland and Scotland, lives that he could clearly see as being various side branches of his family tree. He also had memories of random lifetimes in Africa as some sort of tribesman, and Mexico as well. At first he wondered whether there was some hidden black or Mexican blood in his family, but a thorough search of his genealogy proved otherwise.

Then his daughter married a man of African-American extraction, whose ancestors came from the area he remembered in his prior incarnations. (In fact, he said that he recognized the man immediately when his daughter brought him home; they had been related once long ago.) His daughter proceeded to get pregnant and have three children. At some point he realized that he had been sticking to his family tree after all, but not just the tree of the linear past—he had been incarnating as ancestors of his current life's descendants. He says that he wouldn't be surprised if one of his grandchildren comes home with a Mexican-descended spouse.

(Note: It has been asked as to whether you can bloodwalk forward and see your descendants. As of this writing, we consider the future to be still in flux, so anything in that vein would be vague and no better than a simple divinatory reading. Things are never certain when you're going in that direction.)

Direct Trance Method

You can do bloodwalking without any props, or with the string system I've used, both of which are described below. It's assumed that if you want to try this, you've already had a good deal of experience with journeying and trancework (none of these are beginner techniques). To do it straight up, start by getting yourself into whatever position you use for journeying. Instead of concentrating on going *out*, concentrate on going *in*. Listen to your heartbeat, feel the blood pumping through it, and try to create a connection with your blood. Visualize yourself surrounded by it, swimming in a sea of your own blood. Go smaller and smaller until you can see the chains of DNA that are spun in every cell of your body. See these strands spinning away, toward the strands of the two people who made your body, and from there out further. Follow down the line of the strands, noting each "node" and seeing what images come up for that person.

> Usually when I journey or fare forth or whatever you want to call it, I come back with my body feeling tired, stiff and cold, but whenever I've done the bloodwalking, I feel as if I haven't been breathing enough and need more air, and I'm much more disoriented after doing this than after rambling around between worlds, oddly enough.
>
> –Elizabeth Vongvisith

As you see each node, each image, try very hard to simply absorb it passively. Don't allow your mind to reform them into some kind of romantic vision. I find that it's useful to stay very detached, so if they are unpleasant in some way, it doesn't upset me in the moment. The first time that you bloodwalk yourself, don't look for anything specific. Just see what there is to see and come back, and write it down. Eventually you may go looking for something, but start out just by visiting. You can visit any time you want; this is not a Netherworld, it's your own ancestry, and you carry it with you all the time anyway.

Sooner or later, you will learn how to travel to specific points in your line—to visit the lifetimes of various ancestors. You will also get a feel for how to move back and forth when you want, and possibly how to move from an "outside" perspective as well as moving directly through each person. For some people, moving around at will is easy from the start, while for others it takes more practice. However, because this isn't quite the same thing as journeying into another world, it's likely that you'll be able to move about fairly easily on your first attempt. Bloodwalking is essentially easier than going out of one's body because it's self-contained, and is not the same as faring forth into Otherworlds.

There are a handful of methods that you can use to Bloodwalk that involve physical objects, which can be a lot easier (especially when working with clients whom you barely know, rather than your own familiar ancestry) than just laying down and going out. One method is to use a large body of water, such as a calm lake, where you can stand in there up to your neck. Another method, demonstrated by Hyndla, is found in her lesson at the end of this chapter. Yet another is the multi-string method, which we delineate below.

String Method

I've found it useful to actually use string as part of the tranceworking process. Ideally, this string should be handspun with intent. (Good reasons to learn to handspin, or at least to have some spinners around who can spin with intent!) The intent should be the carrying of bloodline information. I suggest that the spinner ought to do some sort of invocation or short ritual to the Norns, asking for Their aid, and then spin the fiber while imagining people's family trees like many threads, crisscrossing and knotting together and growing new threads out of them.

For each bloodwalking—you will want a different one for each querent, unless they are siblings who share both parents in common— you will want a minimum of sixteen threads, about a yard long. You can have more, but it's difficult to keep track of more than sixteen ancestral lines at once anyway. I recommend spinning or having spun enough thread or yarn to be cut into about a hundred of these lengths, preferably in many different colors so that you can tell one from another by looking. Lay them all together in one fat skein. Place the skein in your lap, close your eyes, and pull sixteen threads out of the end of the skein. (You don't need to pull them all the way out until they're all chosen and your eyes are open.) If you do this work with a client, you will be blindfolding them and letting them choose the threads in the same way.

Put your threads together into a skein, and wipe a little of your own blood on it. It doesn't need to be any more than a drop, but it does seem necessary to charge the skein properly. When you do this for a client, you will need to explain that the blood is necessary. Have sterile stickers on hand, as well as antiseptic and bandaids. If they can't or do not wish to prick their own finger themselves, be prepared to don latex or nitrile gloves and do it for them. Practice on yourself or helpful friends first; as a professional, you don't want to be clumsy at any part of your job. Blood should always be treated as hazardous waste these days. (Alternatively, if the client is a woman between menarche and menopause, she can take the skein home to wait for her monthly bleed and dab a bit on it; if she's bleeding at the time of the visit, just send her to the bathroom with the skein. Menstrual blood seems to work just fine for this purpose.) Make sure that the blood goes on one area in the center of the skein, and loosely tie a bit of cloth around that so that you can avoid touching it; you'll be working with the ends of the thread. If possible, leave the skein long enough for the blood to dry before starting the journeying. The skein will now only be used for that person and their bloodline; have them take it home after you're done and put it on an ancestor altar, or at least keep it safely hidden.

Although it's best to start with your own blood and bloodline—it's there, it's in you, it's easiest and most familiar—it's sometimes tricky to go from doing this for yourself and doing it for a total stranger; the jump from the blood in your veins to the blood on a skein of yarn that you aren't actually touching can be tricky to make. If you have a lover with whom you regularly exchange bodily fluids, and they are willing to give you a drop of their own blood to ingest, you can do an intermediate step. During the half hour or so while their blood is in your body, before it is completely broken down, it will be easier to bloodwalk them than someone whose blood is only keying a charged skein, and it will give you practice.

We'll start this description assuming that you are working with your own skein. Go do some *utiseta*, or lie down, or do whatever it is that works for you for trancework. The first time that I did bloodwalking, I was told to go stand up to my neck in water while doing it. I went down to the local pond; it was after midnight and the fog was so thick that you could barely a few feet in front of you. I could see the edge of the water, and beyond that was an opaque wall of fog. It took a great deal of courage to force myself to walk in up to my neck, after which I was completely isolated in a white world with nothing but solid mist in any direction. But as I worked, the mist around me became like a projection screen, against which images were thrown up—an eerie but very useful effect. I stood there with the skein floating on the water and fumbled my way through it, and visions of my ancestors appeared around me.

If you want to work more closely within a specific line of descent, you also might consider using a string of beads as a prop, perhaps with a certain kind of bead for each known ancestor, and other kinds for unknown family members. You could use this in a manner similar to using a rosary in order to help facilitate your journey. Such a bead string can also be worn or carried as a constant reminder of your connection to the ancestors. For example, if your mother's mother's line is particularly important to you, you could construct a bead string for your maternal female ancestors and use it to bloodwalk along that line of descent. You can also connect different strands of beads together in the same way you would build a web of string as described above.

Whichever method you use, the sensations and feelings you may have while bloodwalking can be very different from those you get with other kinds of journeying. You may actually be able to move along the bloodlines from an outside perspective, drawing closer to investigate individuals. Or you might move directly through the blood, passing in and out of each person's lifetime, one after another. Sometimes there's a sense of claustrophobia. Sometimes, even if you've become experienced at bloodwalking, you might move very slowly and be forced to "push" your way through. At other times you could be drawn very rapidly along, passing individuals at great speed in order to reach a particular person or branch of the family tree.

You might also have vivid and sometimes difficult reactions to who and what you see, depending on what your relationship to your family is like or what kind of people your family members were. Even for those already experienced with trancework, bloodwalking for the first time may be intensely affecting in a way that other kinds of journeys usually aren't. If you managed to remain reasonably detached during the actual journey, you might still feel upset, angry, and/or emotionally drained afterward. This isn't a sign of a lack of skill or ability, but there may be some personal issues you need to address or some additional work you need to do to come to terms with the upsetting things you experienced.

As you move through your lines, you may also notice that some people may stand out from the rest of your family. The nodes representing them may glow brightly or attract you in some other way. This might signify that the person was psychically gifted and/or that they were a mystic touched by their gods, even though their religious beliefs might have been very different from yours. On the other hand, an ancestor's node having a darkened or threatening aspect could mean that something was especially wrong with that person, spiritually speaking. You might want to avoid such people but feel drawn to them anyway; they may have something to teach you, too. Use your own judgment and trust your instincts.

> My grandmother's side of the family was ... different. They "felt" peculiar in a way I couldn't really put my finger on. None of them were particularly out of the ordinary until I was far enough back for them to have been in "the old country" and came across someone who practically blazed with divine fire—I mean, burning like a torch in among all the ordinary people before and after him. I have a strong feeling this person was a priest or church official of some sort, a true "man of God," someone who undoubtedly said Mass in a state of grace ... although he can't have been too saintly, as the line of descent came straight down from him, indicating

that he'd fathered at least one child ... All of the brief glimpses I had into individual lives seemed to come at random, and I don't know that they're necessarily significant to me personally so much as maybe I just happened to see what I saw, if that makes any sense. My speculations about the priest are just that ... speculations, based on the fact that his life-energy felt different from that of the ancestors on my father's side who had psychic or magical gifts, and it seemed very Christian in a way I can't really describe.

–Elizabeth Vongvisith

Going back along your family lines may surprise you with what you discover. Or it might only confirm things that you have long suspected about yourself, your family, and your *hamingja* and *orlog*. It can bring you closer to your ancestors, even very distant ones, and reinforce your sense of place in the lines of your family. It may allow you to contact specific ancestors, or at least learn more about them. It can help you come to terms with a difficult family history, or reveal a hitherto unknown one.

When working with clients, if you're having problems figuring out the vast mass of leaves on that tree, or if you can see the lines but you don't know what's important or where the best information is, one of the things that you can do is to call upon an Disir who may be apparent in that family tree. This was something that I happened upon accidentally; I hadn't ever had any experience with Disir beyond vaguely reading about them. Then while I was doing a bloodwalking for a man who didn't have much information about his ancestry (and people who are adopted, or unsure of who their parents might be, will often be the ones coming for bloodwalkings) and I noticed two specific female "nodes" in his lineage, one on the maternal and one on the paternal side. Unlike other "nodes", which were rather like watching a movie, these two seemed to look right at me and impart vague information. It was as if they said, "Look, here is where I cam from, here is the gift that I gave to my children. See me, see the truth of this lineage!" One was a woman of central Europe in an embroidered peasant blouse who herded goats, the other an elderly Italian woman clad in black with a scarf on her head, fiercely and devoutly Catholic. They pointed me toward the information that he needed. Afterwards, I realized that I had just had a close encounter with the Disir of those two lines, whatever title one might use about them. They were the dead magical guardians, somehow, of the maternal DNA, and they knew the secrets of that line, and where to look for them. So a spirit-worker who is having trouble with a particular Bloodwalking might do well to call upon their client's Disir, and perhaps give them a gift of propitiation afterwards, or ask the client to do so on their own.

Hyndla's Lesson

Bloodwalking

I went to see Hyndla because I'd started bloodwalking for clients. However, the method I had to utilize in order to do it was fairly difficult; I would go to the local lake and stand up to my neck in water, holding onto a handspun thread. The other end of the thread was held by the client, standing on the shore. No doubt some of them were rather bewildered to have to go along with this, although I suppose they mostly just decided that it was part of some weird shamanic thing. But as I live in New England, this rendered bloodwalking impossible for the five months of the year when the local bodies of water were too cold to enter, and often frozen over. I needed a better way to do it, and I couldn't seem to figure it out on my own.

(I get the feeling that many people, while reading these stories of my experiences, will be vaguely disappointed in the way that I continually fail to figure things out on my own and have to resort to the Gods and wights to help me. I can only say in my defense that I have the limitations I was born with, as does everyone, and I haven't gotten to where I am through the sudden development of great super-powers. Instead, I struggled my way up this mountain on my own, and often I had to ask for help—and still do. I hope that my relating my struggles, especially in areas where my native talents didn't cut it, will be of more help than some fantasy of "I just automatically knew how to do everything, because I'm Mr. Super-Shaman!")

After a year of bumping my head against the problem, I pathwalked into Jotunheim and slogged my way up the northern mountains. I'd already asked Hyndla for the appointment, and made her an offering, so I was expected. I knew that she has a bunch of loyal storm-giants who guard her cave and make sure that she isn't bothered or molested, and I didn't want to set them off or get in trouble. Since the air was calm and clear, I figured that I was all right—I got the strong feeling that their first line of defense would just be some nice blizzards to confuse and turn back the unwanted approacher.

The Hag of the Northern Mountains was waiting for me. She was tiny for a giantess, old and wrinkled with long silvery hair that draped all around her, and twinkling dark eyes. She was sitting on a stone platform bed on a pile of furs, and she bade me to come closer. I presented her with a gift, and told her my purpose, which she was already aware of. Hopping down from the bed with surprising *lightness for one so old, she circled me and sniffed me like a dog, nodding her head and clucking her tongue. Was she smelling my Iron Wood blood, or my human genes? Both, I suppose. She asked me how I'd been doing with the bloodwalking, and I explained my inability to do it outside of a large body of water on which to project the images. Hyndla chuckled and said something about there being a lot of the Snake in me.*

Then she ordered me to climb up on her bed and lay down, and I did, feeling a little strange. She hopped back up on the bed alongside of me, straddling me, and proceeded to poke at my belly in various places, whilst sniffing me further, and keeping up a constant stream of chatter in her creaky birdlike voice, which I will not repeat here. Then she told me that she could give me something which would help with the bloodwalking, if I wanted it. She seemed cheerful about it, rather than foreboding, so I cautiously asked what it would cost, and whether it might give me problems. "If you weren't sterile already," she cackled, "you would be after this! That's why most don't want it. Bloodwalking affects the fertility; even doing it yourself without my gifts will slowly make you barren over time, the more you do it. But you're already barren as a winter field, so it won't matter."

So I agreed, and she took her price, and in the process inserted something into my belly. I couldn't quite see what it was, but it was shaped like a narrow cone a few inches long. I can still feel it in me, astrally, just behind my navel. "The place where you are linked to your ancestors," she said as she did it. Then she explained to me how it could be used.

Hyndla's Lesson: Bloodwalking Bowls

Now it is simple—you make a bowl of wood, as big as you can, you paint the inside red, you put the Bloodwalking bind rune on it. Why, you silly thing, where are your wits? It is Mannaz, for the kin and kind, and two of Raido, one on each side, made from the Mannaz and facing in. One for forward, one for back. You should know that. Then you fill it with water, and you prick their finger and let fall a drop of blood into the bowl. And your thread—you know how to spin, of course, so spin thread for this purpose. No, it needn't be red, it can be any color. They will hold the thread, and you the other end, and the middle will fall into the bowl between you.

Then you let your mind go into the thread, and into their blood that soaks it. Yes, it is huge and confusing at first. Start with the parents. Yes, I know, you do not consider them all that interesting. But they are the closest, the most important. Look at them, at the color of the light that you see from their place in the blood-thread. Look closely, because they are the final culminations of their lines, and they combine to make this one.

Go outward, slowly. Slowly. Do not worry if they are sitting there impatiently. This is not to be done speedily, or you will miss things. As your run down the threads, the places where they branch off are like knots, like lights. Sometimes, once in a while, you will find a knot that is particularly big. If you look closer, you will see that there is a third thread running away from it. Perhaps even a fourth, although that is rare. Yes, that is how nonhuman blood gets into yours. You are nodding, you know how that works. Can a whole child of your world be born with only a human parent and a nonhuman parent? Yes, it can be done, but that is even rarer, and they do not live long, they are made wrong and they wither and die as babes.

To track flaws in the blood, that is the next thing. You feel the thread with your hands, you run your fingers down it—not into the water, you will disturb it—and think of that flaw, that problem of the body. You will see it running along the threads like a faint line. Perhaps it vanishes, then comes back in other generations—that happens. You can do this for the unborn child still in its womb, if you have the mother there—let her hold the thread to her navel, see it extending into her. You can see if the flaws in the mother's blood, or the father's, have taken hold in the babe.

Do I mean diseases, when I say this? Yes, that is part of it. But also there are debts, or things done that have made knots in the Threads that the Nornir work, and these can get caught in the blood-threads and passed down. Yes, sometimes they take the form of disease, sometimes ill luck or other things. There is not so much difference as you think. Cleaning those up? That you will have to take up with the Nornir, I only see things.

But the most important thing is that before you do this for them, they must honor their ancestors and make an offering. Such secrets are not to be plundered without giving honor to those who lived them. Have them go out and make an offering; it does not matter what. And the bowl with their blood, that should be carried outside and poured onto the Earth as another offering to those who came before them.

Making Whole:
Repair Of The Soul

I hesitated before putting in a chapter about this subject, but I felt pressured to write something about it, if only because people keep showing up as clients asking for "soul retrieval". They do so largely because they've heard about "soul retrieval" as some kind of neo-shamanic self-help method, much like beating sofas with foam bats or primal screaming, or at the least like some kind of new therapy. Blaming your emotional ills on the loss of your soul feels good to people; it means that whatever it is, isn't their fault, and if a spirit-worker can just get that piece back everything will be all right. The problem is that it's not that simple, and it's not that easy.

Before we get into retrieval of lost souls, we first have to define what the soul is, especially in the northern tradition. In the last section, the Soul Map form of divination gives a good overview of the soul-complex, and complex in this case can be seen not only as a noun but as an adjective. The Northern Tradition sees "soul" as being as multipartite as "body" ... and really, as complex as our bodies are, why shouldn't our souls equal them in that way? This means that if something does get lost, it could be any number of things, and the consequences would vary from hardly noticing to bad luck to illness to death.

Many cultures around the world have a concept of "soul" as something with many parts. The ancient Egyptians saw it as tripartite and sometimes even in five parts: the Ka (life force), the Ba (personality and mortal self), the Akh (immortal self), the Sheut (shadow), and the Ren (name). According to Sarangerel, the Siberian tribal conception of the soul is tripartite: the *ami* (the "body soul" which reincarnates), the *suns* (the carrier of past life memories, which goes to the Underworld after death), and the *suld* (the link to Nature and the Gods, which returns to Nature after death). In some shamanic cultures, an older shaman would literally give a piece of their soul to a younger shaman, in order that something of theirs would be passed on. In some traditions, such as that of the Altaic *kam*, the shaman-soul was a piece that had traveled from one shaman to the next on the advent of the first one's death, usually transmitted through family lines. So the idea of souls as being complex things which could lose or damage parts is not unusual in the rest of the world, or indeed in circumpolar Eurasia.

In researching this chapter, I wanted to cover not just what I and a few other spirit-workers in my tradition did when we "retrieved" souls, but what other people are doing when they bill a session as "soul retrieval". To this end, I researched a large number of practitioners who list "soul retrieval" as one of the services they offer, and carefully scrutinized what they were willing to discuss about their techniques. As is usually the case with modern nonspecific neo-shamanism, much of their language was carefully calculated not to force clients to actually believe in spirits or Otherworlds; there was a lot of talk about "nonordinary reality" and such. Some of the descriptions of the practitioner's methods included journeying to some other place and finding the piece of the soul in the hands of various creatures, or just wandering about lost, and it was recaptured and breathed back into the client. Others described putting the client into a light trance and talking them through "finding" the piece of lost soul themselves.

The gist of it was that, in their perception, pieces of a soul might flee the building if something very traumatic happens to the owner. Examples of this trauma were childhood abuse, the death of a loved one, combat, surgery, or even the breakup of a relationship. One practitioner went so far as to claim that "most of us" have lost pieces of our "vital essence" due to the trauma of most people's horrible lives. The frequently-recurring list of symptoms that indicated a missing piece of soul ranged from depression to "feeling disconnected" to "somehow feeling strongly that this procedure would be useful to you", and did not discuss how different missing pieces might affect people differently. Some stressed that soul retrieval helped people even when they weren't sure that they needed it.

Another possible way that people could lose a piece of their soul, according to this body of knowledge, was giving it to another person (usually a lover, although occasionally a child who they might want to protect) or having it stolen by another person (usually an ex-lover). Practitioners were willing to discuss the process of getting the person to take back the piece of their soul, but were reluctant to talk about what to do if the "thief" (or recipient) refused to give it up. It was stressed in these descriptions that people trading soul-pieces is never good, as they won't be "usable" to the recipient. (I assume that these folks would be horrified at the customs of the Altaic *kams*.) In my experience, other people's soul-pieces are unfortunately quite usable by some individuals, for a great number of purposes.

While I would never argue that many people have painful lives, and that life trauma can cause pieces of the soul to submerge or be damaged, it seems to me that what most of these practitioners are dealing with is not the soul (or the Otherworlds), but the mind and the unconscious. (One practitioner even said bluntly that what the mental health field calls treating dissociation is what shamans call soul retrieval.) That's not to say that this sort of "soul retrieval" can't be useful—it certainly can, especially when it allows the client to feel empowered in helping their own mental healing—but it is not the kind of external thing that most of them claim it, sometimes in a sideways manner, to be. It's more a kind of hypnotic psychological self-help, aiding people to find parts of themselves that they have stashed in their own personal dark basements. The reason that this is a good thing is because A) most people's "missing" parts, the vast majority of the time, are just repressed and not accessible, and this is a very good treatment for that; and B) the fewer people actually wandering around in Otherworlds, fumbling after possibly lost soul parts, the better.

In our tradition, as I pointed out above, we see the soul as having many different parts. Any one of those could be blocked, damaged, hidden, fled, or captured (although the latter two are far more rare than most people would think). This means that if someone comes in asking for a "soul retrieval", and something actually does come up missing, it's important to know which part it is, because that will give you a clue to where it's gone. Some parts don't leave without completely debilitating the individual, and you won't be finding them on your doorstep asking for help (although you may be called in by worried people to look at an unconscious body, if you're someone that they trust to deal with the problem).

Having, in the past, lost a piece of my soul-complex through damage and having had it grow back, I can say that the soul-complex is indeed made to regenerate. While some pieces may theoretically get "lost", more likely they get destroyed and just need time to grow back. The part that grows back is often even stronger than the one that was lost, as the soul-complex adapts to difficult circumstances. I worry about folks who do "soul retrievals" without first checking to see if something's actually gone entirely, not hanging out in an Otherworld (assuming that they are of the minority of practitioners who actually work with Otherworlds, and not just inner worlds full of people's mental sock puppets). I worry because if you've got someone with a hole in them, and you open them up spiritually and open up a door to another place, and say, "Come on, little piece of Soul, come on back," and that piece of soul can't come back because it is destroyed, there's a very good chance that *something* will show up and take its place. Perhaps something opportunistic, perhaps something predatory.

There is also that problems can occur not because a piece is missing, but because a piece has entered that wasn't there to begin with. I'm quite convinced that a few people I've treated who had multiple personality disorder have one or two "riders" in their heads, along with the various "alters" that were originally split off from the core. When someone has that many cracks in their *huge* and *mod*, it's not hard for something small to slip in and make itself at home. It's then in that critter's best interest to keep them continually in that state, never in a safe enough space to heal and integrate, because then it might get ejected. A good spirit-worker will check for "riders" as well as missing pieces, because one can take the place of the other. If you aren't sure what's what, do some divination on the subject.

Soul Work
by Lydia Helasdottir

What do we, in our tradition, actually consider the soul to be? There are many definitions. You could take the definition that takes in all of the parts except for the meat and the energy body directly associated with it. For most people who come for soul retrieval, it's not so much that something is missing as that it's damaged. Missing means ... well, missing where? Where did you go and lose that bit then? Some people will claim that it was stolen, but that's an ego thing—"I'm important enough that some entity came and stole a part of my soul, which means that I am that special and interesting," as opposed to: "I was dumb and did something stupid."

I think trauma damages parts for sure. I've experienced two different things happening. Either that part goes and lives in a safe place, either inside the person or with their patron deity, or it goes somewhere quite separate from the body, perhaps in another world. Or it could be that trauma happens, and that bit gets damaged, or even killed. Usually just damaged, though. These things are made to regenerate.

I have seen very rare cases where some nasty black magician has come and taken your soul away and turned you into a zombie, but that's damn rare. There are plenty of entities out there who can do that, but there's a price to pay when they do that. Unless taking you out is really, really worth it to them, it's too much of a bother—and for it to be worth it, you are probably really good at what you do, in which case you should be pretty well defended. And if they do kill someone—or, I should say, disconnect their soul from their body— that soul goes on as if it were a literal death, but the body keeps walking. Another soul might come to inhabit it, or it might just keep living. But they won't show up in your office asking about soul retrieval, because they will not be aware enough to know that anything is wrong. There will be nobody there to ask for help.

So if someone comes in saying that a piece of their soul is gone, it's likely just damaged, and it will regenerate. As long as the top part, the part that is attached to deity, is still there, the rest tends to fill itself in again slowly … unless it's been put somewhere for safekeeping, or unless the damage was so great that it's having a hard time restoring itself, and it's not getting better quick enough to live. Then you need to either accelerate the healing, or build scaffolding, or do a transplant, or build a clone. For me, whenever I see this, I ask their patron deity or guiding spirit what to do.

Missing bits that have been put away for safekeeping—those I can certainly go find. Most of the time they've just hidden them internally. But then you have to say, "Do you realize what's going to happen when you bring this back on line? It's going to be scary and unpleasant and ugly. Are you ready for this?" I usually have them do a month's worth of prepwork—purifications, meditations, imaginings of what it would be like to have the full thing working again, and preparing a welcome for this bit that they've locked away in the cellar for years. It's like you've locked your child in the cellar for ten years. How is it going to feel when Mommy finally remembers it's there and comes for it? Prepare yourself to be Mommy under those circumstances.

I think that it's diagnosable from the condition that the person's in. You can figure out if there's a bit hidden away, or disconnected. People sometimes disconnect the entire emotional body. They have emotions, but they immediately go away. It's not in the cellar, but nobody's talking to it; it's walking around in an empty house calling and hearing nothing. That's usually just about awareness and reintroduction. For the ones that are locked away, I tend to go down and talk to them first, and prepare them, if they'll let me. On one occasion, Hela had me go down and relocate the creatures inside to another place, so that she could work on them, so that when they did become integrated, it would be more possible. But I haven't seen that a lot. So the basic advice on soul retrieval is that you'll rarely be asked to do it. What you will have to do frequently is repair.

So that brings us to the next question: repair. The first part of diagnosis is to figure out what's wrong, piece by piece. Be aware that none of these pieces works in isolation, and if one part is damaged or missing, the other parts will attempt to compensate, and will likely get thrown out of whack in the process. Someone with soul damage likely has soul sickness throughout their complex; only very strong parts will escape that, and they'll likely be strained from shouldering more of the work. (It's more like a body than most of us like to think.) Start with a soul map reading to figure out what's wrong where, and do an in-depth separate reading (I drop at least three runes) on each remaining part.

Then focus on the damaged or missing part, and try to find out what happened to it. If you can't, go on without that information. Why it's good to know these things is pretty much only to figure out if it happened due to stupidity on the part of the client (which might happen again) or to external circumstances that might repeat themselves (like a family curse or a lover who is an unethical spirit-worker). On the off chance that it is actually gone from the person's soul-complex and you end up going after it, be careful about taking it into your body. Some shamanic workers will actually breathe it into themselves, and then breathe it out again into the client, but this takes practice and care. If it is fairly traumatized (and this holds especially true for the *mod*) then it may perceive you, the spirit-worker, as being a safer haven than the person to whom it belongs, and it might stick in you and be difficult to leave. It might be better to have an object that is charged to be a "trap" that will suck up the piece of soul and spit it out again.

The list below goes through the parts of the soul as they manifest on the Soul Map, piece by piece, and what possible symptoms of damage or loss might be, and how to deal with that. Remember that if you are going to help someone with soul damage, it's best not to go around looking for the wrong thing. Sometimes the client might even have a wrong idea of what's damaged or missing, so it's best to check first.

Hame. This is never missing, if the person is alive and conscious. If it's entirely gone, their body is not going to be moving or even responding. That probably means that they have gone out of their body and not come back, either because they are stuck somewhere, or because they have decided to leave and not come back. If you are looking at someone in this condition, it is probably because frightened people have summoned you to find a comatose person, and this is very rare. The astral body is a big thing, and it doesn't just disappear from trauma. It's deliberate. It will, however, still be connected by a cord, and you can find and follow that. Start by simply finding the cord, tugging on it, and calling them home. If that doesn't create a response, you may have to go out after them.

If the individual is a spirit-worker and journeys often, they may be stuck somewhere. In this case, you can journey out yourself to find them, which may involve laying down next to their unmoving body and faring forth while keeping some physical link to them—holding their hand, etc. Being as a trapped spirit-worker is probably dealing with something that could eat you just as well as them, it may be wise to fare forth with monitors who have orders to forcibly yank you back (by whatever means you give them) every five or ten minutes. It's better to go someplace in fits and starts than to get stuck there as well. However, this can also have its drawbacks. In fact, you might want to team up with another spirit-worker in a case like this; more is better and you can watch each others' backs. Of course, even that doesn't always work; one might recall the tale of the two shamans who were chasing down a missing soul-piece that was held in a trap, and one of them dropped dead in the middle of it, to the horror of the onlookers.

If you're not dealing with another spirit-worker, but simply an unlucky person who somehow managed to get out of their body and go someplace far away, the likelihood is that you'll be able to get their attention with the cord, and perhaps pull them back from wherever they are. In some cases, the individual has left deliberately and does not intend to return, but is not physically dead just yet. In that case, ask the Powers That Be whether it is your *orlog* to go after them and convince them to return. It may not be. If you're not sure who to ask about this, try the Nornir; they may be standing by with the scissors for a reason. For that matter, if you can't find a cord, it means that the *hame* has separated from the body entirely. Severe brain damage, to the point of a vegetative state, can do this. Generally, death will follow fairly soon, even with life-saving procedures—we've seen mysterious pneumonia set in, in spite of all that's done.

Repair of a damaged *hame* requires a lot of *ond*, or energy. Like the physical body, it will heal in time, and indeed feeding up the physical body and making sure that it gets enough nourishment and exercise can help. Conversely, damage to the *hame* will affect the physical body, possibly bringing on illness and malaise, lowering the immune system. This is where infusing the person with a lot of energy can help—from the earth, from other people, from the Gods if possible. Unlike the physical body, the *hame* can generate lost limbs and organs. If for some reason they aren't coming back, there is probably something going on with the individual's Thread, and they may need to craft an enchanted prosthesis, or apply to the spirits to give them one. Be aware that there may be a price. Some wights have given flesh or limbs to a human *hame*, but that flesh isn't human, and acts as such. This can be a gift as well as a problem—Fey feet can run fast, a Jotun nose can smell better, and so forth—but it may also bind them in obligation to that tribe of wights for the rest of their lives.

Litr. This vital force generally isn't missing per se, but it can be either blocked or being leached away by someone or something else. 99% of the time the problem is just that it's badly blocked, to the point where the individual can no longer feel it. Symptoms are lack of vitality, chronic boredom and exhaustion, anhedonia, everything seeming "flat", and—most importantly—a badly impaired sex drive. Usually there isn't a severe depression, just vague unenthusiasm for most things. Blocked *litr* can be caused by mourning, traumatic memories, rape or sexual abuse, gender dysphoria, or certain psychoative medications. It can also be caused by repressed anger, but if that's the case then we aren't talking about being a little pissed for a while, we're talking about decades of seething rage that has been shoved down and covered with a candy-coated smile. Indeed, working out anger is a good beginning for blocked *litr*, as is sex magic (if that's a possibility). A spirit-worker who moves energy can try to unblock the root chakra, which is where the *litr* hides, but a severe block is not going to be able to be shoved open without damage unless the underlying symptoms are dealt with.

If someone else is draining their *litr*, it's likely to be a lover—unlike other parts of the soul, to get to the *litr*, you have to have access to someone's root chakra, and generally only lovers will have that kind of access. In any case, that's a relationship issue that needs to be worked out between them. Giving the lover access to the genitals while blocking the *litr* from them will only succeed in blocking it from the owner of those genitals as well, and you don't want to make things worse. Suggest a relationship reading, and a confrontation if necessary. You might also want to give them a talk about boundaries.

Good sex is also the cure for a damaged *litr*. Generally, damage to this area will be the result of rape or sexual abuse, ongoing gender dysphoria, or surgery that damaged the physical body in the area of the reproductive organs. The best way to fix it is to gently keep sexual energy flowing there as much as possible. While this seems like a contradiction in terms—when the *litr* is damaged, people generally don't want to have sex—tell them to start slow and build up their capacity for it. Daily grounding is a good thing too, especially if the earthy energy is brought up through the root chakra and allowed to sit there a bit, cleansing and healing things.

Vili. The *vili* is also more likely to be blocked than missing, although if it is missing, you can bet that someone else has got it. Mostly, though, it will be blocked, and the person in question will be suffering from a lack of "spine"—courage, decisiveness, and the ability to stand up to others. There may be a good deal of limpness and doormat behavior, or just continually wanting to "go with the flow", even in cases where action to change the flow might be better suited. The third chakra may be soft and spongy to the touch. In very rare cases the *vili* might be being held by another—usually a lover or spouse—and in this case you can bet that it was freely given, and like the situation with *litr*, there needs to be some relationship counseling in order that it might be taken back, or they'll just give it over again.

However, usually it's just blocked—often due to a childhood where the will was repeatedly stomped on—and can be unblocked with difficulty. Expect a huge amount of anger to come up in the weeks following the unblocking of the *vili*. Expect it to be poorly aimed and to spill out onto undeserving bystanders. Warn the client about this problem. They will need to relearn—or, perhaps, learn properly for the first time—how to control their will, rather than letting it run amok. It's a lesson that most people learn in adolescence, unless they have been blocked throughout this time.

Healing a damaged *vili* is like walking on a mostly-healed injured leg, or moving with a healing muscle. A physical therapist will tell you that never moving any painful healing part is the wrong approach to take, leading to atrophy and shrinkage. In the case of the healing leg, you keep thinking that it's not going to hold you—and maybe, sometimes, it won't—but you won't get it to be strong again unless you get up and keep going anyway. Healing the *vili* requires using it constantly, day in and day out, making decisions and commitments and keeping them even when it's difficult. It can be exhausting. Remind the client of the physical therapy comparison, and remind them also that while they can take rests from the exhausting chore of building up the will, even those rests should be actively chosen and not just a matter of collapse.

Unlike healing other parts of the soul, making the *vili* stronger is very much a solitary task. Depending on the help of others—including you, the spirit-worker that they are consulting—will make it tempting to fall back into the pattern of leaning on others, and will just continue the atrophy. This is something that you should be acutely aware of. People with a damaged *vili* will often trigger an instinctive nurturing response in a service-oriented or caretaker-type spirit-worker, and it's exactly the wrong reaction. Keep your emotional distance and keep telling them that they have to go it alone. If you can stand it, encouraging them to get angry at you may help things. Confronting you, the authority figure, with that anger is a step in the right direction; don't punish their attempts at willfulness by squashing it, trying to defuse conflict, or becoming defensive yourself. Instead, acknowledge it, tell them that they have the right to be angry, and encourage them to aim that in a constructive direction.

Mod. The *mod* is one of the most vulnerable parts of the soul complex. Not only is it the most prone to being blocked, pieces of it can sometimes be given away or flee in terror. It is the most prone to being damaged or even killed off ... but it is also amazingly regenerative. I've had most of my *mod* die off due to decades of trauma and pain, and although it took a few years (and I was seriously emotionally blocked during that time) it did grow back entirely. The characteristic hole in the heart chakra that is the mark of a damaged *mod* will be obvious to anyone with the Sight. The heart chakra area will seem flaccid and empty, not strongly energetic.

The *mod* is the thing most often dealt with by neo-shamans, because it is the most likely to be damaged in childhood, and it is also the most likely to be helped by the kind of psychological guided meditation that many of them perform. However, the most common problem, as usual, is blockage. As one might expect, this is often due to various sorts of emotional trauma, generally in childhood. The outer symptoms of walling off the *mod* are disconnection from the emotions, repression, and a profound lack of empathy. The *mod* can be damaged as well as blocked off; this is actually fairly common, as the instinctive response to having one's *mod* damaged is to protect it in some deep, safe place in the unconscious parts of the soul. If the *mod* is damaged but not blocked off, there can be a great deal of emotional instability, so walling off the regenerating *mod* is not necessarily a bad thing. Since it will heal itself, keeping it protected until such time as it is ready to emerge can actually be useful.

The problem comes when the individual has unconsciously hidden their damaged *mod* away in childhood, and forgets that it was ever there. The *mod* comes back to functionality while still in the dark place it's been stuck in, and if it can't get out, it will begin to turn dark and twisted. Then, when it's rediscovered (or bursts out), it will take quite a while for it to be retrained to anything resembling normality. In many cases, it will never be quite normal, but it must be cared for anyway ... because it's what they've got. For spirit-workers, this is especially necessary, because a well-functioning *mod* is crucial to being an ethical spirit-worker. The connection to *wod* will not be healthy unless the *mod* is healthy. The spirit-worker with a damaged *mod* can still connect with spirits, but they might inadvertently attract destructive ones, and they will not be able to connect with the Rules behind the work, which explain which actions are acceptable, and which are not. Spirit-workers with blocked or damaged *mod* problems tend to get in trouble with the forces of Wyrd.

The best medicine for healing a damaged *mod* is love. If the person has no family, they can offer themselves to do good works, or perhaps they can care for animals, many of whom will be fairly unconditional in their love if treated well. The other necessary medicine is time. While the *mod* is amazingly regenerative, it takes its time to do so. Advise the client not to rush things, and to make sure that it isn't walled in when it needs to get out. I find that encouraging them to visualize the healing *mod* as a creature incubating in an egg, perhaps in their heart chakra, is useful. It creates an expectation that the "egg" will hatch when the time is right.

If the *mod* is actually lost, or if a piece of it is gone, it has probably either been given away or it has fled. The first part is the more likely of this unlikely pair, and it will probably be with a lover to whom one has given up a piece of one's self. While one can go asking for it back, and perhaps can create a ritual wherein it is given back, it may make more sense just to cut that piece off and let it grow back. It is very hard for someone to give up a huge piece of their *mod*, even to someone that they love. More likely it will be a small slice, as it were, and this will regenerate in time. Besides, the deal was made on a conscious or unconscious level between two people, and it needs to be undone between them. If the querent cannot deal with seeing the other person again, they need to cut the cord and call it a loss, and take the consequences. Advise them that there will probably be a period of feeling sad and empty, which is a reaction to losing that part forever, and that the most useful and honorable way to spend this period is officially mourning what has been lost, and what might have been.

In the event that a piece of the *mod* has flown of its own accord—usually due to extreme trauma in childhood—ask the Gods where to look for it, and follow their advice. Don't assume that it wants to come back, or that if you bring it back forcibly and stick it into your client, that it will stay there and not vacate again as soon as possible. If the piece of *mod* won't stay, cut the cord and let it go. That sounds harsh, but sometimes it's necessary. If it does stay, prepare the client to deal with all the fear that it has been holding, which is now bouncing around inside them.

Ond. *Ond* is not so much a part of the soul as what keeps it going; comparing the *ond* to things like the *litr* and *vili* and *mod* is like comparing blood to organs. *Ond* is all through the *hame* like blood through the body, although it has specific intake points. If there is no more *ond*, the person is dead, or likely to become so fairly quickly, if they don't get an infusion immediately. On the other hand, *ond* doesn't just all run out like that. If it's left the body, it's because it was either all used up to do something, or someone leeched it out and drained the person in question. That's an emergency situation, which you'd only be there for if you were present and monitoring the magical working that would have to have gone terribly wrong for this to happen.

On the other hand, it's very common to have to deal with people whose reserves of *ond* are low, and who aren't making enough on their own to fill them up properly. This is easily discerned from checking their *hame*; it will be thin, shallow, and close to the body. There can be a variety of reasons for this.

1) First, physical illness can sap *ond*; ask about their health. If there are ongoing physical problems such as a chronic disease, then their *hame* is trying to heal their *lich* with infusions of *ond*, and is running out. Give the *lich* some help, if possible, in order to keep the *ond* reserves from running dangerously low.

2) Second, there can be a leak in the system. Check carefully for a place where the *ond* is leaking out, and patch it if possible.

3) Sometimes the energy is being leeched out by someone close to the individual who is a psychic vampire. This can be a lover, a child, or a parent. Frankly, if the client is being leeched to that extent, it is probably someone who is close to them every day, not someone they meet occasionally. Most psychic vampires are unconscious, and have no idea they're doing what they're doing. While the standard New Age advice is just to stay away from such people, this isn't always possible; the client may object to being told to get rid of an otherwise perfectly good spouse simply for that reason, and you will likely not be able to convince one to give up a minor child who happens to be a vampire.

There's also that the individual themselves may be a primary (meaning genetic) psychic vampire who has just lost their feeding ground (perhaps a lover or parent) and doesn't know how to get fed otherwise. In this case, look for an aura that extends out into many fine "tentacles", which seem to reach toward the most energetic person in the room. As there isn't the room here to discuss issues of psychic vampirism in detail here, I strongly recommend that professional spirit-workers read "The Ethical Psychic Vampire", which has practical and compassionate advice for vampires and their loved ones.

4) If the individual is another spirit-worker, they are probably exhausting their *ond* with their work, and not taking good enough care of their *hame* and *lich*. Question them as to their maintenance disciplines, and refer to the Health chapter in this book.

Huge. If the *huge* is missing, the person you're dealing with is likely to be in a catatonic or semi-catatonic state, conscious but probably unable to speak. The personality and cognitive process does not go on walkabout unless there is serious mental illness involved, usually of the physiological rather than the traumatic sort. Again, this is a rare thing. Even blocks in the *huge* are more about difficulties with a particular sort of brain function—perhaps ADHD or autistic-spectrum issues—than losing one's entire personality. The only time that I ever saw a missing *huge* was in someone with advanced Alzheimer's. Blockages in the *huge* require a good deal of query into the individual's mental state, including neurological problems and mental illness. There many not be much that you can do about these things.

Similarly, a damaged *huge* suggests that there is physical damage from the *lich* that is affecting this part of the soul. I've seen incidence of a damaged *huge* in victims of stroke and brain damage, especially when there is damage to the right side of the brain. People with right-side brain damage don't have the language disturbances that those with left-side damage sustain, but their connection to reality is strained, and they may act in bewildering and unrealistic ways. Infusing the *huge* with healing energy might speed the repair of the physical structure as well. Push energy in through the eyes, which are the doors to the *huge* and *mynd*, especially to the eye that is opposite to the damaged side of the brain (the right side of the brain runs the left side of the body, and vice versa).

> *Huginn and Muninn*
> *fly every day*
> *over the mighty earth.*
> *I fear for Huginn,*
> *lest he not come back,*
> *yet I worry more about Muninn.*
> *-Grimnismal*

Mynd. A missing *mynd* is also one of those things that never happens, except in rare cases of complete amnesia, and more often that will be a *mynd* blockage which can be opened. *Mynd* is the more passive of the twinned head-soul functions, and thus can be pushed around by its more active brother, the *huge*. It is generally the *huge* who is in charge of repressing memories, shoving them into some oubliette in the subconscious for the sake of remaining functional. This means that recovering memories—bringing up hidden parts of *mynd*—can only be done with the consent of the *huge*. If that part of the soul feels that the situation is not safe enough to bring up those memories, then it won't allow it to be done.

Unblocking the *mynd* can cause a lot of problems, as Lydia points out above. Those memories were repressed for a reason, and releasing them without preparation can create a meltdown. At the very least, the client should choose a time when they have no responsibilities for a significant period of time, and can concentrate on dealing with whatever might erupt in all its ugly glory from its mental prison. Ideally, they should have a support system to take care of them, for days or weeks if necessary depending on their own fragility and the seriousness of the blockage.

If the *mynd* is missing altogether—which is extremely rare—that's cause to look for an external enemy. If this is a spirit-worker, they may have stumbled into a place where they weren't welcome, and been attacked for it. *Mynd*-stealing is a traditional trick of the Fey/Alfar/Sidhe-type folk, for what it's worth, although usually they will only steal a small piece of it, creating a gap in the memory. If it's their doing, you can generally forget about getting it back through force (they're stronger than any one spirit-worker) or trickery (they're trickier). Try propitiation, and if it doesn't work, resign yourself to having lost a piece to them.

Godhi/Gythja. The Higher Self, for which we use rather clumsy terms, doesn't get lost or stolen, just blocked. I believe that this is because there are rules of Wyrd that would prevent it from being bothered by someone else. If it is blocked—which isn't uncommon—it has been done by the individual themselves, because on some level (perhaps unconscious) they don't like the glimpses that they are getting of their Wyrd, and they choose to go in a different direction. A blocked Higher Self is a sign to the diviner of someone who is going to balk when informed of what they ought to be doing. It may not be possible to convince them of the rightness of a path they have rejected, unless their entire life is in shambles from avoiding it.

It's rare for the Higher Self to become damaged. Usually it's just walled off, but if damage occurs, the best medicine to heal it is hope, and positive experiences in following one's path. The positive buildup of experience from doing what you're supposed to do, and then having things get better, can slowly strengthen this crown-chakra part. Unlike other parts, infusing energy into the crown-chakra in order to heal damage is not a good idea. It won't be able to take it in properly, and you'll just fry things further.

Fylgja. Here we are using the term *fylgja* not in the sense of outside spirit teachers, but in the sense of a part of the soul which has been split off and used to fare forth for information-gathering purposes. Most people don't have an active *fylgja*, as this is a shamanic trick learned only by a few, so when you do a soul map reading for most people, you'll be dealing with the issue of spirit teachers, and the fact that the individual has blocked them out, or they have left in disgust. However, for the few who do have a conscious, active *fylgja*, it might well turn up missing. It is ironic that the one piece of soul that is the most vulnerable to getting lost or being destroyed is the one piece that most people don't have as a separate entity.

Creating a *fylgja* does to the soul what multiple personality disorder (or whatever euphemism they're calling it by these days) does to the mind. The creator of the *fylgja* gains the ability to send out a messenger to find out information that might be dangerous to the consciousness, and a guide and scout for faring forth, but in return creates a serious vulnerability to their own soul. It is no accident that the Siberian shamans carefully hid and protected their wandering animal-souls; the Yakut shamans tell about how their *yekyua* is hidden in a safe place where no one can find it. They reported bluntly that their lives depended on it.

While another spirit-worker with destructive intent can capture or kill the *fylgja* of another, the main danger to a *fylgja* is from otherworldly creatures who may not appreciate being bothered. There is no guarantee that the *fylgja* of an inexperienced spirit-worker who thinks that all

Otherworlds are their personal Disney ride is going to have good judgment in faring forth, especially since it is only a piece of the soul and therefore tends to think rather two-dimensionally. *Fylgjar* can get into bad trouble if they're not wise yet, which is why the best advice for someone with an animal *fylgja* is to ask the Grandfather spirit of that type of animal to take their *fylgja* on as a sort of apprentice, and teach them to be more skillful.

The act of splitting off a piece of oneself to be a semi-separate entity is not an easy one, and the temptation of the inexperienced spirit-worker is to err on the side of splitting off those things which they most dislike in themselves, and have stuck in an oubliette somewhere. How convenient to just take them one remove further from the soul-complex, making a *fylgja* out of them, and then one doesn't have to ever see things through their eyes! The problem with this, of course, is that you've just made a "helper spirit" which contains everything that you hate about yourself, and that makes them terribly hard to partner with. (The Yakut shamans, when listing off the types of animal *yekyua*, tell about the predator *yekyua*—dogs, wolves, and such—who constantly torment their owners with gnawing and demanding hunger, as opposed to "placid" *yekyua* like cows or rabbits. One wonders if these are the result of splitting off the worst of the soul qualities, and then paying the price.) On the other hand, you could put a lot of good things into the fylgja, and then lose conscious access to those things yourself. The creation of a *fylgja* needs to be carefully thought through, or it won't get along with you. A poorly-created *fylgja* who is disliked by its Dr. Frankenstein owner may well run off and not want to come back.

If the *fylgja* is missing, it is your job to go find it. (This may be dangerous in and of itself, depending on where it's being held.) There will likely be a thread joining it to the *hame* of the afflicted spirit-worker; if not, that's trouble. The thread can be severed, which means that the *fylgja* has been cut off from its source. If this happens, there are a few options. First, you can find the *fylgja*, reunite it with the spirit-worker, and hope that the thread reattaches itself. If it doesn't, the fylgja is lost. The best disposition for it is to send it to be with the Grandparent spirit of its putative species, if it's an animal, or to be with one's patron deity no matter what it is.

The loss, wounding, or death of a *fylgja* will show up as damage to the spirit-worker; this is clear in the legends that tell of people shooting a spying animal that behaved strangely, and the next day finding a sorcerous neighbor lying wounded and ill in their bed. If someone's *fylgja* is dead, they will know it on some level, and they will likely be in pretty bad shape. Whether it is fatal will depend on how much energy and "self" the spirit-worker put into the *fylgja*. At the very least, they can guarantee a long period of illness, low energy, the inability to do much of anything magical, and possibly a period of mental and emotional instability until that part of their soul regenerates. It may be years before that evens out to a period of health, and it will certainly be years (and perhaps decades) before they can generate another *fylgja*. At worst, its death will immediately put the spirit-worker into a coma, and may cause physical effects such as stroke or heart attack, which may well kill them.

Kinfylgja. Not all family lines have a *kinfylgja*—in fact, most of them don't—so if it is missing, that's not as big a problem as with other pieces of the soul that are more personal. If it does come up as blocked (or, more rarely, missing), that means that there was one, but it's gone now. Question the client about their relationship with their ancestors. It may be that their ancestors have turned their backs on them for some reason, and that might not be due to anything that can be remedied. It may be that they do not approve of the client's lifestyle, or the deities that they have been working with. (I remember doing a reading for one man who had been grabbed up by a Pagan deity, and his Jewish ancestors were now having nothing at all to do with him.) Remember how many generations of Christians may be behind a particular Pagan worshiper.

It may also be that the *kinfylgja* (assuming there was one) has deserted the bloodline due to the actions of others in that line. They do tend to be singleminded in that way. However, one can do perfectly well without one, so it's not an emergency. *Kinfylgjas* don't become damaged, they just leave in disgust.

Ve. Since most people have a very limited *ve*, hardly developed, it doesn't get lost. It can, however, be blocked off. In fact, the way children are raised in Western society is almost guaranteed to create blocks in the *ve*, if only through atrophy. With time and patience, it can be unblocked; generally the best way to do it is repetitive meditative and magical exercises. Remind the client that the best way to build up an unused muscle is through constant repetitive action, no matter how boring it is. All fantasy novels aside, there is no quick fix to release the *ve* except through divine intervention, and that's a good thing too, because in the rare cases where the Gods do decide to try that, the individual has a high risk of going completely mad.

I have seen cases of a lost *ve* occasionally, and in every case I was dealing with a fully-fledged spirit-worker who had gotten into trouble with the Gods and wights, and they had yanked the *ve* until further notice. Generally this was due to having broken a deal with one of them, usually the patron deity. (And yes, before you ask, if you break a deal with a deity, they have the lawful right to do that, no matter how much you complain that you didn't understand the fine print before you signed on the dotted line, or that you made a mistake in judgment, or that you just don't want to do it.) In these cases, the only thing to do is to keep the bargain, no matter how difficult and painful that is. There may be interest due as well. This is why all spirit-workers should understand that there is always a price for the aid of the wights.

A damaged *ve* is also a job hazard of the functioning spirit-worker. Its cause is simple: sticking your fingers into plugs that push current too heavy for your wiring, and getting yourself fried. For spirit-workers, the *ve* is used and pushed far more than it is for most people, and it can get broken through misuse. Some readers may have heard warnings about people frying themselves by calling up too much Kundalini energy, and indeed this can happen. Your psychic "wiring" is the size that it is. You can increase its "carrying capacity" to a certain extent, slowly and gradually, through continual grounding, centering, moving energy up and down, yoga, tai chi, and many other sorts of energy disciplines. This will only take you to the limits of what your *hame* will naturally stretch to. Anything further will have to be modified by a deity or major wight. If they refuse to do it, it means that you're not meant to channel anything heavier. It may be that your *ve* would not be able to handle those changes without damaging your mind, or other parts of your soul. Don't take it personally. It may be that the ability to handle that kind of modification is largely genetic—not racial, but only running in specific family lines.

I remember coming across the writings of a woman who had spent time with the Saami *noaidi*, and she commented that the difference between shamans and most modern Western magic-workers was that shamans channeled "heavy voltage". I nodded when I read that; it's true. We have to be able to call down heavy stuff in order to do our work, and that's why we have to die, in order to be in a condition where the spirits can modify the *hame* that brutally. If a magician without those extreme modifications tries to pull down that kind of voltage, they will wreck their *ve*, and possibly other parts as well. It's sort of a punishment for hubris, in a way. Abusing entheogens for their *ve*-enhancing properties is the most common door for this sort of damage.

Healing a damaged *ve* requires starting from scratch, doing gentle energy moving at a low level. It may require a period of abstinence from all psychic work. The *ve* also regenerates slower from damage than other soul parts—perhaps because it is not as necessary for daily life—and may never get back to where it once was. This may also be a built-in safety feature, insuring that it will not be so abused again.

Wod. The *wod* is the part of the soul that is closest to the Gods, and I have never seen it go missing. I would expect that in the very rare circumstances where that might happen, it would go directly to Them, and be safe there. In that case it would simply be a matter of petitioning the Gods to give it back (and accepting whatever They say). More likely, though, it's blocked due to the actions of the client. It may be a case like the *ve* above—breaking an agreement with a deity—or it may be sheer fear. Sharing any kind of soul-space with a god is terrifying as well as awe-inspiring. I've always felt that the Greek myth about the mortal consort of Zeus who asked to see him in his true form and was then burned to a crisp was a good description of reality. Unfettered by the interface that makes them accessible to us, their Presence can fry our circuits. It may be that the individual in question brushed up against that Presence, and got so scared that they slammed the door. This is not something that is going to be fixable in an hour's reading; they need to make their own decision as to whether they want to be in that incredibly humbling place again.

If the *wod* is damaged, it's due to spirit-possession, because the *wod* is the place where there spirits enter. This is not usually a problem for godatheow-folk who have divine owners to watch out for them and set limits on joyriders; it tends to be more of a problem for spirit-workers who are "free agents" and have difficulty enforcing limits on those who possess them, perhaps because those entities are actually stronger than they are. Symptoms of a damaged *wod* include the inability to sense or hear the Gods and wights, although if the *ve* is still intact the ability to move energy will remain accessible. A damaged *wod* is a sign that the spirit-worker needs to stop doing this until they can get better protection. Since *wod* damage is caused by spirit-contact, it can only really be healed by the spirits, and probably only by deities. This means that *wod* damage means propitiation, preferably to Someone Big.

Maegen. The personal power that is *maegen* is earned and built up by giving and keeping one's word. It is lost, most often, by breaking one's word. While breaking your word to anyone will lose *maegen*, breaking a deal with a deity will sometimes wipe out large chunks of it, perhaps depleting you to the point where magic is impossible. While the wrath of a deity will never rip out your *mod* or *vili* or something else necessary for functioning on a mundane level, if you break oath with a God/dess, it is within their lawful power to strip you of those things which make you more than mundane—namely, *ve*, *wod*, *maegen*, and *hamingja*. In most cases, someone who has lost all their *maegen* has betrayed Something or Someone important, and they had better start making their apologies and finding out what can be done to help the matter.

Maegen can also be lost in large amounts by betrayal of yourself. This happens when you do something utterly compromising of your spirit, your honor, and yourself. This has often wiped out people's *maegen*, because holding *maegen* depends on being a whole vessel without cracks. Being whole is another way of referring to integrity, which literally means being all-of-a-piece. When you break your integrity, you lose your *maegen*. It's as simple as that. To get it back, you have to start from scratch and build it up all over again; when it's gone, it goes back into the fabric of the Universe, just as if you spent it on a spell. There's no easy way to fix the problem, just more hard work.

Hamingja. If the luck is missing or blocked or damaged, that's a whole issue unto itself. This is dealt with in the chapter on Luckworking.

Orlog. As it is attached to the Wyrd, the *orlog* cannot be removed, and it doesn't fly off. It can, however, be blocked, obscured, or lost within the individual's deeper self. Finding it is a matter of trust. First the spirit-worker should figure out what the next few steps of the *orlog* are, and the individual needs to do them, even if they have no "feel" for it due to blockage. It's rather like learning to find your way somewhere blind, while trusting that the closer you get, the more you'll be able to see ... but those first few miles are terribly confusing. If there are a lot of tangles in the Thread of Wyrd, this can make dealing with the *orlog* more difficult. If there is an *orlog* problem, always consult the Wyrd as well.

Wyrd. The Wyrd is never missing, just hidden. On the other hand, one's Thread can sustain all sorts of tangling and knots and difficulties. Those are addressed in the chapter on Wyrdworking. All things Wyrd are in the hands of the Nornir, and all questions on that should be addressed their way.

Some northern-tradition spirit-workers refer to the art of soul repair as "wholemaking", as it makes whole what has been damaged or split apart. Whenever doing the art of wholemaking, however, one should first check and see if it is your job to take on any one case. Some people need to stay in a place of being split, until they have learned something important. In these cases, all the good work that you do will get undone—the soul-piece will vanish again, the blocks will go up, the light plunged again into darkness. Having had several clients with actual multiple personality disorder—and a very fractured *mod* and *huge*, of which some parts were quite blocked off—and having had everything I did for them get undone by sabotaging from various parts warring with each other, I have learned that it is some people's *orlog* to stay unwhole until they have worked some things through. If you can't help, the best service you can give them is straightforward honesty about their condition, why it isn't your time to help them, and some divination to determine where they should go from here.

Hamrammr:
Strong In Shaping

Odin could change his hame, and his body would lie there as if
asleep or dead, while he himself was a bird or an animal, a fish or a
snake, and would travel in an instant to far-off lands on his errands
or on those of other men.

–Ynglingasaga

The word *hamrammr*—skin-strong or shape-strong—refers to having a talent for shapeshifting, turning oneself into an animal. (It is eerily similar to the Dineh word for a shapeshifting magician—skinwalker—and even the Spanish word for witch, *bruja*, comes from a word meaning "to skin or peel".) When the magic-worker left their body, they were said to be *hambleyna*—"leaper out of the skin"—and anyone who took on an unfamiliar shape was *hamslauss*—"out of his skin". While we tend to use the term *hamfarir* as a general term for journeying out-of-body with the *hame*, its original meaning was specifically to leave the body in the shape of an animal. This seems to have been the common practice of northern spirit-workers, perhaps because it was believed that one was in less danger of injury and death (or perhaps recognition) if one's *hame* was animal-formed rather than one's own human face. It might also be due to the use of the fetch in northern spirit-work; since the fetch was frequently cast as a beast, the spirit-worker might choose to match its shape when it led them forth.

Northern Europe has a strong tradition of shapeshifting and

lycanthropy, and there are numerous examples in lore—Bodhvar Biarki fought in the shape of a bear while his body lay in trance, and Dufthak and Storolf fought in bull-shape and bear-shape over a piece of land. King Harald's hired shaman travels overseas as a whale, and then of course there are the berserkers and *ulfhednar*, who were believed to turn physically into bears and wolves during battle. The name of one of the Viking battle formations—*svinfylking* or boar formation—has been said to refer to the boar-magic of the warriors involved. In fact, shapeshifting was the most warlike of the Norse magical arts, or at the least it is the art most used as a weapon. As one can read in *Beowulf*, the warriors decorated their armor and accouterments with figures of the fierce animal spirits that they wished to embody—bears, wolves, boars, eagles, etc.—and it is likely that shapeshifting astrally into a fierce beast in order to increase one's battle worth was the most popular and sought-after form of magic. Certainly there are far more tales of it in the surviving lore than those of more peaceful and boring pursuits such as healing and calling fish into the bay.

On the other hand, those accounts usually did not end well. It seems that the berserker, for example, was not only a great warrior on the field but a terror off of it. Some accounts paint the picture of amoral figures given to gleeful fits of insane rage, roaming the countryside and wreaking havoc. A rogue berserker would invite himself to the hold of a small lordling or wealthy peasant, who would be obliged to let him in for dinner by the laws of hospitality. He would then proceed to get drunk, pretend to be insulted by a chance comment, and start a fight, often by the outright slaying of one of his host's men. He would then insult the host, usually with one of the insults that couldn't be refused or the receiver would lose his honor and be unseated by his men, and challenge him to single combat the next day. The host had to accept or lose all face, even though it tended to end with the berserker going into his altered-state battle rage, murdering his hapless victim, and laying claim to the spoils of his home, wife, and wealth. Then, when they were spent, he would move on to the next victim. Wolf-warriors, too, would pull this trick, when they were not held in check by a strong ruler.

The original purpose of the warriors with their altered states and battle-animals was to be a troupe of landless sacred warriors, rather like the Irish Fianna, a God-sent weapon in the hand of their leader. They would don the skins of their animal spirits over naked, painted bodies and rush in to battle. Then they would reach *hamask*—the state of animal fury where they would lose their reason and kill everything in their path. There has been much theorizing over what sort of entheogen, if any, that they used to get there—from henbane to the Little Red Man to simply a lot of ale—but nothing conclusive. It seems likely to me, however, that with practice and motivation—and these warriors had both—they could easily learn to do it without any external chemical aid.

As with so many shamanic paths, dealing with shapeshifting and the attendant altered state is another example of how we spirit-workers use controlled versions of what would otherwise be considered insanity. The warning corollary to this practice is well illustrated in the aforementioned grim tales of berserkers, and the even more gruesome tales of werewolves that lasted well into the medieval period. Many layers of werewolf tales come from Germany, and they are almost all negative, shifting from the tales of shapechanging heroes gone wrong to out-and-out peasant serial killers who murdered and cannibalized people while believing that they were wolves—and for some of them, while wearing wolfskins and acting like a wolf, they convinced escaped victims that they were wolves indeed. Such individuals began to be treated in writing less like shapechanging demons and more like dangerous madmen, and whether or not they managed to actually shapeshift while on their rampages became irrelevant.

On the other hand, the protective sides of shapeshifting were still utilized in some places. In medieval Lithuania, military brotherhoods called *Wahrwolf* societies would transform into wolves and journey collectively to the land of the Dead to fight evil spirits for possession of the year's seed grain. Like the volvas, they carried iron staves to their battle. They claimed to have been doing this for thousands of years; one of their self-proclaimed titles was "Hounds of God". In Arcadia, werewolf legends have other legends alongside of them, claiming that there was once a "brotherhood" of shapeshifters who were sworn to protect the people. Once a year, in February, one of them would go forth clad in a wolfskin and get themselves taken into a wolf-pack as a member. They would then live with the wolves for a year and warn the humans whenever the wolves came too close to raiding their pens. After a year, they would return and a new member would go out to the wolves, as it was feared that more than a year with the wolves would cause them to lose their humanity and stop being a good spy. If the idea of living with wolves and being accepted as one of their own seems farfetched, consider that Inuit children were sometimes taught how to be accepted into a wolf-pack through communicating with their body language, in case they became accidentally separated from their tribe and needed to survive until rescued. They would be the low wolf in the pack, but as long as they gave the right submission signals, the wolves would protect them, allow them to eat some of their meat, and provide them with body heat with which to survive.

As Angrboda points out in her lesson following this chapter, there is a difference between taking on the form of an animal and actually becoming, at least partly, that animal. The former is a human conception of how that animal looks, acts, and thinks. At its best it taps into the archetypal Grandparent wight—wolf-wight, bear-wight, sparrow-wight—and takes something from that, just as one might take some form and energy from a divine archetype. However, even that spiritual information is filtered through human conceptions. In order to go deeper, one needs to have a personal relationship with the animal spirit so that they will do a one-on-one exchange of energy when the time comes, and this requires a bond with that animal spirit that is not easily put aside. That's why it's best to start with the latter technique and get used to that, as the spirits can't be forced. They will come to you or they won't.

This is where personal totem spirits come in. Working with an actual animal spirit is both easier and more difficult than working with human shaping alone. On the one hand, it is harder to run amok in ways that trigger actual mental illness. Wolves don't just run about the countryside killing everything in sight for fun, unless they are rabid (or unless you are talking about Fenris, who is not a wolf-spirit but is a God of destruction in wolf form, which is different). They bond with others, they submit to authority, they shy away from contact with unnecessary strangers. On the other hand, acting like an actual animal while still in one's body can be a problem, and should only be tried in a safe space. The down side of shifting directly with the aid of an animal spirit is that you can temporarily lose some of your human judgment, and if you put yourself into that situation in a space where others could be harmed, it's still your fault when they do. Do it out of body, and make sure that everything is set up to return the entirety of your human judgment to you as soon as you come back. If you must shapeshift your *hame* while still in your body, do it in a place where there are no people around as far as you could run, or where the people are trained monitors who know the risks and can keep things safe.

Wolves were, bar none, the most popular shape to shift into, and the werewolf is still the first thing that pops into people's minds when they imagine taking animal form. In the story of Sinfljoti and his son, the two men are outlaws who come upon two magical wolfskins. Upon donning them, they become wolves—not only physically, but in personality as well—and find themselves stuck in that form for nine days straight (again, the magical number nine). They are released on the tenth day, but not until the father nearly tears his son's throat out in a rage. Other tales of magical wolf-transformations are found from Ireland to the Balkans, all of them remarkably similar.

Animal expert Dr. Temple Grandin, drawing on work done by Robert Wayne at UCLA, writes about how new research is showing that dogs and wolves may have shaped humans just as humans domesticated one from the other. Dogs were the first animal to be bred to human socialization, probably from captured wolf puppies who were raised to bond to a human "pack", and we started burying them in their own graves about 14,000 years ago. Grandin points out that according to this new research, humans started working with wolves as long ago as 135,000 years in the past, when dog DNA began to separate off from wolf DNA, and that even before that time wolf bones have been found in close proximity to human bones. In the process of this ancient bonding, humans took on social traits that are found in no other primate species... but are found among dogs and wolves. We learned about loyal same-sex and nonkin friendships, complex and shifting hierarchical social structures, the ability to freely take in nonrelated members and bond with them, and most importantly, hunting in groups. None of these traits are found in our closest primate relatives, but they are all found in the canines that we bonded with.

Even more strange, at the same time that wolves were becoming domesticated and losing a certain percentage of their forebrains (about ten percent, which happens to all domesticated animals who are now being taken care of and don't need to survive on their own in the wild), mankind also mysteriously lost about ten percent of his own brain capacity. Humans lost size from the midbrain, specifically the parts that deal with smell and reacting strongly to emotions. According to Dr. Grandin, dogs took over many of the sensory and "guard" duties for humans, while humans took over the long-range planning for dog lives. It may also be a key to why Neanderthal died out—they did not domesticate dogs, while their *Homo erectus* neighbors did.

Given this long link with the canine species, it is not surprising that the most common shape for the *hamrammr* is that of a wolf, the oldest fighting partner of our species, nor that so many people take to it so well—just as so many people own and love dogs. Somewhere along the line we humans absorbed a great deal of wisdom from dogs, and they may have "trained" and "bred" us to be more like them even as we bred them to be friendly to us. Wolf-shape (and its corollary, dog-shape) is extremely accessible to our ancestral line, hiding in our distant past.

Other shapes abound, however. We have mentioned bears and boars as warrior-shapes, and ravens are one of the oldest of sacred birds (and shapes), as are eagles, hawks, and various seabirds. Hoofed herd animals such as reindeer, elk, deer, goats, and horses were also popular, both the wild and the domesticated varieties. Whales were also a popular form of *hame*-shape, especially in areas that were near to the ocean. A good deal of cross-oceanic reconnaissance and boat attack by seidh-workers in whale form were recounted in various sagas. The Saami *noaidi* claimed that every shaman needed at least three shapes: a bird-shape for traveling to the upper worlds, a fish or snake shape for burrowing or swimming to the lower worlds, and a four-legged shape for moving around in this world.

What one seems to be able to glean from such writings is that shapeshifting was not merely the province of spirit-workers, although they may have been the experts at it. "Ordinary" people would use shapeshifting as well, most specifically the warrior-elite, and the spirit-worker's job was to aid them in doing it. Many traditions survive throughout Europe where people don masks as part of holiday festivities, perhaps wandering from house to house as outcast spirits might; Halloween is the final holdover from this practice. "Masking" festivals were not uncommon, and many folk would don the shapes of their family totems. Some claimed that they would in this way be able to take on the properties of those totems, and possibly their shapes as well. The line between realities was less finely drawn for our ancestors, and the more likely such things were in their concepts of what could be done, the more likely such things were to actually occur.

Masks have been an important part of shapeshifting since Paleolithic times; archaeologists continually argue as to whether the animal-headed or half-animal figures n the walls of ancient caves are meant to be totem spirits, masked shamans calling on the powers of those totem spirits, or masked hunters acting out a ceremonial episode. It does, however, show that the first masks were the skins of hunted animals, preserved head and all.

Masks are common equipment for shamans around the world, including in Siberia, where they can be doors for a spirit to come through someone's body when the mask is donned. The most common sort in Siberia, the "mask of a thousand faces", in simply a fringe that hangs down over the shaman's face, obscuring their features to onlookers and also closing out visual input that might distract from the trance.

Thus the effects of the mask works both ways, on the viewer and on the wearer, creating unusual liminal spaces for them both. The famous female Saami *noaide* Rijkuo-Maja was said to have done trance rituals standing in the shallows of the sacred lake near her home, wearing a "veil" of reindeer calfskin, described as a bag over her head, for the same reasons.

In northern Europe, masking was a part of magical practice, and this is reinforced by the number of divine and sacred terms around the word mask—*grim* in Old Norse. They include *Grim* and *Grimnir*, epithets of Odin. Boar-masks were also supposedly worn by priests of Frey in order to shapeshift them into his sacred animal. Two of the figures on the Oseberg tapestry, for example, seem to be women (from their trailing skirts, or perhaps they are *ergi* men) wearing masks that cover them to their knees; one is of a crane's head with bird wings and the other clearly wears a boar-mask/skin and carries a shield. Two felt face masks were discovered in the cracks of a Viking ship, being used for caulking; one was a small red undetermined animal face, and the other was a large and well-made bull's face. In Novgorod, where many Scandinavians settled and took over, many leather animal masks have been uncovered well-preserved in the acid soils.

One of the wights that I work with—and have a lot of sympathy for—is Mimir. He is a living prophetic head, a cult object that happens not to have died yet. When I go into trance and prophesy, he is often the one who inspires me. He taught me to make a mask of his face—stark white, almost like a skull with the skin still on it—with long silver hair. The eyes are made of reflective glass disks; they are translucent enough to make out shapes, but not to see well. I took it to a well and blessed it by dipping it in the water—but first, I drew blood from my eyelid with a clean needle and let it fall into the well, then poured in a whole bottle of booze, both offerings. When I wear the mask of Mimir, instead of sitting on a high seat, I lay on the floor. I have a great mantle of shiny dark blue-green silk like the water in a well, and I wrap it about me so that it covers me from head to foot, and lays out onto the floor around my head and shoulders, as if I am a disembodied head in the Well of Mimirsbrunnr. I keep the light dim, with only a few candles at the edge of the Well. Then I go into trance, and he speaks through my mouth. The mask is the key—even just holding it, I shudder. No one else wants to touch it—it's too *unheimlich*.

–Gudrun, seidhkona

The Gods often play with shapeshifting, but some are more *hamrammr* than others. The undisputed master of it is, of course, Loki. His various forms include a mare, a spider, a hawk or falcon, a salmon, a fly, a flea, and a seal, and probably others that we don't know about. He is accused by Odin of spending years underground bearing children, which would suggest that he takes on female form as well when he chooses to, and this is borne out by the experiences of many who work with him. He is the best possible teacher of shapeshifting, if you can deal with working with him. He is also skilled at literally taking one's *hame* and molding it like clay, actively directing the shaping, which can be helpful to those who are having trouble doing it themselves (assuming that they can bear being shoved around like that). It's his way of "motoring one through" the skill, and his physicality in training people helps in that way.

Another good teacher or this art, not surprisingly, is Odin. As noted in the quote at the beginning of the chapter, Odin takes on many forms—an ill-favored Jotun and a snake in the tale of Gunnlod and the Mead of Poetry, for example, and as various other human men while on his wanderings. His various *heiti* describe him as being bear, wolf, and eagle. In fact, it was a common warning about him that he might come in disguise to one's table, and thus one had best be clean about one's hospitality to strangers. Odin's take on shifting is more practical and less whimsical than Loki's, and he specializes in warrior totems and learning to fight in beast's *hame*.

Freya also has been known to do a good deal of shapeshifting in her aspect as Mistress of Seidhr. She appears in bird form in several sources, and has a cloak of falcon feathers that will turn her into a falcon form. While it is not in the lore, many of her followers speak of how much she loves cats, and will sometimes take cat form in order to send a message to someone. For Freya, shapeshifting is often linked to glamour, in the sense that illusory glamour applied to the surface holds better when there is a certain amount of underlying shapeshifting anchoring it. Some spirit-workers have also valued her guidance in using shapeshifting to slowly change the physical body—perhaps to gain or lose fat, add muscle, or other physical changes done in order to make one feel better about one's body. Some male-to-female transsexuals have been greatly helped by her in energetically enhancing their hormonal feminization, and getting their bodies to shape in a more fully feminine way.

In other areas, shapeshifting was also common among Siberian shamans. The Koryak shamans began rites to turn themselves into predatory animals by smearing blood on their mouths. The Chukchi shamans tell of the "Raven Incantation", where a shaman with a black knife would transform himself into a raven, and use his knife as the beak to peck at his foes, a freshly dead corpse being magically linked to their bodies. This was a combination of sympathetic magic and shapeshifting, two techniques that work well together. One strain of Siberian shapeshifting magic transformed "sympathetic" items as well as transforming the shaman, so that he/she could work on an otherwise untouchable problem directly. One example might be transforming a victim's soul into a sealskin, and then transforming small stones into shrimps to scatter across it and let them eat it. Another would be turning their soul into moss, which was then strained through a net, buried, dug up again, and then turned into a dog forced to wander from camp to camp.

This illustrates a useful trick that the northern-tradition shaman can work on: shapeshifting outside objects, not just themselves. In order to do this, you first must energize the object through various means, giving it a *hame*, and then you shape the *hame* to be differently-shaped from that of the object. This way, a short fence of sticks can become a large protective wall on the astral plane, or a long pointed stone become a knife capable of wounding someone's *hame*, and yet remains perfectly capable of being carried on an airplane.

Controlled shapeshifting starts with controlling the *hame*, or at least being aware of it, and being able to move it independently of the *lich*. Being *hamrammr* starts with learning to be "loose in your skin", or having the astral form not so tightly linked to the physical one. That starts with awareness of them as separate. If you have trouble in this area, here's a simple exercise to do: Sit quietly and visualize your astral hands. Imagine that your flesh hands are gloves, and there are other hands inside them. Move your fingers, feeling this "glove" sensation. Then pull on the index finger of one hand, gently, stroking outward. Make yourself feel that you are slowly stroking the fingers of your *hame* out until they are longer than the fingers of your *lich*. See how long you can make them before they attenuate and won't be stretched any further. Touch things with your extended fingers—not the tips of your flesh ones—and monitor the sensations. Try this with your eyes closed as well, and see what you feel.

That's the first step, which teaches you how to separate the *hame* from the *lich* while conscious and moving. The second step is to shape it into something else. By making your fingers longer, you've already started. Now try that exercise again, only this time, shape them into something else—tree twigs, claws, tentacles. It can help to actually shape one hand with the fingers of the other as if you were sculpting clay. If this is still not clicking in your brain, try training for it by actually sculpting clay in this way—stick some clay on the ends of the fingers of one hand, shape it into extended fingertips, then shape it into something else. Do this several times until you have a "body memory" of how that feels, and then use that memory when you try again with just the fingers of your *hame*. You'll know you have it right because it will be a very peculiar sensation that you can't attribute to any specific nerve endings. It will just feel weird.

Of course, once you've done it, you'll have to put it back. Most people find that by shaking their hand, it will all spring back, at least the first time. If that doesn't work, go ahead and use the hand for a while as you normally would, ignoring the "weird" feeling, and it will likely go back by itself. If that still doesn't work, go to sleep—shapeshifted body parts often return to "normal" after sleeping. If you wake up and it's still shapeshifted, deliberately sculpt it back to normal. The reason that I recommend waiting through all these "normalizing" activities before deliberately adjusting it is that it gives you a useful calibration of what your *hame* naturally does when left to its own devices.

Once you've become accustomed to doing a hand, start trying to work with other single parts of your body, shifting them and then setting them straight. Eventually you can work up to shifting your entire astral body at once. Shifting your *hame* while it is still congruent with your *lich* is, of course, going to create some problems of dissonance—if the *hame* has become four-legged, the *lich* is going to do what it can to mimic that in motion and action, with perhaps varying degrees of success. It's going to feel awkward, and you'll probably wonder why you're bothering to do this.

There a couple of good reasons to start out this way, however. First, if you are pathwalking, you'll have to get used to working this way if you intend to shapeshift while traveling. Second, this method is particularly thaumaturgic, in that it involves no lore or spirit-help. It is the most basic and beginning level of shapeshifting, as well as the most conscious and careful one. By learning how to take on different forms by slowly and consciously sculpting yourself, you will never be in a position where you get so stuck in an unfamiliar form that you aren't able to change back. It's a way of building up what we'd call "body memory" if we were talking about the *lich*; instead, just shift the concept to the *hame*. You build up body memory for your *hame* when you practice any kind of energy working to the point where you can just do it automatically, without thinking—and shapeshifting is one of those things that should be built up in this way. When you need it, you often need it quickly and accurately.

Shapeshifting can be dangerous and unhealthy if you do it carelessly or too often. Only a very few people find that they stay shapeshifted for long periods of time without intervention, and these are generally those with a particularly poor *lich/hame* connection (see the chapter on Health for more information on the *lich/hame* connection). If this is you, then you need to work on that connection or shapeshifting could be more trouble for you than it's worth. At the very least, you need to be learn enough body memory for the *hame* to consciously snap it back, as accurately as possible, as soon as you notice that it's still off ... and you need to develop keen and constant awareness of what your *hame* is doing, so that you will bother to do so.

Frankly, tempting as it is to walk around in wolf-form or whatever all the time, being permanently *hamslauss* in a non-human form for long periods of time is not healthy for your *lich*. Even when somewhat detached, the *hame* exerts a powerful effect on the *lich*, and will attempt to mold it in ways that it simply isn't built to go, possibly causing orthopedic problems later in life. Like it or not, we are bound to these human forms while we live, and we must respect what they need. The physical body will keep attempting vainly to change in ways that will only pull it out of alignment and cause soft tissue damage; it is imperative that we respect the boundaries of our flesh. If nothing else, make sure that your *hame* is lined up with your *lich* as fully as possible whenever you go to sleep at night, and whenever you exercise or indulge in any athletic activity.

With that caveat in mind, the opposite is also true: if you are particularly adept at it, shapeshifting can be used as a form of healing, especially when the goal is to build up damaged or atrophied tissue. By keeping your *hame* in a form as close to the way your *lich* was when it was well (or ought to be *if* it was well), you encourage it to pull in that direction. Some folk who have damaged muscles or tendons and find that they are still too tender to work via physical therapy have reported that moving the astral limb regularly encourages the physical one to heal faster, in order to join its counterpart, and to atrophy less.

The second method of shapeshifting, as Elizabeth Vongvisith describes below, is to separate out the *hame* first and then shapeshift it. This is the preferred method for journeying, and the benefits are that it puts very little pressure on the *lich*, although in order to keep up those benefits, you'd better be faithful about shifting all the way back first before reentry. It's not uncommon to be in such a hurry upon returning that you get slammed back into your body; training yourself to automatically shift to your *lich* form on the return journey can help with this. The drawback is that you have to be skilled at spending long periods nearly entirely out of your body, and manipulating yourself and your world during those times. For those who take naturally to that, it's less important to start while still in your *lich*, although still useful for building up your automatic responses. For those who don't, it's better to start out the slow, conscious way.

Beginning to shapeshift while out of the body is a different experience; it's more sudden and organic and you may not remember how you did it (or how to shift back, which is a problem for some people). It's not uncommon for this process to start while dreaming. We often experience ourselves as having different bodies in dreams, and this is sometimes a jumping-off place for the unconscious to mold the *hame*. Fetches are particularly prone to doing this, since by its nature the fetch is dissociated from the main soul and not accessible to the conscious mind. Some people have reported learning to shapeshift by being taught by their own fetch.

The third method is described by Angrboda in the lesson following this chapter, and it is the most specifically shamanic, as it cannot be accomplished without the aid of an animal spirit who is willing to help you. Again, there are drawbacks and benefits. The benefits are that you will be plunged deeply into the experience of being that animal, which can be a powerful thing. It can also temporarily hide your own soul in cases of emergencies. The drawbacks are that while in such a state, you may not care about much of anything that you're actually supposed to do. There's no point in taking on horse form in order to travel swiftly from place to place in another world if you forget that you're anything but a real horse with no mission or agenda, and waste several hours gaily trotting about looking for greener grass. Keep in mind, at all times, that the whole point of learning these things is to be able to do your job more successfully and thus serve others, not to entertain or soothe yourself with interesting parlor tricks.

Hambleyna
by Elizabeth Vongvisith

Shapeshifting is a common skill among the folk of the Nine Worlds. The Jotnar in particular are known for their innate gift — the most well-known example being Loki, who assumes various animal forms during the course of his adventures. The Alfar, light and dark, are generally capable of shapeshifting, although they much prefer to use glamour to influence the perceptions of others rather than to physically alter their own forms. Members of other races are likewise capable. Odin is known for his ability to change his shape, and Freyja's feather cloak (sometimes borrowed by Loki for reasons known only to him) likewise grants its wearer the gift of taking falcon's form. Humans with Jotun blood may find they have the inborn ability to change shape, as might those with Alf blood, but this is neither a guarantee nor a requirement.

I'm not going to discuss the kind of shapeshifting which is said to have been done by berserkers — putting on an animal's skin and taking on the attributes of that animal without changing visible form. Nor am I discussing the actual alteration of one's physical, human body through force of will, if such a thing is possible. All the shapeshifting I've done personally has been on the astral level during journeying, and I am not really certain I could teach anybody *how* — it is an ability which people either seem to be able to do, or not. However, I've learned that there are times when shapeshifting is necessary and useful, and times when it will get you into hot water, so if you wish to use this skill in your spirit-work, you might wish to keep a few things in mind.

First of all, accept that it's not always going to work when you shift your form in order to disguise yourself from others. Ordinary inhabitants of Midgard, or your average Jotun or Duerg off the street might not be able to tell, but in general the populace of the Nine Worlds is far more used to magic than we are, and thus better acquainted with its signs. Many Jotnar can tell that someone is shapeshifted even if they don't know them, because it's such a common trait among their folk. Almost all Alfar will know right away, and as for the Aesir, Vanir and Rökkr...forget it. It's pretty much a given that the majority of folks you meet in the Nine Worlds will be more familiar than you with the peculiar ways of magicians, even if they aren't one themselves. Don't assume that they haven't already seen a dozen or so others try the same thing you're thinking of trying.

If you decide you're going to do something stupid like trespass into someone's hall in an assumed form, know that your chances of getting away with it are pretty much nil—you'd be better off just using extreme care to sneak in under your normal guise. Don't even *think* about shapeshifting into a winged form to fly over walls or otherwise go unnoticed into either Asgard or Helheim—you will be attacked and most likely killed, swiftly and without any warning, by the guardians of those respective realms. Even the Duergar, who generally do not shapeshift nor are inclined to learn how unless they are sorcerers by trade, have ways of knowing when something or someone is not as it appears.

The main reason you shouldn't shapeshift in an attempt to hide your true identity, however, is that in many places it's considered rude to pass yourself off as something you're not, particularly when you are a guest or uninvited visitor to that realm. (The biggest exception to this are the elven lands where the use of glamour is taken for granted.) When you're trying to hide from enemies or are involved in some furtive attack against a foe, that's another matter—all's fair in love and war, as they say. But if you wish to get along with the inhabitants of the other Nine Worlds, I'd advise being honest about who and what you are, which means allowing others the courtesy of interacting with you in your true form unless otherwise requested. True, many of the folk you'll run into in Jotunheim or Ljossalfheim, say, will not return the favor, but the rules that they abide by aren't necessarily the same ones that apply to mortal spirit-workers visiting their worlds.

If for some reason you do have to shapeshift before paying someone a visit, be sure to announce your real identity as soon as you arrive, or else send word ahead that you will be coming to them in another form than your true one. At the very least, this may prevent the guardians of that person or place from setting upon you the minute you hove into view, if by chance they don't see you for what you really are.

So now you may be wondering, *why shapeshift at all?* The answer is to give you abilities that your actual (spirit) form may not possess. This may seem only relevant to who undertake astral journeying or *hamfara* rather than pathwalking, but since your astral form shows up most clearly in the other worlds no matter which technique you use, there will be times when shapeshifting is necessary or useful regardless of how you got where you are.

For example, those whose astral forms do not bear wings may shapeshift into birds or insects in order to fly over difficult terrain, to escape pursuers on the ground, or simply to speed up a journey. Turning yourself into a fish allows you to swim great distances and cross dangerous bodies of water. Taking a form that is small and unnoticeable, like a mouse, can both divert unwanted attention and allow you to get into places that are otherwise inaccessible, like cracks in caves or holes in the ground. Shapeshifting into a form that is many times larger than yours may help you battle a bigger foe if you're attacked, or give you the ability to perform feats of great strength with little effort, depending on the situation (although some folks find that they are still only as strong in another form as they are in their natural one.) And as has been noted elsewhere, the Jotnar are known for shapeshifting during sex, whether to sire or bear a child (as when Loki changed himself into a mare) or for magical purposes, or simply for the experience's own sake. You never know…

Shapeshifting one's spirit-body also has a few practical advantages in on this plane. If you have trouble with maintaining your balance, as I sometimes do thanks to a childhood ear infection, you may find that taking a form with a different center of gravity (or extra limbs) can help you with that. Sometimes shifting into a scary or repellent astral form can deter people from hassling you, if you suspect they are sensitive enough to feel that something isn't quite right even if they don't know what it is. It can also deter various spirits from messing around with you when you happen to enter their territory or realm of influence—if you're forced to spend time in a place where there are a lot of restless ghosts and you aren't prepared to deal with them, shapeshifting your astral form might convince them not to bother you.

Angrboda's Lesson
Mother of Monsters

I've gone to see Angrboda many times. The first was when I was in a bad way, and needed some support, and prayed to Hela who owns me. I'm not the sort to respond well to squishy nurturing mother goddesses, but I felt that I needed something a little more warm and personal than Hela's cold transpersonal compassion. She responded by sending me to her own mother, and I journeyed to Angrboda's hall in the Iron Wood. It's a huge hall, usually guarded by werewolves the size of small horses, hung with painted skins stretched on wooden hoops and lit by a smoky fire.

The Hagia of the Iron Wood was waiting for me. Although she is one of the Mothers of the Rökkr (along with Laufey and Sigyn), she is not a kind earth mother or a receptive water-mother. She is a warrior, and the mother of warriors, and she put her arm around me and took me for a march. While we walked, she told me that there would be bad times ahead, and that they would get worse, but that I was strong enough to bear them. There was warmth and passion to her, but I could tell that she had no patience for weaklings. The strong brought low by circumstance, those she would comfort in her own way, enough to get them back on their feet and fighting again. The ones with great obstacles set against them by Nature, but who refuse to give up, those she cherishes. She was the Wolf-Mother, the pack-mama who defends her litter with her life.

She brought me back to her hall and bade me sing by the fire, and to make it a song that would tell everyone gathered who I was. I'd written the various lines of verse that had come together to be my shaman song, I'd even embroidered them on my skirt, but I'd never sung them before. I sang them then, before all the wolves and trolls and giants and strange, deformed monsters in her hall.

Afterwards, she pointed many of them out around the room, and described how their particular deformities were useful or beneficial in some way, usually for purposes of shapeshifting. "You cannot be one who changes form regularly, a walker between the worlds of the body, and stay the same all the time in your own body. There is a price for everything, and you go ask them if it is worth the price. They will all tell you yes. You need to remember that, for things are going to get worse for you. But you are strong enough, you can manage. You are my grandchild, after all."

She said that confidently, and to this day I remember that moment as an anchor, reminding me of my strength. Then she spoke to me about shapeshifting, a lesson that is retold below.

The next day I went to the doctor's office in the very mundane world. The chronic illness that had dogged my life for decades was getting worse, and tests had been run. That day, the day after my visit with the Wolf-Mother, I was informed that I had lupus, the disease named after the Wolf.

Angrboda's Lesson:

I know that you already know how to shapeshift, how to move your hame around in different ways, but that is just a child's playing. Yes, you can make wings, make your face beaklike, but that will not make you a bird. Yes, you can make paws and a muzzle, but that will not make anything that truly runs on four legs. You will just be a human's idea of bird or beast, not the real thing, and that is not good enough ... because creatures with one shape are made the way they are for a reason. Every part of them works together as a whole; it was Nature who honed them so perfectly. There is no way that you can replicate that with your human eyes and your human mind; you will be a human stuffed into an odd shape, and you will not know how to use it properly, and anyway there will be parts missing, vital parts.

What you must do is to meet that animal spirit, face to face, and ask permission to take on its form. Then it will exchange forms with you, and run in your body on its own strange astral place. Right there you must decide—if you do not want it running about in your form, then don't ask to borrow its form. There must be an equal exchange, a gift for a gift. Some animal spirits will take a different thing in exchange, but many will want to take your form, and you must become comfortable with that. So you wake up with scratches, bruises, exhausted from running? So what. You'll be fine; they will not abuse your form so long as you do not abuse theirs. A few scratches, that is not abuse, that is simply a reminder.

You cannot take on the form of an animal unless there is enough of you that is like that animal, and to find that form, you bring out those things. Easy enough, yes? Then why do you humans always get it wrong? I'll tell you why—it's that you don't really understand the animal, most of the time. You have some idea about what that creature is like, some romantic idea, but it's not real. You don't want to see the real creature, because it spoils the romance. So for you, it is best to start with the part of that animal that you like the least. If you can touch that, you can know that animal well enough.

Let me give you an example. Would you want to be Wolf? Yes, you may think first of its predatory nature, the hunter, the fierce defender of territory. Is there a wolf in you? Wolf is a pack animal; is there a part of you that is desperate to be part of a group, that would suffer being the lowest and most mistreated rather than be alone, that would go mad if it was abandoned? Is there a part of you that would not be able to keep from jockeying for dominance and position in any group, even to being cruel to those beneath you? Were you like that as a youth, would you be like that again, if you could? You can imagine devouring raw meat; can you imagine gulping down bobcat shit, and enjoying it? Those, too, are Wolf. If those are in you, start there. Ah, I see you shaking your head.

But you know your name, yes? What is the Raven in you? The thief? The one attracted to glitter, even foolish superficial glitter? The one who will eat anything, no matter how foul and disgusting? The one who relishes the squelch of a rotting eyeball? The one who could speak the language of the humans, if it wished ... but will not, out of contrariness? The nervousness of a bird, the coarseness of its humor? Is that where you start with Raven? If not, you should. You humans do best at understanding animal nature when going by what is least attractive.

Then you go to them with that part of you in the front, so that they will smell it or see it, and you ask permission to switch shapes. You will be eye to eye, and then your hame will shape to be them—not just some idea you have of them, the real thing—and it will feel natural as your own body did a moment ago. And they will be you, and you will see them like a fetch looking in your eyes just before they fade away. You can run, fly, what you will, but as soon as you grow tired of it, it will end and switch back. Such things are difficult to hold for long, and besides they may grow tired of it first.

If you do it enough, if you have an alliance with that animal spirit, it can happen fast. You are friends, and you need only call them and look them in the eye, and then it is done. But you must feed them, make offerings to them, if you want them to remain pleased with you. It is not an easy thing, or convenient. Could you become a tree, or a plant, this way? Yes, but it is much harder to pull out the part of yourself that is much like a tree or a plant. They are more alien than you think. But it has been done, certainly; some wight-workers have done it.

There is no song for this, except for a creature that sings, and then you had best listen to them and learn their songs. The best thing that you can do is to meet that creature in your world and watch their breathing. Breathe as fast as they breathe, as deeply or shallowly. Remember that breath when you speak to them. If you have the breath first, they will find it easier to link to you if you are both breathing together. No song, just speak their language, whatever that is. You will need to learn it anyway, not to speak in while you are shifted—that will come naturally—but to remember later what was said to you during your time in beast's hame. You will want that, eventually.

And yes, those of us with more than one shape, we pay for this with bodies that are not perfectly put together. But oh, the other side of that mountain! But I am the Mother of Monsters, I know how to love monsters. Can you learn that? If you cannot, you will never learn to love yourself, shaper, wight-worker, *ergi*, made different from birth and from effort. There is nowhere for you to go but there or madness, the self-hatred that will cripple you. The animals, the plants, the people of this tribe—they will not look down on you for what you are. In the eyes of a raven, you are exactly as you should be. Now go, and do not let me hear that you have insulted any of them with your human foolishness.

Part IV:
Keeping
Whole

Power And Restriction:
Spirit-Work Taboos

One of the most disconcerting things that happens to modern spirit-workers, especially when they are following lost traditions with the aid of Gods and spirits whose connection to this world has been lost for a long time, and most especially if they become god-slaves, is the issue of taboos. I use this word because it's the one that we have in our language to describe behaviors that must be done even if they are not necessary for survival. For most people, the word simply refers to cultural rules, albeit ones at odds with the larger society. For others, it has the connotation of strange and superstitious rules that make no sense, and whose origins are shrouded in mystery. An example of the former might be the Jewish kosher laws; of the latter, Burmese women who stretch their necks out with rings.

Yet our society has hundreds of taboos that we don't even think about. Why don't women go topless in public? Why don't children go naked, even in fine weather? Why are there gender-segregated bathrooms? Why can't men wear skirts and makeup? We do these things not because they make sense, but because they make people uneasy and upset when we cross them. It's what people are used to, and most people dislike change. Every society has its cultural taboos, and they all also have a good number that might have been based on a religious or mythical commandment once, but now are simply carried on due to habit.

However, the taboos of the spirit-worker are a quite different thing; they are magical taboos that both restrict behavior and add power. As one gains allies, they teach you things, but then require things of you in turn, sometimes things you'll have to do for the rest of your life. Usually these taboos are enforced directly, in the sense that if you violate them, you lose power, or lose the ability to do something, or perhaps even get sick or physically weak. Taboos that have to do with the body tend to be enforced by the body—if you're not supposed to ingest a certain kind of food or substance, then you will become ill when you do it.

A good example of spiritual taboos in Celtic folklore is the story of Cuchulain, who has amazing skill in battle, but has been commanded by the spirits never to violate certain taboos—eating dog's flesh, refusing hospitality, etc. When his enemies want to rob him of his powers, they set up circumstances so that he unthinkingly violates them all, more out of lack of mindfulness than deliberate disobedience. He then loses his powers and is killed; if there is a moral angle to this tale, it is about learning to manage one's taboos, and figure out where you might run into trouble before it hits you.

This is not the only story where taboos are seen as weaknesses; how many folktales, ancient and modern, have the heroes attempting to take down a sorcerous villain by exploiting the one thing that he can't touch, or can't be near? The more powerful the "villain", the more likely it is that he has an abundance of such things which he protects himself from. If the story was real, the hero would have the same problems, rather than being impervious to all things. But even Superman has kryptonite.

Some taboos come along with an archetypal job. We refer to these jobs as "hats", rather lightheartedly, as in "He was wearing the Chieftain hat and that's why people were listening to him." Each of these "hats" comes with a set of musts and mustn'ts; some will only apply while the individual is actively "being" that archetype; some will adhere themselves to the individual's life as a regular taboo, especially for people who are doing a particular Job most of the time. One example might be the Sacred King archetype, which has taboos against lying in public, and failing to be constantly creative. Another might be the Lady Of The Hall archetype, which might come with a taboo against giving hospitality and meals to people who are disrespectful, or one that requires giving that hospitality to anyone who isn't.

Something that many spirit-workers have noted is the tendency of wight-bestowed taboos to come in a way that might be labeled "whatever is not mandatory is forbidden, and vice versa". One spirit-worker might be forbidden to eat meat, another required to do it. One might be forbidden to cut their hair; another must shave their head. One might be vowed to celibacy or monogamy with their patron deity-spouse, another required to have sex with any willing person that their deity points out. One might be forbidden to use entheogens, another required to do it. One might be forbidden to eat the flesh of their totem animal; another might gain power from doing so. One might be forbidden to tell lies; another (especially one working for a trickster deity) might find themselves required to tell a lie at least once a month. (The safest way that people with this taboo have found to manage it is to tell a fanciful story about nothing important to a total stranger in passing.)

In each case, it isn't that the "forbidden" behavior in question is wrong, or that the "mandatory" one is morally right. These distinctions are human ones that get smeared over the taboo, because we as humans don't like having our behavior restricted for irrational reasons, and so we come up with some moral principle that the Gods and wights must be using. However, the very fact that any given behavior may be forbidden in one spirit-worker and mandatory in another belies that. It isn't about right or wrong, it's about you personally, and what you need to do and not do in order to be the best possible tool of the spirits. Taking your taboo and getting all righteous about it is missing the point. Be assured, somewhere there is someone who is struggling with its opposite, for reasons just as incomprehensible as those of the Wight that gave you yours.

In tribal societies, life in general is bounded by taboos, in order to keep the group cohesive and not offend the spirits without which they would have difficulty surviving. It's almost expected that the shaman of the tribe will ignore and is allowed to break many of those taboos, as are priest/esses and such. (Examples might be touching or even seeing sacred objects, or coming into contact with unclean people safely.) The fact that they can do this is an acknowledgment of both their power and set-apart station in life, and that they will have their own sets of taboos, some of them more extreme than those of the ordinary tribesfolk. Sure, the shaman can touch the sacred statue, but they also have to jump into icy water on a weekly basis to do strange devotions. Sure, they can walk up to a woman in childbirth and not be sullied, but they also have to wear those odd clothes all the time. It's a tradeoff, which sets them apart even more.

In Marie Czaplicka's 1914 book *Shamanism in Siberia*, she lists many of the odd taboos that the shamans of the various tribes had to adhere to, and concludes: "The vocation of the shaman is attended with considerable danger. The slightest lack of harmony between the acts of the shamans and the mysterious call of their 'spirits' brings their life to an end. This is expressed by the Chukchee, when they say that 'spirits' are very bad-tempered, and punish with immediate death the slightest disobedience of the shaman, and *that this is particularly so when the shaman is slow to carry out those orders which are intended to single him out from other people.*" (Italics mine.) This is something that can't be impressed enough on people who have been grabbed up by the Gods and wights and are being slowly (or not so slowly) killed and reborn into being classic shamans. Unlike most spirit-workers, classic shamans are meant to be visibly distinct in some way that marks them out as sacred and dangerous.

This brings us to the issue of the very presence of the classic shaman being dangerous. While this doesn't apply to all spirit-workers, there is a reason that shamans traditionally live in the little hut at the edge of the village. After being killed and remodified by the wights, a shaman never goes back to "normal" astrally. (References to them as "walking dead men" are quite accurate in their own way.) Not only does the shaman have wights hanging around them and bothering them—a situation which can be very difficult for those who live close to them—their very aura may give off a certain sort of energy, which will vary depending on what sort of spirits they work with and how they have been modified.

We have noticed this effect on people who live with, sleep with, or come into physical contact with modern classic shamans, to the point that I now tell any spirit-worker to warn any possible lovers, roommates, massage therapists, etc., just in case. The most common effect is what we jokingly call "Instant Karma Beverage Powder", which somehow temporarily speeds up the power of Wyrd around the individual who has been affected. It can manifest as simply as going home and finding a whole lot of bills that you've forgotten about in your mailbox, or having the car that you've been forgetting to put oil in seize up that afternoon. It can also cause full-on mental illness or life disasters, especially with repeated contact. "Breakups or breakdowns," was the comment of one observer. "Shamanic radioactivity," was the comment of another.

However you call it, it's both sacred and dangerous. While it can be considered a good thing in the long run to deal with all your buried issues, it can be very disconcerting for people to have so many of them leap out at once and force you to face them, now, whether you like it or not. And then more of them tomorrow, and the next day, and the next. This kind of radiation doesn't spread out from all spirit-workers, certainly—at most the Wyrd-speeding radiation only seems to roll off of classic shamans in this tradition, and not all of them—but even the lighter-weight spirit-workers sometimes have strong energies (and strong wights) hanging around them and their living spaces, and those energies affect people. It's become clear to us that some of these taboos, especially those which set the shaman apart from the rest of society and create that wall of isolation—are put up for the safety of other people. Like the veil over Nerthus's face, it's important for non-spirit-workers to keep a safe distance from the spirits most of the time, and that can mean keeping a safe distance from shamans. (That isolation can also exist for the safety of the shaman as well; when people notice that cascades of intense and not necessarily desirable things happen to them after coming in contact with someone, they may strike out.)

This puts the shaman in a lonely place, no question. It's also a powerful place. We are allowed to do what is not normally permitted—to break not only human social taboos, but taboos normally placed by the Gods on what humans may and may not do with cosmic energies—but in return we pay for this with our lives. It becomes the boundaries of our life, the container that holds us, and makes us safe for the people that we serve. Where there's fear, there's power, and breaking any taboo brings us through a fear and releases the power bound up in that fear. At the same time, our power must be bound or it will become dangerous. Great power requires great responsibility.

Sometimes the taboos laid on us seem strange, petty, even bizarre. Why must I wear these colors? Why must I only touch this with my left hand? Why can I do this small petty thing, but not that small petty thing? Why can I say this, but not that? It reminds me of the skeptical tone of the scholars a century ago, writing that the shaman may only lie on the left side of a horsehide, or must enter a hut backwards, or cannot go anywhere without bells sewn to their clothing, or must not pass a burial place without doing some small rite. Sometimes we don't understand why they ask us to do these odd things, and we just have to trust it as a measure of gaining power. Sometimes it's more clearly that they've just prevented us from doing some behavior that they don't like, with the least possible energy invested in the problem.

The big surprise for most beginning spirit-workers, and especially for modern folk who get spirit-grabbed and turned willy-nilly into shamans, is that taboos are enforced quickly and painfully. It's very common for a patron deity to use their own body against them, to entrench the taboo in their flesh. If you're not supposed to eat a particular food, it will simply make you violently ill. If you go where you shouldn't, you'll get sick. If you try to say something when the Gods have gag-ordered you about it, you'll open your mouth and your vocal cords will seize up. I've noticed a higher-than-normal percentage of spirit-workers with neurological problems, such as tics or seizure disorders, which a patron deity finds easy to trigger when they've disobeyed the rules.

Sometimes it's the mind that's used against them rather than the body. One spirit-worker was told to quit smoking; she angrily defied her patron deity and walked into the convenience store to buy cigarettes, wandered up and down the aisles ... and then walked out again, fuming, but unable to make herself go to the counter and ask for them. Gods and wights are perfectly capable of inducing fugue states, phobias, or mental paralysis in order to keep their vagrant servants from straying. It can be infuriating. The only comfort I have on the matter is the advice of decades of watching this in myself, and I can say that whenever the reason for a taboo came clear to me—perhaps over many years of doing it—I realized that yes, indeed, the Gods really did know better than me on this one. So like all things in spirit-work, it's an act of trust.

On Taboos And Service

by Lydia Helasdottir

There is power in keeping taboos, and there is power in breaking them too. It depends on what kind of taboo it is, and where it came from. Breaking societal taboos is a vast source of power, as ergi people and Tantric people have discovered. Keeping taboos, that's kind of part of the ascetic path as well, disciplining and focusing yourself. There are food taboos, taboos against certain kinds of speech—no lying, etc. Some taboos are inflicted because it's just healthier for your particular body, and some are inflicted due to the deity that you're working with at the time.

For baby spirit-workers, I think I'd advise not to rail against them too much. Young plants need sticks to grow alongside. It's scaffolding. Later, they may actually become sources of comfort. Simply from an engineering point of view, you have to have a vessel if you're going to generate pressure. The vessel has to be tight in order for the alchemical processes to work. Some of them are deals with Gods—"I'm going to be your ally, but now you have to do this." Taboo is mindfulness mechanism, taboo is power generator, taboo is an aid to following your path, and taboo is social bonding—when you share particular taboos with people, it's a means of belonging to a particular group, which is helpful on a large scale because it overrides any personal quibble that you might have.

I am personally ambivalent as to whether one should break taboos just for the hell of it, and I get into a lot of trouble because of that. I tend to find out very quickly which ones were there not to be broken, usually painfully. I tend not to break the ones where I've personally made an agreement with a deity... or I tend to try not to, although sometimes I can't help it. Societal ones—well, if I don't recognize the validity of their foundation, I'll break them as I please, especially if they once had validity but the reasons are no longer there and they are outworn.

It's really interesting to see what happens when something gets liberalized. As an example, many years ago it was really wild and out there to have a tattoo. And a nipple ring... heaven forfend! And now it's boring. I had nipple rings at a time when there were only two guys in the UK at all doing genital or nipple piercings, and it was all hush-hush and you had to know somebody who knew somebody. I remember the thrill of actually getting it done was in large part due to knowing that I would be irrevocably even more of an outcast than I was before.

This brings us invariably to the issue of spirit-workers being outcasts. In tribal societies, the spirit-workers are allowed to break societal taboos—such as where men and women can go—partly because they have their own sets of strict taboos, and in exchange for that they are somehow unclean and become outcasts. They usually have to break the social taboos visibly, and that's true today too; a lot of us have to do weird things where people can see them. They are shunned and feared and reviled behind their backs, but called when anything goes wrong. So you're not just allowed to violate those taboos, you're expected to. It shows that you're beyond the normal boundaries, and also that you're more powerful than the people. They will get struck down if they go to the sacred space and drink the milk, but the shaman doesn't. They need that, in order to trust you with problems they can't solve themselves. People have to believe that the shaman is more powerful than they are, otherwise why bother? "I'm not going to give a reindeer for that! Fuck off!"

Shaman Health and Shaman Sickness

You live in a body, and you are here in that body for a reason.

No matter how much you wish you were not tethered to this flesh, it is needful for many reasons ... and you know what they are, if you will be silent and think about it. No matter how often you leave, you must come home to this gift. Yes, it is a gift to you—our gift. Do not insult us by devaluing it.

—Communication from a bunch of Gods to me

We spirit-workers do things to our astral bodies that most people wouldn't dream of. In many respects, we run our astral bodies like an Olympic athlete runs their physical body. This has repercussions on our physical form—the *hame* affects the *lich* and vice versa. As long as you live, there is no way to fully separate the two, or protect them from each other. This means that part of your job as a spirit-worker is to take care of yourself, on both levels, with the intensity that an Olympic athlete would give to their flesh. Ignoring the physical is one of the biggest risks we run, spending so much time as we do outside of it. Sooner or later, though, this catches up with you and interferes with your ability to do your job. Sometimes it can even kill you.

There are three areas of concern when it comes to the health of spirit-workers: taking care of the physical body, taking care of the astral body, and surviving shaman sickness should it occur. We will take them piece by piece, with suggestions from a number of spirit-workers who have dealt with this for years.

(Note: You'll notice that this chapter is on the health and sickness of the spirit-worker, not that of their clients. Healing is indeed one of the main functions of a shaman, and of many spirit-workers. However, it is such a complicated and widespread subject that it deserves, and will get, its own book: *Mapping The Hollow World: Northern-Tradition Shamanic Healing*. In the meantime, no one ever talks about the health of the spirit-worker, and it's about time someone actually started.)

Caring For The Lich

Some of us have the luxury of reasonably healthy bodies, but many of us don't. Modern spirit-workers seem to come with many inborn health problems; it's been speculated that the genetic "wiring" that makes one more easily able to do the work comes with genetic side effects. This conjecture is made more interesting by two further anecdotal details: first, the majority of early-life medical complaints from spirit-workers fall into a few specific categories, and second, spirit-workers who didn't have complaints in those areas from an early age often develop them anyway after doing spirit-work for a few years. This strongly suggests that these are common side effects to being born with, or developing through spirit contact, the "wiring" that makes what we do possible.

First, neurological problems. We've found that the following conditions are frighteningly prevalent in spirit-workers: epilepsy, non-epileptic seizure conditions, Tourette syndrome, and chronic migraines. Lest medical personnel leap to conclusions about all this spirit-work being just illusions caused by bad brain wiring (well, actually, if they're heavily invested in believing that then they will believe it no matter what I say), it should be pointed out that seizures and migraines are some of the conditions developed by some apparently neurologically "normal" people *after* beginning spirit-work.

> The shaman Yetilin had an incessant nervous twitching in his face, [and] the Chukchee said laughingly, that he was probably "with an owl kele" (spirit), comparing his affliction to the jerking motion of the owl's head when it devours its prey.
> —Bogoras, *The Chukchee*

The second area of complaint is blood sugar issues. Both hypoglycemia and diabetes are found in pre-onset spirit-workers, and hypoglycemia is especially prone to appearing in post-onset spirit-workers. The third area of complaint is immune disorders; a malfunctioning immune system is again symptomatic in both cases. There is also a side set of endocrinal problems often found alongside of immune-system glitches: polycystic ovarian syndrome, hypogonadism, and various intersex conditions, all of which present in higher numbers in people who will become spirit-workers. Those sets of problems happen so commonly that new spirit-workers who mention developing them tend to get wry, knowing nods from more experienced ones. It's "part of the deal", although it's difficult to say how it all fits together.

Neurological problems can probably be explained by the stress of running high-voltage energy through a body and brain wiring that wasn't built for it, and as for those who had them already ... well, as my assistant pointed out, when you build a really sensitive receiver, you get static. Blood sugar causes are less easy to track, but may well have to do with the *hame* being frequently out of alignment with the *lich*, and two separate digestive systems giving different information to the brain, which becomes confused about where nourishment is needed. Under normal circumstances, healthy food will nourish a healthy *lich*, which will supply most of the *ond* necessary for a normal *hame*. With the combination of extra *ond*-needs and a *hame* that frequently gives out vastly differing signals from the *lich*, it can be conjectured that the resulting stress, over time, creates blood-sugar problems.

The endocrinal syndromes are a more difficult thing to explain, although simple low-immunity can be spoken of in terms of stress. However, most of the other syndromes are genetic in nature to one extent or another, which lends some credence to the often discomforting idea that continually rears its head: that some people are just more genetically "wired" to be spirit-workers than others, and that these "gifts" come with an associated genetic price. It is also interesting that a few of these conditions—epilepsy and intersex conditions, for example—have been considered signs of being "god-touched" in many ancient cultures anyhow. Again, rather than considering them causal, one could consider them frequently comorbid with spirit-work.

While some spirit-workers will have fairly serious physical obstacles, some may seem entirely healthy in body. Still, spirit-work takes its toll over time, and the intelligent spirit-worker will pay attention to a failing *lich* as a sign that all is not well with the *hame*, and do what can be done to tilt the balance in the other direction. The health suggestions below were all gleaned from interviews with spirit-workers on their health practices. Most of these suggestions were repeated by most of the spirit-workers interviewed, so my cutting of repetition for brevity should be kept in mind. Most of us have found that almost all of these things help.

The single biggest thing is getting enough sleep. That has a much more immediate impact on my ability to do spirit-work than anything else, even more so than what I eat or what kind of shape I'm in. I'm the kind of person who'd stay up 24/7 if I could, reading or writing or doing any of a hundred other things I find more interesting than lying comatose in bed. I used to be bad about not sleeping enough. But when I was shaman-sick, I became subject to prolonged periods of insomnia. I couldn't sleep for days at a time, and it really made things awful both physically and mentally, so that I was even less capable of holding things together while grappling with shamanic insanity.

If I don't sleep for at least six or seven hours, I won't dream, and my dreams are an important part of my life as a spirit-worker — I often have prophetic dreams or get messages through them, which can't happen if I'm awake. Plus it's hard enough to focus on mundane tasks when I'm sleep-deprived, but it's damn near impossible to do anything spooky on not enough sleep. For one thing, I can't hear any of Them very well when I haven't slept enough. For another, I'll start having first auditory and then visual hallucinations, and needless to say, these gravely interfere with my ability to do any spirit-work.

Otherworld journeying is the hardest on me, physically; although I practice *hamfara* or astral journeying, rather than having to physically pathwalk, it still takes a great deal of energy. I'm usually exhausted when I return even if the journey was of relatively short duration. Part of that may be because of the time differential between this and the rest of the Nine Worlds; even if only an hour or two passes in this world, if my journey lasts for days in the otherworlds, then I'll feel just as tired as if I'd been traveling and doing things for an equal amount of time here.

Since lots of spirit-workers seem to have medical conditions like insulin resistance, neurological disorders or chronic pain, having pre- and post-spirit-work procedures already in place to compensate for your existing physical problems is a good thing to do. Doing things like horsing or trancework takes enough out of a person without throwing in blood sugar issues or old injuries acting up on top of everything else. For instance, I'm diabetic, so hardcore fasting is not an option for me. I usually eat at least a piece of raw fruit or two before I undertake a journey, since I don't always know how long I'll be "gone." But because there's always a chance I might have a low blood sugar episode after I return anyway, I make sure to have something to eat or drink ready at hand for when I come out of trance.

Needless to say, if you willfully ignore your body while doing spirit-work, eventually it's going to rebel against all the ill treatment, possibly to the point of severely interfering with your Job. And what would They have to say about that? Probably not something very reassuring, I'd think.

–Elizabeth Vongvisith

Diet is important. That doesn't mean any one particular diet; different people have different needs and there is no one-size-fits-all. If you're not sure what you should be eating, ask your patron deity. They may not tell you outright—what god has the time to list every food?—but you'll probably find yourself drawn to or repelled from certain foods over the next couple of weeks. Pay attention to that. I find that for myself, it's not any variety of actual food so much as simple wholesome foods. I do best when I can identify every part of what I'm eating, and there is nothing that couldn't have been (or ideally was) grown on a local farm.

In fact, I have a visual exercise that I do when I'm wondering whether I should eat something. In my mind, I have an imaginary neighbor named Gunther, who works a small, old-fashioned farm. (As I live in the city, there are no Gunthers near me, so I must imagine one.) Gunther farms like I would were I drawn to that work—no pesticides, no hormones in his herds. Cows, sheep, goats, chickens, geese and pigs wander his fields, well-treated and well-fed. Each of his vegetables, or the fruits taken from his extensive orchard, is carefully grown and harvested with pride. His grain may be cut with a tractor and ground in his mill, but he understands its gift. His wife Breta makes butter and cheese, and grinds the flour. His fishponds teem with fishes, although he will also sell those brought in by his brother Bjorne the ocean-fisherman. Because Gunther's farm is imaginary, it can shift climates and grow food from many areas. Whenever I look at a food in the store, and read its label, I ask: could I have bought all the ingredients of this food at Gunther's farm, and assembled it myself, assuming that I knew how? If not, I usually make myself put it back.

This is something that many spirit-workers have discovered: just cutting out the chemicals makes a big deal. Eliminate the preservatives, the dyes, the pesticides—eat organic and simple—see what happens. You hear things more clearly, you are more sensitive. You would be surprised how much the false food dulls you. It was never alive, never had life to give, and it is profane. A little is not a sacrilege, but the more you consume, the worse it is. With spirit-work it is just the opposite of what some would have: the more alive the food is, the more recently it drew breath, the better. Raw vegetables fresh from the garden are the best precisely because they are still alive and have the most energy. It sounds terrible, but no spirit-worker should be afraid of the cycle of life. We feed on life, and someday we will feed it in turn. That's the other thing that I think of: is what I put into my body making it fit food for worms someday? If my rotting body would poison the earth, something is very wrong.

                                        –Gudrun, seidhkona

After the obvious effects that dietary changes have had, I have become much more sensitive to trance states; whether this is a purely physical thing or not is debatable, but since I think trance states have as much to do with physical factors as they do with spiritual and mental ones, it figures into my way of thinking. Being more sensitive to trance states is beneficial, but it's also troublesome; my current challenge is to become stuck more firmly in my body. Again, this may not be a purely physical thing, but spirit-work has greatly affected the way I fit into and relate to my body, so this has been one of the biggest physical results of spirit-work. I'm much more sensitive to foods, and things like caffeine and alcohol. Various aspects of the work have reduced an already mercurial sex drive to near zero; ironically my early training included sex magick, which changed me in other ways. Things like heavy ritual work, journeying, or working with sacred plants can leave me run down for days; I'm not good for much of anything past making tea and watching daytime TV.

Spirit-work can be exhausting, and when we get tired immunity can be compromised. The exhaustion seems to be a natural part of the work. Keeping healthy certainly helps avoid becoming sick, but it's a tough road until a certain level of endurance is built up; I'd say that the work load is as much to get things done as it is endurance training. Intense energy work can have adverse effects on the body if the right safeguards aren't in place; you can burn out circuits, and that's never pleasant. Unhappy wights have several ways to make sure we don't cross their paths again, and their retaliation can include physical illness. Always keep preventative maintenance in mind; eat the right things, take your vitamins, and get enough sleep (when you can). Stay mentally healthy; make time for recreation and for non-spirit-work activities. Pay attention to shields and personal energy fields, and take care not to anger any spirits.

Above everything else, I have to keep working. My health, particularly mental health, is dependant on my working; if I stop, I'm hit with overwhelming depression, extreme mood swings, and other problems. These problems have direct effects on my physical health; for instance, when I get very depressed, I don't eat very well, which only makes me sicker. I have to pay attention to my taboos and obligations. Neglecting these results in spiritual ailments or affects my ability to do my job, which is what I have to do in order to stay healthy. If any part of my life is ignored for too long (mundane responsibilities or spiritual ones), everything else falls apart. I have to pay close attention to keeping everything in the correct balance.

–Jessica Maestas, spirit-worker

I've struggled with my health ever since I became a spirit-worker. The work that I do has left me with joint and back injuries, a compromised immune system, migraines, blood sugar issues, hormonal imbalance, depression, and stress and anxiety problems. To counteract some of the strain and to keep myself healthy, I do the following regularly: I practice Tai Chi and Chi Gung. I regulate my sleeping habits and get enough solitude to keep stress away. I take a number of supplements daily—vitamins, iron, chromium and magnesium to help regulate my blood sugar, flax seed to regulate my estrogen levels, acidophilus, calcium with extra Vitamin D, and coriolis (a Chinese mushroom that is absolutely wonderful for strengthening the immune system). I take herbal medicines as needed—I find that thanks to the spirit-work and my Jotun blood, my body does not respond as expected to many pharmaceuticals and even when it does, I tend to become immune to them fairly quickly. I do regular cleansings both astrally and physically via herbal detox. I meditate and pray regularly, and I get a health reading once a year from another shaman.

The most common complaints that I've suffered have been exhaustion, migraines, blood sugar issues, and weak immune system. Of course, I think that the nature of the physical strain will vary depending on the spirit-worker and the type of work he or she does, but immune-system issues seem to be pretty pandemic across the board.

Also, there have been times when I've had to engage in astral combat or other protective work and my astral body has taken severe hits that have culminated in physical injury on the temporal plane. (The worst of this was a case of elf-shot that left me with pinched nerves and scar tissue in my lower back.) Usually such astral injuries affect the physical body by leaving scar tissue, debilitating pain, joint problems, even ruptured disks. It depends on the nature of the injury itself. I've also seen astral injuries that bleed energy and strength from a person which results in sickness, malaise and depression. I've known cases where toxins infecting the person on the astral have eventually leaked down into the physical and resulted in tumors, cancers, and infections, but I myself have not yet experienced this.

Being aware that stress can come from simple mundane things is important too. Many of us are kept on a fairly short leash by our Gods, which can include truncating personal relationships. The isolation and marginalization of being who and what we are can create an amazing level of emotional and psychological stress, as can the hostility we often must face on a day-to-day basis from the communities we serve. The cure for this, if cure there is, lies in seeking out and developing a community of spirit-workers, shamans, god-slaves, god-spouses, mystics, et al. as a support network ... people of like mind, who understand and share both the work and the strains. Having that community to fall back on can be immensely strengthening in and of itself.

–Galina Krasskova

Spirit-work, in all its various forms, is rather draining. It's physically tiring, emotionally taxing and spiritually exhausting. It's important to try and keep your general health at a high level. I'm grateful that Hela made me get my health together before all of this started to get really out of hand. Some of it started to happen during that process, but it has snowballed tremendously. My diet is rather strict. I have been essentially vegan for the past two years (though She wants me to change this slowly) and I avoid processed foods: no hydrogenated oils or artificial colorants, no preservatives, high-fructose corn syrup, nor canned products. I eat organically as much as possible, but when it isn't, I avoid the "dirty dozen" crops. I would really recommend trying to get enough rest (easier said than done when one is an insomniac and the spirits are overworking you), eating a lot of good nutritious fruits and vegetables (also easier said than done when one has digestive ailments and monetary restrictions), and using high-quality nutritional supplements when one can afford them. Juicing is also a great way to power up if you can afford to do it. Mix fresh vegetables and fruits with lots of pigments. Exercise is important if you can manage it. I respond particularly well to hiking in the woods. These things really do help.

I have also been doing near-daily cleansing baths which I find extremely helpful. I take them very hot, with Epsom and sea salts. I often use lavender essential oil or a blend of oils designed to help me relax. Conversely I can use energizing oils if needed. This is very good for me physically as well as spiritually and emotionally. Sauna, when one can get it, is also amazing for this. I often meditate and/or perform ritual cleansing while I'm in the bath, unless I am simply too spent. Then I use a simple prayer for aid in my cleansing.

–Steph Russell, spirit-worker

I have to eat a seasonal diet, consisting of whole or minimally processed foods, and my sugars are limited to maple and nutmeg syrup, honey and some (increasingly rare) 'raw' sugars. Also, I have to eat raw meat occasionally (if the source is questionable, I can make it extremely rare) when I work. I also have to find local equivalents to my cultural diet. More and more often I find I have to shift towards game meats instead of livestock meats, which means I have to get to know hunters – or have people 'pay' me in game meat – and buy it in the grocery store. I've noticed that livestock meats are beginning to make me ill when I eat them. Buffalo over beef; pheasant over chicken, etc. If my ancestors could hunt it and gather it, I can eat it ... and they're getting really insistent that I stick to this.

Spirit-work has also changed how my body responds to modern medications. I can't use any modern painkillers, and 95% of modern medicine does me no good whatsoever. The 5% that does work are massive doses of the highest-strength stuff (which naturally isn't covered by my insurance), and I have to use them rarely to continue to be able to use them at all. This means that I get regular downloads of herbal information, and I pick up 'local' herbals everywhere I travel. That proved useful on my honeymoon, as I was in a situation which required medical care, and for which I had to use local herbs. I'm getting this information more and more often to compensate, so long as I continue to demonstrate my willingness to abide by it.

–Aleksa, spirit-worker

Breathe deeply, have good posture, stretch when you can, and move your body whenever you can. I know that we tend to live in worlds connected with our minds and souls, not our physical bodies, but we have to remember to move them on a regular basis. Keeping the body moving keeps the energy channels moving. If nothing else, take walks out in nature.

–Ari, spamadhr

Meditate and drink a gallon of water a day. Drinking lots of water flushes the system and speeds the process. Also basic grounding techniques including eating starchy foods after horsing or journeying helps one be more body aware and less dissonant. Being aware of where the body is at all times when elsewhere cuts down on a lot of mistakes that lead to illness.

–Krei, spirit-worker

Caring For The Hame

On the other hand, the astral body needs its health seen to as well. Energy-moving techniques are the best thing for this. As spirit-workers, we can't afford to let the wiring get rusty, because it's put through so much extra usage. One way to manage this is, of course, just circling your energy, perhaps while you're sitting around waiting in the doctor's office, or on the bus. Run it in a loop up the front of your body and down the back, and then reverse it. One of those directions will relax you, and can be used to help get to sleep. The other will energize you, and can take the place of stimulants. The tricky part is that which is which will differ for each person (regardless of what any energy-gurus may say) and only you can figure out which direction does what for you. However, you'll likely be able to figure it out in very short order, as the effects are noticeable in something like a minute or two. This simple exercise is a quick pipe-cleaner, so to speak; the equivalent of running hot water down the drain. It may not get rid of major buildup, but it will at least keep the channels open.

I get utterly exhausted astrally if there's a lot of work. Oftentimes there are so many balls in the air at that I'm never all in one place, so there is a sense of disjointedness and missing time. Spirits usually have priority over my time, and even those times one might presume are "normal" situations inevitably end up being "on duty" lights. I get nausea a lot when my astral body isn't well, which is usually helped by grounding, centering, and getting some sleep.

Astrally speaking... hmmm, well, depending on the duty at the time I can end up with "electrical cuts" (they look like scratches with a burned tinge), and aches in metaphysical joints (if I had to shapeshift to make the journey, for example). I'll get the sensation of not being all in one place, or of being half present. Centering my attention and retracing my steps usually helps with this. Eating properly helps both bodies. Keep "grounding" foods — salt, meat, chocolate, bread — on hand at all times.

-Aleksa, spirit-worker

Grounding and centering, if not daily then at least every couple of days, helps a lot. Even if you're the most city-bound of spirit-workers, leave the city and find a green place where you can ground and center regularly. It will keep your energy cleaner. Come up with a regular purification ritual—it doesn't have to be a long one, it can be short, and then you can do it every time you take a shower, which means that you don't have to schedule a special time for it.

—Ari, spamadhr

If you are particularly prone to issues of blockage, and especially if they get in the way of your signal clarity and your general work, well ... there's a reason why we shamanic types use altered states of various kinds. Having an especially cathartic altered-state experience, especially if it is done ritually and with the aid of one's various wight-helpers, can blow out the blockages and widen the "pipes". It can also do harm, if you're not careful, so make sure that you take precautions. (For more information than you likely need on all the different sorts of altered-state techniques, please see the next book in this series.)

Cleanliness and purification is a useful thing for *hame* maintenance. Learn to give your *hame* a once-over and check for small parasites which may sucker on to you while journeying. (Useful instructions for grounding, centering, and keeping the *hame* cleansed and monitored can be found in the Journeying chapter of the second book in this series, *Pathwalker's Guide to the Nine Worlds*.) If you're put in a job where you have to be sucking negative things out of people constantly (and you're not a primary psychic vampire who can burn them off naturally, or you are and you're dealing with things too horrid even for that), take precautions. Try putting together a filter to pull the energy through before taking it into yourself, perhaps in an amulet that can be worn and dipped regularly in salt water to clean it. The best way to keep your *hame* clean is to avoid gunking it up in the first place. As in many professions that deal with toxic waste, hygiene is very important.

What you put into your physical body, in general, can affect the astral body and thus psychic ability, or the *ve* as we refer to it here. This is something that mystics and psychic workers in general have known for a long time, thus the elaborate traditions that have grown up in many religions around purification, asceticism, and other ways of clearing the mind and focusing the spirit. This isn't just about food, however, especially in this modern era. Medications can affect the astral body through the physical. This doesn't mean that one shouldn't take necessary medications, it just means that one should be aware of the possible psychic side effects as well as the physical ones. If there is some question as to whether a particular medication should be put into a particular spirit-worker's body, divination should be done to get the opinion of the Gods and wights on the subject.

One issue that has come up recently as an ambivalent debate among spirit-workers is the problem of psychiatric medications and their effect on the ability of psychically talented people to use those talents. This is one are where divination is crucial, especially in the case of SSRIs, antipsychotic medications, and antiseizure medications. Psych meds are highly variable in how they affect someone's mind and *ve*. The same medication can give one spirit-worker the mental clarity to better access their *ve* without blocking it in any way (and some of them learn to work around any psychic side effects of lifelong meds without much trouble), but giving it to another spirit-worker can completely shut down their *ve*, a situation that can anger the wights and cause them to find ways to get that individual off of those medications. Some spirit-workers have even found that this blockage lasted for years after they went off of the medication; they report having to work for a long time to bring back what had been lost, and some claim that it was never the same again. Take great care, then, before making the decision to take any psych med. (I realize that this is easy for me to say; it may be the case that if someone is in such a state as to need psych meds, they may not be using their best judgment. That's why divination, preferably from a neutral party, is a good thing.)

Something that we don't like to talk about is that the human beings of today are very different, genetically, than those of thousands of years ago. We have been radically sculpted in ways that we aren't even aware of by the last few generations of toxic chemicals in the environment and in our food, and also by modern medicine saving people who would have died in previous centuries, and allowing them to breed and pass on their genes. Really, we've changed the course of human evolution, only we've not done it in a deliberate way, or one that makes us stronger as a species. We're weaker, and continuing to get weaker. Don't ask me how to fix this socially; I have no answers ... and the answers of the Gods frighten me.

What I do know is that we who are bound to serve other people and heal them need to address the fact that there are disease conditions going on today that have never occurred before in the history of mankind. Some are genetic, some are triggered by external toxins, some are a combination of both. Traditional Native American medicine people that I've spoken to were the first ones who started talking about the existence of new forms of illness—and especially mental illness—that they, their teachers, and their spirits had never seen before. It was then that I realized I'd been seeing the same things, and the wights that I work with were rather unsure what to do about them. Certainly those wights were also uncertain about the role of modern medicine, and modern psychoactive medication. The wights that I work with aren't static, they aren't two-dimensional shadows. They understand change, and they change. They just need information to catch up. That means that I spend a lot of time reading books and articles about modern medicine and drugs, and I let them see it through my eyes, and they make the connections. I trust that they will learn to help, and to aid me in assisting those who suffer. We just need to give them help so that they can help us in turn. And the wights talk to each other, too, so the more of us that are doing this, the better it will be for all of us.

–Gudrun, seidhkona

I think one thing that isn't talked about nearly as much as it needs to be in modern society regarding medication is that everyone is different. That is not a convenient fact for the pharmaceutical industry (it makes it harder to put cholesterol ads in Time magazine, for one thing). This means that every individual person will respond a bit differently to a medication. That also applies to different times in a person's life when for many (often hard to quantify) reasons a medication may work better or worse for that person.

Sometimes a deity that you're working with will say that a particular person (possibly you) shouldn't use a particular drug. What we need to keep in mind as spirit-workers is that there are times when a medication is totally the wrong thing for us or a student or colleague of ours. I don't doubt that the deity is right in that case. It may be that another anti-depressant might have been OK for that person to use, or maybe that person just couldn't be on that kind of drug at that time and do what spooky stuff they needed to do. It would be tempting for us to say that this means that particular drug is not OK for spirit-work or magic, but it really just means it wasn't for that person in that instance.

There are no easy answers in matters of neurochemistry and spooky-foo. This is an area that most of us in the spirit-work community would do well to acquaint ourselves with. The incidence of neurological and/or psychological issues is quite disproportionate among spirit-workers. I should point out that I am a big believer in using as few medications as is possible while still being able to function and be safe. Witness that I have Tourette Syndrome, and I am willing to go around barking like a dog rather than deal with the side effects of the few medications that have any effect at all on my tics. And yes, some of that is because the medication side effects hinder my ability to function as a spirit-worker (or anything else for that matter), although I would point out that there is a real difference between saying that a medication interferes with spirit-work and that the side effects of said medication do. On an individual medication basis the difference is semantics, but knowing the difference can have a big influence on where you go next.

As spirit-workers, and mentors and teachers of spirit-workers, it also behooves us to be aware of what the consequences of going off of different medications are, and what are the proper procedures for doing so. I know that certain of the medications I take make horsing more difficult, although not impossible by any means. If I know that I am going to be horsing a difficult or unfamiliar deity I will make the necessary changes to my medication in the proper and gradual way that the drug calls for in advance of the horsing (advance enough to give me a few days for it to get out of my system). After the horsing I'll go back on the drug in the appropriate and/or gradual way each drug requires.

A full AHFS Drug Information (like the PDR, only put out by the national pharmacist organization instead of the drug companies) or even the AHFS DI Essentials or AHFS Drug Handbook should be something that those of us who work a lot with students or who use medication ourselves have available for finding out that sort of information. Plus when a student comes to you saying that the Fey are trying to kill her, it is nice to be able to check and find out that paranoid delusions are a withdrawal side effect of the anti-psychotic your student just went cold turkey on *before* you go starting shit with the Fey.

–Wintersong Tashlin, spirit-worker

Some experiential evidence shows that any med, taken long enough, will become absorbed by the system and it's antipsi effects will wear off over time. The more the body "needs" the med in order to function correctly (and in this, I'm adding my experience working with people with seizure disorders, on heavy CNS druggage) the quicker the bodymindspirit adapts to it and it ceases to be a problem.

Specifically, it seems that neuroleptics like Topomax, Dilantin, Neurontin, and the like have a big effect of shutting down psi. However, as the body adjusts, the psi returns in slow doses. Usually I advise people that if the psi doesn't return, it's not the right drug for long term usage.

–Del, spirit-worker

The Lich-Hame Connection

There is a lot of material out there, especially in New Age and alternative health care circles, about people who can heal themselves— sometimes of terrible diseases—through the power of prayer or will or positive thinking. This seems like a kind of magic, a kind of spiritual techniques that you'd think that spirit-workers would have mastered. After all, isn't there a lot of stuff in anthropological accounts about shamans healing themselves as part of the first thing they do? Wouldn't it look like that? And if so, why are there so many modern shamans with chronic health issues?

The answer is complicated, and you won't find it in the think-yourself-well books. There are two ways that healing without any physical cause can happen. The first is that the Gods and spirits intervene, either because someone prayed or because they agreed to do so for other reasons. The latter is what spirit-workers are generally expected to arrange if possible, and the former is probably responsible for at least some of the "miraculous" cures of ordinary people. However, there is a second reason for the "think yourself well" folks, and that is literally what it says that it is—being able to overwhelmingly affect your physical body by your mental state. While a lot of folks talk about that, few are talking about what sort of energy body that requires.

As far as we can tell from our observations, people who are able to do this are people with a very strong *lich/hame* connection. Their astral bodies are so perfectly linked to and lined up with their physical bodies that influencing the one has a profound effect on the other. The down side of this is that these are also the people who can cause themselves great harm from psychosomatic illnesses, perhaps even unto death. But they can heal themselves, if they try.

Spirit-workers are on the other end of the continuum from these people (with the rest of humanity somewhere in the middle). By the nature of the work that we do, we have a much more pronounced split between our *lich* and our *hame* than that aforementioned mass of humanity, and that's necessary. If it wasn't the case, being *ergi* (often a very psychologically painful situation which encourages both psychological and psychic dissociation) wouldn't be nearly so much of an asset to spirit-work as it is. (For more information on the *ergi* taboo, check the next book in this series.) This is especially the case for classic shamans who have died and come back; the near-death modifications cause a permanent separation between the *lich* and the *hame* that can be temporarily bridged with difficulty, but the twain shall never meet naturally or for very long ever again. Even if you're a non-shaman spirit-worker, you work will by definition tend to push the two apart. This is a necessary evil for doing our Work, and if the Work weren't so valuable and important, we wouldn't have to do this thing that is so hard on a human body and soul. Spirit-workers in general tend to be excellent at ignoring pain and discomfort, which is reflected in the accounts of shamans dancing all night until they dropped, and then getting up in an hour to go work in the fields with everyone else.

However, just because we have this necessary handicap doesn't mean that we should just give up and let ourselves disintegrate. Even if you're a classic shaman and your *hame* is never going to stay congruent with your *lich* again until you die the final time, there are ways that this can be temporarily bridged long enough to keep you reasonably healthy. One that has worked with me is acupuncture, although it may take far longer for the *hame* to be trained to respond to it than the *lich*. It took me about a year of weekly sessions to get to the point where I could both physically and astrally work with what was going on as the needles did their work. Other folk have had luck with energy-work sessions to temporarily reconnect the two in order to send appropriate energy along those channels.

A few bodyworkers who work with spirit-workers are learning to do different sorts of massage that help to shape the *hame* when it gets stuck, or to help the *lich/hame* connection. However, about fifty caveats need to be inserted at this point. Bodyworkers and energy workers who do not understand the nature of spirit-work, and especially the nature of the astral modifications of a particular spirit-worker, should not take it upon themselves to attempt to mess with that spirit-worker's *hame*. The Gods and wights can sometimes make permanent changes to our astral bodies that may look bizarre or wrong to an energy-worker with vague second sight and no understanding of why things flow in this weird way. We've heard horror stories of spirit-workers who went in for a simple massage to deal with orthopedic problems, and the massage therapist happened to also be an energy-worker, took one look at their unusual *hame* configuration, decided that it was a terrible problem that needed to be fixed, and attempted to "fix" them without their knowledge or permission. In each case, it did damage to the spirit-worker and took them some time to get it all back to working function. It was certainly a good thing that this didn't happen with spirit-workers who have heavy wards and "booby-traps" on the various modifications to their astral bodies, because that could have gone badly for the energy-worker as well.

All this means is that you, the spirit-worker, have to choose any bodyworkers extremely carefully. If what you're looking for is just physical work that doesn't go any deeper than the *lich*, it might be a good idea to stick to bodyworkers with a highly medical or sports-massage context to their work, ones that see it all as a physical thing and don't hold with all that fluffy Newage spooky shit. On the other hand, if there are weird physical anomalies that are actually caused by the spirit-work, there will be no good way to explain that, if you feel that it's necessary. The ideal, of course, is an energy-trained bodyworker who understands spirit-work, is willing to learn about your particular "system" and what it's been altered to do, and can deftly work around it.

But there are few of those on the ground right now, which means that it's probably up to the spirit-worker to "train" their own energy-worker, should they need one. To be fair, there also needs to be a lot more pooling of information between us about this issue before we can give comprehensive instructions to bodywork schools. For example, we need more information on the different kinds of energy-oriented bodywork and how they affect different sorts of spirit-workers. Craniosacral therapy, for example, has been anecdotally cited as a frequent offender when it comes to screwing up spirit-worker *hame* "systems", and until we have further information we feel that it is strongly contraindicated for spirit-workers with serious spirit-created astral modifications. In some cases, we've heard of even such "harmless" energy as Reiki being ineffective or causing mild damage, so proceed with care.

Make sure you're spending a good amount of time studying and implementing grounding techniques, and that your daily practice includes a scan of both the *lich* and the *hame* for potential issues. Personally, I have found that keeping a pair of bodhi stones help keep me grounded and focused when I'm not "on the clock".

I think the other thing that helps keep me grounded, both in my own body and in the realm of humanity, is not neglecting my real-world responsibilities just because I have spirit-work as well. I still have to do the dishes, keep my laundry situation under control, and take care of my pets. Also, volunteering my time to those for whom all of this would be a luxury—the mentally ill, the terminally ill, the homeless—helps keep me grounded and focused.

–Del, spirit-worker

How do you tie together things that exist on different levels of reality? In pondering this, I'm trying to find some analogy that could give possible leads. How would you tie Earth and Water, when they are so different in nature? Perhaps by combining elements, sympathetic magic could be used. Air and Fire don't seem as relevant. But Earth is solid, and Water unites, slipping through all the cracks. Earth is physical. Water is more like the Astral. Perhaps applying mud on the chakras? All right, time to pause for experimenting.

I just tried rubbing mud onto my throat chakra, rubbing clockwise, from the point of view of someone standing in front me. Throat went up from 6 to 12 (in my intuitive measuring system). Tried it on third eye; it went from 31 to 41. And they're still slowly climbing. I notice my Sight being clearer than usual. It might be just from the clockwise rubbing, but I think the mud makes a difference. When I've previously tried to "spin" my chakras into higher activity, the results were very short-lived. The mud seems to make it "stick".

As the mud dries, the effect seems to decline. Down to 9 and 37 after about 15 minutes, though I can still feel it active, like a warmth. Perhaps covering the mud to keep it wet would help? With the water gone, it's just earth, so that kind of makes sense. Will have to see if there remains some net increase tomorrow. Otherwise, it's just a temporary fix, and not nearly as useful. Maybe earth and oil would work, so it doesn't dry. Skin oils are the only reason the earth is still sticking onto me, after the water's gone, and it seems to still be working. After half an hour, it's at 9 and 36. Interesting...

I get the numbers by asking my intuition, but another method is using a pendulum over the chakra while lying down. You count how many times the pendulum swings a full circle before stopping, and that's your number.

Final notes: The next day, I was still at 9 and 36, and a week later, I am at 12 and 37. The "mud spin" method seems useful in improving the astral and physical body connection in a permanent way, and it increases the function of weak chakras (a 100% increase) more than that of strong chakras (a 20% increase). Though your mileage may vary.

–Linda, spirit-worker

Dead Men Walking: Shaman Sickness

The term "shaman sickness" is not one that you'll generally hear outside of most spirit-worker circles, and that's because we have only relatively recently learned to identify it again, after centuries of not understanding what it is that happens to shamans at the beginning of their careers. The term denotes a period of illness (often seriously life-threatening in some way) which is caused by the Gods and wights in order to completely remake someone and turn them into a shaman. The phenomenon of shaman sickness is found in tribal cultures around the world, with remarkably similar sets of traumas. It is the hallmark of the classic shaman in many parts of the globe.

I should disclaimer two things right here: First, in spite of all references about global shamanic traditions, we are again only speaking for the Northern Tradition. In some tribal cultures, it seems that their spirit-workers do not go through such changes and experiences. I can't comment on that one way or another; however, it seems that in the traditions of northern Eurasia, this is the way things work, the way that the spirits want it, whether we like it or not. Again and again we find references to this in circumpolar shamanic traditions, and also ones in other areas of the world. The following century-old comments by Siberian shamans from Marie Czaplicka's book on the subject are typical both of what many tribal cultures say about shaman sickness, and what modern classic shamans in the Northern Tradition find to be true today:

Whether his calling be hereditary or not, a shaman must be a capable—nay, an inspired person. Of course, this is practically the same thing as saying that he is nervous and excitable, often to the verge of insanity. So long as he practices his vocation, however, the shaman never passes this verge. It often happens that before entering the calling persons have had serious nervous affections. Thus a Chukchee female shaman, Telpina, according to her own statement, had been violently insane for three years, during which time her household had taken precautions that she should do no harm to the people or to herself.

I was told that people about to become shamans have fits of wild paroxysms alternating with a condition of complete exhaustion. They will lie motionless for two or three days without partaking of food or drink. Finally they retire to the wilderness, where they spend their time enduring hunger and cold in order to prepare themselves for their calling.

To be called to become a shaman is generally equivalent to being afflicted with hysteria; then the accepting of the call means recovery. There are cases of young persons who, having suffered for years from lingering illness, at last feel a call to take up shamanistic practice and by this means overcome the disease ... Here is an account by a Yakut-Tungus shaman, Tiuspiut ("fallen-from-the-sky"), of how he became a shaman: "When I was twenty years old, I became very ill and began to see with my eyes, to hear with my ears that which others did not see or hear; nine years I struggled with myself, and I did not tell any one what was happening to me, as I was afraid that people would not believe me and would make fun of me. At last I became so seriously ill that I was on the verge of death; but when I started to shamanize I grew better; and even now when I do not shamanize for a long time I am liable to be ill."

The Chukchee call the preparatory period of a shaman by a term signifying "he gathers shamanistic power". For the weaker shamans the preparatory period is less painful, and the inspiration comes mainly through dreams. But for a strong shaman this stage is very painful and long; in some cases it lasts for one, two, or more years. Some young people are afraid to take a drum and call on the "spirits", or to pick up stones or other objects which might prove to be amulets, for fear lest the "spirit" should call them to be shamans. Some youths prefer death to obedience to the call of spirits. Parents possessing only one child fear his entering this calling on account of the danger attached to it; but when the family is large, they like to have one of its members a shaman.

During the time of preparation the shaman has to pass through both a mental and a physical training. He is, as a rule, segregated, and goes either to the forests and hills under the pretext of hunting or watching the herds, "often without taking along any arms or the lasso of the herdsman"; or else he remains in the inner room the whole time. "The young novice, the 'newly inspired' (*turene nitvillin*), loses all interest in the ordinary affairs of life. He ceases to work, eats but little and without relishing his food, ceases to talk to people, and does not even answer their questions. The greater part of his time he spends in sleep." This is why "a wanderer ... must be closely watched, otherwise he might lie down on the open tundra and sleep for three or four days, incurring the danger in winter of being buried in drifting snow. When coming to himself after such a long sleep, he imagines that he has been out for only a few hours, and generally is not conscious of having slept in the wilderness at all."

However exaggerated this account of a long sleep may be, we learn from Bogoras that the Chukchee, when ill, sometimes "fall into a heavy and protracted slumber, which may last many days, with only the necessary interruptions for physical needs."

Second, this is not something that every spirit-worker is going to go through. On the contrary, most won't. Shaman sickness is something endured by the classic shaman—another reason why, at least in this tradition, I'd like to see the word "shaman" reserved for those who have gone this route, and "spirit-worker" or "shamanic practitioner" (or even "seidhworker", "vitki", or "volva" when appropriate) used for those who haven't. I know that I have no hope of instituting this definition outside of this tradition, and I don't intend to try. However, those of us who work with the wights of this area of the world should understand that for us, this is the division.

There's no need to feel like you're not as good a spirit-worker if you haven't gone through shaman sickness. Rather, you should feel grateful, because it kills people, sometimes quite literally. Every tribal culture whose spirit-workers go through such a spirit-triggered ordeal agree that not everyone survives it, and there is an attrition rate. Not going through this condition means that you retain the ability to make choices with your life. It might also mean that your "wiring" isn't such that it could survive the transition, and the Gods know best about these things. Be grateful that you are still alive, and do the best work that you can with what you have.

When I first met other spirit-workers, many of whom had gone through or were going through shaman sickness, I learned that there were two distinct forms that it took (although some people got hit with both at once at full volume). We jokingly, sarcastically referred to them as the One Road and the Other Road.

The One Road is the Death Road, and it attacks through your body. Spirit-workers on the Death Road come down with physical illnesses, some of them life threatening; there may be months or years of hideous, painful, chronic illness that slowly wears you down and "kills" part or all of your astral body, not to mention bringing your physical body close to death. In fact, the "classic" end to this road culminates in a near-death experience (or in some cases an actual death from which the individual does not return), sometimes with a vision of dismemberment where one is actually taken apart and rebuilt by the spirits. Usually it's not only one specific illness, but a cascade of them—or one which drags on, lowers the immune system or otherwise throws the body seriously off, and starts the cascade. Sometimes it may even start with a severe physical injury, and goes from there. One of the telltale marks of the Death Road is that if modern medical science manages to cure one of the illnesses, it will either recur in a more virulent form, or something just as horrid will take its place. Shaman sickness is remarkably resistant to modern treatments.

I walked the Death Road. Between a combination of medication-resistant lupus and secondary congenital adrenal hyperplasia, I sickened further and further for the better part of a decade, and hemorrhaged quite literally to death at the end. I still wonder if I'd had the luxury of knowing what was going on, and perhaps another human being who understood to help me through it, I might have gotten to the end much sooner. Certainly I'm well aware that I came close to not making it; my patron deity was very clear about that. Still, there was a certain level of physical death that I had to achieve, and there was not going to be any safe or easy way to achieve it. Most of what I went through was entirely necessary to make me what I am today.

The Other Road is the road of Madness. On this road, the death is of the personality that came before, and it can come about through a period of mental illness. The mental instability during shaman sickness is especially difficult, because the individual is legitimately experiencing contact with unseen (to most others, that is) entities—and they are also seeing and hearing them through a veil of insanity. Figuring out what is real and what isn't can seem nearly impossible, especially since any mental health professionals that they consult are likely to be less than helpful. They may concur that there are brain chemistry problems, but they will neither believe in any of the spirit-contact nor understand the need to see the illness through to some end, whatever that is. Psychiatric medication may be prescribed, and the individual may end up in the hospital. In some cases, the spirits may drive the sufferer away from medical help if they think that it will retard the process, even if this has them sleeping on park benches for a while. In other cases, the sufferer accedes to the wishes of mental health personnel, but it doesn't necessarily fix the problem.

Psychiatric medications for people who are on the Other Road are an ambivalent subject. As discussed above in the section on whether spirit-workers should use psychiatric medications at all, it will largely depend on the individual in question, and divination should perhaps be done in order to get a clear answer. On the other hand, if you are walking the Madness Road as part of a spirit-triggered shamanic rebirth, They may well prefer to you to experience it fully, without the buffering effect of drugs—at least for a time. And if a particular psychiatric medication interferes with your *ve* in any way—such as making it difficult to move energy or ground and center—it is unlikely that the spirits will allow you to take it, so as above, do divination first to find something appropriate. This advice includes any herbal remedies, but for the latter, it is imperative that a spirit-worker who utilizes herbal remedies should make an alliance with the Grandparent-spirit of that plant, or it may not be all that effective. (Spirit-workers can't just make assumptions about the use of living things for their aid; we are held to a higher standard, even by wights that we haven't met yet or whose existence hasn't occurred to us.) Also, be aware that herbal remedies can interact in difficult ways with allopathic medications, so be careful.

You may also need to consider how much of the issues brought up by shaman sickness are chemical and how much are trauma that no chemical can help, and that needs to be worked through by itself. If, for example, there's a large chemical component that is preventing you from making any headway on the emotional things, you may be able to bargain a deal where you temporarily go on medication long enough to throw yourself fully into working out your emotional issues (assuming that you are not taking one of the anti-empathic meds that simply repress your emotional issues so that you don't have to look at them). Of course, you'd then have to dedicate every day to making yourself emotionally stable enough to go off the medications and deal with the rest of the shaman sickness process without going under. Other tools of modern psychiatry that some modern spirit-workers swear by for "getting ready to survive the Madness Road" are DBT (Dialectical Behavioral Therapy) and NLP (Neuro-Linguistic Programming).

While one might think that the Madness Road is, if not easier, at least less life-threatening than the Death Road, that would be incorrect to assume. A spirit-worker on the Madness Road may commit suicide out of pain and despair, or do something stupid that gets them killed, or go so thoroughly mad that they burn out their own gifts and live practically catatonic for the rest of their (usually short) lives. One of the big dangers of the Madness Road is being too crazy to realize that you're all that crazy, especially if you've actually got wight-contact going at the same time. It's also common for your judgment to be entirely off about all the important things in your life, even the simplest ones.

What the spirit-worker going down this road desperately needs is a sane, reasonable person that they trust who shares the same or at least a similar world view to them to be their reality check. This "reality check" should give them feedback as to their apparent sanity based on their behavior as a human being, not based on some socially acceptable scale of belief. They should understand that talking to the unseen or doing odd ritual behaviors is, for this spirit-worker, not evidence of insanity. However, being unable to hold a sensible conversation or negotiate reasonably and rationally over some mundane matter might be, as might losing one's empathy or ability to see the world views of others, or becoming paranoid about the motivations of your loved ones and attributing unrealistic and sinister motivations to them, regardless of all evidence to the contrary.

It is important to remember that the mark of a shaman who takes the Madness Road is that they only suffer from those extremes during shaman sickness, and then they recover. A functioning shaman may have odd social behaviors that are the result of his bargains with the spirits, but s/he is fully aware of how they look to others, and can communicate patiently and sensitively past that hurdle. They are able to have healthy relationships and negotiate sanely with others. They need to be sane, in order to do their jobs—not just because the job is so stressful, but because it requires them to understand and empathize with many different clients. They need to be able to live in this world as well as in the Otherworlds, or they are ineffective. This means that in order to function as a shaman, they need to come back from that illness. It's important to have faith in the wights who guide this process, as they understand how to bring someone back from it, but it's also important to have a human support system who can help you with regular infusions of reality about how you look and sound to "normal" people.

At the same time, there will still always be a faint air of insanity about people who have walked the Madness Road, even when they are acting completely sane and normal, just like there will be a faint aura of "death" around those who have walked the Death Road—and for people with the Sight, they may be able to see and smell Death in their auras. (That "smell of death" is difficult for most non-Sighted people to interpret, and they may end up associating it mentally with "evil" or "wrongdoer" or just "creepy". Even if these shamans are lawful and upright people who never harm anyone, people may just "feel" after being around them for five minutes that this is someone dangerous or harmful.) That's because shamans don't ever really come all the way back. One spirit-worker, however, pointed out to me that walking the Madness Road has one significant benefit: A shaman may well be asked to deal with people who are broken in all sorts of ways, and having spent time insane can give insight and compassion in those cases. When one spends time delving into damaged psyches, it's good to know the territory intimately.

I remember seeing a beggar in the New York subway during my sickness. He was shirtless and filthy: he had open sores on his skin and was staring down intently at the concrete, his cupped and dirt-caked hand extended in front of him while his shoulders were hunched like he was getting ready to spring. He was also sitting in a full lotus position: to this day I've rarely seen another American who was able to do that. And I realized that in India he would have become a sadhu, and people would have known exactly what was going on with him. But in our culture he was just "mentally ill".

I wonder about the distinctions between schizophrenia and shaman-sickness. One possible distinction might be: "You recover from shaman-sickness; schizophrenia is a chronic and degenerative condition." But this leads to yet another question. How many cases of "schizophrenia" are just untreated, or badly treated, cases of shaman-sickness? If I had received "psychiatric help" during my 1994 episode of shaman-sickness, I might well have decided I was insane. I would never have listened to the voices. I would gladly have taken whatever medications were required to silence them, and today I'd be living in a welfare hotel and collecting a disability check—or I would be yet another suicide statistic. Winding up on the streets self-medicating with marijuana was one of the luckiest breaks I ever got: things could have been a whole lot worse.

I got better once I stopped fighting the voices and started listening to them. I also noticed that my spirit-voices spoke in complete, coherent sentences (or at least clear thoughts and images). The neurochemical noise, by contrast, tended to be garbled words or sentence fragments repeated inanely. I still get those when I am tired or under stress: I treat them as a warning buzzer and have managed to work with and around them. I'm still given to logic-leaps and mental tangents which are common to schizophrenics and creative folks alike, but I'm able to dial it back to "charmingly eccentric" instead of "drooling nutcase". But the scars are still there. This is one of the things which can make the whole question complicated: "in contact with the spirit world" and "bug-fuck-nutty" are not necessarily mutually exclusive, even after shaman sickness has run its course.

–Kenaz Filan

Modern psychiatry is not, of course, terribly supportive of people's claims that they are hearing spirits talking to them. And, to be fair, only a tiny percentage of cases of mental illness (or, for that matter, life-threatening disease) are actually manifestations of shaman sickness. It is likely that if shaman sickness were an accepted diagnosis in this culture, many mentally ill people would claim it as theirs. We know this because it does happen in cultures where it is accepted. One example of this is the central figure in Margery Wolf's ethnographic paper *The Woman Who Didn't Become A Shaman,* a Taiwanese woman who started having alleged possession incidents and claimed to be speaking to unknown gods. Local shamans were called in and examined her, but decided that she was merely mentally ill and not actually suffering from any culturally acceptable form of shaman sickness. The author, watching the episode from an academic Western (and aspiritual) viewpoint, felt that the reason for the rejection was that the woman in question was of low status, or something equally socially unfair. Not really believing in the "spirits" of the actual shamans, she was mystified as to why those professionals would claim that those spirits were not in evidence for the afflicted woman.

This means that someone who ends up on the Madness Road is going to have to be very, very careful as to what they say to any mental health practitioner. If you are actually hearing spirits in addition to the sock puppets in your head—or hearing them through a field of distortion—then this is something that you're going to have to work out on your own, perhaps with help from a trusted diviner. No psychiatrist is going to be able to address the root of the problem if they don't actually believe in it.

On the other hand, sometimes the Gods want you to clean out your mental problems in preparation for this soul-wearing Work, and they may want your feelings clear and loud so that you can deal with them. Talk-therapy may be useful here, as long as you stay away from spirit-work and keep on the subject of your ordinary human problems, of which you likely have just as many as any non-spirit-worker, whether you believe that or not. If there are major issues cluttering you up that will interfere with future Work, your patron wights will do what is necessary to make you clean them up.

Recently I learned that there is a Third Road, the Art Road. This was described by someone as being the road for the spirit-worker who has dedicated themselves to some Art. They live it, they breathe it, it is their identity and the source of all the joy and creativity in their world. The Third Road forces them into a position where they must give it up entirely and walk away, never to touch it again. I have little more information on this Road—unfortunately—but I would assume that it would lie close to, or lead to, the Madness Road. (There is also that the Roads cross each other. Severe illness can be accompanied by bouts of mental instability, and mental illnesses can have physical side effects. Most cases of shaman sickness will involve a lot of one and a little of another.)

One thing that must be stressed is that shaman sickness is a long process. It's not some sort of weekend-long epiphany after which the individual claims to be completely changed. It is long, slow, and agonizing, and usually lasts for years. It can also recur if the Gods and spirits feel that you have reached a level where more work needs to be done. If you're mired in shaman sickness, understand that it is going to take its own time. Lay in supplies as if for a long siege, and the best supplies are patience, devotion, and doing as much spirit-work as you can manage, given your situation.

We do know this about shaman sickness: It is triggered by the Gods and wights, and once it starts, even they cannot stop it. It has to go through to its end, whatever that may be. While there's nothing that will make it stop, or reverse, there are some things that may help to speed it up. One of these is deliberately going through ordeals. Not everyone is cut out for, or should go down, the Ordeal Path—but for those who can do it, it can bring the body and mind closer to death and thus speed up the process. Taking these multiple trips to the personal Underworld of body and soul brings you closer to Death, and gets you more quickly to the point where they can do their astral modification work and get it over with, and get you out the other side. For more information about the Ordeal Path in the Northern Tradition, look for that chapter in *Wightridden: Paths of Northern-Tradition Shamanism*. For more information about the Ordeal Path in general, we recommend *Dark Moon Rising: Pagan BDSM And The Ordeal Path*.

Shaman sickness doesn't happen to every spirit-worker, but when it does it can be pretty frightening. First, though, I want to distinguish between Kundalini sickness and shaman sickness; they are related, but not the same thing. Kundalini sickness is what happens when you are changing the way your body runs energy from 110 to 220 volts. Kundalini energy is basically this coiled energy that sits in the base of the spine and comes up. Working on that channel connects your genitals to your brain, and has other benefits like making your brain work better. Upping the voltage makes your core go from idle to forward motion within your energy system, but when that comes up, it comes up quite violently. It can break things, if you're running too many volts for your wires—or too many amps. Your wires will melt, things will get damages, your capacitors will burn out, and you can really seriously damage yourself. You can damage your kidneys, you can give yourself migraines, you can fry your nervous system permanently.

A woman that we know actually died from it. She had a website dedicated to the dangers of Kundalini sickness. As it stands, it's quite easy to prevent it from happening. You just need to do your Kundalini exercises carefully, drink lots of water, know that it can happen and back off if it starts to happen instead of doing more. It requires your whole body, eventually. It is a kind of natural modification that slowly rewires everything for 220 instead of 110, as it were. You can go through months of not being able to eat, puking everything up. People go blind for minutes or hours at a time. There are weird wandering depressions.

Some of the symptoms of shaman sickness are related to Kundalini sickness. Some of it is just that the spirits have to get you close enough to death to receive their modifications. Part of it can happen just because they have kickstarted the thing, waking your energy body. There are all sorts of blockages in your energy system because you haven't been using it properly and they will smash through it. Then once they've done that, they start to kill it off. They make sure it's all working, and then they just drain the life away from it. It's terrifying, painful, and depressing. I certainly thought that I was dying. There can be psychotic breaks, despair, long drawn-out illness. You can't get healed. You have to hit bottom somewhere.

There are things that would slow it down, but I'd be more interested in trying to speed it up. Certain meds can slow it down, and so can fighting it, but that will just kill you in the end. I think accepting it speeds it up. Ordeal work can speed it up. The problem is that speeding it up can bring you too close to death too fast, and that can kill you too. The knowledge doesn't come from people, it comes from solitude and suffering. The Inuit will stick you in an igloo for months without much food, for the initiatory ordeal. Of course, maybe that's for the safety of the tribe as well. Because part of your karmic record has to be cleared away, you act out every imbalance that you have, with grotesque violence. So I was just horrendous to be around during that period. You're a source of bad luck, and certainly a source of bad vibes.

We ended up having a full-on funeral for a very large part of who I was. A part of me was laid to rest and chose to die, because I had become so sick and dysfunctional. I was depressed, I had terrible asthma. That part of me—she was so sick and hypervigilant, she gathered all of that into her and took it to the grave with her. And now she's feasted as a hero; she's one of my ancestors now. It was rough, though; it still upsets me to think about it.

How do you choose what part of you gets to die? First you have to know who they are. This requires a lot of meditating and introspection. They need a name, they need a history. Write a saga about them. Write the end of the saga "And then they died to save me." And they need to be ready. Just because you want them to sacrifice themselves and go die now doesn't mean that it's the right time, and that they're going to want to do it. They have to want to do it. You can't just kill them, because you become what you kill and you have to take the karmic load. It's actually much better if they can do it themselves, because then you who are left don't take the karmic load. If you kill them, you still have the karma. If they kill themselves, they take it with them. It's easier on what's left. Of course, some of them don't go down easy. You can ask the spirits to kill them, because then the spirits will take the karma. But then you have to make sure that the spirits will take only them and leave the rest intact. Or you can ask your deity to kill them. Then you have a proper funeral and mourn them, really mourn them.

So I don't know if that has to happen to everyone, but I suspect it's not that uncommon. But that's a big undertaking, to decide that this is what's needed. If you are going to do that, you need to talk to other shamans. If you can't, do lots and lots of divination, and get confirmations from omens, so that you can get a clear idea that the divination is correct. "I want to see a freaking billboard that has her name on it somehow, or I want to drive past something with a huge grave on it, or something. I want that level of clarity." Because if you do kill a piece of yourself off, there's no going back.

Of course, I don't think you should even contemplate it without advice from your patron deity. What I'm concerned about it someone going to a workshop and saying, "Oh, I saw my totem animal guide and it told me that I should kill myself." You need to have a long-term established relationship with a patron of some kind. They can trigger the shaman sickness without showing themselves to you, or you can be too thick-headed to notice that they're there. Usually in anthropological tales, the spirits come first. Those who go through it without hearing their spirit patrons end up dead.

But mainly it's about letting go. Meditations on emptiness. Meditations on letting go. Relaxation exercises. Dissolving work. Letting go as hard as you can.

–Lydia Helasdottir

I was mentally ill for three years. I wasn't even aware of what was happening until I managed to contact a few other spirit-workers online and they told me what was going on, after which things really took a turn for the worse—kind of like, "Okay, so you know what's going to happen to you—hold on, here we go!"

I had several violently psychotic episodes as well as "missing time" and memory lapses. There were numerous bouts of insomnia, some of which lasted as long as four days at a time. I became paranoid and convinced that people secretly hated me, and what little sense of self-worth I had was beaten into the ground. I was severely depressed and overreacted to everything with wild mood swings. My judgment was likewise disabled—once I freaked out completely when I accidentally locked my keys in my car, and had to be talked down over the phone by a friend, who likewise had to solve the problem of my locked-in keys because I couldn't think straight or reasonably.

My life turned into a bad country-western song. I lost my job, my car, my social life, even my cat. My family, from whom I hid the fact of my shaman sickness, kept haranguing me about being unemployed and acting strange, which stressed me out further. Basically, my entire life fell apart and I was helpless to do anything about it. What made all of this even worse, though, was that except for a couple of dear friends who were busy having and raising a baby, I was geographically isolated from everyone I cared about. Days would go by where I wouldn't talk to anyone I knew, or maybe nobody at all if I didn't leave my apartment, and once I figured I had gone about four months without even touching another person. Not having hardly any human contact all that time was in and of itself an ordeal.

I think that for a lot of us, shaman sickness can be described as a Hobson's Choice sort of affair—either you die fast or you die slow. Either you get Cweorth and burn on the funeral pyre, or you get Ear and you rot. I rotted. I don't really remember there being a single turning point in all of this—in that respect, I didn't have a classic sort of shamanic experience. But things slowly began to resolve themselves. My life got rearranged differently. I was being internally rearranged as well—I lost a lot of old emotional baggage, and my self-esteem was built from the ground up, much stronger than before. I lost any uncertainty about my experiences being "real" as well. And I was lucky; despite being unemployed and nearly incapable of taking care of myself for three years, I did not wind up homeless, nor did I starve. My family turned out to be surprisingly understanding when I finally told them what was going on, as did all of my remaining friends.

Then one day, Loki said to me that I was done, the shaman sickness was over. And I managed to survive, somehow. I feel fortunate.

I didn't have a near-death experience like other spirit-workers I know, but there are parts of me that rotted away and were buried and are gone forever now, or that were taken by Loki or Hela and replaced with other things. The most significant aspect of shaman sickness is that whoever you were before it began becomes more or less irrelevant after it's well and truly over—you vaguely remember what it was like being that person and feeling her feelings and thinking her thoughts, but it may have so little connection to who you are afterwards as to seem like another person entirely. So yeah, I think it's true; you don't come back all the way, whether you actually die and are brought back to life in a physical sense, or whether you just get killed off a tiny piece at a time.

What I did, after my initial reaction of "No, this isn't happening to me!" was simply to accept it—that my life was going to implode, that I was going to go crazy, and that there was nothing I could do to stop it. I know that's the last thing most people are inclined to do, but if you're going to be shaman-sick and the spirits are going to put you through the wringer no matter how loudly you protest, you might as well make it as easy on yourself as possible.

Just as people get injured more often in auto accidents because they unconsciously brace for the impact, if you try to resist, you're just going to be hurt worse. You have to go with it—you have to ride the pain and loneliness and insecurity and fear without letting it drag you completely under. It's hard, but it can be done. You have to keep in mind that it will end, and that when it does you will be a stronger person for it, and will look back with amazement and hopefully, some compassion for yourself for the things you went through. Yes, there is the chance you won't make it—some of us don't. Some people die, or are broken forever. But you can decide not to let that happen to you.

No matter how much things suck, no matter how bleak the future looks or how unprepared you feel or how scared you are, you can survive this. If there was no chance of your survival, the spirits would never have done this to you. You are not the first nor the last person to ever go through this, and you are not alone—even if you're geographically isolated or stranded among people who don't understand and are hostile to the whole thing, you are not alone.

–Elizabeth Vongvisith

Mental illness has historically been what I'm hit the hardest with, and this time seems to be little different. I'm emotionally unstable, and prone to wild mood swings, deep depression, anxiety, anti-social behavior, and the occasional manic episode; I can behave very badly and hardly realize it. The depression can be overwhelming; it's arrested my ability to work and if I'm not careful I become sick for not taking care of myself. Even though I've had to live with it my whole life, the instability that comes during shaman sickness is unique (and interestingly enough, when I'm doing my job and not dealing with sickness, my depression is nearly nonexistent; I don't even have to be medicated for it). The mood swings and weird behavior alienate people and I've lost long-time friends over it. My fortune and circumstances have also been screwed over, which seems to be just par for the course.

How to make it pass more quickly? Hop into it headfirst and try not to hang on to any part of your life so hard that it breaks you when it's ripped away. Obeying all necessary taboos will keep things from getting as bad as they could be, and doing your job can win you some small assistance from the spirit world. But you can't go through that kind of crisis—emotional, physical, and spiritual—and not be dramatically changed for it. I can now look at some of what I went through and say, "Well, at least it's not that again!" The relative difficulty of whatever mess is in front of me is readjusted accordingly. It removed the doubt of the validity of what I was experiencing; some things end up written so deeply that no amount of rationalizing or self-doubt can argue against it. On the surface that appears to be a good thing, but speaking for myself, some of the ways I achieved that knowledge were horrible (and others simply monstrously unpleasant). The way I understand it, part of the purpose of shaman sickness is to saturate you with poison; in the way that fever drives out illness, shaman sickness strikes at the illness of your life in order to heal you. Getting to the harmony and "health" necessary for a spirit-worker isn't accomplished by comfortable forms of healing—it's amputation and fever, like cutting out cancer or making the body such a toxic environment that whatever invading parasite is driven out or killed. The life that was originally present is forever altered because it was "sick" by the standards of spirit-work. When you're "healthy" you are by necessity a different person.

-Jessica Maestas

Early on, I was shoved down the path of Madness. I took quite a few steps on that path and sank deeper and deeper into an often suicidal depression. I was blessed by Loki to be given a choice, though: He allowed me to take a long term look down the Madness Path and quickly chose physical death instead. It's a hell of a lot easier—for me, anyway. I still carry shards of memory and scars from my experiences of slowly feeling my sanity and hold on reality slipping away (and there are times where the terror of that time still rises up in some perverse shamanic PTSD), but I managed to not go too far down that path. I instead chose to walk the Death Road.

Once my choice was made, I was immediately struck ill for a fortnight. I was unable to eat, drink, could barely urinate and lay flat on my back in feverish agony. After that, things slowed down and progressed at a more stable pace. Having walked the Madness path for a little bit, I have motivation to keep moving down the Death path. I know that if I hesitate too long in what needs to be done, or refuse certain challenges, I'll be thrown back into madness. It's... um... incredible motivation.

My shaman sickness involved losing myself. I started having intense visionary experiences with the Gods that I was honoring. Then things started being taken from me: I lost my apartment, my job, the physical mobility that I'd enjoyed as a dancer, my career, every single one of my friends, and the religious group I was working with at the time. Had it not been for the kindness of the priestess who had trained me, I would have ended up living on the streets. I was forced into emotional and spiritual darkness and for a time, I thought I was back on the Madness road. I think I did go mad for a time. It was as though my emotional landscape was being ploughed up, forced through a sieve, halved and carefully planted with new seeds that would eventually blossom into skills of priestcraft and shaman-craft.

In many ways, I got off easy. I know that just as I must now go through a series of ordeals, I may be taken into another cycle of shaman sickness. Odin has hinted at this strongly over the past year. I'm not quite sure what exactly this will entail, though Odin seems to favor a workable blend of mental and physical anguish.

I don't think there is anything that will make shaman sickness pass more quickly. I think the way to survive is to surrender to the process and to trust in one's Gods and just bear up and go through it, knowing that if one endures, there is a light at the end of that very dark tunnel. This was the only thing that allowed me to get through it ... that hope and an inborn stubborn streak. Finding a community of other experienced shamans and spirit-workers and having a good spiritual foundation can help immensely too but ultimately the only way out is through.

Of course, the saying is true, you don't really come back all the way. How can one come back fully from the type of traumatic experience that shaman sickness is? The whole purpose of the sickness is to break a person down, change and re-pattern them into something the Gods and/or spirits can use; to open them creating a vessel or tool. The person as they were before the sickness essentially dies. What returns is different, and the person carries with him or her the scars and remnants of their sick-time. It defines their path and work from that moment on.

So if you're going through this, pray. Utilize consistent devotional techniques like centering prayer as a lifeline. Do what you can to keep yourself as physically healthy as possible—no use adding extra strain. Avoid psychiatrists— they don't understand the spiritual and nothing they do will accomplish anything but prolonging the inevitable. You'll likely have no luck with most modern "core"-type shamanic practitioners, because they haven't gone through this and the nonconsensuality of it may frighten them. Try to find other classic shamans and spirit-workers, those who have already been through shaman sickness. They may not be able to do anything to help, but just having a support group of people who understand and can reassure you that you're not going crazy, who have gone through the sickness themselves, can be immensely stabilizing. Unfortunately, I really do believe the only way out is through. Do whatever you have to, whatever your Gods are suggesting to open yourself to the process and just endure. I don't know of any other way to survive it.

–Galina Krasskova

Shaman sickness itself causes drain, never mind when it's synergistically combined with emergent gender issues and emotional rebirthing. I tend to think of them as inextricably linked in the cases where they occur together. In my particular situation, I've dealt with insomnia, major depression, malaise and physical exhaustion, frequent illness, digestive upset, food intolerance, self-destructive episodes, and gender dysphoria. Then there are the bouts of profound self-doubt, extreme spacey-ness, forgetfulness, various kinds of madness, fairly extreme changes in emotional response (including rage which requires a physical outlet) and a desire to run from Deity. Never mind the actual day-to-day world collisions and near dissolution of everything I have financially, romantically and career-wise. Your whole world suddenly becomes very precarious. I've known others in my position who have had these same or similar experiences.

Having a good support system is really important. This can also be tremendously difficult to achieve when the people closest to you are alienated at times by your behavior and inexplicable changes. You're in the process of dying and being remade, and your loved ones may not recognize or like who and what it is you are becoming. Things you are required to do by the spirits seem contradictory to what is sane and healthy behavior; these things may be seemingly injurious to your person, financial stability and ability to help maintain a functional household. It's no wonder that people around a shaman-sick person have a hard time dealing with it. It's important to keep your lines of communication open with any significant others. This can be tremendously difficult when people are judging you harshly, but you absolutely must be forthright. If things are going to fall apart, there is little you can do to change it anyway, so it might as well happen honestly and succinctly. Being as honest and open as you can manage gives the other people in your life the opportunity to either rise to the occasion or bow out. There is, in the end, no use in prolonging the inevitable or in denying yourself potential support.

My advice is to find other people who have experienced these things firsthand. For a quiet introvert like me, finding and accepting community support was a difficult task. It was also one Hela insisted on and I cannot thank Her enough for it. I have found a community of warm and helpful folks who actually understand my predicaments and have useful advice to offer. It's a terrible thing to navigate this experience blind, with most people around you convinced you are simply going off the deep end to no avail.

From my own experience and what I've seen in other situations, fighting Deity and running from responsibility is not something that ever ends up helping in this process; in fact it is personally devastating. I spent a good amount of time being avoidant and it has resulted in punishments and a work backlog. Things seem to go better when you're doing what you're supposed to, and if your experience is anything like mine you're going to be exhausted either way. It's a lot less painful when things are running smoothly ... well, most of the time. Much of the work is grueling and sometimes pain is just part of the process.

The initial stage of shaman sickness seems to me to be a lot like boot camp. You get hazed and ordered to work and be productive, and you scarcely know what you are even doing. For me it's been a sink-or-swim situation a lot of the time, and the only thing I can do is have faith and try. You might get tossed "on-duty lights" that seem way out of your league, all the while trying to navigate your own personal issues. It can be immensely difficult and intimidating, but you have to step up to the plate.

I've spent a lot of time thinking about why things are the way they are and my intuition screams that They do things this way because it's Necessary. I know that my patron Hela in particular is motivated by Dire Necessity and Purpose, two things I constantly work at keeping in mind while I struggle with my work. All my life I've had this sense of needing to do something incredibly important (and frankly being bothered by it), and I've spent a lot of my life wondering what that was. I'm not a very ego-centric person and am not drawn to accolades, so I had trouble wrapping my head around this inward push. I think I'm beginning to understand.

–Steph Russell, spirit-worker

My shaman sickness took roughly 6½ years and resulted in excessive weight gain, extreme depression, suicide attempts and a completely changed personality. Collectively, they created a situation in which my family members rejected me and eliminated my support base. I'd say that it was primarily mental illness, with physical side effects. The only advice that I can give is to stop fighting it and dive right in, as the more you deny and struggle the harder it becomes. Also, contacting friends you trust and people who may have lived through it for venting or guarding you during the difficult period is helpful. Life would have been far easier if I could have just gone into seclusion and dealt with the spirits rather than holding down a regular job, but this is the modern era and there's nowhere for novice shamans to go. If having friends who've survived isn't possible, finding knowledgeable people to explain it to your loved ones (if appropriate) could help.

One thing that might help is to find the culture most akin to the manifestation of sickness and see how they handle the transition. Echo it as much as possible. That's what I did. For those without such a culture, you might review the lore of an accepting culture as well as the lore of yours, and see the parallels — then work the parallels to help the transition.

–Aleksa, spirit-worker

The important thing to keep in mind is that although we have no cultural reference for this experience in Western Culture, it doesn't mean that you can't go to a medical doctor for physical manifestations, or to a psychologist if you get the distinct message that there might be a biochemical emotion regulation issue. Sure, you might not be able to describe it as "shaman sickness", but you can be honest and up front about your symptoms and treat those without getting into the underlying cause.

Contacting your local pagan organization can yield names of pagan therapists, counselors, and social workers, who can help with not only the mental issues, but also negotiating the real world consequences. Some people find that they can no longer hold down a day to day job, so talking to a social worker about SSI income and Section 8 housing will keep you from homelessness. Finally, if you feel all hope is lost, or that your health is truly an emergency situation, please seek some kind of care. Just because this is a spiritual affliction doesn't mean that you should stay at home if you are having a legitimate medical emergency.

–Del, spirit-worker

Know that it will pass and do not act rashly or irreversibly when not sane. Mindfulness of external word and deed is vital. Suicide is an act of weakness, not a sensible option. Perseverance is all one can do. Don't lose your sense of humor or your will. Don't forget how to love.

There is a profound absurdity to a lot of it; see it for what it is.

                                                    –Krei, spirit-worker

Astral Body Modifications

One thing that modern spirit-workers of all sorts are beginning to talk about when they get together is the fact that often our *hamar* are different from those of other people. Some may have mild to moderate changes, and those may have grown slowly, over time. Others may have dramatic astral changes of the sort that can only be implemented by major spirits, as explained above. Nonhuman bloodlines can create *hame* anomalies, which can become more severe if those bloodline-gifts are exploited for spirit-work, as they usually are. Constant shapeshifting can also take its toll on the makeup of the *hame*, and the spirits themselves can move through you and change you, leaving traces of their nature that can build up over time. It's not uncommon for the attributes of a patron deity to leave their mark as well; one spirit-worker whose patron is Odin developed eye problems. My own patron, Hela, limps, and so do I a good deal of the time. Like her, I am not made even bilaterally due to skeletal malformations, and my physical and astral meridians are also very different from side to side—one side is always more "dead" than the other.

One example of a minor spirit-modification that has become immensely popular is a Reiki attunement. When done in the classic way—and not just in the way of many folks who claim to be able to attune anyone in two minutes by waving their hands at them—a bit of your aura is scooped or "cored" out to make room for a "port" that will connect to the Reiki energy and download it through your hands. The various symbols are used for control of the flow. Some Reiki masters warn that for the next 21 days, the astral body needs time to get used to the modification, and may reject it. Many already-modified spirit-workers have found that Reiki attunements just won't take on them; that "port" may be already in use for other purposes.

This is a new and uncharted area, and we are working on tiny scraps of knowledge. One thing that we have noticed, anecdotally, is the issue of the chakras. (Yes, this is Hindu and not northern-tradition, but just as every *lich* has the same acupuncture points, every *hame* has chakras, regardless of what you want to call them.) Chakras have many purposes, but one of them is as attachment points between the *lich* and the *hame*. We've noticed a lot of changes in which chakras are strongly and permanently attached, and which ones are "normally" detached for spirit-workers. The biggest offender in this latter category is the second chakra. Ironically, it is associated with the reproductive organs (as opposed to the sexual organs which are root-chakra) and there is a long tradition of spirit-workers being sterile or childless. In some cultures, women are not allowed to do shamanic work until they are past their childbearing years. While a minority of spirit-workers (especially those who are closer to "priest" or "priestess" than "shaman" in their work) do breed, most don't, even today. This is sometimes due to the pressure of the Gods and spirits—if your entire life is dedicated to them, there's no room for the responsibility of children—but it is strikingly often due to physical reasons. At a recent yearly gathering of spirit-workers from various Western traditions, only one out of the entire gathering had ever had a child, and that one became sterile soon after a single difficult birth. When the bloodline-goddess Hyndla gave me an astral modification in the region of the second chakra, she commented that if I hadn't already been sterile, it would have made me so.

Other anecdotal knowledge suggests that different chakras are used for different sorts of magic, and thus get modified differently, if only through continual use. Sex magic, of course, uses the root chakra the most and tends to make slow changes over time there. Both shapeshifting and body-temperature control seem to make strong use of the third chakra, over the diaphragm. Heart chakras are the second biggest "offender" for being frequently disconnected in spirit-workers, although that may be due more to continual trauma than anything else. Making sure that the heart chakra is at least temporarily connectable is very important for a spirit-worker, who is in a service position and must not fall into contempt for the people that they are serving, nor forget how to love. Throat chakras tend to get slightly modified from doing

years of *galdr* or other "shaman singing". Third eye and crown chakras
are often heavily modified by the spirits, especially the latter if the spirit-
worker is a horse for god-possession. When I underwent my shamanic
death, my crown chakra was permanently shut down and moved to the
back of my head, where it became a sphincter-like "port" that could be
opened to receive information, energy ... and deities, should they wish to
use my body for their purposes. (For more information on the
phenomenon of god-possession, please see the next book in this series,
Wightridden.) Other horses report that the spirits use the existing crown
chakra, or in rare cases the heart chakra.

Many of us have theorized, as discussed in the chapter on bloodlines,
that those of us who are spirit-chosen have been nabbed due to the
nature of our "wiring", of *lich* and *hame* and *ve*. It may well be, especially
for those of us who go through shaman sickness, that we have been
chosen for wiring that can not only manage the basics of spirit-work, but
has the best chance of surviving shaman sickness and the ensuing spirit-
modifications. It may also be that those spirit-workers who do not get
heavily modified and sent through shaman sickness are spared because
the Gods and wights, in their wisdom, do not feel that they are "wired"
in the right way to be a good risk for survival.

Another thing that we've noticed is that no matter how strange and
extreme the astral modifications are, the basic energy meridians and
points described in acupuncture are still where they are in "normal",
unmodified people. We conjecture that this is because moving those
meridians and points would cause the physical body to become
unbalanced, ill, and die. That means that even a modified spirit-worker
can still get acupuncture, use acupressure, and work with those physical
meridians. No matter what is done to us, we still remain here in a human
body, and have to work with that.

It's not unusual for modern spirit-workers to "anchor" an astral
modification to a physical body modification such as a tattoo, piercing, or
cutting. In some cases, the wights actually did the astral modification
simultaneously with the physical one, as in the case of the nine symbols
on my back that gift me with the protections of the Nine Clans of the

Iron Wood. During each piece of the tattoo, I had a vision of the chief of that clan coming to me and putting something into me. Another spirit-worker had a set of modifications done for purposes of signal clarity—the large ear piercing was for better "hearing" of the spirits' messages, the labret (lower lip) piercing was a "microphone", and the tongue piercing made sure that she spoke the messages properly.

Modified Invisibly: Changing The Hame
by Lydia Helasdottir

Astral body modifications are changes to your astral/energy body that make it different from that of usual people. Some you can do yourself, but the big ones generally have to be done to you by a deity or wight. It's not something you were born with yourself. Some might serve to up the amount of power you can handle on different frequencies, or allow you to even work with those frequencies. We see this whole thing from an engineering paradigm, so if you could draw a wiring diagram of the astral body, there'd be a new component.

The milder modifications are usually widening of the pipes that carry the chi around your body and reinforcing them. That's a typical low-end, low-invasiveness mod. You can do that yourself, slowly over time, from doing various sorts of maegencraft, body energy work. Maegen is cognate to the German and Dutch word for guts, stomach, and in Chinese medicine the guts are where the astral battery is kept, which I find to be an interesting coincidence. Anyway, these make your pipes wider. When one starts to build an energy defensive system, or to improve one's aura, or whatever, that's a mod. So maybe you've got a thing that's made of energy and that looks like an egg around you, and it acts like a filter or a pressure suit, depending on where you're going—that's a mod. But those are just enhancements of existing technology.

When we're talking about higher mods that are given to you, you might have a body part that has been replaced on the astral. For instance, my one hand is a Fey hand, and both my feet are Fey feet. I was badly burned, and we were working with the Fey at the time, and I made a deal that I would carry out some activities for them, and in return they gave me new hand and feet skin. This gives me my fleet running ability—it's sort of like having Fey boots that I can't take off, so I might as well call them Fey feet. This sort of thing is also in various sorts of lore—Nuada of the Silver Hand and so forth.

Then we have mods that are related to physical body modifications—tattoos and piercings and other transformations that become a physical carrier to hold the astral changes. These are quite simply wiring modifications. I've got one that connects my power chakra to my heart chakra, like a thick piece of wire on the astral. It makes sure that those two are always connected together, so I won't be evil. I used to have trouble with being either too gullible or too cruel, and when you connect those two centers, you are neither too gullible nor too cruel, because the two have to work in unison all the time.

Another modification—although some people have it as a natural extension—is that when you've done enough internal alchemy that you can manifest both the male and female, you might manifest genital bits of the gender that you physically and genetically aren't. All people can learn to do this, although it's not easy for most, but most choose not to and it's a damn shame.

Then you have things like plant-based mods. You might be working with a vine, for instance, and receive a subdermal mesh of green reinforcements to the connection between your physical vehicle and your energetic vehicle. That's actually a plant, it's not part of your body at all. It's some other creature in a symbiotic relationship with you, just as your mitochondria are symbiotic in your body. Then you've got specialty mods—for example, if you have to navigate strange spaces a lot, your patron deity might give you a little navigational beacon installed in your head. Some of these things can even show up on X-rays—there are three stones in my head that show up on X-rays! In that case, the story was a funny one because these three little emeralds disappeared out of a sealed envelope and could not be found. Then we investigated and it kept saying that they were in my head, and then the next time I had a head X-ray they were there. That was pretty weird. Since then, I never get lost, either physically or astrally. I can just triangulate.

Reiki is an example of an astral body modification. When people get a Reiki attunement, they get an astral mod in their crown chakra that makes a very big pipe out through the hands. Then you have mods that are unfriendly—infections, implants, and so on. This is where it starts to sound crazy, but if various wights can put something nice on you, then they can put something nasty on you.

How do you tell when you're getting a mod? Usually you feel really sleepy and have to lie down. When you wake up you feel weird, and if you scan your body and look at what used to be there and what's there now, you'll find that things have changed. Maybe there's an extra bright glowy thing, and you have to go find out what it does. It's generally believed to be impolite for deities or spirits to install mods without telling you what's going on, unless they own you. But it's rare, so don't assume that every time you fall asleep with a funny tiredness that you're getting some sort of magic modification or something.

You can have them checked by an energy worker that you trust, to see what they look like. But then once you have them, you can't let any old energy workers work on you any more. You have to set up your energy system prior to seeing the acupuncturist, so that whatever they do to you isn't going to screw up the mods. Generally, things like craniosacral therapy are not all that helpful any more, because it will screw with the mods. But if you know about this beforehand, you can protect yourself from whatever the energy worker is doing, if they're clumsy, by roping them off and putting them in a Faraday cage for the time being. If you're very heavily modified, sometimes you just can't do certain therapies. I have a mod that, while I was getting used to it, I just had migraines for two years. Headaches and migraines seem to be a side effect of energy changes, and of Kundalini rising.

There's a lot of debate as to whether it's better to open one's chakras from the top down or from the bottom up—the water method or the fire method. We generally think that it's safer to use the water method, dripping slowly down from the Source to gently relax and open the chakras, so that when it opens all the way down to the root chakra, everything is already open and relaxed. Whereas the more Hindu method, the fire method, winds it up from the bottom up, smacking into the next chakra, and you feel it—"Wow, something happened!"—and if you do it by the water method you don't get these dramatic effects. But what can happen is that Kundalini will hit the next chakra that isn't open, bounce back down and come out, and manifest itself through the chakra below it. Let's say that the heart chakra is blocked, and the Kundalini comes up, and smacks into the heart chakra. It will go down into the power chakra, and you'll manifest all sorts of power chakra imbalances, like tyranny and inappropriate severity. If your throat chakra is blocked, the Kundalini will come up and bounce off of that, and come out your heart, and you'll have emotions you can't talk about, you'll be put upon, unable to speak with command, and get taken advantage of all the time, because your heart's wide open, inappropriately.

A seer can usually see your mods, unless they're cloaked. The other thing is that there's only so many ports, usually, and often the ports on some people are taken up by attachments on either prior relationships or earlier hangups and traumas. If you scan your body, you'll see them as these little feeding tubes coming in. For the most part, you need to unhook them and send them back. That's a perilous thing, though, because sometimes when you unhook them, if the person who put it there was feeding from you in this way, then they'll notice that you've noticed, and that you've unhooked it, and you will get a lot of attention that you didn't really want. But generally these tubes are just emotional ties to parents and lovers and such. If you don't want to be that disconnected from them, you can send out connectors from your heart level which you control, and which hook into their heart instead of involving your power center. How do you notice it? Chi follows zi, energy follows attention. Sometimes they will remanifest if you invite them back.

Some mods you can override and some mods you can't. Generally the ones that deities provide are not easily overriddden. I've also seen things like big information and energy downloads in the back of the head or neck, or other species/race body parts—I've got Jotun blood, but I've got a Fey hand and feet, which gives a lot of internal conflicts. There's a guy I know who is basilisk totem who has a very hot furnace, and he could suck in poison and burn it up in the furnace. He could extend spikes on his back; his armor was always switched on and he looked like the Batmobile. But he didn't realize that he didn't need that, and that the armor will switch itself on when there's incoming nonsense. So we taught him to switch it off at will, and now he has shimmering skin that looks more like fish scales. It's more approachable and sensitive, and he can get more information ... because when you wear plate armor, you're blind and clumsy, and you get tired quickly, and it's dark in there and you can't get sunlight, and you look like you're looking for a fight, which means that you usually get one. So now he looks astrally like a human with slightly shimmery skin, which is more inviting, but when you become aggressive toward him, with energy or with your hand, the heavy black chitin-type armor will pop up automatically as it's needed. That makes it much easier for him to run the system and to get fed. Another thing that he's got is extendable finger-spikes—green ones for feeling the energy, black ones like blades with tiny hooks to reach into someone's energy body and hook out what shouldn't be there, stainless steel ones like hypos to suck things out of someone's arm, and guides in his wrists to let him know what the poison is before he lets it into himself. But sometimes you'll see scared people with monster armor on, and they can't take in energy, and they get starved.

To integrate mods, do energy work that runs your energy through your whole body, over and over, including through the new stuff. Draw pictures of yourself with the new stuff, or wiring diagrams to get used to the fact that it's there now. Use them a lot. They are basically prosthetics ... so how do you get used to a prosthetic? Get out of the wheelchair and walk around on it more and more often. Some can be switched on and off, some are permanently on. Some are like hardware, some are like software—like being able to decode languages quickly.

Keep your tongue up. If you keep your tongue up on the roof of your mouth, the energy will come down around and make a cycle instead of blasting out the top of your head. That can help with a migraine, keeping your tongue up. It's in all the decent ch'i-gong books, but it's just this minor thing that everybody says, "Oh that can't be important!" It's interesting to just do breaths with your tongue up, just do a breath that runs from the bottom of your spine over the top of your head and down the front of your body. Do that twenty or thirty times, then put your tongue down and do the same, and see how it's different. And if you're overexcited and want to go to sleep, you can run the energy up the front and down the back of your body. Try that tongue-up and tongue-down, and see what happens.

Spouses, Partners,
and Other Hapless Bystanders

In the histories, legends, and anthropologies that we collect, it is not at all unusual for shamans and spirit-workers to be single. (The exception is in some tribal societies where marriage is a very different institution from ours, and shamans have a higher status.) In fact, the classic archetype of the shaman is not generally thought of as someone who has a spouse—someone with whom they argue over the breakfast table about whose turn it is to clean the catbox, someone whose anniversary they must remember, someone whose arms they lie in at night and take comfort. Yet this calling comes to many people, partnered or not, and the partner may have no choice but to either stay and hold on while everything takes a back seat to this spiritual whirlwind, or walk out and leave their lover during this most difficult of times.

Probably the hardest thing to come to terms with for a spirit-worker's partner is the fact that you will never be the first and most important thing in your partner's life. The work will come first, always. This is made more explicit when the spirit-worker is a god-spouse and the mortal partner isn't even the primary one, but even those who simply work for and with the Gods and wights will have to put them first. If that means getting out of bed in the middle of lovemaking because there are dead people at your window who need help, or missing your spouse's company picnic because a particular rite needed to be done right now, no delaying, well, that's the price that both people will pay.

One thing is certain: If the partner actually gets in the way of the Work, or if the partner's disapproval or lack of understanding is used as an excuse to avoid the Work, the Gods will arrange to remove the obstacle. Yes, this is a warning to both spirit-workers and their lovers. Don't be that obstacle. Don't let them become that obstacle ... if you want to have any hope of keeping them, that is.

Children are a particularly thorny problem. Unlike the adult partner who can choose to be there and be supportive or walk, children are stuck and have no choice. However, the Gods arc not unaware of this. While the majority of spirit-workers that I've met have been childless (some through choice, some through physical issues), those who have had children have been cut some extra slack during the period of the child's youngest years, and longer if they were single parents. I was given time to see my own daughter to maturity before taking on this job full-time; in the meantime, the deal was that I would learn as many skills as possible in preparation for that time. The Gods, of course, may have a different idea of what "maturity" means. They decided that my daughter was old enough when she was in her teens and still years from being a legal adult.

In some cases, the Gods may also decide that it is better for the other parent (or other family members) to raise the child, leaving the spirit-worker free to work, however painful that might be for them. Generally if this is the order and it is refused, they will do what it takes to lever circumstances until there is no other choice. I've seen this happen worst when someone has been fingered by the Gods, is rebelling against their Wyrd, and getting married and spawning is part of their attempts to get away from their future. That's ended in divorce and loss of full-time custody more times than I can count. If you are going to fight the Powers That Be, my advice is not to bring a helpless child into it.

I spoke to one spirit-worker who had felt the push by the Gods to give up her small child in favor of the Work. She demanded of the mother goddess of her pantheon to only send the primary care of her child away if she could be guaranteed by the Gods to have him pass to a home that was more loving and more appropriate for him than anything she could give. Less than a month later, they visited her brother's farm, and her son fell in love with everything there, including his cousins. Her brother and his wife offered to take her son in temporarily while she got her fluctuating health situation together, with as much visitation as she wanted. Feeling the push by the Gods, she sadly and reluctantly agreed. The arrangement went on until he was an adult, and twenty years later, both feel that it was the right choice.

This does not mean that every spirit-worker should give up their children—as I pointed out above, many manage with the help of other parents, or by making bargains to wait until the children are old enough before taking on the job fully. There is a reason why women, in some cultures, are not allowed to become shamans until they reach menopause—and why their psychic gifts often burgeon at that time. The survival of the young must come first. It is difficult, if not impossible, to take on responsibility to the spirits and the community concurrently with raising young children.

The comments below were gathered from the partners of some of the spirit-workers interviewed for this book. They ranged from the completely nonreligious to those who were spirit-workers of various sorts themselves, and their attitude toward their partner's work varies from skepticism and worry (in the case of J.K.) to complete acceptance. I deliberately kept in the more ambivalent comments, because it's not unusual for partners to go through several of these stages, including the ones that are not all that flattering to the spirit-worker, and they are perspectives that need to be honored. It's not an easy thing, especially in this day and age, to have a lover who has been grabbed up by a path that may seem so bizarre to society. However, the hope and devotion inherent in many of these testimonies tells us that love is possible no matter what the Gods may have in store for you.

As I helped to edit my spouse's unfinished shaman sickness article, I jokingly added certain humorous yet true comments to her text. While I was doing so, she commented that I could perhaps lend some insight into the trials of being on the other side of the fence.

I would imagine, given the nature and severity of such a process, that many relationships falter or fail completely due to the incredible stress put forth by the "awakening". I would also guess that the level of closeness in the relationship would have more to do with the actual ability to accept the inherent changes and alienation occurring during said process. Although I am no stranger to spiritual awakening, I have but a faint murmur at this time, compared to my mate's thrumming spiritual pulse. At times she seems consumed by it, her every waking moment seemingly being spent thinking about her past tasks, lessons, and work to be done.

There are many levels to this transformation that I have watched happening. In her article she wrote: "You're in the process of dying and being remade, and your loved ones may not recognize or like who and what it is you are becoming." This could not ring more true, and as she also stated, it really is reminiscent of a "boot camp" experience. Depending on where you are in your relationship, this alone may cause a disconnection. Once again, communication is key, I know personally that I could not initially accept many of the circumstances that came with this journey. At times I reacted quite poorly, rejecting the notion of it entirely, isolating myself from the truth and reality of the situation at times. Ultimately, though, whether you want to address it or not, having a significant other that is in the shaman-sickness process makes you *part* of that process. It may awaken things within yourself that you may personally be unable to handle, or afterwards, contain. It may cast a light on the spiritual path that you are to take, possibly even shoving you unwillingly onto that path.

This shamanic journey is such a strong thing that you become involved via osmosis. The energies and gods that interact with your mate—in your own home—will affect you, whether you like it or not. It really isn't something to be taken lightly, but talking about things and not harboring resentment is crucial. In order to have an understanding, even when there is hostility, one must think constantly of how this feels to them. They may not be handling this painful transformation very well themselves. In the end, though, it will be much better for everyone if you talk about things rather than hide from them.

I believe that balance is a major part of what makes the "big wheel" turn, and as life during this time will be frequently turbulent, once certain benchmarks have been crossed, it *will* get better. Know that this process is ultimately going to make them become what they really are meant to be, and that if your love is truly "unconditional" (as I'm sure you have told them many times), when they arrive at their "true self" they will be a much happier and centered individual. The person you fell in love with is still there, but over time we all change. These changes are healthy and necessary; remember that. Take heart that many of the problems and baggage that plagued your mate in the beginning will probably be addressed, if not worked though entirely. I have realized that this is all part of the journey, and that dealing with "skeletons in the closet" is part and parcel of shaman sickness. It won't be pretty, and it will likely involve more effort than the energy possessed ... but they need you *now* more than they ever have. Being supportive doesn't mean agreeing with or liking everything that happens, but you will be surprised at how much of an effect you can have on their journey by being a positive influence if you really do love them.

–FX, spirit-worker's husband

Being a spirit-worker myself (though not a shaman), it made the whole process of watching my partner Wintersong's shaman sickness both easier and harder. I could see that what he was going through was necessary, and I could ask Them and get the answer that no, I couldn't help too much, because that was not the point. That all helped, because I didn't feel like I was flailing in the dark. But at the same time, I knew that I was going to have to do something myself eventually—not what he was going through, but something. Seeing what he was going through made me very nervous, no matter how many times I asked and was told that I was going to go through something different. That answer only made think of different and equally painful ordeals that I might have in store for me.

–Fireheart Tashlin

I met Aleksa near the end of her "shaman sickness". My part in the recovery was, and is, being a stable grounding for her to anchor to, and to be there as a steady support mechanism for her while she does her work. We're in many ways the opposite sides of a coin, so I can understand what she needs, and having my own brand of magic makes it easier for me to help out with any required background work.

Sometimes the Ancestors request (or demand) certain behaviors or lifestyle changes, but so far those have all been very rational and easy to take, as well as educational. I believe Aleksa has mentioned the growing insistence on a seasonal, local, and organic diet, for example—sure, it takes some work to shift from our usual supermarket shopping habits, but it's less of an inconvenience than a truly better way of eating and living.

I feel very blessed that Aleksa's work is very much ancestor-based. Because of this, I've never had the issues that some spirit-workers' spouses may have with having to "share" her with a Deity, spirit, or the like. In fact, it's rather the opposite, in that Family (living or dead) is the primary core of her community, so that once the Family (especially her dead great-grandmother, who is her spiritual mentor) had accepted me into the family, there was no conflict. Overall, in my case, being the spouse of a spirit-worker presents far more blessings than hardships.

–James, spirit-worker's partner

When this all began to happen to my wife, I was confused, and then angry, and then confused some more. At first I refused to believe it—I was a Pagan, but nothing like this had ever happened to me or anyone that I knew. As some of the other partners of spirit-workers who were there in the beginning have pointed out, we didn't sign up for this kind of a relationship. We didn't sign up for a partner who has to rearrange the furniture in the house because the Gods want a room all to themselves, just for altars ... and then she would spend half the night in there, talking to no one, as far as I could see. This stuff grew and grew until it took over her life. She quit her job to do runes for pay, but so far it hasn't paid off like her job did before, and I've had to pick up the financial slack. That's been the biggest problem. The second biggest problem is that it takes up all her time, morning and night. It's like being with someone in the Army, with no paycheck.

I would try to help with things, only to have her tell me that I wasn't doing it right ... or worse, that I was doing it with the wrong attitude. That really burned me. OK, later I realized that I was desperately trying to make this part of her life somewhere that I had some say, some control, but at the time I just felt like I was trying and being rebuffed. Why would the Gods care about my attitude? But things that I would buy her and give her for her work would mysteriously break, while the "magical" gifts of friends would stay together. I accused her of deliberately, or even unconsciously, breaking them. She would cry, and I would yell, and it would turn into a fight. Which would always end with her steadfastly saying that she had to do this or that, there was no choice in the matter. I'd storm around the house, trying to get her to see that this was crazy, that she only thought she had to do these things.

Until the day that I, in a rage because she was gone out in the middle of the night for hours after telling me she'd be back soon, I walked by an altar and the hand-thrown pottery chalice I'd given her to use for Freya fell off and shattered in my wake. It was like a cold finger ran down my spine. I went to pick up the pieces and put them back on the altar, and I couldn't do it. I literally couldn't make myself do it. It was like someone had put out a hand and stopped me cold. I know that it sounds crazy, but I felt like a sword had just whistled past my head, deliberately missing me. I had never experienced that before, and I was so freaked out that I had to leave the house for four days.

When I came back, I couldn't approach the altars at all. Not because I think that the Gods will hurt me—although I think that I came really close, there—but because I think that I can barely understand the powers that my wife has to deal with, and they scare me. Maybe I can't hear them, but maybe I don't want to. Anyway, I believe her now when she says that she has to do some things or the Gods will hurt her, or that they break things they don't like. I have more sympathy with her now, although there have been nights when she's come to bed exhausted as the dawn is breaking, from doing what I don't know, and I have to yell at the Gods and curse them. But they don't answer me, and truly I don't know what I'd do if they did.

But having seen her relationship with the Gods, it's changed mine. I used to think of them as entirely kind and good—why I don't know, because I can read the myths as well as anyone else, but I guess I put that down to the people long ago having hard lives and seeing the Gods like they saw each other. Now I know that the Gods have goals, and even if those goals are good ones—and I still do believe that they are—they will do cruel things to people in order to reach those goals. That's something that I can't talk about to my Pagan group.

But the Gods use her, and they use me to support her. If I love her, which I do and I guess the Gods know that, then I can't leave her, I have to stay and do what they want. My relationship with her is worth it, and I see how much she tries to make space in her life for me, to not let them take over everything. I guess I've gone from believing in the Gods and not trusting her to believing in her and not trusting the Gods, and it's hard.

But it's only been a few years and we'll see how I feel about it in ten more. I was proud when we went to a gathering in western Canada and people were coming to her in a flock, asking for help. She worked herself to exhaustion and never got to go to any workshops with me, but I was proud of her. Even if by the end of the gathering I was "the seidhkona's husband". She does good work as a seidhkona. So maybe I'll get used to this after a while, being the seidhkona's husband.

–Haley, spirit-worker's partner

I am kind of a skeptic about all of this stuff. I believe in ghosts and spirits, but not Gods. I grew up in a really traditional household in Korea in the 70's, and my family saw shamans and made offerings, and still see the shaman at least once a year in this country. This means that I don't get freaked out around all of my partner's spells or anything, but I pretty much view it as psychosis of some kind.

I try to be supportive. I have respect for the intensity of her faith, but I also see it as an excuse in a way not to deal with immediate problems or goals. It's much easier to blame the Gods because things are not fortuitous than to change them. When my girlfriend went out and spent $1000 we did not have on archery equipment because the gods told her to hunt (which is hilarious because she is totally uncoordinated and does not eat meat), or spends most of the extra money around the holidays on liquor that goes into the ground, I realize all I can do is support her and chalk it up as her eccentricities.

Early on in our relationship she told me that her religion came first, but I had no idea what that meant at the time. At the time, she had a really high paying job she liked, went to graduate school which she loved, had a great apartment she owned, a big religious community, and lots of friends. Over the past two and a half years, almost all of that has gone away. She's gained lots of weight, been really depressed, started having health problems and lately seizures which she refuses to get help for, and claims to have been told by the gods to quit her job. She is looking for work, and she tries really really hard and stays up all night working on resumes and articles, and fails time after time. She told me that this is called shaman sickness. I think she might be going crazy. There are days where she does not leave the house, she won't go to noisy places, smells bother her, she claims she is forbidden to drink alcohol, and needs a ridiculous amount of time by herself because she needs to meditate or pray or whatever. We were just on vacation in the mountains and she made us leave the area because she claimed to be harassed by elves. It's obviously hard to put up with, sometimes rather like having a child with a zoo of imaginary friends.

She cries herself to sleep a lot of the time because she thinks that the Gods don't care about her. She thinks that they are holding back her luck and nothing she does is right. I don't know how to give this credence. It's hard. I try really hard to be supportive and loving, but I also know that insanity runs in her family. I've also seen people in her religious community exploit her kindness and hurt her time and time again. It hurts me to see her in all of this pain.

Most of the time I just feel powerless to help her, and I just try to understand her within her world view and focus on her goodness and generosity and compassion. She has stopped talking about it with me for the most part, but I do see her psychosis progressing and I am afraid for her. It's my job to make sure she eats and gets out of the house and does not turn completely inward. I see it as everyone has problems and baggage, and hers is a really tortured soul. It's the lesser of many evils, I suppose.

–J.K., partner of spirit-worker

I knew from the beginning that he was a devout pagan and "a shaman", but I didn't actually know much about either of those things. Early on, he sat me down and told me there were two very important things he had to discuss with me. First, he wanted me to know that this spirit-work he did was not a hobby he could take up and put down as he chose. He told me that even if it became a great source of discontent between us, he would always do this work. At the time, I was not a very religious person, but I had a great deal of respect for religion and didn't like to see it treated lightly. I understood this shamanism as a spiritual vocation, not much different than being a minister of any other faith. I assured him that I would hope a clergyperson would not consider putting their romantic affairs above their calling. I understood his priorities, and I respected him for them.

The second thing he told me took longer to sink in. He told me that one of the consequences of doing this spirit-work was that it made him and the people close to him face their issues. He said it speeded up their "karma". Since he is a very intense and keenly insightful person, I didn't doubt that any intimate relationship with him could bring all manner of psychological issues to the surface. We'd already had a number of interactions that had made me seriously rethink things about myself and my understanding of the world. I liked this about him, and tried to assure him of that. I didn't really understand what he meant.

Later that weekend, out of nowhere, I had a big cathartic episode about something I had been doing for the wrong reasons. I hadn't discussed it with him, it had nothing to do with our relationship, and he had no opinion on it. I just suddenly realized that what I was doing was at odds with what I believed in, and instantly I became incredibly uncomfortable with an activity I had done for years without much thought. Afterwards, I realized that this is what he had been talking about. He seemed worried that I would be angry at him—perhaps after years of lovers reacting in this way—but I just said, "Well, this is really going to suck, isn't it?" He still teases me about that.

I don't see it as a bad thing. It just means living under closer spiritual scrutiny, quite literally. The gods and wights are a much more tangible presence in my life than they ever would be otherwise. While I am not a spirit-worker, I have become a deeply religious person. I cannot doubt the presence of the gods in my partner's life—not because I trust his word (though I do), but because I can watch him and see things happen that would make no sense otherwise. Eventually I became exhausted by the increasingly bizarre mental gymnastics required to explain it all away in "rational" terms. After a while, Occam's Razor left me with the conclusion that this is all entirely real. It gives me a certainty in my spirituality that seems unique to the god-touched and those close to them.

I have a new appreciation for "superstition" based on this sure but limited knowledge of powerful and ever-present forces which I can scarcely perceive. If I'm cleaning the table and my partner has left something there that he's asked me not to touch, I'll get clarification about whether he meant that literally before I clean under or around it, and not because I'm worried he will be upset with me. Spirit-workers have things that normal people really ought not to touch. Curiosity is a dangerous trait when you live in the same home. In fact, unless you have good reason to, you'd often do best to not spend too much time handling or even looking at the spirit-worker's things. Spirit-workers are not only trained in how to handle these things properly, they are psychically equipped to handle things that normal folks simply cannot do safely.

I remember watching the Saami movie *Ofelas (Pathfinder)*, and there was a scene where the old shaman had just killed a bear and taken his spirit, and for the whole next day no one is allowed to look him in the eye—or the power of the bear spirit would harm them—except through a magical ring which the young female assisting him holds up to her eye. I wondered if I was the only person in the audience besides my partner who appreciated this as a perfectly rational and necessary safety measure, not some primitive superstition. So not only do you have to put up with your partner's strange activities (sometimes in public), but you can end up doing some strange actions of your own, out of self-defense.

The most difficult thing about spending time with my partner and other spirit-workers is that as his assistant I need to know a great deal about the practice of spirit-work, but I can't actually do any of it. I've studied a bit of magic and energy work in order to do my job, but I have limited aptitude. It is especially frustrating when folks assume I can perceive things which I cannot. I've had to deal with a lot of feelings of inadequacy about that.

My partner doesn't have a great connection to his body, and doesn't always think about taking care of his physical needs. I think a lot of spirit-workers ignore their bodies, which is a terrible thing because spirit-work is actually a very physically demanding job. People often don't realize that. They may not look like they are doing much besides sitting on a stump for a few hours, but they often come back from it starving and exhausted, and in no shape to prepare themselves a healthy meal. The spirits can drive a person to their physical limits, and sometimes the spirit-worker can get so accustomed to it that they don't think to take better care of themselves when they have the opportunity.

There is a good deal of scut-work involved in this work, and as his assistant, I try to take care of as much of it as I can. If he's going to have to drag himself out in the middle of the night into the cold to talk to some wight who doesn't have the good sense to drop by at a more convenient time, there is nothing I can do about it. But I can at least remind him to wear his gloves, get together appropriate food or drink for the wight, and have some hot tea ready when he returns. In the morning I can pull the offering dishes out of the snowbank and wash the grime off the special coat that the spirits insisted he make of white wool, even though he has to run around in the woods in it. It isn't much, but it helps. Every little bit helps.

Living with a spirit-worker, I think you eventually have to either accept that their worldview is basically accurate, or accept that they are profoundly delusional. There isn't a lot of comfortable middle ground where you can both politely accept each other's differing but equally valid religious views and not make a big deal of it. You don't have to like what they do or worship their gods, but if you don't believe that their spirit-work has a strong basis in reality, how can you come to terms with how they live their life? Their religious beliefs and practices guide every decision they make—food, clothing, employment, finances, hobbies, friends, ethics, everything. It isn't as simple as going to different churches, or celebrating different holidays, or not discussing theology at the dinner table. For a spirit-worker, their theology is their reality. It starts becoming your reality too, if you stick around long enough.

Suddenly, gods and wights are everywhere, whether or not you can perceive them. Every single day your partner is doing something for or with the spirits. Altars spring up like mushrooms. Votive figures seem to multiply while your back is turned. Things that used to be fine are now taboo. Every conversation comes back to one spiritual thing or another. More and more of their resources go into this work. They buy gifts for the spirits, and then don't show up to your birthday party because they were "busy". It is worse than them taking another lover, because you can't hope to compete with it. You can't woo them back. Getting angry at them doesn't help. It just keeps escalating and there is nothing you can do but hang in there and hope that when they come through this, there is still a place in their life for you.

A related important job that the partners of spirit-workers often end up doing is being their link to humanity, and reminding them to appreciate being human. Being in such close contact with the spirits can blind them to the fact that most people—even deeply and sincerely religious people—are not. You can end up in the position of mediating between them and the outside world, or explaining one to the other. Spirit-workers often have a hard time knowing how to describe what they do or believe to other people. Their pragmatic and utilitarian view of religious practice can be nearly inexplicable (not to mention irreverent) to the average religious person, who is guided by tradition and what feels right to them, not by what "gets results".

On the other hand, the spirit-worker can have a hard time understanding what the average religious person's relationship to the gods is like. Most religious people would consider themselves blessed to have a single experience of personal, direct divine contact. It would be a defining moment in their lives, not a hassle that got them out of bed at 3 a.m., *again*. Many people can't imagine that level of connection even being possible, let alone ordinary. They shout their prayers into the void, and have to struggle to maintain any sense of connection to the divine presence. If they turn their minds away from the gods, the gods will not chase after them with a stick.

Normal people base their religious beliefs on sacred texts, tradition, emotion, and philosophy because they don't have a whole lot else to go on. You can't really fault them for that. One spirit-worker commented that people arguing over theology looked like dogs fighting over scraps on the floor, because they couldn't see up on to the table. I don't think spirit-workers always appreciate how far away that tabletop looks to most of us. The spirit-worker's job is often such a burden to them, and their experience of the gods so ever-present and overwhelming, that I don't know if they really *can* appreciate how much the rest of us cherish our little scraps, and how easy it is for us to become jealous and defensive over them.

Even though I don't have the same immediate access to divine presence, being partners with a spirit-worker has let me know that it is possible. I get to watch that, if only from a distance. That is world-changing. There are spiritual experiences that I've had and information that I've been given just from being around my partner that I never would have had otherwise. There are many wonderful things about my partner, but to me, those opportunities alone would have been worth all the struggles.

–Joshua, spirit-worker's partner

Mengloth's Lesson
Earth and Air: Mountaintops

Mengloth is the Lady of Lyfjaberg, the Jotun goddess of healing, Eir's Jotunheim counterpart. In the lore, she is left offerings for healing, but all who need her help must get to the top of her high mountain somehow. When I went to see her, it took a lot of walking in order to get to her gate. She appeared as a tall and rather plain giantess, swathed in white robes, with dozens of necklaces jangling from throat to waist. Her attitude was friendly and matter-of-fact; she told me to lay down in the same way that a doctor might tell someone to hop up on the table, although her bedside manner was not exactly full of sensitivity. As she ran her hands over me, she made sideways comments about Hela's breeding experiments being so interesting.

I had been referred to Mengloth by Eir the healing goddess of Asgard, who spoke to me only the once, and only long enough to foist me off on her colleague. Mengloth holds the knowledge of many ancient and lost healing disciplines, from herbs to heat to old shamanic magic. She easily told me the story of her courtship with Svipdag, and the strange truth behind it (published in the Jotunbok). She agreed to take me on, even though I had no gift for healing—"There are things that those with no gift can do," she said, shrugging as if it was to be expected. "One is not always so lucky as to have someone with a gift about. Those I learned from, they learned in the days when there were not many folk about, and each small group had to take what gifts had been dealt to them by Fate. No matter who you are, there is some form of healing that you can manage." So it was that I began the long, slow process that I have half-jokingly referred to as "Mengloth's Med School".

Mengloth's Lesson:

You wanted to ask me about the link between the lich and the hame of a spirit-worker? Have you ever been on a mountaintop? There is a reason why they are sacred places. They are as far as you can get into the sky with your feet still touching earth. Spirit-workers are like mountaintops in that way. You are as far as one can get out of the *lich*, yet still living fully in it—and yes, I said fully. You are as far as one can get out of the world, yet still completely engaged with it, and with the folk who live in it. That is where you are different from the mystics. At your best, you are the sacred mountaintop.

Mountains have roots, and so must you. What are your roots? Your healing will come from there. Leaving the earth bears no healing for you—the winds of the sky will batter you, wear you down, send rains to erode you. It is the roots that pushed you up, like all mountains, and it is the roots that must sustain you. If you are rooted deeply, you can survive this.

So start with Earth, with the body. To ground to the earth, you know that. Any who do not learn that die quickly, in this business, but there is more. That is only the first step. Grounding forms a connection to the Earth, it fills you with the juice of stone and soil and all beneath it, but it is only the first step. You must become one with the Earth, for a little while. You must be a part of it, if only for an hour—joining yourself to its life. In that way, the processes of Earth can take hold of you and do for you what they would do for any piece of soil. The body and soul of Earth are never separated, and thus you will be made congruent, for a time.

Ground and center, then lie naked on the earth in some wild place. If it is a high place, all the better. If insects crawl on you, leave them. If you are being a part of Earth, you will welcome them. If you are truly linking with Earth, they will not harm you. If it is possible, before you relax, find a bit of plant that will give itself to you, and eat it. Thank the plant, and take that place of Earth into you. Then ask the land-wight to take you in its arms and eat you. Don't fear—land-wights can eat you and regurgitate you without harm to you or it. Oh, did I mention that you should make it an offering beforehand? Of course you should, that ought to go without saying.

Ask it to eat you, and then release you in a little while. A land-wight does not understand "hour" or "minute" or even "afternoon"; tell them to release you when the Sun sinks to a certain level of the trees. Then, your job is to surrender and let it happen. Do not fight it. If you have pleased the wight, it will do what you ask, and you should relax. What else to do? Why, wait, of course. Wait until it is done. Then, when it is over, go home and eat something pure. During this time, the few hours—perhaps even minutes—that your *lich* and *hame* are together as one, this is the time to instruct your *lich* to heal.

Then do it again in a month. It will help. It will not fix everything, but it will train your *lich* and your *hame* to understand what it is to be whole, for the moment. Eventually you may be able to call them together as one with your will alone.

There is something else that you must understand. You have done magic, and seen magic done, with nothing more physical than the wave of the hand, the muttered word, perhaps not even that. Yes, it is useful when you have nothing around and you must work, but there is a drawback, at least for a spirit-worker. The physical things that you do—the drumming, the dancing, the singing, the sacred objects that run through your hands—these are more than just focus, more than just useful techniques or repositories of power. As above, so below, do you understand that? As the great, so the small. As your magic works equally in both worlds, so your magic works on you in both worlds. If there is too much of the spirit and not enough of the body as you do a rite—if your hands touch nothing but the *ond* of the Universe, if your body feels no touch of sacred clothing, if your ears hear nothing but the voices of the wights, if your eyes see nothing but what is seen by your Sight … every time you do this, you pull your lich and your hame further apart.

It seems foolish to you, I know, but it is important, more than you understand. The singing, the moving up and down, the strange bundles and bags, the waving of odd objects—this is more than something to focus you or to keep a client off balance. When your own attention is equally spread in both places, you are where you should be, Walker Between Worlds—exactly straddling the middle. In the beginning, of course, the physical world keeps dragging you away. But later, that is the real danger … when you become skilled enough that the Otherworlds pull you across that line in the opposite direction, and you begin to see the physical world as lesser, as something to be fled. That is the beginning of Death. And while Death is no enemy, there is no need to run back down Her road like a fool, yes? So remember that, whenever you feel foolish. Your spirit-work should engage as many of your senses as possible, whenever possible. These actions, these objects, these experiences of the senses, they are your link to Life.

Afterword

The man before the shaman wants something, and he does not know if it is right for him to have it. The stones are cast, the runes read, and things still look ambivalent. It is not wrong, but ... there is that question, always. *Who are you that the Universe should go out of its way for you? Or, perhaps, if the Universe has nothing against it, who are you that my allies, the wights that I have worked to gain this relationship with, should aid you? Favors to them are dearly bought; it is not my job to spend every one for anyone who walks in the door. Just because I serve the people does not mean that my costly pennies should all be spent for them, or I will be of little use in short order.*

So the shaman asks him: who are you? What is great about you? What have you done? This is a favor that will require aid of a warrior god, so he asks him of his courage. What have you done that will impress this wight? Have you served in the military, perhaps? Have you stood up for those who could not defend themselves? Have you spoken up when it was right, but dangerous? Were it a different wight whose help was needed, he would ask other questions. For a love-goddess, well, how have you treated those with love-bonds before? For a god of wealth—have you been generous? Have you opened your home and your hearth?

It takes much time, and the man is annoyed that he should want to know so much about him. The shaman tells him that a doctor would want to know that much about his body, should he come to that, and he is called to know that much about his soul. He is warned not to lie or embellish, but to put forth the truth baldly and bluntly. This is not a god who likes those who embroider their deeds.

It is well, in the end. He has indeed done some brave and honorable things, and the shaman puts these together into a song. Then they go to an outside place, high and cold, and the shaman sings the song—sings of his courage, his deeds, his honorable service, and why he should be granted this thing that he wants so badly. It is not what the man expects, he knows. When other magic-workers do spells for someone's major life changes, they might do sympathetic magic of some sort, or use sigils and talismans to draw certain energies. They do not supplicate themselves in this way. The deserving of the needy is not taken into account; no one need prove themselves worthy of anything save an open wallet and silver across the palm. But when he became what he is, more was expected of him. This is not working with energy, or the footprints of the Gods, or some archetypal shadows. This is working with the entities themselves— ambiguous, annoying, cryptic, ugly, beautiful, awe-inspiring, soul-filling—and they will not be ordered about. They must have a reason to do what they do, or else one must depend on the mercy of the much less personal Universe itself—and for that, one might as well ask one's self, and not waste a spirit-worker's time.

The man goes away, shaking his head, but mere days later he calls back. It has been granted, in a way that he never would have dreamed possible. The shaman tells him what offerings he must make in thanks, and not to toss this off. The man is not comfortable with gratitude; he would prefer the impersonal Universe to whom one need not set out food, or drink, or one's mumbled thanks. Yet the Universe had not cared enough to bend itself for him, and now a God has done so. Gratitude is the order of the day.

Gratitude indeed. The shaman pours his own offering, thanking his allies for allowing him to work with them. For he cannot be other than a spirit-worker—his Wyrd is set and hammered—yet without the good will of the wights, there would be little that he could do. So it is done, and done well.

This, then, is the spirit of what we do. It is our Work, for good or ill. If it makes you flinch, turn away—if you still can.

If it fills you with hope, then sing. Yes, right now, sing for them, whatever comes into your mind. It doesn't matter if your voice is like that of a goose; you will be asked to do far more humiliating things on this path than just sing loudly on the spur of the moment. This is a test: are you willing to do what needs to be done?

For all the Gods and wights who have blessed me, I sing thanks.